THE INTERMARRIAGE HANDBOOK

THE
INTER-
MARRIAGE

HANDBOOK

A Guide for Jews & Christians

JUDY PETSONK & JIM REMSEN

ARBOR HOUSE
WILLIAM MORROW
New York

Copyright © 1988 by Judith Petsonk and Jim Remsen

Library of Congress Cataloging-in-Publication Data

Petsonk, Judy.
    The intermarriage handbook : a guide for Jews and Christians / by
Judy Petsonk and Jim Remsen.
        p.   cm.
    Bibliography: p.
    Includes index.
    ISBN 0-87795-976-5
    1. Interfaith marriage—United States.   2. Marriage—Religious
aspects—Judaism.   3. Marriage—Religious aspects—Christianity.
4. Jews—United States—Attitudes.   5. Christians—United States—
Attitudes.   I. Remsen, Jim.   II. Title.
HQ1031.P45 1988
306.8'43—dc19   88-16776
                                                                          CIP

Printed in the United States of America

First Edition

1 2 3 4 5 6 7 8 9 10

BOOK DESIGN BY LINEY LI

ACKNOWLEDGMENTS

We wish to thank Lydia Kukoff for sharing her time and resources with us so generously. The book also benefited in many ways because we were able to turn repeatedly for advice and insights to Rabbi Nancy Fuchs-Kreimer, Father John Hardwick, Dr. Egon Mayer, Rabbi Zalman Schachter-Shalomi, Sherri Alper, Rev. Timothy Lull, Nick and Joan Weingarten, Joseph Giordano, Monica McGoldrick, Rabbi Jeffrey Schein, Lena Romanoff, Dr. Eugene Fisher, Esther Perel, Jud and Ed Petsonk, and our wise and patient spouses, Steve Eisdorfer and Harriet Katz. Our agent, Diana Finch, and editor, Liza Dawson, also were valuable guides. Bob Sauer, Kent Tyler, and Marion Remsen kept our engines stoked with their faithful transcribing of interviews.

We are indebted to the following people for the careful reviewing of portions of the manuscript: Dr. Manfred Brauch, Rabbi Michael Swarttz, Father William McGowan, Dr. Jan Linowitz, Dr. Robert Garfield, Father Paul DiGirolamo, Rev. John Nesbitt, Debbie Aron, Robin Miller, Sister Gloria Coleman, Rabbi Susan Frank, Dr. William Stayton, Rena Yount, Father John Miller, Rabbi Ivan Caine, Father Charles H. Diamond, Bennett Goldstein, and Dr. Ruth Fischer.

Most of all, we wish to thank the scores of intermarried couples and the children of intermarriage who opened up their sometimes-painful feelings to us. They are the heart of the book.

DA

CONTENTS

UNDERSTANDING YOUR CHILDREN

CHOOSING A FAMILY STYLE

MAKING CONNECTIONS

HANDLING SPECIAL DIFFICULTIES

INTRODUCTION

Marriage between Christians and Jews has skyrocketed in the last two decades. As barriers of prejudice and tradition tumble, the percentage of Jews "marrying out" has shot from 6 percent thirty years ago to a current level of somewhere between 24 and 40 percent.[1] The number of Jewish-Christian couples in the United States has topped five hundred thousand and is growing by about forty thousand a year.[2]

Intermarriage is easier today because religion has become less a determinant of people's lives: In the last generation, America has become largely a secular culture. Frequently, both partners in an intermarriage have lived in similar neighborhoods, had similar educations, and feel there is no essential cultural or philosophical difference between them.

But as they stride along confidently, a mixed couple may suddenly stumble into unanticipated pitfalls. The truth is that the differences have not vanished and the pull of tradition has not died. Sometimes, despite their apparently smooth blend, a couple finds that cultural differences create tensions or misunderstandings. As people get older, latent loyalties can surface. Often, there is community and family opposition.

The community opposition is more likely to come from the Jewish side. Intermarriage takes place in a curious force field, with alarm on the Jewish end and near-silence from Christianity. Jewish tradition has emphasized the importance of maintaining the Jewish people, religion, and way of life distinct from all the surrounding cultures, and has long frowned upon and even forbidden marrying out. Jews have always been a small minority, and the modern Jewish population suffered heavy losses from the Nazi Holocaust in Europe and from assimilation in America. Intermarriage is seen by many Jews as another equally serious threat to the survival of Judaism. As the proportion of Jews intermarrying has surged upward, Jewish leaders have expressed anguish, studies have been launched, and programs are being aimed at this target population. To Christianity, however, intermarriage with Jews is only a tiny minority of Christian marriages. Because of that demographic difference, and because of Christianity's newfound respect for Judaism, Christian institutions have been largely silent and inactive on this front.

We decided to step into this force field because we saw the need for an independent, nondenominational handbook to help couples make their way through the emotional and practical issues that arise. Both of us have had personal experience with intermarriage. Jim Remsen, a lapsed Methodist, is married to a Jewish woman and assists in the Jewish upbringing of their children. Judy Petsonk, an actively involved Conservative Jew, is not intermarried but has dealt with a number of intermarriages in her family.

We've traveled across the country to talk with one hundred fifty intermarried people, as well as forty-three children of intermarriage ranging in age from five to forty-eight. We also interviewed one hundred seventy-three counselors, therapists, clergy, and professionals who work with intermarried couples.

We tried to talk to intermarried people who had a wide variety of experiences and had made widely differing choices, and to look for common patterns. Nationwide, many more intermarried families choose a Jewish orientation than a Christian one, and our range of families reflects that.[3]

We use the term *intermarriage* broadly, to include mixed couples as well as ones where one partner has converted to the other's religion. Though conversion officially confers a one-religion home, the spouses will always have different backgrounds, families, and cultural traits.

The book is organized according to the life cycle of the family. It is designed to be useful both to couples who are engaged or newly married, and to families who are in midstream and suddenly find religion arising as an issue. We think much of the information can also be helpful to nontraditional families, such as gay or lesbian couples, or others who live together.

You will find five types of information:

1) *Practical information* This includes, for example, the major movements' positions on intermarriage, as well as where to find clergy who will conduct weddings for intermarried couples.

2) *Psychological information* This will help you understand what's going on under the surface when a problem arises. For example, we look at the family power struggles that can erupt around an engagement or wedding.

3) *Written and verbal exercises* These will help you draw out your feelings about the issues you face. We suggest you join or organize an interfaith couples' discussion group and do the exercises and talk about the chapters there. Or, do the exercises with your spouse or partner. Keep written exercises in a looseleaf notebook so that you have a record of your journey through the issues and decisions of intermarriage.

4) *Case studies* These are stories of real families and how they dealt with the issue under discussion. Except where stated otherwise, the names of the people and most identifying details have been changed. Some of the families had painful tales of major conflicts. But most felt they were getting on fine. Their initial reaction was, "Why talk to us? We don't have any problems." Yet when the stories began to unfold, we found there was not a single family whose lives had not been affected in important ways by their intermarrying. Intermarriage had enriched many of them, but it had made life more complicated for all. We hope that their insights and experiences will shed light on your situation and help you move toward a constructive solution.

5) *Practical tips and recommendations* We have tried to present a range of options available on the major issues that arise, such as what to do about the wedding, holidays, rites of passage, and religious education. Our goal is to help you avoid getting stuck, to avoid thinking that you must choose between two unacceptable or mutually exclusive paths. Instead, we hope you will see a variety of possibilities and be able to stretch toward a mutually agreeable solution without feeling either of you has forsaken his or her own integrity. At the same time, we have tried to present our observations and best judgment about the strengths and weaknesses of particular approaches.

All marriages require compromise, but intermarriage raises the stakes. At most interfaith weddings, there are two invisible attendants: ambivalence and loss. The ambivalence comes from the pull and counter-pull of the various loyalties and resentments you feel toward your own and your spouse's families and cultures. That ambivalence can cause you to be paralyzed—to avoid decisions about your family's lifestyle—or to be inconsistent, to make contradictory or changing decisions. The antidotes are self-awareness and communication. We hope the book helps you achieve these goals.

The second issue is loss. In any compromise in an intermarriage, someone, perhaps many people, will feel they are losing something precious. This book will help you to discern where any losses are occurring—to acknowledge them, and to deal with them. Often we saw one or both partners shoving ahead to a decision without taking account of the sadness and other sensitive feelings at work beneath the surface. The healthier approach is to weigh everyone's needs openly, acknowledge the trade-offs that are made, and push on, while staying sensitive to shifts in emotions and being prepared to adjust the arrangement if necessary. You cannot make the feeling of loss go away, but you can keep it from corroding relationships.

Remember that you are pioneers. This is the first generation in which marriage between Christians and Jews has taken place on a massive scale. As you explore what it means for people from two religions to live together in love and respect, keep in mind that you are pushing forward on a new frontier.

There are riches to be mined in bringing together your different personalities and heritages. A handbook, of necessity, is a trouble-shooting guide and focuses on problems. But we also hope to give a vision of the richness of possibilities.

PHILADELPHIA
January 1988

A note on Hebrew pronunciation: We use the Ashkenazic (European) rather than the Sephardic used in Israel (e.g., we use *Shabbos* rather than *Shabbat*). We apply the symbol *h* rather than *ch* to denote gutterals (*Pesah,* not *Pesach*).

THE INTERMARRIAGE HANDBOOK

GETTING
STARTED

1. JEWISH-CHRISTIAN HISTORY:

A Legacy of Pain

History forms an invisible backdrop to every life decision discussed in the pages of this book. You need to understand this history—a history of virulent Christian persecution of Jews—because it is bound to affect you in some way.

Jews see themselves through the lens of history as a people who have existed for nearly five thousand years. Most Jews are keenly aware, and most Christians are not, that for the last two thousand years Jews have suffered horribly and repeatedly at the hands of Christians. For many Jews, this history plays like a tape in the mind—a tape that is triggered by symbols such as a crucifix or a Christmas tree, and that repeats: "Crusades, Inquisition, pogroms, Holocaust."

Although young Jews today may never have experienced anti-Semitism, they are the first generation in two thousand years to have escaped it. In the 1930s, American Nazis were able to muster large anti-Jewish marches in the streets of New York City. In the 1950s and 1960s, some residential neighborhoods, private schools, hotels, and resort communities still excluded Jews. Even today we have talked with children who have heard the accusation "Christ-killer" from their Christian playmates.

We often talked to Christian partners (and even some assimilated Jews) who thought Jews were vastly oversensitive or paranoid about this history. Until you understand the viciousness and persistence of the persecution—its reappearance time after time after periods of apparent peace and amity—you cannot understand the reactions of Jewish relatives or the Jewish community to your intermarriage. Therefore we must begin on this gloomy but central topic. Seeing the accumulation of horrors, we hope, will help you to understand the "paranoia." Later we will be presenting many examples of couples who have overcome the barriers created by history. But in later chapters, when we allude to Jewish sensitivities, try to hear the tape playing that says, "Crusades, Inquisition, pogroms, Holocaust." Realize that your parents or in-laws are probably hearing it, too. This will set the psychological context for you.

Christianity began as a sect of Judaism. The first Christians were the apostles; they were all Jews who belonged to Jewish synagogues and abided by Jewish law. But when they began to proselytize among gentiles, they reached a momentous decision: Pagan converts would not be required to observe Jewish law. The early Christians believed that they were the logical evolution of Judaism, and that all Jews should and would join them. When that didn't happen, a reaction set in that some historians have compared to the reaction of a child slamming the door on the parent's home. Christianity began to contrast itself to Judaism and to declare that God's favor had passed from the "old" religion to the new.[1]

Jews, for their part, saw the Christians as having betrayed and deserted the Jewish people—particularly after the Christians fled Jerusalem, refusing to join in an uprising against Roman rule. Some of the apostles were persecuted or killed. The style of the time was inflated rhetoric, and bitter words were exchanged. Unfortunately, this bitter rhetoric became part of the founding theology of Christianity and laid the groundwork for centuries of wholesale persecution of Jews by Christians. Some passages in the New Testament (particularly in the Gospel of John) were used by Church authorities to justify anti-Semitism, whether or not that was the Gospel writers' intent. The story of Jesus and the Pharisees, reiterated annually in the Easter liturgy, was used to inflame hatred of Jews.

In part, there was a political problem: In the early centuries of the Christian or Common Era, both Christianity and, to a lesser extent, Judaism were missionary religions competing for the same pagan population. But there was also a theological problem. The early Christians had expected the imminent return of Jesus and the ushering in of the last days. When that didn't occur, they developed a new view: Jesus would return when all the world had come to believe in Him. According to

Christian theology, the Jewish faith was destined to wither away and be replaced by Christianity.

But the Jews persisted as a separate people. They did not all flock to embrace Christianity. They were an embarrassment. And they came to be seen as an impediment to the uniting of the world under Christianity. Instead of being regarded as people who remained loyal, often against great odds, to their own precepts and way of life, they were seen by the Christian leadership as people who had defiantly rejected the Truth of Christianity.

Two ideas provided the theological justification for later Christian persecution of the Jews: The first, originated by Saint Justin (who lived from the year 100 to 165), said that Jews were ejected from Jerusalem and their land ravaged as divine punishment for the death of Jesus. Although crucifixion was a Roman punishment, abhorred by Jews, and Jesus in fact was executed by the Romans, the idea that Jews were Christ-killers and were collectively responsible for the death of Jesus became rooted in the Christian Church. While never an official part of church doctrine, neither was it officially repudiated until the Second Vatican Council (Vatican II) in the mid-1960s.[2] The second doctrine, developed by Saint Augustine (354–430), said the Jews were kept alive by God much as Cain was kept alive after he murdered Abel—with a brand on his forehead. God had decreed that the Jews would be perpetual wanderers, serving as living proof of what happened to people who reject Christ. This doctrine was later used to justify forced conversions and mass expulsions of Jews from many countries.

The words hurled from the pulpit by early Christian leaders who became saints of the church are shocking to modern ears: In the fourth century Saint John Chrysostom, patron saint of preachers, who is particularly venerated in the Greek Orthodox church, delivered six sermons from the see (bishop's throne) of Antioch, in which he called Jews "the most miserable of all men, lustful, rapacious, greedy, perfidious bandits . . . they murder their offspring and immolate them to the devil." He charged that the synagogue is a house of prostitution and that Jews worship the devil. The Jews are guilty of deicide (killing God), he said, and there is "no expiation possible, no indulgence, no pardon." He said God hates the Jews and always hated the Jews. "He who can never love Christ enough will never have done fighting against those [Jews] who hate him."[3]

He was only one of many saints of the Christian church to unleash vituperation against the Jews.

When Christians succeeded in converting Emperor Constantine (306–337) and Christianity became the official religion of Rome, discrimination against Jews became standard practice throughout the empire.

The Church leaders and Christian rulers of the next few centuries were faced with what they saw as a dilemma.[4] The teaching of Saint Augustine which so influenced this and later eras had two sides: Though Jews were destined to suffer, they were also destined to be preserved, as a witness people. Though extensive efforts could be made to persuade them to convert, they could not simply be exterminated or forced en masse to convert, as was done with pagan populations. At the same time, these Church leaders and rulers were very anxious to preserve Christianity's dominant position, and to make sure that neither Jews nor Judaism became attractive enough to lure Christians away from the faith.

Although both Church law and Roman law made it clear that Jews were not to be harmed, and that Judaism was to be tolerated, at the same time, specific legislation severely restricted Jewish rights. Over the next three centuries, a series of laws were promulgated, sometimes by regional church councils, and sometimes by imperial Rome, which outlawed intermingling between Jews and Christians and which crippled Jews economically. Such legal restrictions continued to be enacted in various places through the sixteenth century. Although not all the laws were in effect at any one time or place, and there were periods in various parts of Christian Europe when Jews enjoyed acceptance, wealth, and even prominence, the net effect of these laws was drastically to undermine the status of Jews in the larger Christian society. As historian Raul Hilberg has pointed out, nearly every legal restriction placed on Jews by the Nazis echoed an earlier measure taken by a regional council or synod of the Church.[5]

The Council of Elvira (Spain), in 306, forbade Christians and Jews from marrying each other, having sexual intercourse, or eating together; by the following century, Jewish-Christian intermarriage was punishable by death. The Synod of Clermont, a region of France, in 535, and the Council of Toledo in Spain in 589 barred Jews from holding public office. The Synod of Orleans (France), in 538, and the Council of Toledo also prohibited Jews from employing Christian servants or owning Christian slaves. (Since agriculture and industry of the time were conducted through slave labor, this effectively prevented Jews from competing with their slave-owning Christian neighbors and they were driven out of agriculture and industry and restricted to small business and crafts.) Jews were barred from practicing law or becoming civil servants or officers in the army. The sixteenth council of Toledo in 693 ordered Jews to stop conducting businesses and to forfeit all land acquired from Christians.

Other measures were taken during this period directly to ensure that Judaism would always remain a minority religion vis-à-vis Christianity. Construction of new synagogues was prohibited and even repairs could not be made without permission. In 415, a synagogue built without permission was destroyed. In 425, the emperor abolished the traditional Jewish leadership, the patriarchate. It was a crime for Judaism to seek converts. Christians who converted to Judaism lost the right to their inheritance. (On the other side, the third Lateran Council in 1179 decreed that Jews could not cut off inheritance to a child who converted to Christianity.) And later the Synod of Mainz in 1310 defined conversion to Judaism by a Christian, or reversion to Judaism by a baptized Jew, as heresy, for which the punishment was burning at the stake.

The severity of the legislation varied from place to place, with Spain at certain periods being among the worst. In the mid-600s, in Spain, Jews were forced to sign an oath which, if followed, would make it impossible for them to practice their religion.[6] Failure to keep the oath was punishable by burning or stoning. The Synod of Toledo, in 681, ordered the burning of the Talmud, the most important Jewish religious book after the Bible. The seventeenth council the following year banned all Jewish religious rituals and decreed that all Jewish children over the age of seven were to be taken away from their families and educated as Christians.

There were also Church-sponsored attempts to ridicule and humiliate the Jews and their religion. In Toulouse, France, for three hundred years from the mid-800s to 1160, each Good Friday a Jew was summoned to be publicly slapped by the bishop, symbolizing the belief that all Jews were responsible for the crucifixion of Jesus. Another custom, traces of which persisted until modern times, was to make special mallets for a Holy Week ritual symbolizing the killing of Jews.[7]

In various parts of Europe, Easter was a season not only of humiliation, but of danger. Clergy preaching against the Jews in Easter sermons would inflame the common folk, who would ravage the Jewish district, killing and burning. Easter riots continued in Eastern Europe down to the early 1900s.[8]

Even though official Church teaching forbade forced conversion, periodically, local rulers allied with local clergy ordered entire Jewish communities to convert to Christianity under the threat of exile, confiscation of property, or death. In Spain in the seventh century, some ninety thousand Jews underwent forced conversion; the rest lost their homes and property and went into exile.[9] Many brave Jewish souls suffered martyrdom or committed suicide rather than undergo forced conversion. Jews called this martyrdom *Kiddush Ha-Shem*—sanctification of the name of God.

Despite all the social and legal restrictions, in many places Jews and Christians continued to live in the same communities and to conduct business with each other. At certain times of the year, especially at Christian holidays, there would be threats and harassments, but between times, there would be relatively cordial interactions between neighbors.

But the situation for the Jews deteriorated dramatically after the year 1000. It was a time of turmoil for all Europe, and frequently the fear and frustration was taken out on Jewish bodies, Jewish homes, and synagogues. Many Christians had believed Jesus would reappear at the millennium. When the waited-for Second Coming did not occur, the Church was thrown into a crisis. Christianity sought a new direction. Muslims had captured Jerusalem and closed it to Christian pilgrims. In 1095, Pope Urban the Second called for the liberation of the Tomb of the Holy Sepulchre. Many of the faithful believed that this holy war was the beginning of the events that would culminate in the Second Coming. Thus began the Crusades—a three-hundred-year nightmare for the Jews. One reason many Jews cannot see the cross as a symbol of Christian love is that Crusaders marching beneath the banner of the cross massacred Jews by the thousands. During the first Crusade alone, Crusaders on their way to Palestine killed some five thousand Jews in the towns of Europe, then burned Jews alive in the synagogues of Jerusalem where they had taken refuge.

Some popes rebuked the Crusaders; many of the bishops and some of the nobility tried, with various degrees of effectiveness, to protect the Jews. Others, like Pope Innocent III (1198–1216), fanned the flames.

Prejudice, superstition, and a distorted version of church teaching fused into a generalized hysteria in which the Jews were seen as demons; in medieval art, they were depicted with horns and tails. In 1171, the Jews of Blois, France, were accused of ritual murder (using the blood of a child in their Passover matzoh), and thirty-three men, women, and children were burned at the stake. This slander was revived more than one hundred times in Western Europe as an excuse for executing Jews. The charge of ritual murder became a persistent part of the folklore of some parts of Christianity, with frequent trials through the eighteenth and nineteenth centuries in some parts of Europe. The most recent trial on this charge was held in Russia in 1911. The accusation even surfaced (to be quickly dismissed) in the United States in 1920 in Massena, New York.[10]

In 1298, based on a rumor that Jews had desecrated the communion bread, or host, an army of Judenschachter (Jew-slaughterers) marched through Germany and Austria killing an estimated one hundred thousand Jews.

The hysteria against Jews intensified with the arrival of the bubonic plague. Jews were accused of poisoning the wells. In the 1300s, tens of thousands of European Jews were massacred on this charge. Religious fanatics—flagellants—though condemned by the Pope, roamed Germany and France, stirring up some of the attacks. Over two hundred Jewish communities were destroyed. Greed as much as fear triggered many of the charges. In some places, the Jews' belongings were parceled out to their accusers before they were even put on trial. In Strasbourg, on the basis of the poisoning charge, two thousand Jews were burned alive on a scaffold over a huge pit—in the Jewish cemetery, on the Sabbath. Their credit records were burned with them. The men died wrapped in their prayer shawls.

In the midst of all this chaos, Church councils continued to issue legislation restricting the rights and degrading the social position of the Jews. The Third Lateran (Roman) Council, convened by Pope Alexander III in 1179, banned Jews throughout Christian Europe from appearing in court as plaintiffs or witnesses against Christians. The Fourth Lateran Council, summoned by Pope Innocent III in 1215, made universal for all of Christian Europe a number of the restrictions that had been enacted earlier by regional synods. In addition, it added two particularly injurious laws. As had been required earlier of both Christians and Jews by one of the Muslim rulers, Jews would be required to wear distinctive clothing. (In some places, they had to wear badges, in others, pointed hats.) And the Council said that those who joined the Crusades would be absolved of their debts to Jews—a step which devastated the Jews economically. Moneylending was one of the major sources of income for some, since they were barred from many trades and industries. Ironically, this council, so devastating to Jews, was of profound theological importance to Christians. It was here that the doctrine of transubstantiation of the Communion wine and wafer was acclaimed, and that the minimum religious duties of a Christian (annual confession and communion at Easter) were defined.

New legal restrictions continued to be announced by regional authorities. The Council of Bezier (France) in 1246 decreed that Christians who patronized Jewish doctors would be excommunicated. The Synod of Ofen (Switzerland) in 1279 prohibited Christians from selling or renting real estate to Jews. The Council of Basel in 1434, which like the Lateran was an ecumenical council applying to all of Christendom, barred Jews from getting academic degrees and from acting as agents in the conclusion of contracts between Christians.

Attacks on the Jewish religion also continued. The Synod of Vienna in 1267 prohibited Jews from arguing about religion with average Christians. Sometimes Jews were ordered to debate the relative merits of Judaism and Christianity—a debate whose outcome had already been decided. Following one debate (after the pope had called for an investigation of Jewish books) in 1240, in Paris, twenty-four cartloads of copies of the Talmud were burned.[11] From the ninth century on, but particularly in the thirteenth century, Jews in various parts of Europe were compelled to attend sermons where Judaism was denigrated, Christianity extolled, and their conversion sought. In some places, their ears were inspected to be sure they weren't wearing ear plugs.

In the 1200s, the Inquisition began—the Church's tool to combat heresy. Although others were trapped in its coils, the most infamous of the Inquisitions, in Spain, was primarily directed at converts from Judaism—*Conversos*. The Spanish clergy and nobles—after forcing Jews to convert—doubted the authenticity of their faith. Despite the pope's objections to the conduct of the Inquisition in Spain, in one twelve-year period in the late 1400s, the Inquisition there burned at the stake thirteen thousand men and women who had converted to Christianity but were charged with secretly practicing Judaism.

In 1492, 170,000 Jews who would not accept Christianity were expelled from Spain. The voyage of Columbus was partly financed with their confiscated property. But even those who stayed and converted could not escape Christian fury. They were called *Marranos* (pigs). By *limpieza* (blood purity) statutes, they were excluded from living in certain towns, and from public and religious offices, guilds, and colleges.

The Inquisition in Spain was not abolished until 1836.

During the late Middle Ages, an increasing number of cities adopted regulations forcing the Jews into ghettos. In some places these were simply quarters or sections of the cities. In other areas, they were walled compounds, locked from the outside, narrow areas crammed with people and prey to waves of plague and of fire. The Synod of Breslau, Poland, in 1267 and the General Council of Basel, Switzerland, in 1434 were among the earlier church councils to adopt policies of compulsory ghettoization; by the sixteenth century, they were common.

The Protestant Reformation called into question many Church practices, but not the theology of anti-Judaism. Martin Luther, frustrated in his initial attempts at friendly conversion of the Jews, called for the burning of synagogues "in order that God may see that we are Christians, and that we have not wittingly tolerated or approved of such public lying, cursing and blaspheming of His Son and His Christians."[12]

Exile was another result of the convergence of state power and Christian influence. Repeatedly, Jews were forced to leave homes where they had lived for generations, with nothing but the clothes on their backs. Sometimes the exile meant a lifetime of wandering and poverty, since many towns were closed to newcomers and many of the guilds which controlled the practice of crafts were closed to newcomers or to Jews. Christian society succeeded in creating the wandering Jew—the situation which Christian theology predicted. In the 1200s and 1300s, the Jews were expelled from England, France, and parts of Germany.

Many of the exiled Jews went to Eastern Europe, particularly Poland and Russia. They flourished for several centuries, but later it became apparent that in Eastern Europe, too, neither their religion, their property, nor their lives would be safe. From the early middle ages, through 1264, when they were given a charter of rights, to the mid-1600s, they were treated very favorably by the Polish kings. They eventually had their own parliament, with almost complete autonomy. They became traders and financiers, and were appointed tax collectors by the kings—a role which led to their undoing. From 1648 to 1667, there was an uprising of Eastern Orthodox Ukrainian cossacks, in which thousands of the Roman Catholic Poles who dominated the region were killed. Jews, who served as middlemen between the Ukrainian peasants and the Polish rulers, were the target of special fury. According to historians Margolis and Marx, some "victims were flayed and burned alive. . . . Infants were slit like fish or slaughtered at the breasts of their mothers or cast alive into wells. Women were ripped open and then sewed up again with live cats thrust into their bowels."[13] Some were given the option of forced baptism rather than death or torture.

Potok quotes a letter that seems to prefigure the Holocaust, describing the scene in one town where seven hundred Jews were killed: "Some were cut into pieces, others were ordered to dig graves into which Jewish women and children were thrown and buried alive."[14]

During this same century, Poland endured a series of invasions. Jews suffered from both ends of the invasions. First they were attacked by the invading Russians, Cossacks, and Swedes. When the invaders were repelled, they were attacked by the Poles, who claimed that they had collaborated with the invaders. By the time this bloody century was over, one fourth of the Jewish population of Poland had been murdered. Estimates of the deaths range from one hundred thousand to half a million.

Thousands of Jews wandered from town to town with no permanent home.

Russia was another major center of Jewish population. According to Chaim Potok, in 1850, there were 2,350,000 Jews living in Russia. Most were confined to a crowded region known as the Pale of Settlement. Once again, says Potok, the Jews were caught between an oppressed underclass (the peasants) and an oppressing ruling class (the noblemen), and became the target of blame and rage. There were frequent pogroms (violent mob attacks) and other difficulties for the Jews. The government added legal disabilities: economic restrictions, expulsion from villages and cities, forced conscription of young boys for twenty-five-year terms in the army, banning from academic schools, a special tax on the candles used by Jews for religious purposes. In the 1870s, the government removed many of the restrictions and there was a brief, enthusiastic flowering of Jewish culture—a mini-Renaissance. But then in 1881 Czar Alexander II was assassinated by a bomb. It was blamed on the Jews. There came a new wave of pogroms and restrictive legislation. The head of the Russian Orthodox Church, Konstantin Pobedonostsev, announced his hope that "one-third of the Jews will convert, one-third will die, and one-third will flee the country."[15]

Although this bitter history explains the suspicion and anger many Jews feel toward Christians or Christian religious institutions, it isn't the whole story. Just as many Christians are ignorant of how the Jews suffered at the hands of official and unofficial Christianity, on the other hand most Jews have an unfairly monolithic view of the relationship between Jews and Christians during the centuries of Christian hegemony in Europe.

There were both clergy and Christian rulers who attempted to protect the Jews and sometimes even to elevate them to positions of privilege and honor.[16]

Pope Gregory the Great (540–604) forbade the bishops from intervening in internal Jewish affairs, prohibited forced conversions, and in cases where synagogues had been violated, ordered that they be returned to the Jews and restored to their former condition, or compensation paid. Other popes in the coming centuries followed his example. In fact, "disrupting Jews at worship" was an excommunicable offense. Many of the restrictions and expulsions were promulgated by secular rulers, often over the objections of Church officials.

There were also devoutly Christian rulers who treated the Jews fairly and had good relationships with them. The Frankish emperor Charlemagne employed a Jew as an ambassador. His son, Louis the Pious (814–840), granted letters of protection to Jews, permitted Jews to employ Christians, and instituted a large fine for the murder of Jews. Louis himself had a Jewish doctor.

The popes and many bishops consistently condemned the blood libel and well-poisoning charges.

Even when Christian leaders outlined a policy of discrimination against the Jews, they often set limits upon it. Saint Thomas Aquinas (1225–74) wrote that it was all right "to hold Jews, because of their crime, in perpetual servitude, and therefore the princes may regard the possessions of Jews as belonging to the state; however, they must use them with a certain moderation and not deprive Jews of things necessary to life."[17]

To understand the context in which the events described in this history occurred, it's also important to remember that the Europe of the Middle Ages was not made up of nation-states as we know them today, but was often splintered into small kingdoms and fiefdoms. For most of this period, neither popes nor emperors had real control over these many principalities, or even over the regional clergy, some of which enacted policies toward the Jews which were in conflict with the expressed wishes of the Church authorities in Rome.

If you are Jewish, the pogroms are the thing that most immediately shaped the attitudes of your grandparents' generation. Many of these grandparents lived through the pogroms or fled Europe to escape them. You may have heard a grandparent talk, for example, about the Kishinev pogrom of Easter Sunday, April 6, 1903, which left forty-nine Jews dead, five hundred injured and two thousand homeless.

The attitudes of Jews of your parents' generation were profoundly shaped by the Nazi Holocaust, in which six million Jews were killed. One of the most frightening aspects of the Holocaust to American Jews was that it originated in Germany, which, like America, was a place where Jews, to all outward appearances, were quite well integrated into society. Many American Jews cannot forget that there have been previous periods in Europe (in both Christian and Muslim Spain around the year 1000, for example) during which the Jews enjoyed social acceptance, prestige, wealth, and apparent security—only to find everything they had built smashed in a new round of persecutions.

Given the suffering Jews incurred at the hands of Christian Europe, apostasy—voluntary baptism or conversion to Christianity—was viewed as the ultimate betrayal of the Jewish people.[18] Intermarriage to a Christian was seen as almost as bad. Most voluntary conversions to Christianity were looked upon as cynical opportunism—done not out of religious conviction but to escape the economic and social discrimination against Jews. Common people would spit three times when they met a voluntary apostate from Judaism, and would recite a verse from Isaiah, "Those who ravaged and ruined you shall leave you."

Although Jewish religious law holds that a born-Jew never loses his membership in the people, the vast majority of Jews until very recently regarded one who converted to Christianity as dead, irrevocably cut off from the Jewish community. Even today, most Jews view baptism as betrayal. Nearly all would say it is impossible to be Jewish and Christian at the same time.

Given the history of bloodshed and mutual suspicion, it is remarkable that we find ourselves where we are today. America itself has been a positive influence on Christian-Jewish relations. Jews found in America a more open society, free of many of the legal and social strictures that had so limited their options in Europe. In spite of the prejudices that erupted following the waves of immigration by Jews and other Europeans, they were gradually able to become assimilated into the larger society in a way that had never been possible in Europe. Especially since World War II, the relationship between Jews and Christians in the United States has changed dramatically. Jews have been economically successful, are socially respected and are seen as desirable marriage partners by many Christians.

The organized religions have changed markedly. As a result of the Holocaust, the Christian world has begun to come to grips with its history of anti-Semitism. Some Christian theologians and historians have called for a recognition of how Christian anti-Judaism laid the groundwork for the non-theological and Godless anti-Semitism of the Nazi era. Vatican II reassessed Catholic teachings about the Jews. The Church's new teachings state that Jews have a valid covenant with God which has never been revoked, and that an understanding of Judaism is essential for a valid Christian faith.[19]

Most importantly, the declaration *Nostra Aetate* (In Our Time) specifically repudiated some of the most destructive ideas about Jews voiced by the Christian thinkers of earlier times. The Synod stated that although some Jewish leaders in Jesus' time may have pressed for His death, their actions "cannot be charged against all the Jews, without distinction, then alive, nor against the Jews of today." The Synod added that "the Jews should not be presented (in Christian teaching or preaching) as rejected or accursed by God."[20]

Since the declaration, the Roman Catholic Church has undertaken a sweeping evaluation and revision of parochial school texts and curricula and retraining of teachers. The object is not only to root out negative references to the Jews, but to promote a positive understanding of Jewish culture and its contributions to Christian beginnings as well as to the world of today.

Protestant denominations have also taken steps to take responsibility for and redress some of the injuries done by Christians to Jews.

The World Council of Churches (WCC) in 1948, five years after the end of World War II, while continuing to stress its intent to evangelize the Jews, stated that "Anti-Semitism is sin against God and man," and acknowledged that "churches in the past have helped to foster an image of Jews as the sole enemies of Christ, which has contributed to anti-Semitism in the secular world." The WCC called upon "all the churches we represent to denounce anti-Semitism, no matter what its origin, as absolutely irreconcilable with the profession and practice of the Christian faith."[21] In 1968, the WCC declared that the survival of the Jewish people in spite of all the efforts to destroy them makes it clear "that God has not abandoned them." In fact, said the declaration, the survival of the Jews is living proof that God also cares for those who do not believe in the divinity of Jesus.[22]

There has also been a wave of scholarship and theology exploring Jesus as a Jew, and the Jewish roots both of his teachings and of many church practices.

Thus, those who attended Protestant or Catholic Sunday schools since the mid-1960s were taught a very different outlook on the Jews than was prevalent earlier.

In addition, both Protestant and Catholic Churches have made extensive efforts to develop mutually respectful contacts with Jews, through dialogue groups and other means. The Vatican, in setting up its Office of Catholic-Jewish Relations in 1969, stated that the dialogue must include "respect for the other as he is, for his faith and religious convictions. All intent of proselytizing and conversion is excluded."[23]

It is in this radically changed atmosphere that young Jews and Christians today are meeting and falling in love.

Although we have stressed Jewish-Christian relations in this chapter, those dealings were a minor theme for both religions during this two-thousand-year span. Christianity did not exist merely to persecute Jews, nor Judaism merely to deny the divinity of Jesus. Both religions have their own grand and beautiful traditions that developed on their own terms along their own trajectories. These traditions offer much to sustain their members, as we make abundantly clear throughout this book.

But as life-affirming as Christianity can be, as full of goodwill to Jews as it now seeks to be, most Jews still feel the scars inflicted by the churches. Older Jews are generally either unaware of the changes in the outlooks of the churches or are skeptical: They may not believe that forty years of good relations between Judaism and Christianity are enough to ensure the definitive end of nearly twenty centuries of bad relationships. Thus, when intermarrying couples are considering such steps as a co-officiated wedding ceremony, or raising of their children in both Judaism and Christianity, they must appreciate the psychosocial residue of Jewish-Christian history. Many Jewish families will view their child's participation in any Christian ritual, or even entering a church, with horror and anguish. And the Jewish community in general will not accept attempts to fuse Jewish and Christian ritual or Jewish and Christian identity.

If you are Jewish, you may not feel an instinctive reflex against the church and its symbols. Or if you do, it may be something you want to "get past." But be aware that these feelings can return to you at unexpected moments and for unexpected reasons. Your family and members of the Jewish community quite likely will have the reflex. Remember that it is deeply grounded in a very real history.

2. SHOULD YOU GET MARRIED?:

An Early Appraisal

Asking an engaged couple to think about whether they really ought to marry seems a little like asking a woman in labor if she really wants to have a baby. It often appears that a powerful and inexorable process is in motion that nothing can stop.

But that's not true. In reality, thinking about whether you should get married is a lot more like thinking about whether you want to have sex. Even in a permissive era, if the stakes get high enough—if you're worried enough about an accidental pregnancy or a fatal disease—you proceed carefully.

In marriage, the stakes are high. When you commit your life and your heart to another, there is the potential for broken hearts and wrecked lives. Yet if you heeded all the dire warnings people threw in your path, you would never drive a car, start a career, or buy a house, much less climb a mountain, ride an ocean wave, or fall in love.

How do you mix prudence and caution with passion and exhilaration? How do you make a reasonable evaluation of your chances for a successful marriage without being unduly swayed by anxious or prejudiced relatives and clergy? Those are questions that every engaged couple faces, but they're even more urgent for you and your partner because you would be intermarrying. An intermarriage *does* pose more genuine difficulties and complexities, and you need to consider them—and your own relationship—soberly and dispassionately.

Yet the warnings you encounter will not necessarily give you a fair, realistic picture of the risks of intermarriage, nor of your ability to cope with them. And the warners probably aren't interested in the riches that may come from the joining of your two personalities and cultures.

All the chapters of this book are designed to give you a fair and in-depth picture of the complexities of intermarriage and of how potential problems might be turned into opportunities. If you are engaged, you will benefit from looking through the entire book for a glimpse at issues you could face in the future. But it also pays to examine ways you and your partner interact right now. The best way to evaluate your potential for a good marriage is to have a good engagement—to spend the time *now,* before the wedding, working out the patterns of relating that you will use throughout your marriage.

Once you've decided you want to get married, you have to be sure that you both want the same things in a marriage. Because you are from different backgrounds, you might use the same word but mean different things by it.

Here's our working definition of a good marriage:

A lifelong committed relationship in which each partner is cared for, cared about, and permitted to grow to his or her fullest potential. A unified home, in which the partners are able to support each other and work together in the physical and psychological nurturing and moral guidance of children.

What do you and your partner each mean by a good marriage? If you use our definition, be as specific as you can about what you mean by "full potential," "commitment," "unified home," and "moral guidance." Spell out the details.

EVALUATING YOUR RELATIONSHIP

When people warn you about the perils of intermarriage, we urge you neither to close your eyes and ears nor to run scared, but instead to think as carefully as you can about whether any of these perils apply in your case. If they do, decide how you will deal with them and whether you are willing and able to make the necessary compromises. Although this evaluation may sound cold and calculating, you actually do it all the time. During the course of your young adulthood, you have probably rejected any number of potential mates with the realization that for you, they were not good "husband or wife material." Even in the midst of falling in love and deciding to get married, each of you were making some of the same evaluations about each other.

It will take some extra effort to include intermarriage issues in that evaluation. Chances are neither of you has had the experience of living for a long period at close quarters with someone whose background is different from yours. Several things can help you make your evaluation more honest and more accurate.

Have a Prolonged Engagement Try to go through an entire year together as an engaged couple before you get married. Use that year to identify and try out some of the issues that may come up during your marriage. Several of the most troubled couples we talked to had met, decided within a month or two to get married, and were wed a short time later. Their energy went into planning the wedding and being in love, and they glossed over severe problems. Even if circumstances such as geographic separation seem to dictate a short engagement, reconsider.

Go for Counseling Consult a clergy person of the religion that you intend to be married in. Try to select one who has had some training in family counseling. Ask if the person has any compatibility tests the two of you can take. Use the tests to highlight potential problem areas, and work on them during your engagement year. (Some clergy also wisely ask couples to agree to come back after the wedding for a "six-month checkup.")

Assess Cultural Differences Read Chapter 5 (Ethnic Background). List what you see as your areas of difference. Check out areas of potential difference by doing things together that you are likely to have to do when you're married. Buy some expensive and durable items together and see how you mesh in tastes and attitudes toward money. Prepare a holiday meal for relatives and see how your attitudes toward food and celebration fit. Babysit together during the day to see how your child-rearing styles mesh.

A potentially corrosive issue is sexuality. The Jewish and Christian traditions have different messages about sex, as Chapter 21 explains. Therefore, explore your views on contraception, on abortion, and on sex in the years after you don't want any more children. Ask yourselves: How frequently do you expect to have sex? Who do you expect would initiate it? What practices do you look forward to, what would you be uncomfortable with, and where are you open to experimenting? Do you know what turns you on sexually? Can you talk about it with your partner?

If you have different views, it's important to come to an agreement now that you both can live with, or to admit now that your needs are irreconcilable.

Visit Each Other's Parents Try to spend at least a week to see what it's like in each other's cultures. In an intermarriage, each of you must make a partial "move in" to the other's culture. A visit will help you imagine what it will be like to live for the rest of your life with this person's special ethnic flavoring. Keep in mind that ten or fifteen years from now, when you have children, your partner probably will be a lot more like his parents than he is today.

We know one New York Jewish woman who was engaged to a Southern Protestant man. She went on a two-week camping trip with his parents. By the end of the trip, she realized that she could not go through with the marriage. His parents' way of relating together jarred with her personal style. She began to see the ways her fiancé resembled his parents and realized that over the long haul she would not be happy living with him.

Explore Your Spiritual Inclinations Religious troubles in intermarriages often spring not so much from differences in formal religious labels as from differences in each partner's need for some spiritual expression. In many couples, one partner is intensely spiritual and the other is not. One needs a relationship to religion or God, the other does not. Unlike many issues in a marriage, this one can't be reasoned through, negotiated, or compromised on; it's a need, a sensibility, a matter of temperament and training that goes deep. It's an area where it's often difficult for partners to understand each other.

As you read the chapters on "Finding Your Spiritual Path," notice any differences in the ways you respond to the issues. Try to anticipate whether you can respect the differences or whether they will eventually become grating areas of mutual intolerance.

Gather Information Take courses in each other's religions. Even if you don't intend to practice any religion in your home, this studying will give you a far better idea of each other's backgrounds and unspoken assumptions.

Consciously seek information from your own family and your partner's about their lifestyles and values. Draw them out. These conversations will be a valuable base for your future relationship with them.

Talk with couples who have long, successful intermarriages. Ask how they handled religious and cultural issues. What were the hardest problems for them? What problems had they not expected? What problems remained unresolved? In particular, ask them about how their relationship to religion and culture changed over the course of their marriage. If possible, talk also to someone who was intermarried and is now divorced. You may see where some intermarriage issues, such as family pressures or ethnic differences in handling conflict, played a role in the breakup, and gain new insight into how to avoid those problems yourselves.

Negotiate Some Preliminary Agreements Pick out some of your current disagreements and consciously negotiate them. These could be such things as how much time to spend together, how much time to be with family, how much money to spend on a particular item, how to spend your vacation. Watch yourselves as you negotiate. Do you face issues squarely or come up with temporary compromises that don't solve the underlying problems? Does one partner always win? Are you both satisfied with the arrangements you come to, or are you ambivalent? Watch yourselves fight, too. Does the same issue come up over and over without getting resolved? What fighting techniques does each of you use, and how do you feel about those?

A related consideration: Even though you can negotiate solutions to many problems, there will always be some that are unresolved. Try to evaluate how good you are, and how good your partner is, at living with differences. When your partner does or thinks something different from you, does it rankle? Or can you just shrug and let her do it her way? When you do something in a way your partner disapproves of, is she compelled to interfere? To succeed in an intermarriage, you must be fairly flexible and tolerant. Rigidity is a virtue in some situations, but not here.

Write a Marriage Contract Cover hard practical issues, such as finances, sexual fidelity, what you will do if one of you becomes disabled. In addition, try to spell out what emotional support you need and what day-to-day responsibilities you expect each partner to take. Include a detailed agreement on holiday observance and children's religious education. As in the traditional Jewish marriage contract, talk about what minimum financial settlement you would make in the event of a divorce. The issues that you find it hard to think about or agree on are likely to be the ones that are most problematic in your marriage.

Practice Your Solutions If you plan to follow certain religious practices and to divide up the holidays between families in a certain way, do that during your engagement. Attend religious events of friends' children, such as a first communion or a bar mitzvah. If you're going to keep kosher, start doing so. If either of you feels uncomfortable, now is the time to voice your doubt. This gives you a chance to work out a new solution or to reconsider the engagement.

Try to Anticipate Changes Over Time Make time lines of your parents' marriages and the marriages of older friends. Were there periods when they were more or less involved with religion? Make a time line for yourselves. Was either of you more involved in religion as a child than you are now? How do you expect you might change over the course of your life? Talk about how you would revise the agreements you have made if one of you wants to become more involved with religion. Will the other one view that as a breach of your agreements?

Evaluate Outer Pressures These might be parental opposition or community and job pressures. Watch how each of you deals with stress. Do you have the strength to let your own relationship evolve independent of the pressures and not simply in reaction to them? Do stresses and problems strengthen your trust in each other or make you doubt?

On the other side, how do you do when you're not under stress? Do you have anything to say to each other on a boring rainy evening when you don't have a date and there's nothing pressing to discuss? Are there quiet activities other than sex that you enjoy together? Also, are you able to let each other go off and do things separately?

Some relationships thrive on conflict. We talked with a number of mixed couples who fell in love partly because they were so different and had so much to argue about. If both of you have a sense of humor, this "debate-team" style of marriage can work. But if not, one of you is likely to tire of it. Can the two of you feel any sparks without the drama of your differences?

Listen to Your Own Ambivalences and Doubts List your fears and misgivings, share your lists, and talk specifically about how you will deal with each problem you foresee. Which of your doubts are realistic and which are not really problems?

Listen to the Doubts of Others Make a conscious effort to separate the realistic from the hysterical. Try this exercise: Divide a paper into three columns. In the first column, list the names of people who have warned you against intermarrying. In the second, list the warnings you think are unrealistic, and explain why you think each is unfounded. In the third, list the warnings you find realistic and how the two of you plan to cope with each.

After you have dealt with all the warnings, go to each important person who has warned you and discuss your responses, dealing with the warnings that have merit first. This will help both you and them to have more faith in your ability to handle potential problems.

Many couples skim over their differences, sailing into marriage without ever sounding for the rocks below the surface. One woman, now separated from her husband, says interfaith issues were not what caused them to split up. But she was so busy dealing with her parents' opposition to the wedding, so busy defending her fiancé as the most wonderful man in the world, so busy with the million details of planning a wedding, that she and her fiancé never faced the real problems in their relationship. Eventually those problems caught up with them.

Not every issue, not even the issue of how to raise the children, will be neatly sewed up by the time of the wedding. But it is important that couples begin to talk and negotiate about difficult issues. Patterns of communication are being set that may last throughout the marriage.

3. DEALING WITH PARENTS:

Push and Pull

"I WANT JEWISH GRANDCHILDREN!"
The cry is burned in Jeff's memory. When he and his Italian-Catholic fiancée, Angela, told his parents they intended to be married, his mother burst into tears. She stood stock still in the middle of the kitchen and wailed loudly, "I want Jewish grandchildren!"

Her anguish shows grippingly how intermarriage can pit your parents' needs and hopes against your own. Every child, to become an autonomous person, must at some point separate from parents. When you marry, you have to transfer your loyalty from the family you grew up in to the new family you're creating. You must develop the ability to decide what's right for you as a couple, independent of the desires of your parents.

On the other side, most parents have religious and cultural values that are important to them. It is a blow if you appear to be choosing a drastically different life. As a result, when you announce your intention to intermarry, you're more likely to get a cry of pain, or stony silence, than hearty congratulations.

Sociologist Egon Mayer found that out a decade ago when he surveyed intermarried couples for the American Jewish Committee. He found that 43 percent of Jewish parents and about 30 percent of Christian parents openly opposed their child's intermarriage. Only 20 percent in each religion approved. The couples in Mayer's group found that if they went

ahead with the marriage, the rupture with parents healed.[1] But our interviews have shown that in a significant number of families, the wounds
remain raw for a long time.

In this chapter, we look at some of those wounds and at how an
intermarriage can get caught up in deeper family dynamics, particularly
in the struggles of young adults trying to break free of their parents. And
we'll offer practical strategies for dealing with, or heading off, problems
with parents.

PARENTS' REACTIONS TO INTERMARRIAGE

Guilt and humiliation are often the first and strongest feelings parents
have when they learn their child plans to intermarry, as Rabbi Sanford
Seltzer points out in a useful booklet.[2] The parents accuse themselves of
failing to raise their child properly. They're probably afraid relatives and
peers are accusing them, too. Parents may push hard to have a rabbi or
priest perform the wedding because they hope the clergyman, an authority figure, will certify by his presence that they haven't really failed.

Guilt may rapidly be channeled into anger, first at the son or
daughter, then at the intended spouse. Guilt may give way to denial.
Some parents will push for a conversion regardless of the fiancé's wishes
or beliefs. In their guts they feel conversion—even a "paper conversion"—erases the unpleasant fact of their child's marrying out.

There's another feeling that's even stronger than guilt and anger:
loss. Every parent feels somewhat abandoned when his children marry,
and the pang is sharper when you are marrying someone of another
religion. Your parents may fear that you will no longer participate in the
holiday celebrations that make the family feel like a family.

Your parents may also feel rejected—especially if you decide to
convert to your partner's religion.

The intermarriage intensifies another fear that parents may not admit is there: the fear of aging. Often they have already had to bear an
adult child's moving far away. The intermarriage may sharpen their fear
of being left totally alone in old age.

On a more immediate level, the intermarriage may shatter many
of their hopes concerning grandparenthood: the right to brag to their
friends, the right to become the wise elder, passing on values and traditions.

Finally, your parents are likely to be apprehensive of the alien
world from which your spouse comes.

These feelings are intensified if your parents are products of an
Old World culture that encourages strong family bonds.

If your parents protest at your intermarrying, it is easy to cast them as the hidebound bad guys. We urge you instead to recognize their perspective. Their protest might be principled and heartfelt. Jewish parents, for example, may feel a real commitment to preserving the Jewish way of life. Just as your peers might encourage your intermarriage, your parents' peers might be urging them to oppose it. In addition, they may fear that you are choosing a perilous and painful path.

Understanding Your Own Guilty Feelings Don't blame your parents for whatever guilt you may feel about intermarrying. Guilt is not something your parents do to you—it's either a mental club you use to beat yourself, or it's your own way of reacting when your actions don't match your values. As you grew up, you rejected some of the things your parents taught you, but others became part of your value system. If you feel guilty about intermarrying, you have to figure out your own values. Do you yourself have strong feelings about wanting to carry on your ethnic or religious heritage? If so, it is important that you own up to that ambivalence.

If you are Jewish, think hard about whether you think Jews have an obligation to remain in the fold, and if not, why not. If you are Christian, think about whether you believe your marrying out jeopardizes your children's salvation, and if not, why not. Gaining clarity on your own feelings and convictions has obvious benefits for you. It also will increase your chances of resolving matters successfully with your parents. When you know, securely, where you stand, you will be able to be more confident, calm, and consistent with them.

Reassuring Your Parents Because your parents are suffering an extra loss through your intermarriage, you need to give them an extra measure of reassurance. Make clear to your parents that although you are choosing a lifestyle that may be different from theirs, you still share and respect many of their values. Give them credit for the good things they have taught you. Tell them how you intend to continue to use those lessons. If your new family's practices will be similar to your parents'— in other words, if you will continue to practice Judaism or Christianity— be sure to reassure your folks of that. Tell them you will still visit at holidays. At the same time, note any accommodations you are making to your spouse's needs and ask them clearly to respect those differences. If your religious lifestyle will differ from your parents', let them know that although you understand and respect their feelings, you feel compelled to go ahead with the course of action you have chosen.

Philadelphia psychiatrist Robert Garfield, a Jew whose wife, Linda, was raised as an Episcopalian, took his mother aside before the wedding and told her that he understood her qualms and had some of the same fears himself, but that he felt the relationship was strong enough to survive the extra stresses of an intermarriage. The conversation calmed her and helped avert conflict, he says.

If your parents can see the intermarriage as a manageable, if sad, consequence of modern life, you can work with them at adapting. "The hope," Dr. Garfield says, "is that parents, by getting familiar, will soften up over time and begin to accept that this new way of living in the family is legitimate."

INTERMARRIAGE AND SEPARATION STRUGGLES

Of course, there isn't always such an easy resolution. That's because the intermarriage can become caught in the web of the family system. Both the child and the parents can project their own meanings onto the new person and onto the intermarriage—meanings that go far beyond religious difference. The underlying issue is often what therapists call individuation: how healthily the adult is able to separate from his or her parents, and how well the parents are able to let go. You, the child, may see the intermarriage as your quick ticket out of your family. Or your parents, because they are having trouble letting go of you, may become invested in seeing your intermarriage as a personal betrayal. We're not talking about parents who state their principled objection once or a few times, listen to your response and are willing to work toward reaching an equilibrium. We're talking about parents who keep objecting and won't quit.

Let's look at some of these unhealthy reactions, first of the parents and then of the intermarrying children.

Richard and Martha: A War of Attrition Richard's family called themselves Orthodox. But his mother broke so many Jewish laws that her own mother called her a *goy* (a sometimes contemptuous term for a non-Jew). Richard, seeing his family as hypocritical, looked elsewhere for religion. As a young man during the 1960s, he tried all sorts of cults. He spent two years living in a Buddhist house. When he got involved with Martha, it was actually a sign that he was coming back to a more stable period of his life.

Martha had been raised as a Protestant in the deep South. Though Richard didn't care two hoots about Judaism, Martha was quite interested in it. She thought Jews were sensitive, intellectual, successful people.

They represented a way of life that she had dreamed about and never thought she could achieve.

Martha was stable and sensible and fed Richard's confidence. But Richard's mother could see nothing good about her, and kept up a steady program of harassment, trying to persuade Richard that he should leave Martha. She criticized Martha's housekeeping. She dropped newspaper clippings on the table (where Martha could see them) warning that the children of a non-Jewish woman would not be accepted in Israel. When Martha and Richard lost their first child, Richard's mother told him it was God's punishment because he had married a non-Jewish woman. When their second child, a boy, survived, Richard's mother would phone several times a day to criticize the way "that *shiksa*" (non-Jewish woman) was raising him.

The reaction of Richard's family is not so unusual, according to Rabbi Edwin Friedman, a family therapist in Washington, D.C., who has had twenty years of experience counseling over two thousand Jewish-Christian couples. Friedman says he has seen "almost psychotic" reactions to intermarriage in some Jewish families. "I have seen Jewish mothers threaten suicide and Jewish fathers go into severe states of depression," he told a family therapy conference in Tel Aviv. "I have heard of threats to cut children off emotionally and financially. I have witnessed harassment in the form of daily letters or weekly phone calls. Whatever the form of reaction, the rationale is usually phrased in terms of the survival of the Jewish people. 'How can you do this to us?' 'Remember the Holocaust?' "[3]

Religion as a Smokescreen The families might try to present these disputes as battles over religion. But although religion is a sincere concern of many parents, *religion is hardly ever the real cause of severe, protracted conflicts* between an intermarried couple and their families. This point was stressed time and again by nearly all the family therapists, psychiatrists, and clergy we interviewed. Religion, in troubled families, is a smokescreen—a convenient new focus for old power struggles.

Rabbi Friedman has noticed, for example, that the severity of Jewish parents' reactions to an intermarriage is independent of their degree of involvement with Judaism. He writes: "I have seen survivors of the Holocaust not react negatively, saying, 'We have had enough turmoil in our lives,' and I have often seen so-called assimilated fathers take to bed for weeks. . . . Parents who have not been in a synagogue for 20 years can become defenders of the faith overnight."[4]

Richard's mother, for example, had never been a synagogue-goer and used to serve breaded pork chops, winking and calling them veal. At Christmas, she hung stockings on the fireplace and told her children Santa Claus had filled them.

In these families, arguments about religion allow people to veer away from the real issue—individuation or separation.

Rabbi Friedman has developed a theory to explain why some families go off the deep end in reaction to an intermarriage. This theory, which he spelled out in a paper called "The Myth of the Shiksa," has had a great deal of influence on family therapists working with mixed couples.[5] *Shiksa* has come to mean non-Jewish woman, but its root is the Hebrew word for abomination. In ancient times it meant the forbidden ritual objects of idol-worshipping foreign religions. Friedman says Jewish families, in particular, justify their interference in the lives of an intermarried couple by a myth: that the *shiksa* will seduce a Jewish man to abandon his faith and his family. In real-life America, says Friedman, the opposite is usually true. Gentile women who marry Jews tend to be interested in Judaism and often push their husbands toward greater Jewish involvement.

Why do over-reactive Jewish families believe so tenaciously that the *shiksa* is an evil temptress? Friedman says it's because the child who marries out occupies a key position in the family. Subconsciously, the parents can't afford to let that child go. In fact, Friedman asserts, the child marries out because of a subconscious need to help the parent make the break.

Though separation from parents is a process that goes on in all families, each ethnic group has problems that can only be understood by looking at its cultural patterns and history.[6] Mediterranean cultures including the Jewish, Italian, and Greek, tend to have tightly knit, emotionally expressive families that discourage independence. Family bonds were so strong that children were not expected to separate from their families. This patriarchal or matriarchal pattern was useful in the lands from which they came. But when the values collide with American values of independence and mobility, the result can be a family trauma.

The difficult history of the Jews has deepened this trait of family closeness. Generation after generation, Jewish families have faced arbitrary violence from their neighbors. Even in America today, it is a rare adult who has not experienced anti-Semitism. So history has encouraged Jewish mothers to hold their children tightly and Jewish families to cling together.

Richard's family, and other troubled Jewish families, have an excess of the qualities typical of their culture. They interfere excessively in their children's lives and have great difficulty letting go of them. But

Friedman points out that such reactions are by no means limited to Jewish families and others from Mediterranean cultures. In every culture, some parents clutch at those who marry out.

THE CHILD WHO BREAKS AWAY

Sometimes an intermarriage is a more or less conscious attempt to wrench free of family. That was Sarah's case. She is the child of German-Jewish refugees from World War II whose practice of Orthodox Judaism was shaped by their rather cold and formal personalities. Sarah remembers the Sabbath not as a day of joy, but as a weekly ordeal. Every piece of silverware had to be polished, every piece of linen ironed, and every rule and restriction observed to the letter. She hated it.

Beginning in high school, Sarah rebelled. Her life became an experiment on every front. An artist, a bohemian, she began practicing yoga and joined a "New Age" sect that stresses spiritual liberation. And she married a German Christian—a man whose father had fought (unwillingly) in Hitler's armies.

Sarah says she never made a conscious decision "to be the opposite, or to do the opposite" from her parents.

> It was more like, I don't want to live my life this way. I don't want to be the nice Jewish girl who marries a nice Jewish boy and sits down and has nice Jewish kids in a nice Jewish house, and suffocates. . . . I was just looking for a place where I could breathe the way I needed to breathe and chew my food the way I needed to chew.

According to Friedman, in any religious culture the child who is most likely to marry out is the one who has been most important to holding the parents' marriage together. Family members overreact to the marriage because they "confuse feelings about their ethnicity with feelings about their family."[7] Sometimes the parents' marriage may be paper-clipped together mostly by their shared worry over the "bad" or "sick" son or daughter. Sometimes one or both parents' needs are met by a strong attachment to a favored child. Very often in such cases, the intermarrier is the "good" son or the "responsible" daughter, the one everyone thought was least likely to marry out. That was the case with Jeff and Angela.

Angela and Jeff: Closely Watched Friedman notes that a disproportionate number of intermarriages take place among eldest or only children. Angela, a third-generation Italian immigrant, was the eldest of five children. She was the first child in the extended family to leave the Italian ghetto in Brooklyn and go to a suburban high school and a private college. She recalls:

> When I was being raised, the whole family, all forty-five or fifty of them, were watching. My father saw right away I could be trained mentally and socially to succeed. He really was interested in that and paid a lot of attention to me.

She became the privileged one: Her father often took her on special excursions, leaving the other four children at home with their mother.

Angela's family was nominally Catholic and strongly Italian. But her father gave mixed signals about his attachment to Italian ways. The family had moved out of Brooklyn and into suburban "WASP country."

> We had our little Bass Weejuns and A-line skirts, and went off to school, and pretended we were Americans, and came home to the fanfare and the food, and the art, and the opera, and the whole business that only went on in our house and that nobody saw.

Her father encouraged her to go to a prestigious private college on scholarship. "My father thought he would send me into this fire, and I would come out the image of a person who had really come from a Brooklyn Italian ghetto."

In his own mind, Angela's father was laying down an invisible line between the Italian world and everyone else. But Angela didn't realize that until she had crossed the line. She met Jeff at a party while she was in college. In the old-fashioned way, Jeff told Angela's father he wanted to marry his daughter. The reply: "There's a question of religion." He didn't mean Jeff wasn't Catholic; he meant Jeff wasn't Italian. That became clear when Angela's father later stopped speaking to a cousin who "married out" to an Irish Catholic.

Angela's father threatened to disown her when he learned she was living with Jeff. He began speaking to her again when she "made things right" by getting married. But later, her father disowned her again when she took her sister's side in a family quarrel. This second disowning made it clear the issue wasn't religion after all. It was crossing the will of the patriarch.

Jeff's parents were also very upset when he decided to marry out. He was the youngest in his family and was his father's favorite. When he was a boy, his father used to encourage him to set up his own little businesses. As an adult, he chose to go into the same field as his father, and often consults him on business decisions. He is also very close to his mother.

You've already heard about how Jeff's mother wept in the kitchen when he and Angela announced their plans. But instead of tossing Jeff out of the family, his parents rushed to bring Angela in.

Although their parents' behavior was opposite, Angela realized that her family and Jeff's were very much alike: two close-knit families that reacted strongly to the one who tried to get away. Explains Angela,

> Jeff's family is the kind of Jewish family, it doesn't matter what you do, you could murder somebody, you're still their kid. They would still love you, they would still come to the trial, they would still hire the lawyer. My family, there's the line. You cross the line, that's it, we will not speak to you again. That's the stage we're at with my family. It doesn't matter what I do or what I write or what gifts I send or what funerals I attend. . . . They do not want me. And that's really painful. It's Southern Italian culture. That's it.

The problems and cultural patterns in the families of Sarah, Angela, and Jeff vary widely. But they all fit Friedman's theory of a "most important" child who marries out.

The theory also explains why some Jewish families that are not particularly religious put heavy pressure on the gentile partner to convert. The family feels the only way it can maintain its previous closeness is to make the new spouse an indistinguishable cog in the larger family machine.

False Independence Parents are hardly the only culprits in unhealthy family behavior. Sometimes it is the intermarrier herself who has made the marriage a symbol—a symbol of liberation from parents.

In cultures that encourage family closeness, what feels like an embrace to the child may feel like a half nelson to the young adult. If you felt strangled by your parents and hoped that intermarrying would spring you free, you have fallen into a terrible irony. If you have not already separated adequately from your parents, marrying out only intensifies the problem.

Rebels like Sarah who hoped to catapult themselves beyond the grasp of their family find the opposite is true. Conflict, whether an outward battle or inward guilt, keeps the adult child and his parents emotionally entangled with one another.

Parents and children who are cut off from each other, observes

Philadelphia psychologist David Greenwald (a specialist in marital and family therapy), "are likely to be the most emotionally involved of all. Their psychic or inner lives may revolve around this person they never see."

Some people see themselves not as rebelling but as escaping—steaming out of their parents' harbor, with a new partner, toward a new way of life. "An ethnic group," says Barbara Breitman, a psychotherapist and ethnicity specialist with the Jewish Family and Children's Agency of Philadelphia, "is just an extension of the family—especially a small ethnic group and one that was physically enclosed. So [people think] if you want to get away from home, marry out."

The escape is foiled if, like Angela, breaking free of the overwhelming closeness of her own ethnic family, she suddenly finds herself clutched to the bosom of her partner's equally overwhelming tribe.

But other intermarriers gladly seek the embrace of the new family. They are usually gentiles from emotionally austere Northern European backgrounds who have idealized Jewish family closeness and welcome it. Problems can set in when a Jewish partner who is running away from family closeness marries a gentile who is running toward it. Their instincts and needs are tugging them in opposite directions.

Sometimes the gentile partner sees a different kind of liberation in Judaism. Gentiles who lost their taste for Christianity during adolescence may develop an appetite for the Jewish tradition of intellectualism and informed debate. Martha, who was fleeing the narrowness of her Southern white childhood, was delighted by the tolerance and intelligence of her Jewish friends. The lack of dogma and the emphasis on ethics rather than faith makes Judaism more palatable to some gentiles. These values reinforce their self-images as independent, thinking human beings, separate from their parents and making autonomous choices.

But because Judaism comes in a complicated package, where religious ideas and values are intertwined with family, culture, and an almost tribal sense of identity, the gentile partner may find herself pulled in two opposite directions—attracted to the ideas of the faith, but shying away from the enveloping demands of culture and family identity. After all, she has just succeeded in separating from her own parents—why should she allow herself to be swallowed up by a new set of parents?

You may have chosen to marry someone who appears very different from your parents, or in particular from the parent with whom you have conflict. But this strategy, whether conscious or unconscious, often backfires. Says Barbara Breitman:

> People can pick non-Jewish partners and replay exactly the same relationship they had with their Jewish mothers . . . (Men) see the quieter appearance, and the blond hair, the cultural difference, which looks to them less loud, less aggressive, less domineering, less over-protective, and more feminine. But the unconscious finds its mate, which will be somebody who will run the same trip. The unconscious is like radar. . . . If you didn't work out (the problem) in the original relationship, you're likely to marry it and repeat the performance.

Sarah, for example, found herself married to a man who was just as distant and uncommunicative—as formal and classically European—as her parents.

Some people succeed in picking a partner who is genuinely different from the parents—inwardly as well as externally. But in a short while they begin to suffer a sort of hallucination. They attribute thoughts or qualities to the partner that are similar to those of their parents. A man who feels as if he has been dominated by his mother will begin to feel dominated by his wife regardless of whether she has done anything to cause such feelings. Or he will begin to act in the same dependent ways he acted toward his parents, and will provoke more dominating behavior in his spouse.

There's another reason you can't slip away from your parents by marrying out. They are part of you. You can't pluck the parent out of your own personality. A woman who detests her dominating mother may end up duplicating the behavior she detests.

Barbara Breitman points out two principles:

First, separation problems take forms which may appear to be opposite, but are actually just variations of the same underlying problem. In one family, the parent leads by the nose a docile child who can't say no; in another family, the parent cracks the whip to curb a rebel who can't say yes. In both families, a healthy separation has not taken place.

Second, each person tends to marry someone at his own level of independence. Thus, the problem of separating from parents is likely something both partners would need to work on. Jeff found it hard to say no to his parents no matter how often they wanted to see him. Angela was completely cut off from her parents; her father had disowned her. Although their families handled their getaway attempts in opposite fashions, their parents still loom large in both their psyches.

How Separation Struggles Can Undermine Marriages When one member of a couple is having problems with her family, the anger or anxiety are passed on to the marriage just as a billiard ball passes along its motion to the ball it hits. The new ball may go off in a different direction, but you can trace the energy right back to the cue.

Jeff and Angela have had a tug-of-war for years over how close to be with his family. "There are about forty different Jewish holidays," explains Jeff, "and my mother wants us to be there for all of them." Says Angela, "We don't just see them four or five times a year. We see them like once or twice a week. . . . They want us to live next door to them, and anything that does not rise to that level is not satisfactory."

Angela recalls that her family

> wanted us to come up for Thanksgiving and Christmas and this birthday and that birthday. Jeff's family was doing the same thing. So we were like jackrabbits just jumping from one thing to another.

Angela and Jeff are fortunate because they know that they have unresolved problems with their parents that are causing problems in their marriage. When the friction gets too severe, they go for marriage counseling. But often, partners in an intermarriage simply transmit their parents' hostility without realizing they are the conduit. They begin to see in their partner the faults that the parent has been criticizing. They are not aware that the parent may have an unconscious emotional stake in seeing the marriage fail.

Why should you take the trouble to find out if you fit any of the patterns of false individuation? Because marriages built on the rockpile of rebellion can collapse in a heap of rubble. First, if both you and your partner have not gone through a healthy separation from parents, there's a risk that your partner will get tied up in fighting your parents—transferring his or her struggle to your arena. When your partner bursts into a rage at your parents, it may look like support, but it actually makes it harder for you to solve your own problems. In a healthy marriage, the spouse who isn't in conflict with family maintains a sympathetic but detached position.

Second, the rockpile may tumble if one partner begins to grow up. Comments psychiatrist Robert Garfield, "They do well as long as both are at war with their families of origin. When one begins to change, it begins to upset the balance of power that's been the major underlying dynamic" of the marriage.

Separation Struggles and the Larger Community One final point: Separation issues are likely to affect not only how you relate to your families and your spouse, but how you relate to the larger religious or cultural community from which you came. When you are vacillating about how close you are to your family, you are also likely to vacillate about how much connection you have with the larger community. This is logical, because we look for the same things from a community that we look for from our parents: approval and security or a sense of belonging. According to Breitman, "When you have the ego strength to define yourself vis-à-vis the parent, you also have the ego strength to define yourself vis-à-vis the larger religious community."

During the time when Richard was struggling to free himself from his mother's interference, he was alienated from the Jewish community. In spite of the vilification from Richard's mother, Martha was eager to affiliate with a synagogue and see that her son received a Jewish education. When Richard learned to assert himself with his mother, he became ready to reaffiliate with the Jewish community, and they found a synagogue which accepted them as an intermarried couple.

Home Free We've been discussing intermarriages where separation from parents is a problem. But obviously, the magnetism that draws people together does not always spring from a neurosis. A number of studies show that there are also many cases where an intermarriage occurs for the opposite reason: People have already successfully separated from their parents. Their pool of eligible partners is not limited to those of whom their parents would approve.

Egon Mayer, the sociologist, found that intermarriers marry at a somewhat later age. And a significantly high percentage had been divorced. In his book, *Love and Tradition: Marriage Between Jews and Christians,* Mayer notes that second marriages were about 50 percent more likely to be intermarriages than were first marriages.[8] In fact, he jokes, "some have suggested that divorce is the leading cause of intermarriage."

Mayer suggests that divorced people are less likely to be hassled by their parents about marrying out of their group. They have already gone through the family trauma of breaking a taboo. In addition, because they are older and divorced, their pool of eligible mates within their ethnic group is smaller, and parents are just relieved to see them married again.

The couples we interviewed mentioned a variety of other factors that led parents to take an intermarriage more calmly. Sometimes a brother or sister had previously intermarried. Sometimes the person's previous dating pattern had been so rebellious that the present choice of an interfaith partner seemed tame by comparison. Sometimes the couple lived together for a number of years before marrying. (On one hand, their parents got used to their being together; on the other, parents were so relieved that they had finally made things legal that they didn't make a fuss about their child's choice of partner.)

EVALUATING YOURSELF AND YOUR FAMILY

If you and your partner have successfully separated from your parents, you are not dependent, physically or emotionally, on them. Nor do you have a gnawing anxiety about getting their approval. Some people spend much of their time reacting to what they think their parents would think. Sarah calls it "an inner dialogue, or monologue." Her parents were too proper and polite—"too European, too German," she says—to create a scene about her choices. But her mind hissed with the judgments she was sure they made. Though she didn't believe in circumcision, she circumcised her sons because she couldn't deal with the guilt of not doing it. Sometimes she would feel crushed by guilt about having married "a German, of all things. . . . I felt like my ancestors were sort of peering over my shoulder saying, 'What did she do?' "

Individuation problems aren't always obvious—especially to the people involved. Over and over, couples assured us there were no problems between them and their families. But as they began talking, the feelings and memories welled up. So it pays to do some self-assessment. Ask yourself the following questions:

First, do family fights seem to follow the same old patterns? Has the style of fighting remained the same, with a new subject (religion) replacing the things you used to fight about?

Second, do your parents regularly question your adequacy or your competence?

Third, do you get upset when you think about or talk with your parents? Do you and your spouse fight whenever you have contact with your parents?

Fourth, how important are your parents in your daily life? Do you hesitate to do things you very much want to do because it would upset your parents? Do you turn to your parents for advice before making most significant decisions? Do you turn to them for consolation regarding the routine frustrations of daily life, including problems in your marriage? Or (of equal significance), have you been estranged from your parents for six months or more?

If the answer to any of these questions is yes, you need to shore up the shaky foundations of your independence.

First you need to transform your emotional relationship with your parents. The essential element in modifying the relationship is to forgive them. You must make a conscious decision to let go of your resentments. To live in the present and not in the past. And to make the present something you create.[9]

The most important tool in improving your relationship with your parents is empathy. Try some inner calisthenics. Somersault out of your fixed vision of the world and put yourself in their place. Try to get a clearer picture of your parents' upbringing. Find out what life was like in their town or city when they were growing up. Reflect on things they have told you about their past. Read social histories. Find out more from other family members. How many Jews, or Christians, have they ever known well? America is 97 percent gentile and only 3 percent Jewish. There are many Christians who have had virtually no personal contact with Jews. And since Jews are concentrated in urban centers, the reverse is also true. Don't see hostility where there is only ignorance or discomfort.

To aid you further in transforming your relationship with your parents, take a look at the exercises and information in *Making Peace with Your Parents,* by Harold H. Bloomfield, M.D., and *Cutting Loose: An Adult Guide to Coming to Terms with Your Parents,* by Howard M. Halpern, Ph.D.[10]

Your second task is to solidify your own convictions on how you want to live your married life. As you go through this book, try to come to a holistic vision of the religious life-style you want. In addition, come to a clear sense of your bottom line on specific issues.

The final step is to solidify your agreements with your partner. You need to know what kind of life-style and home your partner wants, and to negotiate agreement in any area where you start out with different aims. Once the two of you have decided your terms, believe them and support each other. Prepare to resist efforts at undercutting your resolve. A number of couples spoke of the great necessity of a united front.

"You really have to start thinking as *we*," says one intermarried Jewish woman. "We have done nothing that I would not have done had I been married to a Jewish man, but I think the key word is we, that you have to start thinking as we."

SOLUTIONS: MOVING AHEAD

After you go through your inner calisthenics and establish your united front, you'll be ready to use the "tactics manual" which follows, to take steps forward in your relationship with your parents. Choose the techniques you think will work for you. Remember that your parents don't have all the power. Either side can take the initiative to change the relationship.

Develop Common Ground You can't expect your parents and your spouse or fiancé to love each other when all they know about each other is a name, a face, and a religious label—a label which tells them the other person is foreign. If you were introducing two people at a party, you would do your best to stress the things they had in common. You would tell them about each other's enthusiasms. You would tell them a few nice things about each other. That gives them a basis for starting a conversation. Do the same for your parents and partner.

Find Neutral Turf It helps to get your parents and spouse or fiancé involved in pleasant activities together on neutral ground. Go to a musical or a museum. Take a walk in a public garden. This search for neutral turf can also be for your benefit. It can help you break out of your parents' or in-laws' force field. Suggest new activities, such as potluck dinners or rotating dinners at each other's homes, instead of command performances at their homes. Angela was able to break down some of the barriers between her parents and Jeff by suggesting that all four of them go out for dinner and dancing, an activity that they all enjoyed.

Be Considerate When you visit your partner's parents, bring a small house gift, a bottle of wine for dinner, or some other token of your consideration. Send cards on birthdays and special occasions. Dress with sensitivity to their tastes.

Be Diplomatic You'll get nowhere if your parents feel that you're jamming your point down their throats.

If you feel yourself becoming angry, take a breath, and stop for a moment until you are clear about exactly what is angering you. Don't squelch your anger or avoid the issue, but wait until you can state your point of view clearly, calmly, and without malice before you speak.

Be sensitive to the timing. If you are about to tell your Christian parents that your children will be raised Jewish, do not tell them on Easter or Christmas.

Be receptive. After you have spoken your piece, let your parents talk without interrupting them. Voice your understanding of their point of view, or, if you don't understand, ask politely for clarification.

Set Your Own Pace If parents try to initiate a discussion about religion before you are ready, tell them in a friendly way that both of you are aware that it's a difficult issue, and you are talking about it together. But since you haven't made any decisions, you're not ready to discuss the topic with them.

Express Your Love In sensitive situations where you will not be practicing your religion of birth, Sherri Alper, a counselor for the Reform Jewish movement in Philadelphia, suggests you say something like, "It's true that I am going to be married to someone who is Jewish. I may be with his family for some holidays. But I will still always be your daughter. I will always still love you. Just because I'm changing my religion doesn't mean I'm changing my family. I'll still be there with you for holidays. It won't be my holiday, but I'll be there with you because I love you and it's important to be together."

Take One Step at a Time Try to introduce your parents gradually to your spouse's religion and culture. Begin with situations that are less emotionally loaded. If your parents are threatened by the idea of coming to a Passover seder, invite them for Thanksgiving first.

Give them pleasant, non-threatening ways of participating in your celebrations. Lena Romanoff, director of the Jewish Converts Network, tells how she gave her Italian-Catholic parents a role to play in Hanukkah. Deep-fried sweets are traditional food on the holiday, so she invited her mother to bring the homemade donuts that were her culinary pride and joy.

As time goes on, instead of avoiding any mention of religion, share your enjoyment of what you are doing. Talk about your preparations for upcoming holidays. Send parents or in-laws a calendar so they are aware of your celebrations.

Share on Their Turf Even if you do not normally practice their customs, do so on occasion. Let them have the joy of your company on Christmas Day or for a seder. Attend their services at special times. It is a loving statement that even if you've got a new life, you still respect where they've come from. And it tells them, and you, that they do not have to do all the adapting.

Give Them Grandparent Roles Make clear to your parents that you will continue to welcome them into your life in certain roles, such as grandparents to your children. If they feel able to participate in a ceremony such as a circumcision or christening, give them the role of holding the baby at some stage in the ceremony. Or invite them to say a few words for the child.

In many families, the birth of a child bridges great gaps. All you need to do is let it happen.

Give Them Clear Ground Rules Decide with your spouse what your rules for relating to parents will be, and then tell them in a friendly but firm way. For example, Lena Romanoff told her parents they should give her children Hanukkah gifts, not Christmas gifts, and that the gifts should be wrapped in Hanukkah paper. She also told her parents that the children would in turn send them Christmas gifts wrapped in Christmas paper.

Know How to Set Limits If your parents do things that are destructive to you or your family, tell them. But tell them in a clear, not angry way. Be sure to preface your requests by reassuring your parents of your love and your appreciation of them. (Psychiatrist Harold Bloomfield suggests that you say, "I love you *and* this is how I need you to behave." Not "I love you *but*," which suggests that you will stop loving them unless they change.)[11]

Richard, the Jewish man whose mother sniped at his Southern wife, made it a practice to cut short the conversation as soon as his mother began criticizing Martha. He recalls:

> Every time she would say something wrong, I would just hang up the phone and I wouldn't answer it again. So eventually she learned that if she wanted me to come over and visit, she had to accept my wife and that I was an individual. Since then, things have smoothed out very well.

Don't Retaliate It's easy to let petty problems escalate. There were nearly forty people at Neil's family seder. His wife, Anita, a Catholic, got upset because she was given a folding chair while the other daughter-in-law, who was Jewish, was given a padded chair. The next time her mother-in-law was over for dinner, Anita set the cracked dish at her mother-in-law's place. More important than the dish was the hostile feeling that went with it. The war was on. The best tactic toward a hostile in-law, says Lena Romanoff, is to "kill them with kindness."

Enlist a Third Party's Help Get help from a powerful member of the family—someone who outranks your parent, such as a grandmother or respected uncle. Tell them that you are convinced the choices you have made are right for you, but that you have no desire to be at war with your parents. Ask them to help bridge the gap.

Talk to relatives who are bohemians or rogues, who don't fit the family pattern, and ask them how they broke away. Talk to aunts and uncles who are close to your parent for advice on smoothing ruffled feathers.

Sometimes a family therapist, or a rabbi or minister who is liked and respected by the parent, can mediate.

But a word of caution about mediators: Know who you're recruiting. If you enlist a rabbi, be sure that he has a sympathetic attitude toward intermarriage; most rabbis object to intermarriage on principle. Most also will be unwilling to talk to your family unless they know you personally. If you enlist a relative, the same cautions apply. Many relatives are more interested in keeping the peace than in trying to bring about real communication. They may say one thing to you and another to your parents, so that you're no closer to understanding each other than before.

Don't Create Triangles If you try to enlist an ally in the family, there's another trap you mustn't fall into: creating triangles. The family member should be brought in *once,* to break a deadlock. Once you and your parent are face to face and really talking to each other and listening to each other, you must continue to deal with each other face to face. Don't get into the habit of calling a relative or intermediary to complain about your parents, and letting that person pass your remarks along. The reverse is also true. Don't allow complaints to be "sent" to you through a third person. Deal directly with the person you're upset with, and insist that your parents, spouse, and other relatives do the same.

Don't Cut Off Contact When you cut off contact, you are likely to fall into a common psychological trap: projection. The only parent you're relating to is the fantasy parent in your head. You attribute feelings and motives to your parent that may have nothing to do with reality. There's another danger to this fantasy parent: It is incapable of change. It's much better to be in contact with your real parent: That way you both have an opportunity to change, grow, and adjust to new realities.

Take Richard's case. He felt so divided, so pulled in opposite directions by his mother and his wife, that at one point he considered running away to California and cutting off all contact with both of them. But he decided to stay and cope with the dilemma. He now realizes, "You keep the telephone lines open so they can call you and talk to you.

Eventually everything sort of reaches a common ground, everything reaches equilibrium."

Even extreme conflicts such as estrangement can usually be ended if one of the parties is determined to do so, according to our experts. Angela wouldn't remain "dead" to her father if she refused to stay dead, said one family therapist. She could go visit the family, reestablish her relationship with other family members and force the issue. Sometimes humor helps. For example, Angela could send a "rebirth announcement," explaining that she is no longer willing to remain dead.

Be Persistent Realize that over time, most parents will moderate their position. Intermarriage is much more common today. Articles are appearing about it in the media. Your parents are likely to have friends whose children have intermarried. As they realize that they are not alone, their attitudes may soften. Strive to be consistently friendly and open. Hostility and anger are exhausting emotions. Most people can't keep them up forever. Kindness can outlast hostility as water wears away stone. Continue to send cards at birthdays and holidays even if you think they go unopened. If you get nasty letters, ignore them or send them back. A hostile parent may never fall in love with your spouse, but over time, tolerance will probably develop. And tolerance, as Lena Romanoff notes, "is better than nothing."

In Extreme Cases

In spite of what we have said about the dangers of cutting off contact with your parent, in a few extreme cases, you will have to break the wrestlehold and extricate yourself. Temporarily separate yourself in time and distance, then go back and reestablish the relationship. This is especially true in cases of a parent who is mentally ill or abusive, or with parents who are chronically hostile and interfering. It is a step that should be taken thoughtfully, not in a moment of anger. We suggest you first consult a counselor or therapist. If you decide, alone or in consultation with a therapist, that this step is necessary, don't feel guilty. Know that you are not alone: Others have had to take this route. But even in this case, leave the door open. Don't let pride or vindictiveness prevent you from reestablishing contact at an appropriate time.

Give yourselves time, away from your parents, to decide how you want to run your household, to solve whatever problems may come up between the two of you, and to get your routines established. When things are going smoothly, recontact your parents. Tell them, "This is the way we do it. We invite you to join us" for dinner or some other occasion.

All the steps in our tactics manual require one essential element: patience. Change takes time. Even if your parents rage, and you fume initially, appreciate the possibility that you both will soften as time passes. Take to heart the words of Rabbi Mayer Selekman, of Broomall, Pennsylvania, who was speaking to a group of the parents of intermarried but could have been talking to you:

> Don't make a moment into an eternity. You're feeling this for the first time. You have to allow for a process. . . . You see, when you get clobbered with one of these things, you automatically escalate into a nuclear holocaust. It's not a rational response initially, it's an emotional one, and all I'm suggesting is, you have to live with it for awhile.

You also need to understand that you cannot insulate your parents from the complexities of life any more than they could protect you. Many of the choices you make in life are bound to disappoint, bewilder, or trouble your parents. You cannot mold your choices to their wishes or needs. The most you can do is to reassure them of your love.

Finally—consider your children. It's important to resolve separation issues with your parents not only for your own peace of mind and the sake of your marriage, but also for the sake of your children. Your children get their inheritance from two different cultures. They need to know their grandparents in order to know their roots. They need to experience these heritages as being different, but not in conflict.

Remember: Separation issues, like other unresolved issues in a family, can be passed from generation to generation. If you don't untangle the knots in your relationship with your parents, your children might have to deal with similar problems with you.

4. THE WEDDING:

A Mixed Blessing

The wedding is supposed to be the best of times but can feel like the worst. Many of you have dialed the phone till your fingertip was numb, trying to find a clergyman to officiate.

And the difficulties can go far beyond that. The wedding is a *public* ceremony. In your cozy corner, listening to the same sweet violins, you could ignore the differences in your backgrounds. But all of a sudden you're supposed to conduct the orchestra—together. Settling on the specifics of the ceremony is often your first test of negotiating as a couple.

Then comes the large matter of your parents. The wedding is a life-cycle event for *them,* too. Do they have any right to call the tunes?

Your wedding mingles people from two different cultures. An occasional jangling note is almost to be expected. We've heard, for example, about the gentile groom who was handed a glass at the end of the ceremony, didn't know what to do with it, and dropped it upon the floor. Whereupon there was a chorus of shouts from the Jewish side of the room: "Step on it!"

One agnostic Jew says the closest he's come to praying was his fervent wish throughout the wedding day that nothing would happen to offend the family on either side.

As we've traveled the country talking to interfaith couples, we've heard about the problems. But we'll also tell how—with patience and cleverness—many couples coped and triumphed.

We hope this chapter will help you understand why people act as they do about weddings and—if the big day is still ahead—to design it in the way that is best for you and your family. The Appendix at the end of the book contains a listing of referral services for finding an officiant, a summary of each denomination's rules on intermarriage, and a sample ceremony.

As you design your wedding day, we suggest that you think not only about your practical options but also about your own deeply held values concerning what the marriage ceremony means; about the larger-than-life visions of weddings that we all pick up from our society; about your parents' wishes and fears; about the changing relationships in your two families.

Your interfaith wedding presents not only problems but opportunities. The situation forces you to think more deeply than many other engaged couples do about what you want to achieve through the wedding ceremony. In so doing, you have a chance to create a day that can be exceptionally meaningful and beautiful.

THE WEDDING AS A LIFE-CHANGING EVENT

Before you start your planning, it's helpful to understand the enormous emotional freight a wedding bears in virtually everyone's lives. In our American culture, it is often seen as the day when a woman is transformed for an instant into a queen, with a royal gown and attendants. In every culture, it is designed to be a peak experience, full of mystery, symbolism, and emotion. And through the veil of the rituals you glimpse the scary realities: a major new commitment and responsibility, and a major change in life status.

Even if you have been living together, the wedding is a key psychological turning point in your life as a couple. Rabbi Linda Holtzman, director of practical rabbinics at the Reconstructionist Rabbinical College, points out, "There is something about standing up in front of people and saying, 'We are married.' It brings a sense of permanence, solidity to the relationship . . . a determination to work things out."

Your wedding represents a major change, not only in your life but in the lives of your two families. Think about it: There are only two ways to gain membership in a family—to be born (or adopted) and to marry. Even if you have been away from home for some time, your marriage represents almost as big a psychological change in the life of your parents as your birth did. Your wedding launches ripples that will travel through all the other relationships in your family.[1]

Because of this great significance, the wedding is a time when families tend to make grand, even extravagant gestures. Matters of location, music, color, that at other times would be just quibbling differences in detail, assume mythic and symbolic proportions. An interfaith ceremony complicates and magnifies the meaning of such details. Rabbi Roy Rosenberg of New York City's Temple of Universal Judaism, who has officiated at hundreds of interfaith weddings, told us of one couple who chartered a jet and flew the entire wedding party from London to New York because they could not obtain permission to have a co-officiated ceremony in any church in England. "We had a *huppah* (Jewish wedding canopy) and yarmulkas in St. Patrick's Cathedral," he said.

So if you're finding yourselves erupting in periodic emotional geysers, if you feel mired in details and decisions, tell yourselves it is natural. This would happen whether you married someone of your own faith or a different faith. At the same time, it pays to understand how interfaith issues can increase these normal stresses.

To plan your wedding, each of you must sift through your own values and needs. How do people of your culture and religion view the wedding? How many of these values do you and your partner share? A wedding is a public statement. What kind of statement do you want to make? The wedding is also a way of solidifying your commitments to each other—making them formally and publicly the foundation of your lives. What kind of commitment or vow do you wish to make? In arriving at answers to these questions, use Chapters 5, 9, and 10 to explore your ethnic background, your personal beliefs, and your spiritual heritage.

FINDING AN OFFICIANT

One of the most difficult challenges you will face is finding someone to officiate at your wedding. First, in order to choose your officiant, you will have to sort through your beliefs carefully and to deal with all the internal and external pressures—the guilt, the demands of families, the societal criticism—that each of you might be experiencing. You may have to face some genuine differences in beliefs and needs. Second, your search for an officiant puts you squarely up against the religious movements, most of which have limits as to what they consider a valid ceremony. The challenge is to find a ceremony that expresses your values while remaining in an amicable relationship to your families and your heritages.

You have four basic choices of officiant. You can choose to be married in a traditional ceremony in one of your two religions, following the rules of that religion and using one officiant—a rabbi, priest, or minister. You can choose to be married by a neutral non-religious person, such as a judge. You can try to have a co-officiated ceremony, with both a rabbi and a priest or minister presiding. Or you can choose a compromise religion such as Unitarianism, which doesn't make any traditional demands. Within those four choices, you can make various accommodations to your two families.

In selecting an officiant, you are making a public statement about the spiritual pattern you wish to set for your home. If you and your partner have different ideas about who you want to officiate, it's very important to sort through any differences in values and beliefs that may underlie your diverging visions of the ceremony. Your choice of an officiant should not be a makeshift compromise, but should truly reflect the values you have agreed upon for your home and your children.

In choosing the style of officiation, you also need to be aware of the tremendous controversy this issue has caused within Judaism.

Jewish Opposition Rabbis who perform intermarriages—and particularly those who co-officiate—face heavy opposition. When Rabbi Mayer Selekman agreed to perform an interfaith wedding for the daughter of concentration camp survivors, he received an anonymous threat that his home would be burned down and he and his family would be killed. (He went ahead with the ceremony and the threats never materialized.) He has also dealt with people who believed he only did this for the money and who tried to bribe him to prevent him from officiating. Rabbi Rosenberg received an anonymous letter that said, "You are worse than Hitler."

If you have had to search long and hard for a rabbi to marry you, you may have felt the Jewish hostility toward intermarriage as a personal attack on you. It's not. From the historical account in Chapter 1, you have some idea as to why Jews are so concerned about intermarriage, per se. Many rabbis will welcome an intermarried couple into a synagogue once the marriage has taken place, but still refuse to officiate at such weddings—and particularly to co-officiate with a clergyman from another faith. This may seem like contradictory behavior. But there are four reasons for it, rooted in Jewish history, values, and beliefs.

First, a major tenet of Judaism dating from the giving of the law at Mount Sinai over three thousand years ago is that Jews are not to take on the religious practices of any other group.[2]

Second, in Judaism, a wedding is a binding legal contract between a Jewish man and woman who agree to live together and to follow the laws of Judaism. This Jewish contract has no standing when entered into between a Jew and gentile.[3] As a Jew and gentile, you can have a valid civil wedding, but not a valid Jewish wedding.

Reconstructionists, Reform Jews, and even many Conservative Jews today don't consider the law as God-given or binding, but to be modified by the Jewish people. Why are they more stringent about weddings than other points of law, such as keeping kosher?

This brings us to the third reason for Jewish resistance to interfaith ceremonies: the fear that the Jewish people will disappear after thousands of years of continuous peoplehood. This fear has been heightened by the Nazi Holocaust which killed one-third of world Jewry. Even when their views on the details of religious observance vary, Jews of these newer denominations are often deeply loyal to Judaism as a civilization with a distinct mixture of ethnic and family loyalties, intellectual heritage, ethical and spiritual values, and cultural traditions. Some Reform and Reconstructionist rabbis will marry a mixed couple only if the partners agree to pass Judaism on to their children and not to practice any other religion in the home.

The fourth reason some rabbis feel they cannot perform interfaith weddings is that the family (not the synagogue) is the center of Jewish life. The wedding, along with the *bris* (ritual circumcision of the son), is one of the most important rites in Judaism. Marriage is considered the ideal state in Judaism. Judaism teaches that men and women must marry and have a family to achieve the fullness of their humanity, as given to them by God. Since the home in Judaism is the equivalent of the altar or communion chalice in Christianity, many rabbis feel they, as representatives of the Jewish people, cannot consecrate a home which might not be Jewish.

Some rabbis who feel they cannot officiate at interfaith ceremonies will still make great efforts to welcome couples to the community. Rabbi Sally Finestone, director of the Hillel at the University of Houston, will offer to perform premarital counseling, refer a couple to a judge who does interfaith ceremonies, suggest congregations where they will be welcome, and call six months after the ceremony to see how they are doing.

It is much less difficult, at least in America today, to find a Christian clergyman to co-officiate, because most Christian denominations see themselves as growing from or including Judaism; there is nothing in the Jewish ceremony that violates Christian beliefs.

If you are determined to have a co-officiated ceremony, you might be able to locate a Christian clergyperson who has co-officiated simply by calling a large Protestant church or the Catholic diocese. You can then get a referral to the rabbi who has co-officiated with him. Rabbis and cantors who make a business of co-officiating sometimes advertise in the personal classified ad sections of magazines and newspapers. You will need to weigh the advantages of having both religions represented against the disadvantages of having an officiant with whom you may have no personal or spiritual connection.

The issues in choosing an officiant are complex. For example, as you can see from the above discussion of Jewish opposition to intermarriage, choosing clergy as officiants rather than a judge is not necessarily the most spiritual route, or the one that shows the most respect for your religious heritage. You and your partner will have to strike a balance between your own beliefs and desires, the beliefs and desires of your families, and the beliefs and rules of the denominations and clergy with whom you wish to work.

Let's look at how two couples sorted through the issues.

Ann and Evan: Honoring the Tradition Ann Eisenstein is one Jewish woman who took the concerns of traditional Judaism seriously. When she married Evan Johnson, her own religious convictions and those of her family dictated that the ceremony must be conducted by a judge rather than a rabbi. Ann comes from a distinguished rabbinic family. Her father, Rabbi Ira Eisenstein, is the founder and former president of the Reconstructionist Rabbinical College. Her grandfather, the late Rabbi Mordechai Kaplan, founder of the Reconstructionist movement in Judaism and author of *Judaism as a Civilization,* is considered one of the giants of modern Jewish thought.

Although we use pseudonyms for most couples, Ann and Evan agreed we could use their real names so people could see how a prominent family, deeply committed to Judaism, coped with intermarriage.

Ann, a psychotherapist and social worker with a brush of thickly curling light-brown hair, a warm smile, and a direct, look-you-in-the-eyes manner of speech, went to a Jewish day school and predominantly Jewish college (Brandeis) and grew up in a house where Jewish topics and observance dominated every day. She remains a committed Jew and attends a Reconstructionist synagogue. But the other love of her life is music. Her mother, Judith Eisenstein, is a musicologist and a specialist in Jewish music. Ann, a cellist, got to know Evan, a professional violinist, as part of a chamber music ensemble. Evan was in some ways the consummate White Anglo-Saxon Protestant. As reticent as Ann was outspoken, he had grown up in Tulsa, Oklahoma, while she had lived all her life in

New York and Chicago. But, leaving aside the ethnic and religious labels, their families were in some ways remarkably similar. His mother, to whom he was close, was also a musicologist. His family, members of a Unitarian church, were as intellectual and socially concerned as Ann's.

When Ann and Evan announced they were going to marry, Ann's father immediately asked Evan if he would convert to Judaism. But when Evan said no, the matter was dropped. Although he had always felt comfortable with Jews and had had a Jewish girlfriend before Ann, Evan says, "I wasn't Jewish. I didn't feel Jewish."

They had agreed to raise their children Jewish (their son Aaron goes to a Jewish day school). So it would have been possible for them to find a Reform rabbi to marry them. But Ann's father, without malice, told them that in principle he could not marry them. Ann agreed. A Jewish wedding "would be somewhat hypocritical," she says. "The fact is, I was marrying a non-Jew."

A judge who was a member of Ann's congregation agreed to marry them. The ceremony, held in the living room of a cousin's home, was built around their common love, music. Members of their string quartet played a processional. After the ceremony, Ann and Evan joined the group and provided music for their own reception. There was one Jewish element. To close the ceremony, Ann's father gave a traditional Hebrew benediction, but one not customarily used in weddings: ("God bless you and keep you"). The ceremony "felt very true to who we were," Ann recalls.

Ann's grandfather, Mordechai Kaplan, was too old and ill to attend the ceremony, but he wrote them a letter. He underscored his wish that they would raise their children as Jews, but he said that no matter what they did, they had his blessing.

Some Reconstructionist rabbis will not co-officiate but will agree to be "a Jewish presence" at a civil wedding and to say a few words from the Jewish tradition. One woman who chose this option explains, "A wedding is a public statement about how you intend to lead the rest of your life." She and her fiancé had agreed to raise their children as Jews, and she felt the wedding should make that clear. "I wanted some Jewish content so my family and friends that were there knew I hadn't forsaken Judaism, that it was still important to me, that at some level it was still going to be a part of my life."

Leon and Diane: Finding a Place for Both Traditions Leon, a strongly identified "cultural Jew," and Diane, a committed Christian, had met on summer vacation. Before they had finished their first afternoon together, Leon—a man who considered himself a realist and didn't believe in love at first sight—was sure that he would marry Diane. By their second date, they were immersed in heavy discussions about whether they should continue seeing each other despite their religious differences. The problem: Leon, a dark-haired computer programmer and semi-professional worrier, was an agnostic who went to synagogue only once a year at the High Holidays—but he couldn't imagine not raising his children as part of the Jewish people. Raised in a Conservative Jewish home, he had rebelled against the theology back in his Hebrew school days, but he read Jewish books, told Jewish jokes, gave money to Jewish causes, and worried about Jewish political issues. Diane, an ebony-haired dental hygienist with a warm smile and soothing sympathetic manner, was a devout Christian. Diane's own family was more strongly Italian than Catholic. She had many private disagreements with the Catholic Church in which she had been raised, and no longer belonged to a church. But she truly believed Jesus was her savior. Until she met Leon, it had never occurred to her that her children might not be baptized.

Leon had always assumed he would have a standard Jewish wedding. But it was obvious that that would not be satisfactory given the strength of Diane's Christian faith and her attachment to cultural tradition. They began to discuss co-officiation. But they ran into both inner and outer obstacles.

At first, the inner obstacles were the most serious problem. Leon, like many Jews, was squeamish about participating in a service that had any Christian overtones. "Diane would say we have to be willing to compromise. That word made me cringe."

Most Jews are keenly aware that for centuries the Christian church in Europe was a chief persecutor of the Jews. As a result many Jews, even non-observant ones, feel they would rather be married by a judge than hold their wedding in a church or participate in a co-officiated ceremony.

But Diane felt strongly that she wanted her marriage to be blessed by God, and for her that meant having clergy perform the ceremony. They read about the rules, rituals, and symbols for the traditional Jewish and Catholic wedding services to see if they could come up with something to meet both of their needs.

It was important to Diane and her parents to have a priest present at the service. Although neither her parents nor Leon's had raised objections to their marrying, Diane could see that her parents were hurt when she told them the children would be raised Jewish. She felt a co-officiated ceremony would be an important statement that she was not totally rejecting her past.

Before a priest is permitted to officiate at an interfaith wedding, the Roman Catholic Church requires the Catholic partner to make a verbal promise that he will do everything in his power to see that the children are raised as Catholics. But its position on using a rabbi and priest in the same ceremony is relatively liberal, as you can see in the summaries in the Appendix. Still, it took a number of phone calls before Leon and Diane were able to locate a priest who would work with them. Finally, Diane's parents were able to find a young priest in their parish. The meeting with him was cordial, if a bit uncomfortable. He said, "Leon, you know that Diane has promised to do everything in her power to raise the children as Catholics." Leon said, "I know." To himself he said he was just acknowledging the statements that had been made.

"We lied," Diane says simply. (The Church's position is that if after the wedding occurs, the couple disagrees strongly and needs to come to a different decision about child-rearing for the sake of their marriage, then the matter is no longer in the Catholic partner's power, so she isn't violating her pledge.) [4]

Diane came to feel that the pledge about children was an elaborate charade the priest had to ask her to go through so he would not be violating the rules of the Church. "It's the same God," she says. "The religions started out to be the same. I think we're doing a nice thing, bringing people together. But priests and rabbis can make you feel like the most awful person in the world."

Eventually the priest agreed to develop a ceremony that would be acceptable to a rabbi as well.

But things got even stickier when they tried to find a rabbi to co-officiate. Leon belonged to a Conservative synagogue, and though he knew his rabbi would not officiate, he started, "as a courtesy," by asking him. What he got was a lecture about how this was a violation of Jewish law, which made him feel both guilty and angry. Friends gave him the names of six Reform Jewish rabbis who would perform intermarriages, and he called them all. He met with two of the rabbis, and he and Diane met jointly with a third. Unlike rabbis in the more traditional Jewish denominations, all of the Reform rabbis Leon contacted were willing to perform a marriage in which the non-Jewish partner did not convert to Judaism. But none was willing to officiate jointly with a priest, and each of them required a promise that Judaism, and only Judaism, would be practiced in the home. Diane and Leon had agreed that they would tell the children they were Jewish and would send them only to Jewish religious school, but would celebrate both sets of holidays in their home.

One rabbi told Leon, "If you're celebrating both holidays, your children are not going to be Jewish."

Another rabbi said, "I hear what you're asking me to do, Leon, but

I don't think you're saying what you really want."

This rabbi's remark upset Leon because it was right on the mark: Leon was feeling very ambivalent about having a joint ceremony and practicing both sets of holidays. "I was willing to do it because I love Diane, but I was thinking wouldn't it be nice if she'd drop this idea of co-officiation."

He thought of arguing with her about it, but now says he's glad he didn't. "It's a matter of equality and sharing. I wouldn't feel comfortable depriving her of things she believes in and the chance to make her family happy. It's good to have a ceremony that includes both traditions. Now, when I talk to the caterer and florist, I find myself almost bragging about it."

They heard of one rabbi-without-pulpit who has almost made a profession of doing interfaith marriages. But they also heard that he was something of a charlatan ("have *huppah* will travel," as Leon puts it). They felt they wanted a person of genuine faith to officiate at their wedding.

Eventually, Leon and Diane got the name of a deeply committed Reform rabbi who would co-officiate. This rabbi, Mayer Selekman of Temple Shalom in the Philadelphia suburb of Broomall, has been extensively involved in ecumenical activities. He struck Leon and Diane as a man of faith.

Says Selekman, "God is the father of us all, and He has given us autonomy. I can't see that He objects that two of His children want to marry. I co-officiate out of my concern for the couple. To have two clergy side by side, and to have blessings from both, is a powerful statement of rootedness and of the different approaches to revelation. Here are two people who are coming through their respective traditions and not in opposition to them. I will even go into a church for a ceremony. That is as much God's house as a synagogue, though we are not used to it."

Selekman says he is not sure if there is a theological grounding for this position. But he says, "The commitment to the future of the tradition does not rely solely on the statements of the past. The past has a vote, not a veto."

We have talked with some clergy in each of the denominations who sound like charlatans or shallow smoothies, but also with some who perform intermarriages out of deep conviction that this is a needed service that grows out of their religious calling.

Reform Rabbi Irwin Fishbein of Westfield, New Jersey, says, "A Jew comes to a rabbi usually only once in his lifetime and says, 'Rabbi, be with me.'" The birth and death rites are involuntary, says Fishbein: The wedding is the one ceremony for which an adult Jew, in his own right, seeks the support of his religion. "It's certainly not a helpful thing for the relationship to Judaism to get a rejection slip." In his thirty years as a rabbi, Fishbein says he has officiated at over two thousand interfaith weddings and counseled up to five thousand couples.

Rabbi Roy Rosenberg estimates that about one hundred rabbis and cantors in the United States will co-officiate. Most of them are renegade Orthodox who got their ordination outside of the major recognized rabbinical channels, and have no official rabbinic standing, he said.[5] This does not affect the validity of the marriage, he said, because in Jewish tradition, the marriage is accomplished by the man placing the ring on the woman's finger in the presence of witnesses.

Once you understand your own bottom line and your partner's, if you genuinely love each other and possess the determination and skills to negotiate, you can find many mutually respectful compromises on officiation and related issues. For example, if one of you feels strongly about wanting a church wedding and another feels strongly about *not* being married in a church, it should be possible to find a non-denominational chapel at a college or military base (the United Nations Chapel in New York is such a place) which will have the sacred atmosphere desired by one partner and the religious neutrality needed by the other.

But be cautious as you work out your compromises. Sometimes, if the only acceptable compromise is a co-officiated ceremony, it's a warning signal: Neither of you really feels able to accept the other's religious ways. At some point down the road, most likely when you have children, the makeshift compromise struck by having a co-officiated ceremony may fall apart.

DESIGNING YOUR CEREMONY AND RECEPTION

Ann and Evan developed a wedding ceremony and reception that reflected their shared values, such as their love of music, and that also showed their respect for their families' values. In designing your wedding ceremony, your first task will be to ponder your own and your families' values and decide how to incorporate them into the ceremony. What ideas do you want the ceremony to express? How do you want to symbolize or convey them?

There are a number of other factors to consider. First, learn about the traditional wedding rituals and symbols of your own religious traditions. You may decide you want a traditional ceremony in one religion.

Even if you decide against this, it is helpful to use the contents of the traditional services as reference points to help you decide what you want.

You could depart from the traditional service but retain a few of its symbols to help your family feel it is a "real" wedding. Rabbi Selekman notes that Jewish parents "focus in" on the fact that "you have the *huppah* and you break the glass." These "little *shtickele* (things, or ways) . . . are monumentally significant because of the feeling of discontinuity that an intermarriage generates. You give them something to hold on to."

The Traditional Ceremonies Although there are many cultural traditions associated with Christian weddings, the essence of the ceremony is the vows said by each partner. The traditional form of the Catholic vow is: "I (name), take you (name), to be my husband/wife. I promise to be true to you in good times and in bad, in sickness and in health: I will love you and honor you all the days of my life."

The priest may begin by asking the couple, "Have you come here freely and without reservation to give yourselves to each other in marriage? Will you love and honor each other as man and wife for the rest of your lives? (Implying that divorce is not to be considered.) Will you accept children lovingly from God, and bring them up according to the law of Christ and His Church?"

In the Protestant wedding, the minister often states the vow as a question, with the partners each responding, "I do." Traditionally, there is also an exchange of rings.

The Jewish ceremony has three essential elements: The betrothal, which is the declaration by the couple that they are consecrated to each other; the marriage contract, which is signed by two witnesses and read aloud; and the exchange of an item of value (traditionally a ring), which seals the contract.

In addition, three symbols are almost always associated with a Jewish wedding: the *huppah,* which represents the home, the marriage bed, and God's sheltering love; the sharing of wine, a symbol of rejoicing; and the breaking of a glass, which is a reminder of sorrow amid joy, and particularly of the destruction of the ancient temple and exile of the Jews from their holy land.

There are also traditionally seven blessings which are recited by friends and family or by the rabbi.

The Jewish and Christian wedding ceremonies differ somewhat in their religious meaning, and consequently in what is considered an appropriate place for the wedding ceremony.

The Jewish wedding was traditionally a community-wide celebration. Since about the sixteenth century, it was held whenever possible in the public square where all in the community could be witnesses and share in the rejoicing.

The Christian wedding, on the other hand, was supposed to be held on sacred ground, and an outdoor wedding was not appropriate. In Protestant theology, the marriage is an individual covenant modeled on Israel's covenant with God. This much more private view of the ceremony can lead to the Jewish and Christian partners having very different feelings about how many people and whom should be invited to the wedding. Although couples often don't know the details of their religion's stand on these matters, they are part of the culture and attitudes with which we are brought up. These different backgrounds can lead couples and their families to have very different viewpoints on what "feels right" as a location for the wedding.

Making Decisions About the Service Negotiating over what religious or cultural symbols you will have in your service is a good way of getting a deeper understanding of each other's values. Rabbi Linda Holtzman suggests two useful pieces of pre-wedding "homework" that come out of the Jewish tradition: Write a marriage contract; and find seven readings that express your ideals and hopes for the marriage. If you are following a Jewish model, make these agreements and blessings part of your ceremony.

Deciding what religious elements to include can be complicated. The Christian side might be fairly flexible. More questions arise vis-à-vis the Jewish tradition. For example, some rabbis and families prefer using the traditional Jewish ceremony with only slight modification. They may substitute "Be thou consecrated to me according to our sacred traditions" (which refers to both Judaism and Christianity) for the standard "Be thou consecrated to me according to the laws of Moses and Israel." Other families and rabbis, however, feel such a ceremony gives a misleading impression that this is a legal Jewish wedding. If you agree with this viewpoint but want the ceremony to show your respect for Judaism, you can choose readings from the Hebrew Bible that are not part of the standard Jewish wedding ceremony, such as passages from Song of Songs or the betrothal speech by the prophet Hosea.

Be sure to talk over your feelings about the ceremony with the person who will officiate. One couple, a nonpracticing Jew and a disenchanted Catholic, had agreed to be married by a Methodist minister who was a long-time friend of the woman. Since neither cared about religion, they had left the content of the ceremony to the minister and concentrated instead on the reception. When the actual ceremony occurred, there was a traumatic moment. The minister asked the Jewish man to make his vow "in the name of Jesus Christ." The startled groom couldn't say a word. He might not be actively Jewish, but he was not ready to swear in the name of Jesus. Finally, he mumbled something and the ceremony ended. Don't get caught short like that.

You may find that for any number of reasons—inability to agree on the form of a religious service, failure to find acceptable clergy, concern for family feelings, or personal principle on your part—that you want to avoid an openly Christian or Jewish service. Here are some "neutral" options:

Civil Ceremony Judges are used to doing a standard civil ceremony, but most are usually open to changing the wording, to having Jewish symbols like the glass and wine, to talking about God or religious values, and to having a clergyman speak. They also are likely to agree to conduct the ceremony nearly anywhere. Counseling varies and sometimes is minimal.

Many jurisdictions have judges who are known for performing intermarriages. Ask your marriage-license bureau for names.

Unitarian Society Though its buildings are commonly called churches, its teachings are universalist and it has been a haven for Jewish-Christian couples for generations. Unitarian ministers are free to do joint services with other clergy and to have Jewish symbols and readings included.

Ethical Culture Society This humanist organization is open to Jewish-Christian weddings and will accommodate different touches in the service. Be mindful that the group normally includes no references to God in its weddings and other ceremonies. A given member of its clergy, known as a Leader, may be amenable to saying a prayer, but might wish to preface it as being a "reading" that has special significance to the couple or family.

Quaker Ceremony A simple option in some locales is to marry each other without benefit of clergy or any other officiant. All one needs to do is obtain what is called a "Quaker wedding license," which has language to the effect that the two people will unite themselves in marriage. The license will be granted regardless of whether the ceremony is going to be conducted under the auspices of the Society of Friends (Quakers). To be legal, you need only have two witnesses whom you designate sign the license, although the custom is to have everyone who attends the wedding sign as well, or to sign a separate document that bears words to the effect that they bless the marriage by their presence.

You can write your own vows or readings, and if you wish, invent or choose your own symbols.

In the Appendix, you will find a list of books with inspirational readings you can use to design your own ceremony.

THE JOINING OF TWO FAMILIES

As you plan your wedding, it is helpful to keep in mind that a wedding is more than the joining of two individuals. It is the joining of two families. You may be feeling a great deal of pressure from your families, and you may be making a lot of decisions just to stave off violent family reactions. It pays instead to understand what's going on under the surface.

You as a couple are imbedded in a whole network of relationships with the two families from which you came.[6] Your chances of succeeding as a couple will be greater if you have developed a satisfactory ongoing relationship with both families. It's important that your families see a place for themselves in your wedding—that they see some validation of them and the way they brought you up. A young couple has a tendency to think the wedding ought to be solely for them. But consider what relationship the two of you want to have with your parents ten or twenty years from now. How do you want them to relate to your children? The way you handle the planning of your wedding sets a foundation for that future relationship.

Try to understand your parents' hopes and expectations for the wedding. Some Jewish or Italian families, for example, have looked forward for years to their children's weddings. It is a traditional opportunity to go all out, to display their status. It is also their chance to demonstrate that they have fulfilled their duties as parents by marrying off their children.

Veteran family therapist Rabbi Edwin Friedman points out that the wedding can be a powerful turning point for the entire extended family. Weddings, funerals, and bar mitzvahs, he says, are "hinges in time."[7] During these ceremonies, relationships in the family are in flux. It is possible to restructure relationships. For example, the wedding, as a formal rite of passage, can make it possible for families to let go emotionally, when they might not be able to do it any other way. During the powerful moment-in-time of a wedding, longstanding wounds in the family can be healed; or on the other hand, powerful divisions can be opened that may take a generation to overcome. At a wedding, you can bring together your two separate families in a way that may not be possible again until the birth of your child.

Some couples think co-officiation is the only way to acknowledge both families in the ceremony. But there are other techniques. Consider these:

Wine Exchange In the traditional Jewish wedding ceremony, the bride and groom share two cups of wine with each other. Rabbi Selekman has adapted the ceremony to have the couples share the wine with both sets of parents as well. This is accomplished by having the parents stand beside the couple during the ceremony (a custom that is new to Christian parents but one that he finds they take to readily).

Flower Ritual Rev. John Nesbitt, a Methodist minister, suggests that couples, whether intermarrying or not, include in the ceremony a special section called the leave-taking. The woman takes a bouquet of roses and gives them to her own mother and to the father of the man she's marrying. The man gives roses to his own mother and to his wife's father. Each partner thanks the parents for raising such a fine son or daughter, and each expresses a hope to have a good relationship with the new family who will be grandparents to their children. In this way, says Nesbitt, the rite of passage is made concrete. Parents do realize that they have to let go of their children. But they also see that there is a different role for them in their children's lives, and that a new member is entering their larger family circle. "Parents love it," says Nesbitt. "They feel validated."

Special Blessings The person officiating can address the cultural differences directly at the start of the ceremony by telling the families that it is an occasion for rejoicing when two people from different backgrounds can overcome their differences and fall in love.

Applause That's right, applause. Try "planting" a couple of friends in the congregation to start a round of clapping and cheers after the breaking of the glass or after the bride and groom kiss. At the moment of kissing, everyone is emotional and wants to reach out and embrace the couple. Applause provides the perfect release. Philadelphia Common Pleas Court Judge Marvin Halbert, who gave us this tip, says applause "connects people, breaks down barriers, makes them feel part of the moment."

The Toast A gentle, lovingly humorous, and appreciative toast to your families can help give a different perspective on some of the paradoxes or misunderstandings. One rabbi loosened things up by announcing that the wine would be a mixture of Manischewitz and Christian Brothers. Caution: Humor on sensitive issues requires a deft touch!

Diplomacy Ask an outgoing person in each of your families to be a special ambassador to the other family, to draw people out and get them talking to each other during the reception. If you have a sit-down wedding dinner, make sure people from one family are seated with people from the other family.

Mixed Touches Even if one partner converts to the other's religion and you have a traditional ceremony according to that faith, it is possible to design the reception so that the other family feels included. Lena and David Romanoff love to talk about their "Jewish-Italian wedding." Although the ceremony was a traditional Jewish one, the food and the music made Lena's Italian family feel it was very much their celebration, too.

Bread and Butter The special openness and opportunity for bridging family gaps continues for awhile after the wedding day. One couple took time after the ceremony to write a special note to each set of parents telling them how much their presence at the wedding was appreciated, and how they hoped that they would continue to be part of each other's lives and celebrations.

Heading Off Trouble It's also possible to bring families together by doing some advance work. We think of one tall blonde whose ancestors came to America just after the Mayflower. She recalls that when she first visited her fiancé's short dark immigrant Jewish family in Brooklyn, "I felt like I was in one of those first-grade workbooks that says, 'Circle the thing that does not belong.'" She many times heard the word *shiksa* muttered in her presence. But she and her fiancé lived together for five years before they married. During that time, she made extensive efforts to get to know his family—even visiting his elderly relatives in Florida. She also made sure that her mother and her fiancé's parents got together a number of times before the wedding. They would never be bosom buddies, but at least they were not total strangers.

Advance Warning Go over your wedding plans with your parents several times before the ceremony. In particular, be sure there are no surprises in an interfaith ceremony's religious content.

DEALING WITH A BOYCOTT

Even in cases where family hostility seemed impossible to overcome, we found that determined couples were usually able to bridge the gap. When Grace became engaged to Joel, she faced a steady blast of hostility from Joel's mother. The mother's intellectual New York liberalism became an excuse for anti-Catholic bigotry. She fumed about Catholicism being an idol-worshipping, slavish religion. Joel told his mother he would not put up with that attitude. He and his mother didn't talk to each other for months. His mother said she wouldn't come to the wedding, and his father was unwilling to come without her.

In such a situation, it helps to realize that even if the dispute has taken on a nasty and personal tone, it has nothing to do with who you really are. The family can't see you realistically because of what you represent to them.

Family hostility can get extreme: Rabbi Fishbein recalls one groom who was kidnapped by his Jewish family on his wedding day to prevent him from going through with an interfaith wedding.

Fortunately, says Joel, he and Grace had a year-long engagement, and, "Time does work things out. People who draw the line in the sand and say they're not crossing can be made to cross it. But things do take time."

Several things helped during the engagement. First, Joel continually made clear to Grace that no amount of family hostility was going to force him to break the engagement. Second, even though Joel had not suggested it, his brother, relatives, and friends of the family called his mother to try to reason with her. Third, Joel kept the door open. Periodically he took trips to his parents' home to tell them that he and Grace still wanted them to attend the wedding. About two months before the wedding, he told his mother, "I'm not just concerned with our wedding day, I'm concerned with the day after. We will be husband and wife then, and I don't see how you will be able to face us if you haven't attended the wedding."

After that visit, he continued to call at intervals and urge his mother to come to the wedding. None of the strategies seemed to be working. Joel's mother never announced that she would come. But six weeks before the ceremony, she began talking about what kind of dress she was buying for the wedding.

Rev. Melvin Hawthorne, who runs the nondenominational United Nations Chapel in New York, has counseled many couples whose parents initially refused to come to the wedding. He says Joel's mother is typical: Often at the last minute, the parents will decide to come, but to save face, they will never admit that they changed their minds. They will invent some excuse to be there—often a slightly insulting excuse, like saying, "We knew you could never earn the money to pay for this, so we figured we'd better come and bail you out." Hawthorne recalls a time when the parents didn't announce they were coming until the morning of the wedding. Fifteen minutes before the ceremony, the father overheard the minister giving last-minute instructions to the couple, and interjected, "But what about me? You don't think I'm going to miss the chance to walk my daughter down the aisle."

Keep the Door Open If parents threaten to boycott a wedding, don't make ultimatums. "They will come around if you give them a way back in," says Rev. Hawthorne. Without begging, continue to tell them that their presence will be valued. As the months go by, keep them informed of your plans.

Understand the Parent Process Often parents feel their child is making a serious mistake. Refusal to come to the wedding is a bargaining chip. Once they've taken a strong stand, they feel they've discharged their parental responsibility: "They're clean," says Rev. Hawthorne. Often the pressure is most intense about three months before the wedding, when they still believe they have a chance to influence your decision.

Write a Letter Let them know that you understand how much pain and upset they are feeling, and you are not asking for their agreement, only that they also understand what you are feeling. Tell them that, as much as you would like them to be at the wedding and to give their blessing, if it would be too painful for them to do that, it would make you feel better for the parents to avoid the situation that is causing them pain. Rabbi Selekman had one couple try this: Although there was never any response to the letter, the parents sent a check to help pay for the wedding, and on the wedding day, they showed up.

Let Them Save Face When they change their minds, don't rub their noses in it. Nine times out of ten they will come up with their own face-saving formula, but if not, you can suggest one, such as coming to the ceremony but not walking down the aisle, or not coming to the ceremony but joining in at the reception.

Give Them a Role Go out of your way to involve your parents in the planning, even if they say they won't come to the wedding. Ask the mother of the bride to help pick out the wedding dress, or consult the mother-in-law on the photographer or flowers or cake. Often parents' hostility is rooted in their anger or sense of loss at losing control over their children. When you offer them a last chance to do something helpful, most can't resist.

Enlist the Help of Clergy A clergyperson, as an outsider to the family and a person with some authority, can confront your parents with the underlying issues in a way that you can't. Rabbi Selekman requests a meeting with both sets of parents. He tries to help them get past the anger to admit the pain underneath. He tells parents that they have a right to make their wishes known but that if they insist on demonstrating that they are the boss, it will take a toll on their future relationship with the children. As he told a group of parents,

> Parents have a basic choice when kids get married. They put a blessing on the marriage or they put a curse on the marriage. You have to decide what you want to be responsible for . . . You can give them the space to become who they have to become, or you can set up incredible barriers and loyalty tests that may not really give the marriage a chance.

Joel and Grace, using some of these techniques, were able eventually to overcome the boycott. They had a lovely wedding, with both sets of parents in attendance. At the reception, the two families were seated at adjacent tables, and they talked together and even danced with members of the other family. "It was surprising," says Joel. "It was very satisfying. But my mother had come with the attitude that if she was going to do it, she was going to do it. And she did it."

COPING WITH INTERFERENCE

If some parents want nothing to do with the wedding, others want everything. Parents who try to dictate every detail of the wedding planning are unconsciously trying to keep the children involved with them a little bit longer.[8] If this is your problem, think about the long-range meaning of the wedding to you. Is the color of the tablecloths that important? If not, you might let that be an area where the mother calls the shots.

Parcel Out Jobs You could tell your parents that you want control of the ceremony and they can take the lead with the reception. Or if you're not ready to give away that much, you could give them a number of smaller tasks, such as arranging for the wedding cake and the photographer and the flowers and the accommodations for out-of-town guests. If your parents have a penchant for interfering with details, you and your partner should decide what will be the negotiables and non-negotiables, and then turn the negotiables over to the parents.

Pay Your Own Way A number of couples mentioned that they had fewer problems with parental interference because they paid for the wedding themselves. They held the wedding on their own turf rather than in their parents' neighborhood. This was hard for some parents to understand, so one couple chose to be married in the nondenominational United Nations chapel in New York but imported the priest from the bride's home parish.

Rise Above It You and your parents may get embroiled in details as a way of avoiding facing the powerful feelings that go with this event. This is a time to be more mature than your parents, because they are caught up in emotions that they may not understand. One way to keep things in perspective: Donate 5 or 10 percent of the cost of your reception to feed the hungry.

Check Chapter 3 (Dealing with Parents) for other suggestions on coping with parental interference or hostility.

Finally, as one man said, "The only way we could get through it all was to say: It's our wedding. It's our life. We're gonna try and do things that will not be obnoxious to anyone, but you can't satisfy everyone. It worked out. I think what we did was quite pleasing to everyone."

And keep in mind, based on the long experience of many clergy who have dealt with interfaith marriage: The wedding-day disaster you and your parents may fear is not really likely to happen. "When you finally have the ceremony and go through with it," said Selekman, "the response is, it was beautiful."

Each of you will have your own issues to resolve as you plan your wedding. But don't get so bogged down in details and logistics, or so mired in hostilities, that you forget the most important aspect of the wedding. It is the doorway to marriage.

If the planning of a wedding is a stressful time, it is also a time of great opportunity. The wedding is your birthday as a new family. A new entity has been born into the network of relationships that make up your larger family and community.

UNDERSTANDING
EACH OTHER

5. ETHNIC BACKGROUND:

Your Cradle Culture

You may breakfast on croissants now instead of bagels. You may dine on steak instead of spaghetti. But you don't lose the imprint of your cradle culture when you grow up and become a citizen of the world. You may develop a new, adult identity as a doctor, lawyer—even a religious convert. But ethnic traits, as one psychologist told us, are "etched in people's bones."

If you think you came from a no-culture, from White Anglo-Saxon Protestant Americana, you need to realize that this mainstream culture is your ethnic mold.

Perhaps you think that, as a modern couple, there are no meaningful cultural differences between you. But you and your partner remain different in deep-in-the-gut ways. Your marriage may suffer if you are unable to recognize and accept those ethnically based personality differences.

Therapists have begun realizing that, apart from the differences among individual families, people are profoundly shaped by the cultural patterns of their ethnic group, as well as by the way that ethnic group has been treated by the larger society. Of particular use in our work has been the pioneering research of Judith Weinstein Klein, Joel Crohn, Esther Perel, Lori Santo, and others sponsored by the American Jewish Committee's Institute on American Pluralism, headed by Irving Levine. Family therapist Joseph Giordano, director of the Institute's Center on

Ethnicity, Behavior, and Communications, along with Rutgers University researcher and family therapist Monica McGoldrick and John K. Pearce of the Cambridge Family Institute, have edited a book outlining some of the major characteristics of ethnic groups that therapists would need to be aware of if they were to be effective in helping families solve their problems.

We think you, too, will be more effective in solving the problems that crop up in your family over the years if you know something about your partner's ethnic group, and how differences in ethnic backgrounds may contribute to misunderstandings between you. In this chapter, ethnic-group descriptions are primarily distilled from the book by McGoldrick, Pearce, and Giordano, and from a paper written for the American Jewish Committee by Crohn. Descriptions of Irish characteristics were taken from a chapter by McGoldrick, descriptions of Italians from a chapter by Marie Rotunno and McGoldrick, descriptions of British-Americans from Pearce and David McGill, and descriptions of Jews from a chapter by Fredda Herz and Elliott J. Rosen.

It's a cliché that opposites attract. Many people fall in love with a quality in their partner that is lacking in themselves. A distant, cool person will be attracted to a warm, emotional person, and vice versa. Intermarriages are especially likely to be opposites-attract marriages because many personal qualities grow directly from our ethnic roots. But this opposite quality—the quality that most attracted you—may also be the most difficult to live with because it is the most different from you. San Francisco psychologist Joel Crohn, who studied intermarried couples for the American Jewish Committee, says that when couples begin bumping up against their differences, one of two things happens: either they synthesize (they adjust to each other and become a little more like each other) or they polarize (they overreact to each other and grow further apart). Either the cool partner learns to beam out a little more emotion and the warm partner learns to allow a little more distance, or the cool partner retreats into a shell and the warm partner runs after, digging and shouting.

When couples are learning to live with each other, it's easy to take these different styles personally—to think that your partner is cool because he doesn't love you anymore, instead of remembering that he's always cool. Each of you may begin to judge the other's typical reaction as "bad" or "crazy." If you flame up while he remains calm, for example, he may fear that you're hysterical or condemn you as immature and unwilling to control yourself.[1]

Understanding, instead, that your partner's behavior is natural for people from his background, "takes a lot of the sting out" of it, says family therapist Joseph Giordano.

In the remainder of this chapter, we'll outline some ethnic differences, discuss conflicts that may arise because of them, and suggest how you can handle them. First, here is a written exercise to help you and your partner see your own ethnic styles:

AN ETHNIC SELF-TEST

Number a piece of lined paper from 1 to 12. Beside each number, write A or B, depending on which statement is closer to the message you got from your family. Don't look at your partner's answers until you're both done.

A	**B**
1. Money is to be spent only when necessary.	Money is to be enjoyed.
2. Success is to be pursued by all legitimate means.	Success should not be pursued at the expense of family ties.
3. Women's primary role is in the home.	Women have a right to achieve as much as men.
4. A person has a right to be openly proud of his achievements.	Modesty is noble; boastfulness is crude.
5. You can only solve a problem by acting on it; talk is a waste of time.	You can best solve a problem by talking it through.
6. Words can be used for effect. Exaggeration is just a way to make the point.	Words are to be used carefully, not wasted.
7. Marriage is between two people.	Marriage is between two families.
8. Anger is expressed by continued fighting and debate.	Anger is shown by distancing and silence.

9. The authority
of the parent
is nondebatable.

All family rules
can be negotiated,
by everyone.

10. Your problem
is my problem.

Don't interfere
in other's affairs.

11. Food is an
expression of
giving and love.

Food is for
sustenance. Eat
with moderation.

12. Cleanliness
is next to Godliness.

A little clutter
just makes a house
look lived in.

There are no "right answers" to the exercise, no way to tell how you did. The purpose, instead, is to show that differences in style and behavior do not occur randomly but tend to be culturally based. Take time now to talk about the differences between your responses and your partner's. Have these issues come up in your marriage?[2]

Both the special ways you and your partner complement each other and the particular problems you encounter in your marriage are likely to depend in part on the particular combination of ethnic backgrounds you and your partner bring to the marriage.

MAPPING YOUR ETHNIC TERRAIN

Thus, a marriage between a Jew and an Italian-American is likely to face different problems than a marriage between a Jew and a White Anglo-Saxon Protestant. Using information from sociological studies and clinical psychology, we've sketched out below some of the differences for the four main groups involved in Jewish-Christian marriages: Jews, Italians, Irish, and WASPs.[3] If your own ethnic group is not represented here, we hope that you can use the capsule descriptions as models to figure out your own and your partner's cultural traits and how they may fit together.

We present this material with two cautions: First, these are "off-the-rack" generalizations, not tailored to you and your unique history. They may fit in many places, but they're bound to pinch in some spots and billow in others. Just as there can be tall, strong women and short, frail men, so may you differ from the profiles of your group. The descriptions make no allowances for degrees of assimilation, generation gaps, region of the country, etc. If your partner is from a second or third-generation family, less of the description may apply. Second, even if the description fits, you will have to use the ideas with great sensitivity, avoiding the danger of stereotyping. We urge you not to use the ethnic profiles to judge your partner or, fatalistically, to avoid attempts to change yourself. Use them instead to get a clearer insight on your own and your partner's needs. (Although we use the pronoun *she,* most of the ethnic descriptions can apply to either sex. In a few instances, sex roles may either magnify or minimize ethnic group differences. For example, a WASP man is likely to find it even harder to talk about feelings than a WASP woman.)

Sociologists and psychologists note that ethnic groups tend to differ along four key social dimensions: emotional style, values, routines of daily life, and child-rearing patterns.[4]

We'll start by sketching each culture's worldview. As you read the profiles that follow, try to remember that the worldview is this group's way of adapting to the events of its history. In a historical context, this way of being makes sense.

Italians were the first large wave of non-English-speaking people to enter America. Partly because of language barriers, partly because of discrimination, partly because of their own history and culture in Europe, that generation tended to be family-focused: to create barriers to the outside world and to wrap themselves in the protection of the family system. Fatalistic about the future, they were nevertheless adaptable and prepared to enjoy the present. Jews are keenly aware that in America, as they had been in Europe, they are a tiny minority within a Christian country. Many have finely tuned antennae for picking up implications of anti-Semitism. They, too, have turned much of their emotional energy inward toward the home. But at the same time, they have prized success in the larger world and have loosened the family ties to allow it. WASPs are a can-do people with little truck for fatalism. They value rationalism, competence, and self-determinism. They will push on in the face of obstacles, but they do so as individuals, with little sense of group strength or loyalty. A bitter history left the Irish immigrant generation a paradoxical lot, both jovial and gloomy. Their past was full of rebels and fighters, yet they tended to defer to authority—particularly to the Church. The Catholic concept of sin and salvation had permeated the psyche of that generation.

A. Emotional Style

Expressive/Restrained Jews and Italians are the most "intense," a difference that psychologist Crohn measured by looking at "rapidity and pressure of speech, surface anxiety, interruptions and frequency and expansiveness of non-verbal gestures."[5] Italians tend to be colorful and emotional, Jews articulate. Although the Irish may not want to intrude on others, once in a conversation they show a definite way with words. But charm may be a smokescreen to avoid dealing with feelings or coming to grips with hard facts. By contrast, WASPs do not "waste words." As John Pearce and David McGill write, "A British American does not share thoughts, feelings and experiences 'just to hear himself talk.'"[6]

A Jew may be attracted to a WASP's reserve or an Irish partner's charm, while the WASP or Irish partner may be attracted to the Jew's expressiveness and honesty. But they may polarize if the Jew feels frustrated that it seems impossible to talk out issues, and the WASP or Irish partner feels that the Jew wants to talk an issue to death or to probe too deeply.

A Jew may be first attracted to, then intimidated by, the Italian's forcefulness. The Italian may be attracted to, then overwhelmed by, the Jew's fluency. If they polarize, the Jew may inhibit expression of feelings to avoid tempests; the Italian may suspect that the Jew is carrying a grudge.

Nurturance/Distance Intimacy of the type we now seek between spouses did not come naturally in the traditional cultures of any of these groups. Sharply defined sex roles kept Italian husbands and wives moving on parallel but distant tracks. Sexual repression springing from fear of sin often strangled the intimacy and mutual enjoyment between Irish mates. Jews often showed caring in a backhanded fashion, through worrying or criticism. WASPs, barricaded behind their ideal of autonomy, lapsed into emotional isolation and self-containment. To the extent that you have internalized these models, you will have to struggle against your own grain in order to get close to your mate.

We each have another model for intimacy in our families, however: the relationship between parents and children. Many of your instincts spring from that relationship. Jewish and Italian mothers are solicitous and nurturing to their children, sometimes to the point of suffocation. WASP parents give their children plenty of space, sometimes to the point of emotional abandonment. Irish and Jewish mothers tend to idealize their sons, so that the son may feel guilty and resentful but unable to express the anger buried under the affection.

A Jew and an Italian will probably feel compatible in the area of mutual nurturing. A Jew may be attracted to an Irish-American's charm or a WASP's poise and independence, while they in turn may be attracted to the Jew's nurturing. But if they polarize, the WASP may feel suffocated by the Jewish spouse, and the Jew may feel abandoned by the WASP. The Irish partner married to a Jew may feel trapped, while the Jew may feel she was promised an intimacy that never materialized.

Handling of Conflict WASPs and Irish-Americans shun open conflict. They prefer to keep up appearances and avoid embarrassment. Disapproval is expressed through the "silent treatment." But once they have acknowledged a problem, WASPs will reason it out and work diligently to solve it. Though an Irish-American will talk, he may obscure the truth because he is likely to fear it will show how bad he is. Yet he also probably feels a deep sense of responsibility, and once he acknowledges a problem, will set out conscientiously to do what he feels is right. Despite the Irish reputation for hot tempers, Irish hostility is directed against outsiders, and within the family it comes out only indirectly, often through teasing and ridicule. Where there is serious personal hostility, it is likely to build up silently and to result in deep and long-term cutoffs.

Jews and Italians, by contrast, are quite ready to vent their angry and upset feelings. Jews are quick to argue, criticize, nag, or curse each other out. Fredda M. Herz and Elliott J. Rosen write that Jews also tend "to devalue brief, logical explanations and solutions to problems in favor of more complex, feeling-oriented ones." Jews would frequently rather talk than act.[7]

A Jew may be intimidated by an Italian partner's thunder, chilled by the icy silence of a WASP, or baffled by the evasive dance of an Irish partner. These partners may in turn tire of the Jewish partner's desire to pursue an argument down every alley.

Bridging the Gaps in Emotional Style Differences in emotional style are among the most difficult issues for many couples. Perhaps, like Sharon, one of the Jewish women we interviewed, you felt Jewish men were weak and you chose a vivid, macho, Italian husband. But now you discover that he wants you to be submissive and supportive instead of the opinionated Jewish woman you are.

At this point, it's easy to develop a vicious circle. Every display of authority by your husband triggers your need to argue back, which in turn drives him to more stridency.

You can interrupt the vicious circle. But you have to let go, to some extent, of what you expected in a relationship—the expectations you brought with you from your culture about how your partner would behave. You didn't marry someone from your culture. You married someone who behaves differently.

Instead of trying to change the way your partner acts, deal with your own reaction. Don't blame the other. You may not like what he's doing, but his anger is not "causing" your resentment.

How can you change your own reaction? Sit down with a pencil and paper and develop your own "new reactions plan," based on the following seven strategies:[8]

First, try to feel what your partner feels when you respond in your typical way. If you have an interfaith couples' group with a trained leader, it's very effective to play the game of switching roles. Set up two chairs facing each other, and act out a typical fight—but switching parts. The one who is usually quiet plays the one who usually emotes, and vice versa. Ham it up—and be ready to laugh at the portrayal of yourself.

Second, look for opportunities to act inconsistently with your partner's expectations. Remember that you and your partner are a system, an interdependent machine. A change in one of you can change the whole system. For example, if you usually burst into tears when your partner gets angry, do something different this time. Yell back. Stick out your tongue. Tell him that you're tired of crying and you're not going to do it anymore, so you hope he gets as tired of yelling as you do of crying.

Third, recognize that the vicious circle escalates—becomes a spiral—because each of you feels that you have no control in the situation. Agree on an approach that lets you both behave the way you need to. For example, you might agree to establish a "time-out" which gives the withdrawing partner the right to withdraw, followed by a "time-back" which gives the pursuing partner the right to reconnect at a definite time.

Fourth, affirm the contrasts. Remember how the traits you now see as troubling were once the magnets that attracted you to each other. Recall how your partner's emotional style has been helpful to you at key times.

Fifth, make a decision to learn from your partner instead of reacting to her. Consciously model yourself on aspects of your partner's emotional style. (Do this in an appreciative way, not as retaliation!)

Sixth, at the same time affirm the worth of your own style. You have something to give to your partner. Don't suppress your own nature for the sake of avoiding conflict.

Finally, set up a regular monthly check-in time to talk about how each of you is accommodating the other's emotional style. Don't store up resentments.

To make up your "new reactions plan," number your paper from one to seven. Write down exactly what concrete action you intend to take for each strategy. For example, how will you act inconsistently with your partner's expectations during a fight or disagreement? What will you do differently, and when will you start doing it? Although many of the strategies in this book are to be done jointly with your partner, this is one place where you must make the changes by yourself. In fact, don't share your "new reactions plan" with your partner. This is your own private strategy for changing your personal reactions. Don't try to change everything at once: Set one strategy in motion at a time. Give yourself a date to start each strategy. Set a self-evaluation date several months down the road. Be gentle in your evaluation: Give yourself credit for effort, and for even the smallest change. Don't judge yourself by whether your partner's behavior has changed; you're only working on your own reaction.

B. Values

Family and Group Loyalty/Independence Jews stress geographic as well as emotional closeness. Though a Jewish family will allow separation for schooling or career, the offspring are still expected to fulfill family obligations. Italians are even more enmeshed than Jews. Separation of children from parents is not desired or easily accepted. Any disgrace to the Italian family is considered a grievous crime.

McGill and Pearce describe WASP culture as "hyperindividualism."[9] WASPs extol self-reliance and self-control, usually to the exclusion of group and family ties. While Jewish and Italian parents often fear that their children will leave too soon, WASP and Irish parents worry that their children will be too dependent. While Jews and Italians think of marriage as linking two families, WASPs generally regard it as a tie only between two individuals.

A WASP or Irish partner may quarrel with the amount of time, money, and energy a Jewish spouse is willing to spend on family; a Jewish partner in turn may think that an Italian spouse goes overboard in this area. Two possible points of conflict are gifts, and care of sick family members.

A corollary to family closeness is ethnic group closeness. Italians, and to some extent Jews, historically, and even today, tend to live in ethnic neighborhoods within the womb of their culture. Most of their social connections are likely to be with extended family or members of their ethnic group. Conversations are likely to revolve around the family or the ethnic group. A Jew, for example, may read a great deal, yet read almost exclusively books by Jewish authors or about Jewish topics.

A WASP or Irish partner who feels culturally disconnected may initially feel attracted to the strong family bonds of his Jewish partner's culture. But once inside, he may find the web too enmeshing.

A Jew may expect to raise his children as Jews even though he and his parents were never involved with Jewish institutions. He developed a Jewish identity by osmosis—through social connections and family atmosphere. It may not occur to him that his partner can't give children a Jewish identity in this subliminal way because she doesn't have Jewish relatives, Jewish friends, and Jewish concerns which dominate her thinking and conversation. The gentile partner may in good faith agree to raise the children Jewish, then later find herself struggling to understand the nebulous thing her partner wants her to do.

Both Jews and to some extent Italians have a strong awareness of being a persecuted minority. They will want any outsider who comes in to demonstrate loyalty—to make it clear that the newcomer will stand with the group if someone comes after them. An outsider marrying into one of these cultures may feel that members of the group are paranoid; his partner's family and cultural peers may feel that he doesn't fully appreciate the extent of their sufferings.

Manners/Politeness WASPs and Irish have clear rules governing behavior. They emphasize propriety and quietness. The Irish and WASPs are very concerned with appearances and want greatly to be accepted and respected. Jewish and Italian families permit and even expect raucous, argumentative behavior. Jewish families are somewhat chaotic, with unclear roles and a rather tumultuous emotional climate.[10]

Education and Achievement Learning and success are nearly worshipped by Jews, and there is keen pressure on children to achieve educationally, financially, and socially. Children are expected to go to college or beyond. Success is seen as reflecting favorably on the family. However, because the Jewish family also can foster dependency among the children, Jews may feel inadequate no matter how successful they become. While some Italian-Americans have proudly applauded their children's success, others have taken a dim view of upward mobility, and seen ambition as selfish. Their focus is on the family; occupational or personal success, or even going to college, may be perceived by some traditional families as jeopardizing family solidarity. WASPs share the success ethic with Jews, although they may not express it as overtly. WASPs tend to equate hard work with virtue. As McGill and Pearce point out, since WASPs often have trouble expressing emotions, work and hobbies may be their main outlets for both aggression and companionship.[11]

There seems to be a strain of fatalism in Irish culture. For some, this may mean substituting dreams of glory for action and achievement. At the same time, they yearn for respectability, and have striven hard to make it into the middle class and beyond.

An Italian or Irish man or WASP woman may be attracted to a Jewish partner because they see an opportunity to fulfill the intellectual side of their nature; a Jew, conversely, may see these partners as providing some relief from the intense pressure for success in Jewish culture.

Sex Roles Italian sex roles have traditionally been rigid, although they are beginning to loosen. Theirs is a strong patriarchal system, with fathers acknowledged as heads of the household even when their spouses actually run the show. Traditionally, the women were expected to stay at home (and to cook as well as their mothers) while men were allowed to roam the outside world. Italian women are likely to fear violence from Italian men even if it has never occurred. For WASPs and Irish, sex roles are also clearly differentiated. For the WASP woman, the traditional sex role has meant relatively isolated dependency. The WASP man, groomed to work, is programmed to feel irrelevant as a parent. Irish women have been encouraged to be strong-willed and have traditionally dominated family life. In Irish families, men have traditionally been viewed as the weaker and more fallible sex. Women took the double role of backbone of the family and martyr. In Jewish families, sex roles are ambiguous and are often exchanged. In Eastern Europe, the woman was often both breadwinner and the dominant personality in the home, while the man was a retiring scholar or a humble workman. Jewish women often feel torn between expectations that they be Supermothers and professionally successful.

In recent years, Jewish men have achieved a reputation among some gentile women as "ideal husbands." They are seen as dependable, kind, and loving. More than one gentile woman has told us that she always intended to marry a Jewish man.

An Italian or WASP may believe that a Jewish partner will permit her some escape from the sex-defined limits and demands of her own culture; the Jew may be attracted to the more intensely defined "maleness" or "femaleness" of the Italian or WASP. But role expectations die hard: The Italian man may not want to play the macho role, but he might expect a lot more submissiveness than his Jewish wife will find tolerable. And she may want a more forceful husband, but she'll be upset if he doesn't help out with the dishes and the kids.

Bridging the Gaps in Cultural Values People coming from different cultures may have genuinely different values. However, many times needs and symbols from early childhood masquerade as values.[12] If you find yourself engaging in harsh judgment instead of positive suggestion (such as, "you have no taste" rather than, "I would prefer a simpler design"), you're probably dealing not with values, but with important psychological symbols in your family or cultural group. Take a look at the next section, on routines of daily life, where we talk about how to deal with psychologically loaded cultural symbols. How can you tell if you and your partner have a genuine values difference? A value is something you're willing to defend publicly; something to which you devote time, energy, or money. But it is also something you have freely chosen.[13] If you "inherited" a value from your family and culture, have you taken the trouble to examine it, to compare it with alternatives? Have you made an independent adult decision to reclaim it or affirm it as your own value?

Here is an exercise to help you get out of the rut of reflexively defending an old value, and to examine what you really believe in today.

EXERCISE: EXAMINING YOUR VALUES

For each value on which you and your spouse disagree, write a paragraph or two about how you came to "own" this value—about the experience which caused you to reexamine the value and decide you still really believed in it. Mention the counter-arguments you considered, and the reasons you reaffirmed your belief in this value. If you have never gone through this reexamination, do so now: Take a piece of paper, and divide it into two columns. In the left-hand column, write as many arguments as you can think of in support of this value. In the right-hand column, write as many arguments as you can think of against the value. These don't have to be arguments you think are correct; they can be things you have heard other people say, or that you speculate they might say. Put the paper in a drawer. One week later, come back and read it over. Do you still feel absolutely sure of your value? If not, begin to do some reading and thinking and talking to people about the value. If you still feel sure of your position, tear off the column with arguments against it, crumple up that half of the paper, and throw it away. How do you feel when you do this? If you feel calm and unruffled, you're probably comfortable with your value. If you feel *very* good, triumphant, as if "I got those so-and-sos," you are probably being defensive rather than open-minded about your value. You may be defending it because it's yours, rather than because it's right. If you feel somewhat uncomfortable when you throw away the paper, you may suspect that you have rejected the counter-arguments without considering them fairly. In the latter two cases, it's time to do some reading, talking, and thinking.

When you and your spouse have to make a decision about which you have genuinely different values, here are some steps you can take:[14]

First, state your own values clearly.

Second, affirm your respect for and understanding of your partner's values. Showing respect is not easy. It takes stretching to come to the point where you can firmly believe that you're right about something and still entertain the possibility that other people, based on their experiences, might also be right. Listen with an open mind. Not listening is the surest way to communicate disrespect. Be able to summarize your partner's point of view as she would state it. Communicate clearly that, even if you disagree, you haven't passed judgment on your partner. Don't put your partner down, particularly in front of third parties (including your children). Learn to state your disagreement in a way that demonstrates your mutual respect.

Third, look for commonalities. Recognize that values can be, and often are, complementary rather than conflicting. There are many courses of action that respect both sets of values.

Fourth, use the techniques in Chapter 8 (Learning to Negotiate) to arrive at a mutually acceptable compromise.

C. Routines of Daily Life

Eating and Food In both Italian and Jewish families, meals are a symbol of love. They are the hub of family life. WASP and Irish families treat food and eating matter-of-factly, as "nothing to make a fuss over." Portions tend to be small and measured. WASPs and Irish value remaining thin and fit; Jews and Italians traditionally thought pudginess was attractive. Some Jewish and Italian women diet, binge, and hate the way they look. They are expressing the ambivalence that comes from having their guts in a family culture which revolves around eating, and their heads in a larger society which venerates slimness.

Gentile women who marry Jews often pore through recipe books learning East European Jewish cuisine. But it's harder to acquire the unwritten attitudes. Pity the poor WASP wife who slaved over her first dinner for her in-laws. She proudly noted that she had measured everything precisely; there was not a scrap of waste. Her Jewish husband berated her: "I was humiliated. Were you trying to starve us? Do you want my parents to think I don't make enough money to feed you right?"

Handling of Pain and Illness According to a 1960s sociological study, there are significant differences in the way different cultures handle illness.[15] WASPs tend to be stoic, willing to "grin and bear it." Irish often try to ignore the problem altogether. Jews and Italians both make much of illness, with the patient complaining and the family hovering. Jews are skeptical about the doctor's ability, while Italians and WASPs are more likely to accept the doctor as an authority. The Irish have a much higher tolerance for pain. If they say they are suffering, they are unlikely to be exaggerating.

Money The memory of poverty dogs Jewish, Italian, and Irish families, but they have responded in different ways. Because many couples quarrel about money and its uses, and because Jews have long been plagued by the gentile stereotype of the stingy Jew, it's worth pausing to consider what money has meant in these four cultures, and why.

The Jews of Europe were forbidden from working the land and excluded from many crafts; skill in the use of money became one of the few routes to survival. Jews became peddlers and merchants. When trade and capital began to develop, Jews were in a unique position: Because money lending was forbidden to Christians, Christian rulers and capitalists borrowed money for their ventures from Jewish merchants. With land ownership closed to them, Jews who achieved wealth could only use it and display it through personal possessions and charity. In America, many Jews faced grinding poverty and discrimination. But they had a strong drive for education and for financial success, and unlike the rural peasants who immigrated from other parts of Europe, they had many of the skills needed to succeed in an urban industrial world. Gentiles regarded their success rate as remarkable and enviable.

Jewish-Americans from the post-immigrant generation generally want to use money to achieve something: to get an education in a high-status profession, for example. Some families also want to display their success with lavish homes, weddings, or bar mitzvahs. Donations to charity are a priority in many Jewish families; public generosity is a sign of both virtue and status. At the same time, there's an opposite strain of attitudes toward money. Thriftiness, finding a bargain, making a sharp trade, was a virtue in the poverty-stricken ghettoes of Europe and the Lower East Side. In addition, because Jews were repeatedly evicted from countries with nothing but their clothes on their backs, it became important to have cash stashed away. One man said he was brought up on the teaching that you always have a packed suitcase and a full wallet at the ready, because even in America you never can tell when the tide might turn against the Jews.

Italian-Americans also have a recent memory of poverty and of the transitory nature of financial success. Members of the immigrant generation often believed in spending money immediately, while they had it. Among traditional and even among more assimilated Italian-Americans, generosity toward family and personal adornment are often the top priorities. Because of the high value on family and ethnic solidarity, traditional Italian-Americans were as likely to decorate a humble house in a working-class neighborhood as to move up and out to a prestigious suburb.

In middle-class and working-class WASP and Northern European families, frugality was one of the highest virtues. Northern Europeans were strongly influenced by Calvinist ethic: Getting rich was a sign of God's favor and making money was to be encouraged. But lavishness in display was a trait of what they saw as the decadent Papacy (actually feudal and Renaissance cultures). Virtue lay in a stern and simple (if quite comfortable) lifestyle. In wealthier and better-educated families, money was first to be multiplied, through prudent investment, and then to be spent, but in understated ways; furniture, clothing, and homes were expected to be of the best quality, but in simple, classic styles.

The Irish, and the more assimilated German Jews, both sought to acquire respectability by imitating this British and Northern European ethic. Thus they may emphasize frugality rather than spending and good taste rather than ostentation.

Today's young adults may have reacted against or rejected their parents' attitudes toward money, but may still be strongly influenced by it. Because money is a powerful symbol, clashes over it can be intense, with each side seeing the other's way of spending and saving as "selfish" or "stingy" or "foolish." It's easy to lapse into stereotypes, and even name-calling. Even when the husband and wife share similar values, they may get entangled in money disputes with in-laws.

Bridging the Gaps in Routines of Daily Life Everyday experiences like eating and spending are overlaid with meanings because of the family dramas that are acted out through them. Although these details of life seem trivial, they often have unconscious symbolisms rooted in our cultures.[16] One partner may associate having lots of food with being taken care of. It's not really something you can argue him out of, because it's deep in his subconscious. The other partner may associate food with restraint and self-control and may see large amounts of food as loss of self-control. Similar symbolic meanings may be attached to money, neatness, manners, appearances, etc.

One way to be alert to those underlying needs is to notice how you respond. If you feel like jumping away when your partner asks how you like a dress, you may be sensing the strong need for reassurance that underlies what seems like a simple question. Once you're aware of the need, you can choose how to respond to it. For example, you could decide to make a point not only of complimenting your partner at this time, but of giving unsolicited compliments at other times. Keep in mind that your partner's needs are part of the total package you married. You can't be expected to satisfy them all, and neither can you expect your partner's nature to change suddenly so they don't exist.

Your search for solutions to your own problems of everyday life will be more effective if you have successfully identified what these routines mean and what needs they meet for you and your partner.

When a trivial routine of everyday life becomes a difficult issue in your marriage, ask yourself what this routine means to you and the family you grew up in. How did people feel when they engaged in this activity? What were they saying to other members of the family, and to the world?

For example, shopping is a sore point for Salvatore, an Italian, and his Jewish wife, Sharon. Neither is fully aware of the unconscious symbolisms that make this seemingly trivial issue so hard for them to deal with. For Salvatore, buying gifts is a symbol of family loyalty. He gets a lot of his sense of security and self-worth from being part of a large, mutually obligated extended family. For Sharon, money is tied to issues of self-restraint and self-protection. She gets a lot of her sense of security and self-worth from controlling her impulses and planning for the future.

You can't eliminate these differences in response. But you can defuse some of the needs by satisfying them in other ways. Salvatore could make regular phone calls and visits to family, give homemade gifts, and brainstorm about new, non-monetary ways to show his thoughtfulness and caring. Sharon could set up a long-term automatic savings plan or other financial measures that would make her feel secure.

D. Child Rearing

Members of the traditional Italian extended family often expect to be involved in day-to-day parenting. Many Italian-American parents, even today, may be relatively authoritarian and expect children to be obedient and respectful.

WASPs are the most detached from their children. Parents encourage independence and exploration of the outside world at an early age. They may at times expect a level of competence the child feels unable to meet. WASP parents often exercise control through silent disapproval. Being task-oriented, a parent may have a relationship with a child that consists largely of sharing chores around the house. While Jews and Italians make much of passages in a child's life, such as going off to school or graduation, WASPs tend to receive them in an understated fashion.

Irish parents, imbued with the traditional Catholic sense of right and wrong, want very much to raise upright and obedient children. Even today, they are often relatively strict. They may tend to demand respect in an authoritarian manner. They may discipline through ridicule and shaming. Irish children traditionally were not likely to be praised by their parents or to be made the center of attention, for fear of giving them a "swelled head."

Jewish parents play an ambiguous role. They tend to be protective, permissive, and reluctant to punish. They are more likely to listen with interest to their children's opinions. They tolerate challenges to parental authority much more than do parents in other ethnic groups. They tend to keep children in line through high expectations and guilt. This permissive, protective parenting style is typical even of most assimilated Jewish families.

Child-rearing can become an issue when Jewish permissiveness collides with Irish or Italian authoritarianism, or with WASP demands for cleanliness and order. The gentile partner may sometimes feel like pinning back the sheltering wings of an over-protective, hovering Jewish parent.

Crohn recalls one WASP woman (a convert to Judaism) who said, "My family does not worry. When I was thirteen, my father gave me ten flying lessons for a present."

Responded her born-Jewish husband, "I was lucky (at that age) to be able to cross the street by myself."[17]

Bridging the Gaps in Child-Rearing Perspectives Parenting styles are almost reflexive. We learn them when we are children ourselves. They reflect our deepest instincts about how people in families ought to behave.[18]

Keep in mind that the differences can be contradictory or complementary. If you countermand each other's decisions, you will confuse your children or teach them to be manipulative. But if you recognize your differences and support each other's styles, you can give your children a more well-rounded foundation than either of you could give alone. Communicate both your standards and your partner's. For example, if your priority is the child's learning to think and express herself, and your partner emphasizes respect, say, "You will get a chance to speak your mind, but not until it's your turn," or, "We want to hear your opinion, but only if it's given in a respectful way."

In talking about parenting, we need to mention a common problem in intermarriages: the fear of "losing" the child to the other parent. It helps to realize that your child's personality, willy-nilly, will reflect both of you. The bonding between parent and child is so fundamental, and the instinctive imitation begins so early, that it occurs on a level almost beyond your conscious ability to affect it. Recognize also that every child encounters an assortment of influences. If you two are a mix, it's only one part of the complex of mixtures that makes up American culture.

Richard and Martha: Living and Learning Richard and Martha, a middle-aged couple who have been married nearly twenty years, have learned to cope with some classic differences in ethnic style. In some ways, they've gotten more alike. In other areas, they've learned to shrug and accept their differences with gentle humor.

Expressing anger was a big issue. Martha, a Protestant from a small Southern town, says her family was "very quiet and reserved. . . . Anger was not speaking, not expressing, it was the silent treatment."

As Richard says, "To her, yelling at someone meant you were *really* mad at them. It was as bad as slapping them around."

In Richard's family, which is of Russian-Jewish background, "Everybody flares up and screams and yells and the next minute it's quiet."

Their arguments were horror shows at first. Richard recalls, "When I would yell in an argument, not meaning any malice or anything, just yelling, she would start to cry. I kept yelling at her, 'That's not fair. You're not supposed to do that. You're supposed to yell back.' Eventually she got the idea, and now she yells like the rest of us."

Martha recalls that in the early days of their marriage, she would respond to Richard's anger by saying, "'It doesn't matter, do what you want to do, just do it.'

"After a while, I could offer my opinion. We still have a difference of opinion, but he made me realize I do have an opinion, and have worth as a person to express an opinion."

Richard has changed as well. He has tried to tone down, knowing that Martha "can still be hurt a lot easier than the people who were raised up here and are used to it."

Martha still broods. On those occasions, Richard uses one of their favorite techniques: "I keep chasing after her until I make her laugh."

As Martha says, "Humor can get you through a lot."

Another area of discordance was food. Martha describes it:

> I can remember when Richard and I would eat at his mother's, she would walk around the table and talk. I used to come home with horrible indigestion, because there was so much noise and confusion at the meal table. Richard describes it as Horn and Hardart's. . . . Six courses in twenty minutes. Like, grab the dishes and go, then throw out more dishes. Even at Thanksgiving, they're eating the turkey while he's still trying to carve it.

She says that large meals remain symbolic for Richard. "He still wants to sit down to big meals every night, and it's not important to me. He misses that great sense of affection with food. If I have a piece of bologna and bread, that's fine." It's a problem they never fully resolved. Their schedules are so busy these days they settle for simple meals eaten on the run.

As often happens in intermarriages, child-rearing throws the differences into high relief. But they can accept their differences, and laugh. Richard describes how he falls back on guilt to try to motivate their teenaged son, Phil.

> Richard: "For instance, I'll say to Phil, 'Are you gonna do the lawn?'"
> Martha: "Instead of saying, 'Phil, the lawn needs doing,' *I'll* say, 'Go do it and if you don't, you can't do so-and-so. You'll be denied something.' Richard will say, 'The lawn is three feet high. I don't know why you don't do it. I come home and the lawn isn't done.' The next day he'll say, 'Phil, the lawn is four feet high.' And it'll go on and on. Then he'll say, 'I guess I have to do the lawn. I'll have to spend the weekend doing the lawn. My back is hurt,' and all this stuff."
> Richard: "I'll say, 'I have a fifteen-year-old kid and I can't get the lawn done. What's going on here?'"
> Martha: "Instead of looking him in the eye and saying, 'Phillip, go out and do the lawn.' That would be very simple."
> Richard: "That's the way I was brought up. Everything was a guilt trip. The thing is, the thing to really understand, is that [Mar-

tha] and I come from totally different backgrounds. In order to live together, we've just got to understand the fact that we come from different backgrounds. Some of the things that she does that I don't like in most cases just get overlooked. I just overlook it. I hope she does the same thing. Obviously she does."

Martha: "I think it's just a genuine appreciation of the differences in our cultural backgrounds. There comes a point when you can be as angry as you can be, and then you realize there really is humor in the situation."

To learn from each other, as Richard and Martha have done, rather than becoming polarized, takes work. Don't expect massive change. Psychologist Joel Crohn has said that "successful marriage always has [an] element of mutual completion."[19] But a successful marriage, he told us, is one where the partners move a quarter-inch closer together, while in an unsuccessful marriage they move a quarter-inch farther apart.

One woman told Crohn that she wished she could put her parents and her husband's parents into a blender—instead of having two sets of disagreeable parents, they'd have one ideal.[20] In an intermarriage, you put yourselves into the blender. Whether you succeed in creating a blend or merely in grinding your gears depends on the patience, tolerance, and humor with which you approach your life together.

6. ETHNIC AMBIVALENCE:

Love That Blonde

Being a member of a minority group is like being a beet in a flower garden. There may be lots of nourishing, juicy stuff down by your roots, but you may feel that the part that shows to the world is dowdy and unappealing.

It's important to understand both your positive and negative feelings about your ethnic group. As you'll see in this chapter, negative feelings that you haven't reckoned with can undermine both your marriage and your personal confidence. As you'll see in the next chapter, positive feelings that you haven't acknowledged can pose a different kind of trap: You may be perfectly happy to have no connection to your culture at the start of your marriage, and later feel an unexpectedly strong need to reconnect.

To evaluate your feelings toward your ethnic group, write down or say aloud your answers to the following four questions. In each blank, fill in your ethnic group. Have your spouse do the same with her group, and compare your answers.[1]

1) What is it that you love, appreciate, are proud of about being a
_____(Jew, Italian, WASP, black, etc.)?

2) What's difficult for you about being_____?

3) What is it that you dislike about other_____s? About _____men? About_____ women?

4) What is it that you never again want to hear "the others" say about your group?

Talk over your answers with your spouse or interfaith group. You may find yourself digging up a muck of negative feelings even if you don't come from a historically oppressed minority. Psychologist Joel Crohn found that WASPs saw their families as dull, bland, repressed, and emotionally distant. The Irish sometimes saw their parents as strict and punitive.[2]

Many of the intermarriers we talked to chose their spouse at least partly as a way of escaping what they saw as the negative qualities of their own ethnic group. Take Sharon and Salvatore, New York natives now living in a small Midwestern city. Sharon's parents were left-wing Jews who limited their Jewish observance to festive holiday meals. Secretly, she longed for faith and envied the many Catholics in her neighborhood. She says, "I liked the idea you could confess and be done with it, pay for it and get it over with (as opposed to Jewish guilt)."

Salvatore grew up in a Brooklyn working-class neighborhood. His parents, Italian immigrants, are devoutly Catholic, but he no longer practices. As an upwardly mobile intellectual, Salvatore felt a kinship to Jews. In college, he was often the only Italian in his classes. He joined a Jewish fraternity.

"I think we both wanted someone from out of our backgrounds," says Sharon. "I sort of stereotyped Jewish men: Men who got pushed around, might have been professionally effective but weren't that effective in their families or with their women. Men who were not very physical. Salvatore has a certain way of handling his body that is definitely not Jewish. He's very aggressive. Jewish men in my experience were not aggressive."

Sharon sees herself and her family through a stereotype similar to the one she applies to Jewish men. "I would like to be in most ways different from my parents. They were ethical people. But in some ways, both were very passive. I think I'm a lot like them, but I wish I weren't."

There's a problem in this type of motivation: A person who marries out because of ambivalent feelings about his own people can't see his partner clearly. His spouse is at least partly a symbol, rather than a real person. And he can't afford to let her be herself. We frequently found, for example, that the gentile woman in an intermarriage wanted, for her own reasons, to draw toward Judaism. But often her Jewish-born husband was hostile to this interest. He needed her as a living symbol of his rejection of Jews and Judaism. This rejection was often entangled with hostile feelings toward his own family.

Lena Romanoff, director of the Jewish Converts Network, recalls a startling letter she got after speaking at a synagogue forum. The letter-writer's message: "My wife was a very nice *shiksa* (non-Jewish woman). Then she converted to Judaism and became a castrating bitch."

If you have negative feelings about your ethnic group, it will help both you and your marriage to figure out why.

THE FORCES OF SHAME

Members of minority groups often suffer from "internalized oppression."[3] Internalized oppression has four characteristics:

First, people start believing the bad things the larger society says about their group. They may have difficulty seeing themselves as admirable or sexually attractive. They may feel impotent and helpless in the face of insults or discrimination they encounter. They may have a persistent feeling of shame.

Second, they often project the insults outward, onto members of the opposite sex of their group. America glorifies the Nordic ideal of beauty: square-jawed men and svelte women with straight blond hair. Blacks, Jews, and members of other oppressed groups may be "turned off" by the males or females of their own group and "turned on" by outsiders who fit this ideal. Minority group members can "desexualize" each other.

Third, they may go through a psychic flip-flop and begin to see members of their own group as the villains. Thus, the Jewish man may feel oppressed by a dominating mother or a demanding "Jewish princess" girlfriend, even though it is actually the hostile and belittling majority society which has robbed him of faith in his own masculinity.

Fourth, since they haven't the power to return the mistreatment they received, members of an oppressed group may act out their angry feelings by in turn victimizing the less powerful members of their own group—especially the children. Thus, parents who grew up in a society that ridiculed them (as happened to many Jews) may be highly critical of their children, undermining the children's confidence even when they most want to help them. Parents who were subjected to physical mistreatment (as many minorities were) may physically abuse their children. An opposite pattern may also occur: Parents who were unable to protect themselves and their children from mistreatment may become suffocatingly overprotective concerning the circumscribed areas where they do control what happens to their children.

Jews and blacks are especially likely to feel ambivalence or shame about their own groups. The Nazi Holocaust and American slavery and racial discrimination are overwhelming examples of oppression that generate great self-doubt in the victimized groups. "Unlearning" this shame can free you to have greater confidence in yourself, to communicate more pride and approval to your children, and to more fully trust your partner. (After all, how can you trust her judgment if she married a member of a group you despise?) It can also free you to be nurtured by, rather than isolated from, the riches of your heritage and people.

How can you reclaim pride in your ethnic roots? One way is to join an "ethnotherapy" group. Ethnotherapy is a form of counseling that is designed to help people work through their negative feelings about being a member of a minority group. Ethnotherapy groups for Jews (and sometimes for their partners) are springing up in a number of cities; you may be able to find one through the Jewish Family and Children's Agency, Jewish Federation, or YM-YWHA in your area. Groups also exist for members of other ethnic minorities, but they are still rare.

Ethnotherapy groups use a variety of strategies to defuse negative feelings.[4] One is simply to bring all the negative feelings to the surface and talk them out. In ethnotherapy groups for Italian-Americans in New York, women attacked men as noisy babies who wanted to be taken care of, while men dumped on women as bossy and controlling. By seeing each other as Babies and Mommies, they completed the work of desexualizing each other that the Nordic ideal had begun. After the participants discharged their anger and heard each other's viewpoint, they were able to call a truce—to begin to see each other as individuals.

(As you may have noticed, "in-group stereotypes" are in certain ways very different from the slurs of popular bigotry. Italian men, for example, are generally seen by non-Italian women as virile, not as Babies. Italian women are generally seen by non-Italian men as vivacious and sexy, not as Mommies.)

A second strategy of ethnotherapy is to understand that stereotypes are tools, rather than truths. The majority "uses" the minority group as a way of projecting, or blaming on someone else its worst fears about itself. Since stereotypes serve the unconscious needs of the people and societies which use them, they change arbitrarily to meet those needs. For example, in Europe Jewish men were seen by non-Jews as lustful lechers and dangerous rapists (much as blacks are seen in America). In America, Jewish men are stereotyped as impotent wimps. Jewish women in Europe were seen by non-Jews as promiscuous; in America, they're often stereotyped as frigid.

A third strategy of ethnotherapy groups is to put the stereotypes in historical context. Thus, in ethnotherapy groups, Jews who were ashamed of the meekness of some of their grandfathers in Eastern Europe, and blacks who were ashamed of the shuffling "Uncle Toms" among them, have learned to see these traits as a way of coping with overwhelming odds, with a situation in which the majority was viciously violent, fighting back was hopeless, and simple survival became a priority. They learned how in these cultures, where men were forced into a submissive posture, women stepped in to fill the power vacuum in the family. They saw how the majority society then ridiculed the behavior it compelled. And they saw how their own minority culture developed self-hating stereotypes of its members, being ashamed of behavior they had been forced to take on to survive.

By discharging the negative feelings, you can begin to reclaim pride: to talk out loud about the things you value in yourself and other members of your group.

One warning: Going to an ethnotherapy group confronts both partners in an intermarriage with some sad and ugly facts. If you are a non-minority partner, you will be forced to realize the role your own group may have played in shaping your partner's pain. You will also see that, in aligning yourself with a minority group, you take on its troubles as well as its attractive qualities. You will have to ask yourself whether you are ready not only to confront prejudice yourself, but to give your children the strength and pride to resist it.

Even if no ethnotherapy group or intermarried couples' group exists in your area, each of you can be an ally in helping the other reaffirm his roots. Share your positive memories of family and culture. Your partner is probably interested in learning more about your culture if you will let her. Tell what you like about each other, then about how your ethnic group encouraged you to develop the traits your partner admires in you.

As you work on any negative images of your own ethnic roots, take some time to explore your attitudes toward your partner's culture. You will probably find that along with your admiration, you have prejudices. These stereotypes are areas of extraordinary vulnerability for your partner. In arguments, be careful never to make an accusation that will re-open these wounds. For example, even if you make no reference to his Jewish background, asking a Jewish man why he can't stand up for himself will wound him deeply because it hits him right in the center of a stereotype. Similarly, one of the worst things to say to an Italian or a Pole is "You dumb—" Try to develop the habit of hearing critical comments with your partner's ears. Think about how your remark would sound to someone from his culture.

Self-hate is a corrosive force that intermarriers must be alert to. Reckoning with it is part of the process of accepting your past and clearing your marriage of hidden agendas.

7. THE LIFETIME TRAJECTORY:

Changes over Time

As you get older, a curious thing begins to happen. As sure as the gray hairs and crow's feet will arrive, your needs change. Many people who were alienated from their roots as young adults develop a need to reconnect. People who thought of themselves as secular may come to want a spiritual home.

This sudden reawakening of ethnic or spiritual needs can feel like a flower unfolding. In other cases, though, it can strike the marriage with all the force of a psychological time bomb—especially if one partner feels the need to change and the other doesn't. If this happens, it's vital that you find a mutually acceptable way to deal with these evolving needs.

Jeremiah and Barbara were unable to agree on a way to deal with their changing needs. Marital problems that they thought they had solved began to reignite. In the beginning, Jeremiah and Barbara were in flight from their families and their cultures. Jeremiah, reacting against his emotionally buttoned-down New England Yankee family, was attracted by Barbara's warmth and expressiveness. She, a feminist reacting against an enveloping, intrusive Jewish family, was attracted by his independence. They helped each other escape from ways of life that appeared to them to be stifling.

But then Barbara, at the birth of their child, grew interested in reconnecting with her family and their Jewish culture. Jeremiah felt betrayed. That wasn't part of their "contract" with each other. Seen from a life-cycle point of view, however, it was perfectly natural.

This chapter will take you through the stages of the life cycle, showing how your relationship to religion and to your cultural heritage may change at each stage.

THE STAGES OF IDENTITY-SORTING

One of the central tasks in our lives is to become ourselves, to achieve an integrated identity. It's a task we never accomplish once and for all, because at each stage we find ourselves asking new questions, and having to disassemble and reassemble our identities to find the answers. As part of that process, our relationship to our culture and religion may change profoundly several times.[1]

Intermarriage can play central, though opposite, roles in the identity-sorting process at different times in one's life.

Separating The first major identity transition usually comes when we are adolescents or young adults. Some people marry out as part of breaking away from parents. Additionally, because we are in an experimenting time of life, we are truly less like our parents and our ethnic group than we may later become.

Reconnecting Marriage and children put you back in the stream of generations. You may find yourself wanting to duplicate the traditions of your childhood. Having established your differentness, you need to come to terms with the ways you are like your parents, the ways you were molded by your heritage.

Having a partner from a different background can complicate this necessary life process. You may suddenly find you have to negotiate a whole set of cultural differences that didn't seem important before. One or both of you may want to avoid the issues. Yet if you don't go through the sorting process, deciding what you will and won't take from your parents' way of life, you may remain stuck in adolescence. You own only half of yourself.

Buried in Routine Once the family has been established, identity-sorting may enter a third stage: Having gone back and established a more traditional life-style, you may feel that the "I," your individuality, has gotten lost in a morass of routine. Women may feel panicky that they have no identity but wife and mother. Men may worry that they are nothing but "organization men." At this stage, too, intermarriage may complicate the identity-sorting process. For example, a gentile woman who has converted to Judaism may suddenly feel that she has irrevocably cut off the "self" of her childhood. She may feel a need to withdraw from the Jewish community in which she has been immersed. This surge of doubt or alienation can be especially powerful if it coincides with the end of the convert's usual period of "infatuation" with her adopted religion.

One woman we talked to had been happily living with her husband and children as a Jewish family for ten years. But when her rabbi suggested that to ensure their acceptance in the broader Jewish community, she and the children should formally convert to Judaism, she panicked. "Perhaps when I married and did want to merge, perhaps I became submerged," she said. "I feel like this [converting to Judaism] would be the last giving up of my own identity . . . I sometimes wish I'd kept my own name. I don't want to do anything else I might regret."

The Teen Challenge When your children are teenagers, questioning everything, and going through their first major identity crisis, they are likely to propel you into a new identity-sorting process of your own. They may look backward to your parents (their grandparents), picking up pieces of the religion or culture that you had rejected and forcing you to relive, question, or defend your choices.

Larry and Nancy came to one of our interfaith couples groups in a state of turmoil. He had been raised as a Jew, she as a Catholic. Each of them had firmly rejected their religion, seeing it as a symbol of some of the worst aspects of their childhoods. Their son had not been circumcised, and they had raised their children with no religion. But now their son was a teenager, and demanding to have a bar mitzvah and a Jewish religious education. They found all the old bad feelings of their childhoods stirred up, and the ripples went throughout their marriage.

The Empty Nest As you come to the end of your career and parenting years, you may find yourself again sorting through your relationship to the culture and religion of your childhood. At this stage, some people make the break for freedom that they never made during their adolescence. They may feel that they fulfilled all the prescriptions of their culture but got too little satisfaction as individuals. There may be divorces after twenty years of marriage. Many of the remarriages are intermarriages. Often an older man is marrying a younger woman: he and she are at different stages of the identity-sorting process. While he may be fleeing from a culture which he feels shackled him all his life, she may be moving toward a culture which seems to promise a haven from some of the rootlessness of adolescence and young adulthood.

Finally, in old age, we look for a way of integrating and understanding our lives. People who were secular all their adult lives may return to the culture or religion of their childhood.

THE STAGES OF RELIGIOUS GROWTH

Along with changing feelings about your ethnic roots, spiritual needs also evolve as you age. James Fowler, a Protestant minister who is one of America's foremost researchers on the psychology of religion, believes all people go through a similar series of steps in faith development. These steps are linked to our emerging capacities for reasoning.[2]

Fowler's first two stages are discussed at greater length in our Chapter 13 (Children and Spirituality). Fowler says most adults start out with what he calls Stage 3 or "Synthetic-Conventional Faith." Values and beliefs of some ideology (usually that of one's parents, peers, and the church or religion of one's birth) are accepted without much questioning. The ideology provides comfort because it explains the world and one's place in it. These beliefs are seen as natural, true, and inherent in the nature of the world. People who do not hold this ideology are alien. The ideology crystallizes somewhere between age thirteen and age twenty. Many adults stay comfortably at this stage of faith development for the rest of their lives.

But other young adults in their twenties go on to what Fowler calls "Stage 4" or "Individuative-Reflective Faith." It is a time of demythologizing. The young adult "leaves home," not only physically but psychologically and spiritually as well. The person begins to question the beliefs with which he was brought up, as well as his own assumptions. Usually this person adopts a rationalist view of the world. A person in this stage may deny subjective feelings, experiences, or needs that don't fit with the presumed superiority of the rationalist viewpoint. Often values such as social change or competence take precedence over belief and ritual. The person may either seek new communities that share his views or operate as an autonomous individual, without community. Intermarriages often occur when people are in their twenties and are Stage 4 rationalists. The ideologies they grew up with are no barrier because each partner has rejected the religion of his or her childhood. They often share a common commitment to social change or to an occupation.

Many people remain comfortable at that level of development for most of their adult lives. In others, a personal crisis, a restlessness with limits, or some inexorable process of the life cycle pushes them on to Stage 5 or what Fowler calls "Conjunctive Faith." This often occurs when people are in their thirties and forties. They develop a new interest in exploring the questions of religion. They begin to wrestle with the paradoxes of life. They have experienced some defeats, have made some personal commitments which both guide and narrow the direction of their lives, and have faced some of their limits. They may be vividly aware of injustice and human pain, and may be dissatisfied with their own actions and their failure to live out their values.

People begin trying to cope with ultimate questions such as the meaning of life and death that cannot be approached strictly through logic. They experience a new openness in many facets of life—what Fowler calls "a second naïveté." Part of this is an openness to ideas of transcendence and nonrational elements, and a willingness to explore how these ideas can coexist with the rationalism learned in Stage 4. People have a new openness to symbols, rituals, myths, and communities, because they glimpse deeper realities that are contained in these things. People begin rethinking their pasts. They also experience a new openness to the truths of people who have taken paths different from theirs—an ability to see them as "real people," too. Most people who arrive at this stage remain there, Fowler says—with the mysteries of life acknowledged but still unresolved. They have extended a taproot into the richness of human spiritual experience but have not arrived at any permanent sense of peace or resolution. A danger of this stage is paralysis, inaction, passivity in the face of the acknowledged paradoxes.

It can shake a marriage when one partner's spiritual needs go through change while the other's don't. A person who is deeply rooted in a conventional faith may feel betrayed if his partner drops the faith and becomes a Stage 4 rationalist. But a Stage 4 rationalist may feel equally betrayed if his partner drops her rationalist, universalist view of the world and becomes interested in spiritual search. It helps to realize that religious ideas—including rationalism—do not necessarily reflect objective fact or ultimate truth. All our concepts to some extent reflect the needs we feel at particular stages of growth to understand life and our place in the world. One idea is not "better" than another. They grow out of our evolving human needs. You can't get rid of a need by arguing against it or ridiculing it or even by ignoring it. You have to deal with it. It also helps to realize that a person who was a rationalist and who then becomes interested in religion is not going backward. That person is finding a way of wrestling with the new questions that life has presented.

People who have reached the wrestling of Stage 5 often have a yearning to go further. They may be frustrated or full of doubt about the worth of their own spiritual strivings because they feel that they cannot achieve a centered, confident faith. At various times in his research, Fowler suggested that a few extraordinary individuals are able to pass beyond Stage 5 to Stage 6—a unifying, transcendent vision of the world. They overcome paradox by becoming incarnations of their ideals—acting self-lessly and totally out of their faith-vision. They see the ultimate unity among all people and all visions of God. At other times Fowler has felt that there is no Stage 6: Stage 5 is as far as we humans can go.

If you and your partner are having problems because of your dif-fering spiritual needs, or if you suspect that either you or your partner is making a transition from one stage of spiritual needs to another, Chap-ters 9 and 10 on adult faith can help you wrestle with some of the ques-tions that arise.

The Special Hold of Jewish Identity Although people from every group will have periods when they feel compelled to draw closer to their roots, this is particularly so for Jews. Many historians have speculated over how Jews could maintain their religio-cultural identity in the face of severe persecution, over so many centuries of dispersion among other cultures. What happens on a group level is also true for individuals. We have met a great number of people who had no religious tie to Judaism but who, in positive or negative ways, were living much of their life in reaction to their Jewish identity.

In a speech at the Second National Conference on Intermarriage, psychologist Joel Crohn told this story about the amazing persistence of individual Jewish identity: A female patient of his had a Jewish father and a Christian mother. The girl had been brought up without any appreci-ation of Judaism. At one point, the patient suffered a serious depression and was about to commit suicide. "At the moment she was about to commit suicide, she had this vision of this long string of Jewish ancestors behind her, and she couldn't do that." She felt that she couldn't break the chain.

We think this identity persists because the family is so central to Judaism. Jewish rituals, celebrations, laws, all center on the home. The history and mythology are primarily the story of one continuous family. This belief system was reinforced by the Jewish history of ghettoization. All people, at some point, need to reckon with their ethnic heritage. But Jews are particularly likely to experience the compulsion to reconnect.

How can you assess whether you are going through, or need to go through, one of these periods of identity transition? Take a mental snapshot of your life at this moment:

EXERCISE: PICTURE YOUR PRIORITIES

Make a pie graph. Draw a circle. Divide it into wedges to show how you allocate your time in a typical week. Include work for pay, child care, household work, religious or political activity, recreation, education, solitude, time with extended family, or ethnic community. Are you living a life that no longer meets your needs? Redraw the lines on the pie graph to show the balance of activities you would like. Would the religious part, and the extended family or ethnic community part, grow or shrink? Talk to your partner about changes you would like to make.

This sorting process can be frightening. When one partner goes through an identity crisis, the marriage does, too.

How can you get through the identity transitions and feel united as a family again?[3] First, keep talking to each other. Talk about what you're feeling and what you're thinking. Second, keep up your social contacts. When families are under stress, they tend to withdraw from the social network. Isolation intensifies the stress. Keep reaching outward, even when you don't feel like it. Third, use the negotiating techniques in the next chapter to help you and your partner arrive at a new "marriage contract" for this new stage in your life. Fourth, realize that identity transitions are fruitful change points.

If you willingly struggle through the difficult transitions, you will grow. And in most cases, your marriage eventually will be stronger.

8. LEARNING TO NEGOTIATE:

An Acquired Skill

A marriage, and particularly an intermarriage, is like an alliance between two nations. Couples in successful marriages use negotiating techniques remarkably similar to those used by diplomats. You can learn these techniques. Using them makes it more likely that each partner will be listened to and that neither will be left nursing unresolved grievances. Negotiating techniques can help you work out decisions about life-style, child-rearing, holidays, ceremonies, and relationships with extended family.

In this chapter, we will outline a six-step process of negotiation. We will also talk about how power differences and ethnic patterns can complicate negotiations.

Sherri Alper, outreach coordinator for the Union of American Hebrew Congregations (Reform) in Philadelphia, has developed the following exercise to teach negotiation to discussion groups of interfaith couples. Try it now, with your spouse.

EXERCISE: RECONCILING OPPOSING POSITIONS

Herb and Mary Kushner have just had their first child, a boy. They had never discussed birth rituals previously, feeling they would make the necessary decisions when the time came. Now that their son is born, they are aware of very strong feelings on the part of both sets of parents. Herb's parents are concentration camp survivors who lost their entire families in the Holocaust. They are very excited about the *bris* (ritual circumcision) that they are sure will be held for their new grandson. Mary's father, Edward O'Brien, is dying of cancer. He has been a good Catholic all his life, and he has expressed a strong desire to have his grandson baptized.

1. What are the *feelings* of each person above? (When in doubt, imagine!)

2. What should Herb and Mary do? List three *funny* solutions. (Be outrageous!)

3. List three *possible* solutions or approaches.

4. Select the best solution from the above and be prepared to discuss your reasons.

Sherri Alper's exercise illustrates the six basic steps in negotiation. These steps are outlined by Roger Fisher and William Ury in their classic negotiating guide, *Getting to Yes*.[1] We have adapted their suggestions slightly to fit the needs of intermarried couples. These same steps are suggested by family counselors as well as by professional negotiators dealing with business, labor, or international relations:

1. Don't try to decide who is right, or who should win; instead focus on developing a problem-solving process.

2. Begin by acknowledging feelings.

3. Learn about the history (family or culture) that underlies each side's demands.

4. Stop pressing for what each of you *wants*, and instead focus on what each of you *needs*. Instead of mechanically splitting the difference between your two original proposals, search for an alternate solution that meets both partners' needs.

5. Multiply your vision of the available options by using humor and brainstorming.

6. Agree upon criteria for evaluating proposed solutions.

Ethnic Differences in Handling Conflict This talk about needs and feelings and brainstorming may hit each of you differently. One of you may love the ideas. The other may run for cover or turn away with a sneer. What is behind these responses? Often it is ethnic differences. If you and your spouse are having trouble even agreeing to negotiate, take a look at Chapter 5's discussion on cultural differences in response to conflict. Use ethnic descriptions to alert you to possible problems in your own negotiating behavior and to help you make allowances for the way each of you needs to operate.[2]

Hopefully, out of your commitment to each other, you and your partner will work through any resistance and make a sincere effort at negotiating. Be sure to acknowledge each other's attempts and to be gentle in your persistence.

Dealing with Power Differences You have come a long way if you can agree your goal is no longer to win the argument, or to have the family do things your way, but to find a pattern of living that meets both of your needs. For that way of living to be acceptable to each of you, you must arrive at it jointly.

To make this joint process work, you have to deal honestly with power differences in your relationship. Realize that if either one wins, you both lose. The one-down partner is likely to become resentful and withdraw. The one-up partner is likely to become insensitive and lose the ability to connect with the mate. As you talk, try to see what triggers each of you into your power modes (bullying or submissive, for example). Try to understand what behaviors each of you uses in a fight (such as talking louder or faster; withdrawing and tuning out; nursing private resentments; complaining later to friends or family). Don't accuse your partner: Instead, take responsibility for recognizing when you have fallen into your power-difference behavior. Say, "I realize that I'm withdrawing and backing down, and I don't want to do that," or, "I've started raising my voice. I'll stop."

Ethnic differences, as well as male-female differences, may color a power struggle. Men from macho cultures, such as the Italian, Greek, or Hispanic, may raise their voices and lean or move forward. Men and women from verbal cultures, such as the Jewish, may try to out-talk their mate.

If you have dealt with your ethnic and power differences and agreed that your goal is a mutually satisfactory solution and not a win for your side, you're ready to negotiate. Here's how:

Dealing with Feelings Maybe you are a silent simmerer, storing your resentments. Or maybe you're a clattering pressure cooker, ready to explode. Either way, before you can settle down to solving the problem, you need to let off some steam.

But expressing your feelings is not just a way of clearing the air—it is basic to your central task, the task of truly understanding how your partner feels, and why. When each of you expresses your feelings, you become closer; you know each other more intimately. It is this intimacy which is the foundation for the shared solutions you develop in your life together.

When you talk about the feelings a particular issue generates in you, be careful not to lay blame. Take responsibility for your own feelings. Use "I statements," not "You statements." Don't say, "You make me angry," or, "How can you do this outrageous thing?" Instead, say, "I feel angry when you—" or "When you do such and such, I feel scared."

Agree that one of you will speak at a time, and will be allowed to continue without interruptions until he has said everything he wants to say. Then it is the other partner's turn.

If your partner expresses strong feelings, or cries, or gets furious, don't get scared, and don't take it personally. It doesn't mean you are bad or wrong. If strong feelings come out, that's a good sign, not a bad one. It means you're getting to the bottom of something important. You're providing a safe place for your partner to get the feelings out, so that both of you can deal with them. So when your partner gets emotional, don't comment, judge, or defend. Don't even reassure, or try to "patch it and make it better." Don't do anything to cut off the flow until your partner is done talking. Just listen.

When your partner finishes, see if you can restate his point so that he feels your words exactly reflect what he was trying to express. Keep working at it until your partner feels satisfied that you understand.

Then take your turn. If necessary, remind your partner that you also must have a chance to talk your feelings out fully, without interruption.

Remember: You're not talking about content, or how to solve the problem at this stage. You're talking only about feelings. And you're not placing blame. If you can stick to these two rules, you'll find that, without attacking your partner, you can release some of the bottled-up inner pressure and free your energies to find a common solution to your common problem.

Dealing with Family History The second step is dealing with the family history and ethnic group history that underlie your feelings. Just as a lot of the pressure Herb and Mary felt came from their fathers' histories, so your family and cultural experience influences your approach. Visualize moments in your family when the issue came up. Who was there? How did each person act? How did you feel? What was most important to you about that experience? What do you want to preserve? What do you want to avoid, or do differently? Talk over these memories with your partner.

Developing Lists of Needs Write down the two or three things you *need* regarding this issue: not what you *want*, but what you need. In the negotiation exercise earlier, Mary may want to baptize the child and Herb may want to give him a *bris*, but what they each *need* is to avoid guilty feelings or a family rift.

Developing Goals and Objective Criteria Now develop a list of joint goals, or hopes. Herb and Mary may each have such goals as affirming their love and loyalty to their parents. Their joint goals may include welcoming their child into the world and creating a happy family event.

Based on your goals, draw up a list of objective criteria you can use to evaluate any proposed solutions. For example, Herb and Mary might agree as a yardstick that they would not develop a ceremony that either parent would feel unable to attend. You and your partner may be negotiating about money. You disagree about how to spend it. But you agree on a common yardstick: Any solution must permit you to live within your income. Remember that criteria are not solutions; they are mutually agreed-upon yardsticks for evaluating possible solutions.

Expanding Your Sense of the Options First, free yourself from your past ideas about how to solve the problem. Brainstorm together on six or more silly solutions. Take turns tossing out ideas. Teach yourselves to laugh about the area of your dispute.

Next, brainstorm to generate at least ten serious options. Brainstorming is a way of freeing your mind up to think creatively. You free-associate, saying whatever comes into your mind. There are two key rules for brainstorming. One, there is no right or wrong. And two, there's no discussion. You simply hop from one idea to another. Take turns. Consciously create a joint process. Be as free and fluent as you can: Imagine you are a popcorn popper popping with ideas. Don't stop until every kernel of thought in you has burst open. Suspend judgment at this stage. Don't comment on any option until you've generated as many as possible. You're not looking for the best answer yet; you're looking for the widest array of possibilities to choose from.

Evaluating the Options Now, winnow through the options. Are any unsatisfactory to either one of you? Have that partner explain the objection, then let the other respond. Consider modifications to make it acceptable to both of you. Otherwise, drop the option from your list. Talk about what is attractive or unattractive to you in each of the remaining options. Use this process to learn more about what your partner needs.

Use your jointly developed criteria to choose the best of the remaining options. Ask yourselves: Does this option meet both of our needs? Does it "feel right" to both of us? Does it fulfill our joint goals? Does it satisfy our objective standards? Does it have any important drawbacks?

Don't assume that any option is an either/or proposition. Could you modify an option to better meet your needs?

Giving it a Trial Run Now try out the option which seems best to both of you. Make it concrete. If you're going to share the cooking, decide who will cook on which days of the week. Remember that this is a new way of acting, and it will not "fit" well immediately for either of you. If you've agreed that the man will do some of the cooking, the woman is going to have to refrain from interfering while he burns a few pots. After a period of testing, make adjustments if necessary.

Looking Forward, Not Back As you deal with a particular issue, keep in mind that your goal is to make something new, not to undo what's already happened. Don't try to settle the blame. Learn to respond not to the past, but to the real person standing before you today. Focus on the future. If you find yourself using the words *never* or *always*, it's a clue you're dredging up the past. It's also a clue that you're blaming your partner rather than taking responsibility for your own feelings.

Knowing Your Bottom Line Not every partner is willing to try these negotiating techniques. And not every issue is negotiable. You have to know your bottom line. Can you live with this? Or is this a separation-or-divorce issue?

In some marriages, the cultural canyon is too deep and the partners eventually realize they must go separate ways. Sometimes that is the only choice that lets the partners emerge with their personalities intact. But with the right negotiating techniques, the right attitudes, and some effort, most couples will find that most gaps can be bridged.

FINDING YOUR SPIRITUAL PATH

9. YOUR SPIRITUAL NEEDS:

Looking Inward

"**W**hat's the big deal? Neither of us is religious."

That is how many people in intermarriages feel—at least at first. But over time, faith turns out to be an important issue to many couples—even when both are nonbelievers. Most couples don't end up arguing directly about religious beliefs. But they find that many key decisions, such as what to do about the religious education of their children, depend on what they believe.

Several couples, for instance, participated for a number of years in an interfaith couples' discussion group. The group was started by parents who wanted to discuss what to do about their children's religious upbringing. There were no clergy involved, and most of the parents considered themselves religious skeptics. Yet repeatedly they all found themselves drawn toward heavy philosophical discussions—trying to figure out what they believed. They found they couldn't settle any of the other, more practical issues until they figured out that one.

There's another reason why religion is especially likely to become an issue in interfaith marriages: even when couples have the same philosophical viewpoints, they often have different spiritual needs. One needs to be part of a religious community. The other needs solitude and quiet. One finds comfort and beauty in ritual. The other is repelled by ritual. We talked with a number of couples who had begun marriage with similar religious viewpoints but whose spiritual needs had changed over time. After years of marriage, even when other aspects of their relationship were going well, they were out of synch on this one.

To untangle these issues, you have to take four steps: to figure out your own beliefs and needs, to understand your partner's beliefs and needs, to understand what religious options are available to you as individuals and as a family, and to find a respectful common ground. This chapter will help you to sort out what you believe and don't believe. The next chapter will help you to understand and bridge spiritual differences between yourself and your partner. The final chapter of this spirituality section explores the complex question of religious conversion.

We found that one of the big problems in intermarriage was selective silence: People hesitated to talk with each other about their beliefs. In important ways, they didn't know each other. As you go through this chapter, make a conscious effort to open up your communication about personal beliefs. Only after both of you have sorted out your own beliefs and found ways of communicating with each other on religious issues will you really be ready to tackle the practical decisions concerning child rearing, rites of passage, home style, affiliation, and religious education, which are covered in later sections of this book.

Figuring Out What You Believe Every person has some sort of faith. That is a tenet of Dr. James W. Fowler, a Protestant minister who heads the Center for Faith Development at Emory University in Atlanta, and is one of America's foremost researchers in the psychology of religion. To Fowler, faith is how you place your bets in life. It's whatever you do to make sense of the world. It's whatever you truly trust. Or (citing Protestant theologian Paul Tillich), it's the object of your "real worship, [your] true devotion": work, power, wealth, family, nation, love, sex—and possibly God.[1]

Take a few minutes, using Rev. Fowler's definitions, to crystallize your ideas about your own personally defined faith.

What ideas do you find sustaining or strengthening? What makes it possible for you to slog on in uncertain situations? Where do you turn in crisis?

To what extent do you feel part of something greater than yourself? What are those things? Family? Community? History? Nation? Earth? Cosmos? What feelings do you get from that sense of being part of something greater?

What are the things that are truly important to you in this world—the things to which you devote your time, energy, money, and love?

How do you act on your values?

Do your values seem to be based on mere common sense, a standard that is necessary for the smooth running of society? Or are they connected to your sense of what is holy?

Do you believe in some sort of God? How do you imagine or define God? How does your belief or nonbelief fit in with what you see of human suffering, and with what you feel is the purpose of your life?

It helps to write out your answers. Does your partner know what you believe about these basic life questions? Do you know what he or she believes? Take time now to share your answers.

You may think of your faith as a purely personal thing. But it is helpful to realize how much of what you think and feel is shared by others. Try the following exercises.[2]

EXERCISE 1: YOUR SPIRITUAL HISTORY

Spiritual experiences are those that shaped your nonfactual ideas: your values, your sense of the meaning of life. You have such ideas regardless of whether you believe in God.

A good way to understand your spirituality is to get in touch with experiences that have stirred or inspired you.

1. Name a place that was important to you, or where an important positive thing happened to you.

2. Name a person who has had great positive impact on you.

3. Talk about a formative experience in your life.

4. Recount the happiest and saddest experience you remember.

5. Now take your list and apply the following labels:

Call the place Holy Ground, and the person with the greatest impact Spiritual Beacon. Call the formative experience Personal Awakening; the happiest, Vista; the saddest, Religious Questioning.

Applying these labels can help you realize that your experiences are not unique or a result of happenstance: They are universal experiences and needs that everyone has. Take time to share these important experiences with your partner.

* * *

Part of understanding your own beliefs is exploring any negative feelings you have about religion. Unless you work through these feelings, your reaction to religion will be a mere emotional reflex, defined and limited by childhood experience.

EXERCISE 2: DEALING WITH THE OLD GOD

1. Keep a journal. Start by talking about what God means to you. List all the things you think are obnoxious about the concept of God you learned as a child. If you are a nonbeliever, list the objections you have to the idea of God. Keep a record of how you think and feel when you consider the idea of God.

2. Hold an imaginary conversation with that childhood God. Tell Him how you felt about Him when you were a child, how your ideas changed, and if you don't believe in Him anymore, why.

3. When you begin to untangle your feelings about God, you have to reckon with your feelings about prayer. In your journal, answer the following questions: Do you think children should be taught the meanings of God and of prayer? Do you want your children to pray, or would you prefer that they learn about religion, but not pray? Why? Do you pray? Why or why not? Did you once pray but not any longer? If so, why did you once pray, and why did you stop? What did you pray for? What were you taught about prayer? How do you feel about that teaching? What was the intent of the people who taught you? Was prayer helpful to you? Do you sometimes feel sad that you can't pray? If so, why?

Talk to your spouse or hold another imaginary conversation with God about what you wrote in your journal about prayer.

You may have only positive feelings about religion. You may believe deeply in God and find nourishment in the religion in which you were raised. Or, these exercises may have confirmed your nonbelief. But in our interviews, we found that many people belonged to a middle group. They were neither atheists nor committed believers. They felt spiritual needs (some had vague longings, some a sharp yearning) but were turned off by the religion they grew up in, and as a result had not pursued their spiritual impulses.

The next exercise will help you examine your feelings about organized religion.[3]

EXERCISE 3: DEALING WITH RELIGIOUS TRADITION

A. Collect some religious objects: a Jewish star, a menorah, a prayer book, a matzoh, a cross, a Crucifix, a picture of Jesus, a Christmas card, an Advent wreath, etc. While the Jewish objects are on display, play or hum some Jewish music. "Experience" the objects for fifteen minutes. Do the same with the Christian objects, while playing hymns and Christmas carols. What feelings well up? What experiences shaped those feelings?

Pick up the Christian object to which you have the strongest reaction. Describe to the object some of the memories and feelings linked to it. Let the object answer back. Keep talking with it until you reach a resolution. If you can't get anywhere by talking, act out your feelings on the object. Kiss it, stamp on it, etc. Then deal with the Jewish object that stirred you most.

B. "Talk back" to religious authorities: Place a chair facing you. Conjure up a mental image of the priest, rabbi, or Sunday school teacher who represents whatever you object to about organized religion. Imagine that person is sitting in the chair. Tell him (or her) everything you object to about the religion he represents, and everything you object to about him personally. Remind him of any incidents you are angry about. Keep talking until you have nothing more to say. Then let the person answer back. Keep going until you come to some sort of resolution.

These exercises may have stirred up strong feelings. In the next section of the chapter, we'll help you take a look at some of the childhood experiences that molded these feelings.

Your Religion and Your Family You may think you arrived at your beliefs about God and life in the cool of adulthood, but family experience is an important factor in what you think and feel about religion. Bernard Spilka, a professor of psychology at the University of Denver, has conducted research on God-concepts among adolescents. He found that if the youngsters' perception of their parents was loving, they saw God as loving. If they saw their parents as controlling, they tended to see God negatively. He also found that the higher the youngsters' self-esteem, the more likely they were to have a loving-God image. Parents were the ones to seal this connection, both by praising and encouraging the child and by talking of a loving God.[4]

Children tend to base their God-concepts on their parents, especially their father. The father is usually the more distant one who comes in and makes somewhat arbitrary decisions. If you had a good relationship with your father, you are more likely to have a positive feeling about religion. If your father was emotionally unavailable or absent, you are more likely to feel that God is remote or nonexistent.[5]

How does *your* faith (or disbelief) grow out of your life experiences? Who molded you? Who turned you on, or off? Write your answers in your journal.

As we explained in Chapter 7, your spiritual concepts and needs evolve as you age. Think back over how your ideas changed as you progressed through Sunday school, college, and later important experiences of your life. How long has it been since your ideas about religion went through a major change? If you had negative or unfulfilling experiences of religion in your childhood, you may have frozen in your attitudes about religion.

When you went through the exercises in the first part of this chapter, you may have found that you are happy with your religious status quo. Or, you may have become painfully aware that you are unsatisfied spiritually. If you fall into this latter category, the next section of the chapter will be helpful. It contains concepts and experiments to help you define your particular spiritual needs. It will also be useful if you have no spiritual yearnings at present but your partner does. It can help you understand your partner's needs and find how those needs can be met without violating your values and sensibilities.

As an adult, you have the option of seeking your own spiritual path—to reset your course guided by your own needs and values, even if these diverge from the religious forms you were taught in childhood.

Four steps are helpful in this process. The first step is to forgive, to let go of long-held resentments. It's particularly important to let go of any anger you feel toward your own parents. (Harold H. Bloomfield's *Making Peace with Your Parents*[6] has a number of techniques to help you do this.)

Second, it's important to understand your own "spiritual mode." There are many ways of expressing spirituality. As you read the next section, consider which mode works best for you.

Third, you can embark on "spiritual experiments." Because spiritual needs often are murky and difficult to express, you may find it hard to understand your needs and feelings until you take some action. Experimenting with new approaches to God, prayer, and ritual can help you gain that understanding.

Fourth, you can find your own way of reconciling with your heritage, fusing parts of it to new things you have learned about your own spiritual nature and needs.

What is your spiritual mode? What makes you feel most spiritually centered, "in touch," or at peace?

People have five chief paths for connecting with their sense of the sacred:

1. *Sacred Spaces* The lofty arches of churches, the stained-glass windows, and choirs, are all designed to create a sacred space. But many of the intermarried couples we interviewed found their sacred space out-of-doors. One couple liked to spend Yom Kippur, the Jewish Day of Atonement, gazing quietly from a mountain overlook. One couple took their son to a "prayer rock" beside a stream. In the winter, they held a Hanukkah-Christmas ritual there, lighting candles on a snow-hung tree. If you find yourself drawn to nature, make such spirit-treks a regular part of your life. You can also set aside a special place in your home for meditation or family rituals.

2. *Sacred Times* Some people tune in best through sacred times: warm family celebrations at holiday seasons; quiet bedtime reflections with the children; morning meditation. Music can create sacred time. The Friday evening Sabbath dinner in a Jewish home is a good example of sacred time. The candles, white tablecloth, braided bread, and sparkling wine cups all help to make this a special moment of the week. As with sacred spaces, sacred times work best when they're part of a rhythm: when you have daily, weekly, and seasonal sacred times.

3. *Community* For some people, the spiritual tuning-in occurs through community. You may find yourself most "centered" or "connected" when singing in a choir, sharing food at a potluck dinner, calling up a sick friend, planning a political demonstration, or hearing voices all around you saying the words of a familiar prayer. If community comforts you, take a look at the various traditional and nontraditional community options described in Chapter 17 (Affiliation).

4. *Ritual* For some people, the spiritual tuning-in comes through ritual. The ritual may be as simple as the fifteen minutes or so of quiet that starts off every Quaker meeting, or as laden with complex symbolisms and pageantry as a Catholic Mass. For many people who feel spiritually blocked, ritual can open the door. If you want more spiritual connection, take one simple ritual, incorporate it into your life and see if, over a period of months, it changes your inner spiritual climate. It might be a short blessing before dinner every night. Or you could choose the Jewish Sabbath ritual: beginning with the blessing over candles, wine and bread every Friday night, and ending with Havdalah (blessing over candle, wine and spices) on Saturday night.

Live with this one added ritual for awhile and don't try to push forward on other spiritual fronts. See if the ritual helps to open you to other spiritual expressions.[7]

5. *Prayer* Prayer has two meanings in our culture. One is its association with organized religion and the prescribed prayers of religious services. The other is that gasp of pain and longing from the heart that represents our deepest wishes and needs. People frequently feel a conflict between these two aspects of prayer. As a result, people sometimes bury their early experiences with prayer in a rarely opened vault of memory. In our interviews, people often found themselves unexpectedly tearful when they tried to talk about their personal experiences with prayer.

We think prayer may be an instinctive human need that goes beyond belief. Even if you are a nonbeliever or uncertain what you believe, prayer may be the spiritual avenue that works best for you. In this case, prayer is not an expression of belief—it's a deliberate process of opening oneself up to new possibilities. You start by honestly admitting what you feel, fear, or want. You dare to ask for things no human can give you—like inner strength, inner peace.

Try doing this over a period of time—six months or a year. Then take a mental stethoscope and listen to your heart. Does prayer make you feel more centered, more "in touch"? If so, you can benefit by pursuing this spiritual mode.

In making these spiritual experiments, it helps to think of the God-concept as a tool. For a person who has no definite faith, the God-concept is not a description of some objectively known truth: It's a way of reaching out past the limits of human experience toward some kind of transcendence that we sense or hope may be there. No human has an experience of anything beyond three dimensions. Yet mathematicians can do calculations in four, five, or six dimensions. If you're going to do mathematics, you have to develop a skill of the imagination that permits you to work and think in a realm outside human experience.

If you think in terms of a God-concept, rather than of God, then you can make experiments with your God-concept. You can see what works to help open you to your sense of the sacred or transcendent. Thus, some feminists have found that they can connect to the transcendent more readily when they stop using male language for God, and instead think of God as a powerful and nurturing mother.

EXERCISE 4: EXPERIMENTING WITH YOUR GOD-CONCEPT

Try imagining what God would be like if you wrote the script. What kind of God would be acceptable to you? How would the world be different if the kind of God you imagine had created it and were running it? Tell God how you think the world should be and He/She should behave. Try imagining God in different ways and praying to those different mental images.

If you try these techniques—forgiveness, experimenting with spiritual avenues, experimenting with rituals and prayer and God-concepts—you will have a fund of new spiritual experiences with which to rethink your relationship to religion. It will be easier for you to form a spiritual outlook that genuinely reflects your current stage of life and your current thinking, rather than clinging to an idea you formed when you were younger and had different experiences and needs.

Talk with your partner about the spiritual modes that work best for each of you. See if there are activities that you can do together that meet spiritual inclinations of both.

We suggest two further steps. First, do some reading. Acquaint yourself with recent thinking in Judaism, Christianity, and other traditions. On the Jewish side, read works by Harold Kushner, Eugene Borowitz, Martin Buber, and Abraham Joshua Heschel. On the Christian side, try works by Paul Tillich, Henri Nouwen, and Hans Kung. On the Eastern or mystical traditions, check out Marilyn Ferguson's *The Aquarian Conspiracy*. On humanism, look at Paul Kurtz, *In Defense of Secular Humanism*.[8]

Second, visit secular and religious communities. See which most nearly speaks your language. Talk over with your partner what you are thinking and feeling as you explore.

Secular Humanism: The Other Way If you are a nonbeliever and your spouse is attracted to religion, we urge you to be neither defensive nor intolerant. To avoid defensiveness, learn to talk in terms of what you *do* believe, rather than what you *don't* believe. The credo of the nonbeliever, positively put, is secular humanism.

Humanism stresses ethical interactions between human beings, rationality, and such values as democracy, discussion, and negotiated solutions. Humanism has a distinguished past, with many heroes, from Plato to Thomas Jefferson to Adlai Stevenson.

There are two shortcomings to secular humanism as a family values base. One is that it can be isolating. Humanists are generally not joiners (although in Chapter 17 we list a few humanist organizations you can contact). The other is that secularism may itself become a rigid dogma. You may be perfectly happy to spend the rest of your life marching to the 4/4 drumbeat of objective rationalism. But your spouse or children may long for a more ethereal sound.

If you are a secularist and your partner is a believer or a seeker, don't look down your nose at her and assume that you have reached the intellectual high ground while your spouse remains on the benighted plain of superstition. Try to look at yourself over time. Rationalism may be your life-long credo. But it may also be simply a stage you are passing through. At some other time, you may develop a need to seek a spiritual dimension in your life. What you now espouse may be rationally defensible, but it is not Truth. "The surest way to lose truth," says theologian Gordon Allport, "is to pretend one already possesses it." [9]

Matters of faith and the spirit, of what you truly believe about life and death, are among the most intimate of topics. We spoke with a number of couples who were able to talk rather freely about sex and orgasms but who had never shared their spiritual lives. Talking about what you really believe, about your deepest hopes, fears, longings, and doubts, about your own special experiences of insight or faith or trust or despair, can help you and your partner grow in trust and can open doors for both of you.

10. HOW THE RELIGIONS SHAPED YOU:

One Couple, Two Languages

One of your most important tasks as an intermarried couple is to build a common spiritual foundation for your marriage and your family. You must become more conscious of the spiritual values you and your partner share. Yet you must do this in a way that respects differences. It is a delicate task and one that we saw many couples faltering over or avoiding. The ones who were successful stood out like beacons.

In the last chapter, we talked about your private and personal beliefs. But even if you became a nonbeliever, your view of the world was shaped by your religious background and training. Now it's time to see yourself and your partner against the backdrop of your different heritages. In this chapter, we'll take a look at the Jewish and Christian religious traditions and the conscious and unconscious ways they may have influenced you and your partner. We'll look at how you can bridge any gaps and at how you can draw from your religious traditions to enrich and strengthen your marriage. Throughout, we will consider the differing needs of believers, nonbelievers, and that middle group which has some religious loyalties or vaguely felt spiritual needs but no clear faith.

Just as your ethnic background shaped your personality, your religious background shaped the way you think. A tolerant understanding of your backgrounds can help you to accept and even enjoy your differences in viewpoint instead of lapsing into debate or recrimination. This knowledgeable respect is obviously essential if either of you is still involved in a religious tradition. But the religion you grew up with shaped your world view even if you no longer believe in its tenets. Rev. Timothy Lull, head of the theology department at the Lutheran Theological Seminary, observes, "There are different types of nonbelievers, depending what religion it is you don't believe in."

Religions are a way of making sense of the world. They are "reality maps." Each religion has a central story through which the world is explained. The holidays, rituals, morality, and philosophy of life all grow out of this story.[1]

Judaism and Christianity began with the same story. But at a certain point along the way, they branch apart from one another. As we describe those stories, think about how what you were taught shaped your values and your view of the world.

The story, for both Judaism and Christianity, begins in the Hebrew Bible. Both religions teach that God not only created the world, but made a decision to communicate His will to the world and to be a living presence in the world, to accompany human beings on their journey through time.

The Jewish World View Judaism's story begins with God's making a covenant, an agreement, with Abraham and his descendants. From its earliest days, Judaism was the story of a group of families—the families descended from Abraham—which grew into a people with a special relationship to God. According to the Jewish story, God made His presence known and understood in the world through miracles performed for this chosen people. The central event in Jewish history is the Exodus from the slavery of Egypt, which is celebrated every year in the Passover seder. For Jews, the liberation from Egypt represents the possibility of new beginnings—redemption—for both individuals and society as a whole. Whether they are religiously involved or secular socialists, nearly all Jews are inspired by the Exodus. Remembering their enslavement in Egypt, they identify with and empathize with the oppressed. Remembering the Exodus, they are convinced that humans ultimately can throw off tyranny and bring about a just world. (Traditionally, Jews believed that a Messiah, or liberator, would come to usher in the era of peace and justice, but the modern Reform and Reconstructionist wings of Judaism hold that the Messianic Age will come through humans striving to live ethically and to right the wrongs of society.)

After describing the liberation from Egypt, the Hebrew Bible goes on to trace the evolution of the Jewish people through two more key stages: God's giving of the law at Mount Sinai, and the establishment and later destruction of a Jewish kingdom in the land of Israel. These three ideas—liberation, law, and promised land—become the reigning ideas of Judaism. All of them are founded on the notion that redemption is a social phenomenon. Redemption would come when the whole society lived according to God's laws.

After the Jews were driven from the land of Israel, the Biblical commentators and rabbis focused much of their attention on elaborating the basic Bible commandments into detailed codes on how people are supposed to live. These laws covered not only ethics, but every concrete detail of home and communal life. The home and family in particular became the center of many rituals; Jews felt that God's presence could continually be reencountered in the mutual bonds of family love. During their years of exile in Europe, North Africa, and the other lands of the Middle East, Jews developed a tightly woven fabric of community. Within that community, there was a consensus that God's laws applied to every activity, and His presence could be felt in every activity: eating, dressing, speaking, doing business in an ethical manner. At the same time, even though they became an urbanized community, their seasonal holidays kept alive the keen sense of God's presence in nature that they had developed during their history as shepherds and farmers in Israel.

Thus, to understand a Jew's spiritual outlook is to understand a system in which God's presence is felt in this world through the bonds of family and community, the events of Jewish history, the beauties of nature, and the reverent living of daily life according to prescribed laws. Even when modern Jews don't follow these laws or don't define themselves as having a faith in God, they often have this faith in the goodness of human beings and the beauty of nature and of life itself. And they often feel rooted in the Jews' long history as a people.

From shortly after the destruction of the second temple in 70 c.e., Jews had no central hierarchy or authority. The details of Jewish law and Biblical interpretation were worked out in debates among scholars, sometimes meeting in academies or houses of study (which evolved into modern synagogues), and sometimes through written opinions and responses. Thus, an important part of the Jewish spiritual outlook came to be that no one had a monopoly on the truth. The best way to move toward truth was through human debate. Jews developed a deep respect for education and the use of human intelligence to solve problems.

The Christian World View The Christian story begins in the Jewish story, up through the establishment and destruction of the Jewish kingdom. But the final chapters went in such a different direction as to be a whole new story. In the Christian story, the key events were centered in one person: Jesus. Christians believe that God, seeing that humans were enmeshed in a destructive cycle of sin, chose to be incarnate in Jesus and through Him to redeem human beings. God chose to come to earth in human form to give a message of forgiveness and of faith. Although God had set up a moral law, He understood human frailty and would forgive humans for their violations. Since humans could never adequately atone for their many transgressions of God's law, Jesus freely offered up his suffering and death as a vicarious atonement. Through the Sacraments, Christians participate in that willing sacrifice and atonement. The Christian Bible, the New Testament, tells the story of Jesus' miraculous birth (during the waning days of the Jews' residence in the land of Israel), of His years of teaching and ministry, and above all of His death and resurrection.

Many of Jesus' teachings grow from the Hebrew Bible and prayers which He had studied as a child. But the Resurrection of Jesus takes the faith in a new direction. As the Exodus is central in meaning to the faith and world view of Jews, the Resurrection is central to the faith and world view of Christians. Jesus' resurrection and return to heaven was a sign of hope that all people could experience a similar renewal in their own lives. By believing in the power of Jesus' resurrection to redeem them, they could let the sinful and imperfect part of themselves die, and have the strength to begin again as pure and unspoiled spiritual newborns. But even more important, through faith in Jesus they could transcend death and attain eternal life. In Christianity, the idea of the Messiah was transformed. Although it was believed that some day He would still come back to usher in the Messianic era of peace and love on earth, equally important was the second level of redemption: eternal life—available now to all people of faith.

To understand the Christian faith, or world view, one must understand how powerfully the story of this one man, Jesus, influences everyone who grew up in a Christian culture. Even Christians who do not believe in the divinity of Jesus may measure themselves by the selflessness of His life. As Jews find common cause with the downtrodden because they were once slaves in Egypt, Christians are inspired to reach out to the needy because of Jesus' insistence on doing so. Seeing Jesus as intrinsically part of God gives Christians a very personal way of relating to God; believers can often experience a very intimate and personal trust. It gives them a concrete assurance of God's existence. God is a Person, accessible through prayer and faith.

To understand each faith, you must see it in the context of history. While Judaism was evolving after the exile from the land of Israel, Christianity, after the era in which Jesus and his disciples lived and preached, also went through its own long and complex evolution. The Jew Saul of Tarsus, who became a follower of Jesus and was called Paul, galvanized the fledgling community of believers to reach beyond its Jewish base and spread the new faith among the gentiles. Christianity grew into a world power, with its own internal government—the hierarchy of the Church.

As Christianity gained gentile adherents, it could no longer depend for its unity on the family and historical bonds which united Jews. The central bond among the disparate followers of Christianity was faith. Defining the creed—developing unity through a commonality of belief—became of central importance. Church leaders fought against what they saw as potentially divisive heresies. In Christian thought the issues of sin and the afterlife became of central importance. Since faith could help human beings to transcend sin, to be absolved at the time of judgment, to attain eternal life and salvation, and to be in the presence of God, it was crucial to understand what true faith was, and how human beings received it. Splits began to appear in the unified body of the church as people debated issues of faith. Today, although ecumenicists are working to overcome them, there are still great divergences in the Christian world, and many varieties of faith. In Catholicism and the "high-church" denominations of Protestantism, such as Lutherans and Episcopalians, there is a greater emphasis on ritual and hierarchy, and on the importance of the church community as the vehicle for salvation. The Church, in fact, is seen as the living body of Christ, continuing his work. The hierarchy, particularly in Catholicism, is seen as inheriting its authority from the apostles who founded the church and who were designated by Jesus to spread the faith. In "low-church" Protestant denominations, such as the Methodists and Baptists, there is a turning away from ritual and hierarchy and toward the Bible as a source of authority. There is a greater emphasis on the autonomy of individual churches, and the importance of individual conscience. Although the church community is an important aspect of every Christian denomination, and faith is important in every denomination, in the more fundamentalist Protestant churches there is often a greater emphasis on the redemptive importance of an individual and personal faith in Jesus.

Even a nonbelieving person from a Christian background may still look out at the world through the lens of such concepts as sin, salvation, faith, and revelation, or may still brood over the question of an afterlife.

But to understand the faith of a Christian partner, one must also know something about his or her denomination, which very much colors both faith and nonbelief. For example, an "ex-Catholic" may be angry at hierarchy and authority, while a "lapsed Methodist" may have left the church because she disagreed with some of the theology or never felt a fervent faith. A believer may identify with one particular part of the Christian world, sometimes to the exclusion of others.

In the last half of the twentieth century, many of the barriers between Christians and Jews have been falling, and they have been increasingly influenced by each other's thinking. The Second Vatican Council in the 1960s instructed Catholics that to truly understand the Christian faith, they needed to understand Judaism. Catholics and liberal Protestants have become very interested in learning about Jewish ideas of community. On the other side, many Jews, largely without realizing the source of their attitudes, have adopted Christian, especially Protestant, viewpoints such as that faith is a private matter. But, partly because the history of persecution and proselytization by Christians has made them wary, Jews in general have found it much harder to understand Christian ideas about authority and have been unwilling to explore such Christian concepts as salvation or the centrality of faith.

How much was your world view influenced by your heritage? Do you understand how your partner's views were shaped by her heritage? Talk to your partner about what elements of your heritages each of you would like to incorporate into your own household and your teaching of your children. At this point, do you see any important conflicts between what each of you wants to teach? Do you see points of agreement? Do you see ways in which your perspectives can complement or add to one another?

DRAWING TOGETHER

The task of finding a common religious ground is harder if one or both of you have a strong attachment to a particular faith. How can a Christian who truly believes that faith in Jesus is central to inner peace in this life and salvation in the next live and raise children with a Jew who finds his center of faith in a world that does not include Jesus? And how can a Jew, who does not believe in the divinity of Jesus and to whom Christian ideas of salvation and creed are foreign, respect a Christian who does hold these beliefs? Our prescription: *Value what your partner's beliefs do for him or her rather than attempting to judge their content.* Perhaps the simplest way to get the idea across is to contrast a couple who have not achieved this mutual respect with a couple who have.

Don and Peggy are trying to raise their children in both Christianity and Judaism. But although they love each other and share in many areas, each has contempt for the other's religion. Peggy, a devout Catholic, says she feels sorry for Don and all Jews. "I think they missed the boat" by rejecting Jesus, she says. Don thinks Catholics are rigid and unquestioning and that the Mass is like a "primitive tribal ritual."

Neither respects the other as a spiritual being. Neither understands the other's spiritual mode. Peggy's belief in Jesus gives meaning and hope and purpose to her life. Don, imprisoned by his anti-Catholic prejudices, can't respect the sustaining power of her faith and can't understand her need for the prayerful "holy space" created by a church.

Peggy thinks of Don as having no faith, and thus having nothing to give the children spiritually. Don has a deep faith in life itself, but Peggy can't understand that kind of faith. She doesn't see how Don's spirit is nurtured by being in contact with his people and with nature. She can't understand his need to be spiritually comforted by feeling rooted in that world.

Although their children are still young, we think eventually the youngsters will sense this mutual contempt and be torn by it.

Another couple we met, Blaine and Rena, have taken a different tack. Parents of a five-year-old daughter and two-year-old son, they are gentle academics who live in an urban neighborhood where the streets ring with accents from around the world. Rena's whole family was deeply involved in their Conservative Jewish synagogue during her growing-up years. Blaine, whose Air Force family moved many times during his childhood, found his roots, his "home," in the Episcopal church.

Blaine and Rena have not tried to convert each other; each maintains his or her own beliefs. But they participate in each other's faith communities, and each has found something valuable in the other's world. Rena and the children go to Blaine's Episcopal church. She is a member of several committees at the church and values the sense of community there. During church services, she joins in the parts of the prayers that she agrees with and skips those that jar with her Jewish beliefs. As Rena puts it, "I don't participate in the Christian parts of the service, just the God-worshipping parts, so to speak."

Blaine in turn goes with the children to Rena's synagogue and is active on a community-wide interfaith council.

When their first child was born, they wanted to have a naming at the synagogue and a baptism at the church. But when they talked to the rabbi, they learned that this dual identity would be unacceptable in the synagogue. They reconsidered and agreed that they would give the children a Jewish identity rather than telling them they were both. Says Blaine, "It's always been our position that you've got to be accountable to the congregation, the community, that you belong to. . . . It is particularly true in Judaism that somehow this identity has to be instilled strongly for a person to feel Jewish."

Instead of withdrawing resentfully from the synagogue, Blaine was able to understand the congregation's concern for the survival of the Jewish people. He agreed that the children, while being exposed to his church and understanding and appreciating it, would be told that they were Jews and would be given their religious training solely through a Jewish school.

Still, they never considered cutting back their involvement in the Christian church and holidays. Explains Rena, "We were so intent that the children, even if they were going to have one identity, have a thorough knowledge of the other religion."

Blaine and Rena understood that each of them derived strength and a sense of rootedness from their separate faiths. Rather than attempting to decide which beliefs were right and wrong, each focused on appreciating what the partner gained from his or her faith. As you'll see in Chapter 14 (Child Identity), there are strong arguments for not giving children totally "equal time" in two religions. Blaine and Rena's children are young, and it remains to be seen whether they will be confused by the dual exposure they are getting. But however they come out on religious identity, we are certain they will be spiritually enriched by their parents' model of loving respect and cooperation.

How can you attain respect for beliefs you don't share? By practicing the following three attitudes:

1. *The Integrity of a Point of View* First you must be willing to see your partner as a whole person. And you must be able to see your partner's religious background as an entity with its own integrity and validity. Look back at the first section of this chapter. See if you have a sense of the wholeness of the religion. Appreciate how this religious background helped make your partner the whole human being he or she is.

Courses of study in each religion are helpful because they provide a neutral ground for asking questions and probing areas you don't understand or find difficult to accept. You may find such courses useful for understanding each other even if you are nonbelievers who don't intend to practice either faith.

2. *Dialogue: Learning to Listen, Learning to Speak* The National Conference of Christians and Jews has issued a booklet on how to conduct a dialogue. Authors Dean M. Kelley and Bernhard E. Olson define dialogue as "a frank and free discussion of what we genuinely believe in an atmosphere of mutual respect and trust . . . Dialogue is not just speaking to the other . . . it is listening and being listened to."[2]

In a dialogue, neither side is trying to convert or convince the other, to accuse or defend. At the same time, Olson and Kelley stress, dialogue means listening with a genuinely open mind—"a willingness to entertain the possibility that *change will take place in us* as well as in other persons."

If you and your partner have found it hard to talk about religion, joining an interfaith dialogue group can be helpful. This takes your discussion out of the narrow and potentially explosive arena of your personal relationship.[3]

3. Willingness to Learn The third key attitude is a willingness to be enriched by your partner's perspective. A tribalistic Jew, for example, can learn from the universalism of his Christian partner. A hair-splitting Christian can learn from the Jewish tolerance for differences in outlook.

A Jew can learn from his Christian partner to trust, and to humanize what may become an abstract concept of God. A Christian may learn from the Jew to be in partnership with God, to challenge God, to acknowledge the limits of his or her understanding of God's purposes for human beings. A Christian can learn from the Jew's toleration of ambiguity, a Jew from the Christian's willingness to probe questions of faith and afterlife.

The Christian can learn from the Jew about infusing the home with reverence, and making religion concrete and immediate through home rituals. The Jew can learn from the Christian about creating an atmosphere of awe and beauty in communal worship.

Even if you are a religious skeptic, you can be enriched by your partner's viewpoint. You and your partner may both be committed to charity or social action, but have different perspectives on it. The Christian can learn from the Jew about treating charity matter-of-factly, not as benevolence but as basic matters of justice and decency incumbent on everyone. The Jew can learn from the Christian about extending oneself personally to others in one's charitable or political work.

Talk with your partner about what you have already learned from her. Take a fresh look at your areas of disagreement or misunderstanding; can you turn them into opportunities for learning?

Finding Your Shared Beliefs But this appreciative and informed tolerance is only the first building block of your common spiritual foundation. You must go on from there to create a shared set of beliefs that can be an anchor for your family.

In talking about your beliefs and in studying together, you will discover that Jews and Christians share many elements of faith. Both hold that there is a basic and desirable human morality which is in some way inherent in the world—it is not foreign to human beings, but is to be expected of us. Both have a concept that we sometimes fall short of this morality, and that we can't remain forever burdened by guilt but have to pick ourselves up and move on. Both have a notion of redemption, that we can overcome human failings and realize our full potential of creativity and goodness. Although there are real and important differences in how Jews and Christians understand and use these ideas, one can focus instead on the common elements of faith.

By talking in a patient, trusting, and exploratory way about mutual beliefs, you can work toward shared understandings that will strengthen your marriage and give you a common area for teaching your children. Even if you are both nonbelievers, for example, you share the ethical heritage of the Ten Commandments and the Golden Rule. Talk with your partner about how to make those shared beliefs come alive for your children. What can you do as a family to act on your beliefs?

RECONCILING YOUR DIFFERENCES

We've talked about the positive ways to build on your religious heritages. Now let's talk about some of the negative ways religion can affect a marriage, and how you can deal with them. The couples we interviewed generally faced one of four obstacles: prejudice, ignorance, strong commitments to separate religious expressions, and differences in spiritual intensity. Here are strategies to help you cope with these obstacles.

Confront Prejudice in Yourself and Your Partner Put yourself in your spouse's shoes and hear your remarks with his ears. Hear your own hostility, your judgments, your disrespect. Or, if your partner talks in a prejudiced manner and can't hear what he's saying, tell him how it makes you feel.

Discard the Idea of a Single Truth Realize that what seems sensible to you and what seems patently false has nothing to do with objective fact; it has to do with how you were brought up. Instead, think of theologies as spiritual tools, prods to the imagination. If one religion's story inspires or nourishes your partner, be glad he has a tool that works for him. See it as part of the strength of the person you love.

Don't Ask Your Partner to Squelch His Spiritual Needs A devout partner, in particular, must be permitted to practice his faith. One of the saddest couples we talked to was David and Carmen. She was from a pious immigrant Catholic family that had stretched its finances to educate the children in Catholic schools. He had been raised in a lukewarm Reform Jewish family, but had rediscovered Judaism on his own through a program of reading and was entranced with it. They each felt so sure of their religious commitments that they never worried about dating this interesting outsider. Marriage seemed an impossibility.

But in the spring of their final year of college, when they had to face the prospect of parting, they got down to serious negotiation. David offered a take-it-or-leave-it proposition: He wanted to marry Carmen, but could do so only if the children were raised exclusively as Jews. Carmen, acquiescent by nature and training, struggled inwardly but eventually agreed. They married and now have a young daughter.

Although they love each other dearly, Carmen is in constant spiritual pain. As part of her commitment, she has stopped going to Mass. She has even stopped praying to Jesus and has tried to redirect her prayers only to God. It hasn't worked. Jesus is still vividly alive in her mind, but He's on the far side of a barrier that she feels she can no longer cross. She feels lost, bereft of a major support in her life.

Clearly State Your Own Needs It's quite common in intermarriages for the partner who is more domineering to call the shots religiously. We don't think that's healthy. But neither do we think it's entirely the fault of the dominant partner. As in many families, Carmen failed to state clearly the depth of her spiritual needs to David. She played the submissive role she had learned in both her Catholic and her immigrant subcultures. Only when both partners can clearly state their bottom-line needs and when both are committed to finding a solution that is mutually satisfactory can tragedies like Carmen's be avoided.

Develop Compromises Vicki and Burt found an innovative way to meet their different needs. Vicki, a community organizer, is the daughter of a Protestant minister. She is married to Burt, a Jewish labor organizer who is a militant atheist. Vicki missed the sense of community she had in her father's church. But Burt was allergic to all religious institutions. Finally, at Vicki's suggestion, they organized an "un-church." It was a social club made up of their liberal, politically active friends. They held weekly potluck dinners, art classes, and community-service projects. The group met Vicki's need for a caring community without violating Burt's scruples against organized religion. In fact, it expanded his sense of possibilities by adding a personal and communal dimension to their political work.

Barbara, a social worker, and Kurt, a physicist, worked out a more conventional but equally useful set of compromises. Barbara and Kurt have a great deal in common. Both are atheists. Both have their roots in the liberal intellectual culture of Europe. Both were victims of the Nazis: he a Catholic war orphan and she the child of Holocaust survivors. But they have reacted to the Nazi horror in diametrically opposed ways. He is skeptical of all self-defined groups and all orthodoxies. He calls himself "a member of the human species within the animal kingdom." She is passionately committed to Jewish survival.

When they decided to marry, Barbara drew up a "shopping list" of all the areas of religious life they would have to deal with, and they hammered out agreements on each. It took them a year to go through this process. Barbara's bottom line was a Jewish identity for the children. She would have preferred to send them to a Jewish day school; Kurt would have preferred no religion in the home. Their compromise: the children would go to public school, supplemented by Hebrew school and Jewish camps. But the children would also be taught to question and encouraged to see things from many points of view. They would celebrate Jewish holidays in the home, but only Barbara would say the blessings and perform the rituals. Kurt would be present, drinking the wine but voicing no prayers. The Jewish holidays and cultural events would be balanced by "Kurt days," on which the calendar is open and Kurt is free to do as he likes.

Another way of compromising is to find a mutually acceptable community. Look in Chapter 17 (Affiliation), where you will find a range of choices that may be comfortable to both of you.

Look for a Common Path Sometimes the issue is not different needs. Both partners may have similar needs, but they may not be certain about what they want to do. These spiritual seekers need to talk and share and help each other. Ideally you will find an approach that is satisfying and enriching to both. The delicate task here is pacing. If you're becoming involved in a religion which is new to one of you, keep asking each other as you take on new levels of commitment: Are you ready for this? What do we need to do to make this comfortable for you?

Doug and Leslie are exploring together, in a slow and steady manner, and finding it a mutually enriching process. He is a social worker who was raised in a mildly Reform Jewish family. She is a lawyer who was raised Unitarian. They both want to be more religiously involved than their parents were. Having a child propelled them forward. They are creating a Jewish home.

During her pregnancy, Leslie bought a primer on Jewish family celebrations that allowed her to take her first religious steps at home, "without it having to be a public thing or having to find a congregation to join."

They have evolved gently as a Jewish family, with Leslie bringing an adult curiosity to the process. She took pleasure in learning the prayers and Hebrew folksongs and in picking out Hebrew letters. They experimented with some customs and tried building a sukkah. They lit candles, said the Friday night kiddush over wine, took it easy on Saturday. These are things that Doug finds "perfectly comfortable and familiar."

"Somebody who was real religiously Jewish might have been a difficult person for you," Leslie says to Doug. "You were exploring. You were ahead of me on the alphabet and lots of identity kinds of things, since you're Jewish and I'm not. But you never built a sukkah before, either. So there's some ability to learn together."

In addition to their home experiments, they pushed out into the community and found a beginner's *havurah* (fellowship for study and worship) at the local Reconstructionist congregation. Leslie says the fellowship is comforting and not intimidating. They also have affiliated with the synagogue and go to High Holiday services there. The services were liberal enough in format that Leslie was able to relate to them from her own experiences, as when the reading of a poem brought back memories of a beloved grandmother. She thinks group services help her to reach beyond the "controlled, intellectual sides of our lives" toward a more spiritual dimension.

Doug takes it slow and easy. "I'm a pretty cautious, compromising kind of person. I'm not one to pursue things in a radical, throwing myself to the wind kind of way. So what I do can't be grossly inconsistent with the rest of my life.

"Pursuing something spiritual is a goal . . . It's probably not going to be a deeply profound religious experience or spiritual experience because I don't think we can tolerate that. It's pursuing something in that direction."

Says Leslie: "What I've given up is trivial, the Christmas tree. What I've gained is—who knows if I'll reach a spiritual level beyond what I see now—but what I've seen along the way already has a lot of its own rewards. This is richer than a life lived without it."

Treating Your Marriage with Reverence We've talked about finding common ground in your religious heritages. We've talked about the techniques for coming to mutually respectful compromises. But there is a third task that confronts you as an interfaith couple. That is to build a sense of the sacredness of your marriage—a glowing core of commitment to each other. Regardless of what you and your partner believe about God and religion, your marriage will be deeper and stronger if you see your life together as a holy task and each other as sacred individuals, consecrated to each other. By searching your personal beliefs and your religious traditions, you can find fuel to help you keep alive the reverence you felt on your wedding day.[4]

Both Judaism and Christianity believe humans were created in the image of God. Promise each other that you will keep that notion uppermost in your mind—that you will look for and find the image of God in each other. If you don't believe in God, look for the essence of goodness and beauty in your mate.

If you take on the challenge—to probe your own beliefs, to truly understand your partner's, and to find a set of beliefs and values that you genuinely share, you will reach a level of intimacy that many couples, intermarried or not, never achieve.

11. CONVERSION:

Heart and Soul

During the course of your engagement or marriage, someone is likely to ask if either of you is willing to convert to the other's religion. This is especially likely if one spouse or one family is very involved in a religious tradition. But it also can happen even when they seem to be attached by only the slenderest thread.

This chapter is designed to help you think through your response. You must first decide what is right for you. Then you must figure out how to deal with family and community reactions.

Later sections of the chapter will deal with the actual conversion process and with how to adjust to your new lifestyle if you do decide to convert.

What Conversion Means To make an informed decision about converting, you need to know what conversion means. It means very different things in Judaism and Christianity. In Christianity, you convert to a faith; in Judaism, to a people and way of life.

The central ritual of conversion in Christianity is baptism—immersion or sprinkling with water. This outward ritual is a symbol of a powerful inner transformation—an acceptance into your being of the idea that Jesus is your Redeemer. Christians believe that God, in His grace, chooses to enter your heart through the Holy Spirit, and to give you this faith. Although the nuances of belief vary among denominations, Christians believe baptism, through this inner acceptance or faith, cleanses the individual of sin and gives him a new life—one which will not be ended by death but will continue into eternity.[1]

Conversion in Judaism means entering into the covenant between God and the Jewish people. According to the Hebrew Bible, God made a covenant with Abraham, father of the Jewish people, promising to make Abraham's descendants into a great nation. As a sign of this covenant, Abraham circumcised himself and all the men and boys of his household.

According to traditional Jewish law, the gentile man who wishes to enter the covenant must go through a three-stage process, the woman a two-stage process. The three steps are *milah* (circumcision or cutting off the foreskin of the penis—a step which obviously applies only to men); *kabbalat mitzvot* (acceptance of the commandments, which is done before a *bet din*, a three-person rabbinical panel or court); and *tevilah* (immersion in the *mikvah*, a special pool of water). (If the man has already been circumcised a symbolic drop of blood is taken from the area where the foreskin had been.) These acts symbolize the convert's willingness to be committed to the Jewish people—to become part of the worldwide Jewish family and to adopt its way of life.

The rabbinical court questions the convert not on matters of belief but on his or her ability to make this commitment. But as you'll see later in this chapter, the various branches of Judaism differ greatly in what they mean by the commitment to live a Jewish life, and even in whether they require the convert to go through these three traditional rituals.

Between 33 and 40 percent of Jewish-Christian intermarriages involve a religious conversion. In the vast majority of these cases, the gentile converts to Judaism. An estimated ten thousand people convert to Judaism annually, mostly women engaged or married to Jewish men.[2]

THINKING ABOUT CONVERSION

The first thing to understand, before we go into further details, is that conversion has to be right for you. It has to come from your heart or you shouldn't do it. If you allow yourself to be pressured into a conversion that you're not ready for, the conversion probably won't "take"— you may never feel that you are part of the new religious group. And you, your spouse, children, parents, or in-laws may end up being hurt.

Does Converting for the Sake of Marriage Make Sense? Traditional Judaism frowned on the idea of converting in the context of marriage.

Conversion was supposed to be a matter of personal conviction, independent of practical pressures or advantages. In practice, however, the Jewish movements have adjusted to the reality that most gentiles, even if they've been interested in Jewish people and ideas for some time, don't actively consider conversion until they're romantically involved with a Jew.

Christianity has always welcomed converts and even urged conversion, and has assumed religious conviction on their part even if the conversion came in the context of marriage. But more recently, many liberal priests and ministers have begun to help the prospective convert sort through the emotions and pressures and to think of alternatives if there is not a heartfelt faith.

Although you should convert only if it "feels right" to you spiritually, there are definite benefits to converting in the context of marriage. The family you create will be more unified in status and life-style. If you want to raise your children in one religion, conversion helps both of you to be respected and fully involved religious role models. As we point out in Chapter 14 (Children's Identity), conversionary families have a better chance of imparting a sense of religious group belonging to their children than do mixed families.

The act of converting can also jog you and your spouse into having a spiritual life, a need that might stay unmet otherwise. Converting, as a deliberate act taken in adulthood, can be enriching on spiritual, intellectual, and behavioral planes.

Understand the Pressures Before you try to figure out your own wants and needs, it helps to understand and defuse the pressures on you. You need to understand why many people in all sincerity will urge you to convert.

Both the Jewish and Christian communities have strong agendas for wanting a person who is intermarrying to convert to their religion. Jews are concerned about the survival of the Jewish people and the Jewish way of life. The mother's conversion to Judaism before the birth of any children can assure that the children will be recognized as Jewish. Believing Christians, for their part, are concerned about the propagation of the faith. The more fundamental or traditionalist branches believe that the spreading of Christianity is necessary both for the saving of individual souls and for the redemption of the world. Even in the more liberal branches of Judaism and Christianity, clergy and community members are likely to feel that the family will be healthier and more religiously committed if both partners are members of the same faith.

Although you may find it hard to deal with conversion pressures from your partner's religious community, the more agonizing pushes and pulls can come from your two families.

Frequently, family pressure for conversion comes not from religious conviction but from an unhealthy need to keep the family tightly bound and unchanging, notes rabbi/family therapist Edwin Friedman.[3] The parents in those cases don't want the son or daughter to escape. Subconsciously, they feel that if the son- or daughter-in-law converts, the new member can be absorbed into their family system. If you feel such pressures, here's an exercise to help you sort out and cope with them.

EXERCISE 1: DEALING WITH CONVERSION PRESSURES

1. Write, or talk aloud, about the pressures your partner is placing on you and the pressures you think he is feeling from his family, his community, and his religious training. Be as specific as you can. Describe exactly what he or his family are doing or saying and how it makes you feel. Then describe the causes as you understand them. Discuss the social factors: What positive or negative experiences did your partner or his family have with people of your background? What were they taught about your people? What positive or negative experiences did they have with their own group?

2. Now think about internal family factors: Who holds the power in your partner's family? How is that power exercised? What happens to family members who challenge that power? How does that powerful person see you? Who is the family member your partner loves most? How does that person see you? How is your partner seen by the other members of the family? Does marrying you change his position or usual role in the family?

3. Next, write about any pressures you are feeling from your family, the community you grew up in, and your training. What social and family factors are behind these pressures? What were you taught, and what were your parents taught, about your partner's group? How does the powerful figure in your family (or the one you love the most) see your partner or his group?

4. Take several sheets of paper. On each one, draw a stick figure to represent one of those pressures. One might represent a grandparent, another a priest. You can also use stick figures or other symbols to represent abstractions, like the Holocaust, or summer camp. (If you feel comfortable doing so, you can use a blank paper or a special symbol to represent Jesus or God or the covenant.) Label each figure. Hold an

imaginary conversation with each one. First summarize, as well as you can, that figure's point of view. ("I know that you think or feel . . .") Then say to it that although you understand its point of view, you have to do what is right for you. Tell the figure how you suspect it sees you. Tell it how you *really* are. Tell it about the pressures it is placing on your spouse or on you and how you wish it would behave instead. Let the figure answer. Keep talking until you come to some agreement or reach impasse. Tell the figure again that although you understand its point of view, you have to do what is right for you.

5. Then decide what you want to do with the piece of paper on which the figure is drawn. Do you want to crumple it, rip it up, write a message across it, fold it carefully and put it in a pocket next to your heart, kiss it and explain what you are going to do, or put it away until you have cooled off and try again to talk to it? You may simply want to put it into your looseleaf notebook until you have done more reading and thinking.

Do Some Learning You can't make a meaningful decision about whether to convert unless you know something about the tradition you would convert to. But equally important, you must have a fair, realistic and up-to-date picture of the tradition you would be leaving and what it has to offer.

Insist that both you and your partner take courses in the two religions. Unless you are actively interested in converting, it is probably best at this stage not to take the standard course for converts in either religion. Try instead to find a course on the religion given by a college or adult education program that is directed at the general public.

Go regularly to a synagogue or church in the denomination you are thinking of joining. In addition, ask the rabbi or minister to connect you with an adoptive family or older mentor. Share holidays with them and ask them to show you the practical points of religious observance and the cultural ways of the religion. Practice in your own home what they are teaching you.

Set aside a regular time to talk about what each of you is learning. Ask each other: Has anything changed your preconceptions? What has been interesting? Exciting? Distressing?

During the course of study, don't forget to look back as well as forward. Go several times to a church and synagogue of the type you grew up in. Did you find yourself reexperiencing any old feelings of affection and nostalgia or anger or fear? If either of you has difficulty with an idea or practice of either religion, talk about it. Perhaps even the partner who is attached to the religion has trouble with this idea. How does he rationalize it or live with it?

If you decide to convert, it should be as a logical outgrowth of your personal spiritual journey. To help you assess whether conversion is a step you have already been headed toward, try the following exercises.

EXERCISE 2: YOUR SPIRITUAL AUTOBIOGRAPHY

In Chapter 9, we took you on a process of exploring your religious past and development. Let's continue that process here. Describe your memories, feelings and beliefs about God and religion, from your earliest days to the present. What do you remember about holidays, family rituals, religious school? What did you believe? What did you doubt? How did that feel? Did you pray? Have religious experiences? When you get to the present day, be sure to talk about how your partner has influenced you. Has he challenged your beliefs and left you feeling more confused? Has he opened new vistas?

EXERCISE 3: TRACING YOUR SPIRITUAL JOURNEY

Take a piece of paper and draw a long line on it. At one end, put a dot and label it with the age you were at your earliest memory. At the other end, place a dot labeled with your present age. Along the line, put dots to represent different events and realizations in your spiritual autobiography and the ages at which they occurred. Label these points along the line. Do you feel as if your line, your spiritual journey, is moving toward something? Continue the line a decade or two into the future. What do you hope will be happening along that line?

Understand the Magnitude and Limits of the Change A religious conversion is a major identity change. It's almost as basic a change in your sense of yourself as a sex-change operation. It requires a new sense of what you are, what category you're in, whom you are related to. This is particularly true in conversion to Judaism, because with your conversion, you acquire a history. If your conversion "takes," when people talk about the victims of the Holocaust, you'll come to feel, "they're talking about us." When you hear an anti-Semitic remark, you'll feel not only outraged on behalf of people you care about, but that you must rise in your *own* defense.

Lydia Kukoff, director of the Commission on Reform Jewish Outreach in Los Angeles and herself a convert to Judaism, told us, "I think there's a kind of pioneering instinct [among converts]. You are going to a new country, a new land . . . It takes a certain kind of personality to carry that off. I would say in my anecdotal, nonscientific way that people who do it are people who are able to make enormous change and to emerge enriched from the process."

This change in your sense of yourself is so thorough-going that it can only take place over time. Rabbi Zalman Schachter-Shalomi, a "New Age" rabbi who has served as spiritual adviser to many converts and returnees to Judaism, says that ideally, a prospective convert to Judaism should go through a "novitiate." Like a person becoming a nun or priest, she would have a lengthy period, perhaps as long as seven years, to "try on" the new way of life, live with it, grow into it, and see if it feels like the direction in which she was meant to grow. Although there is no official novitiate for converts, you have the option of doing it this way. You can live the way of life, gradually coming to the point where you feel ready to formalize your commitment.

But in addition to realizing the magnitude of the change, you must recognize its limits. You can put on new clothes but you can't grow a new skin. In many basic ways, you will always remain the person you have been, deeply shaped by your family, your ethnic background, and your religious training.

Rabbi Schachter-Shalomi says he wishes there were a "charm school" for converts to Judaism that would alert them to the ways of speaking, laughing, arguing, eating, the in-jokes, the family quarrels, that are part of Jewish identity for born-Jews. Certainly to be comfortable in an ethnically Jewish world you will have to understand some of these folkways. But it's not realistic to expect that they will become part of you. You have your own folkways. Although you may feel fully committed to the Jewish people, Jewish ideas and commandments, if you came from a Christian background, your Judaism will be colored by the Christian expectation of what religion is. You will have to learn to accept yourself as a Jew, and accept your own way of being Jewish as legitimate, even if different from the ethnic Jews in your partner's family or community. Keep in mind that there are many assimilated German-American Jews who are no closer to the East European ways than you are. In any case, by the time your children grow up, ethnic differences will be far less important.

For Jews who convert to Christianity, the biggest problem is external, rather than internal: dealing with the sometimes intense anger of the Jewish family and community. A few of those who convert may feel severe inner conflict or guilt, but most had never felt much identification with Judaism.[4]

Understand the Conversion Process The emotional, psychological, and spiritual process of converting to Judaism is very different from that in Christianity.[5] In most conversions to Christianity there's an epiphany, a moment of illumination or acceptance. It may be a leap of faith or a gradual deepening of conviction, but there's a point when the convert says, "I do believe this." As Adam, a Jew who converted to Roman Catholicism, told us, "It's a sense that I know Jesus is there with me, that I can surrender myself . . . I believe I will be taken care of." Though Adam is an urbane businessman with an Ivy League education, his faith, he says, is "the faith of a peasant." It's the simple sureness that appeals to him.

People who grew up as Christians and decide to convert to Judaism often expect a similar moment of conviction or faith. It won't come. Judaism is not a faith or belief in the same sense as Christianity. It's an identity, and it grows gently throughout life, as all aspects of your identity do. Becoming a Jew is somewhat like moving to a new city. If you are a Midwesterner who moves to New York, you only gradually come to think of yourself as a New Yorker. At some point, you realize that you feel more like a New Yorker than a Midwesterner. But there's no epiphany, just a gradual accumulation of experiences and points of view.

If you decide to convert to Judaism, you can make your declaration at any point along your identity development. You can decide to take the plunge at the beginning and let the identity grow. Or you can decide to live the way of life for awhile, until you say to yourself, "I don't feel fully Jewish yet but I feel a whole lot closer to being Jewish than to being Christian. I'm going to commit myself to this direction."

Cindy, who converted to Judaism when she was pregnant with her second child, is typical of the lifelong unfolding that characterizes many people who eventually decide to become Jews.

She is a pert woman whose gentle drawl belies her outspoken and gutsy temperament. Cindy was raised in Southern suburbia, and from an early age found herself quietly disagreeing with the tenets of her parents' conservative Protestant church. "During my confirmation, I said, 'I don't believe this stuff.' There were ideas there that did not make sense:

'You can do the right thing, but if your motive is wrong, you've committed a sin.' "

By the time she went to college, she thought of herself as an agnostic. She was attracted to the intellectual, colorfully ethnic Jews she met. She and her Jewish husband were married by a Unitarian minister. In the early years of her marriage, she was busily involved in liberal social action and intellectual pursuits, living among Jews but not with Judaism. When her son was born, she decided to give him a *bris* (ritual circumcision). Her husband, Bruce, couldn't have cared less. Cindy began to feel a vague need for a religious affiliation. Over the years, she found herself talking to and arguing with God. She wanted a relationship with the transcendent, but not a submissive one. Cindy explored Unitarianism and the Society of Friends but took no action. Her husband remained aloof from all religion. One day, when Cindy was pregnant with their second child, their son, who by this time was five, came home from school talking about Jesus being God. "Something inside me just went, 'Oh, no!' " said Cindy. She decided to make a decision about religious affiliation.

Shortly afterward, problems emerged in the pregnancy and she was confined to bed. She found herself reading eagerly about Israel, Jews, and Judaism. She felt a surge of excitement—a reawakening of a dormant need, a sense of spiritual direction.

Cindy found Judaism speaking directly to her. "A lot of the things about it I believed: the idea of taking time out to rest, of not having original sin, that man was basically good but could be perfected, that we were expected to right wrongs but not to beat ourselves over the head about it all the time. It seemed to be a good prescription for mental health."

Flat on her back, she rolled the ideas around in her head and decided a Jewish life would benefit her children and enrich her as well. Judaism was a system that would affirm open-ended dialogue, that nurtured what she calls "a partnership with God." She felt herself going through an emotional passage with the force and certainty of a swift labor. "I decided I would convert during my pregnancy. There was no reason not to, because I really had a strong feeling for it."

She never considered holding back, of not converting but merely cooperating as a non-practicing gentile. She had fallen in love with Judaism. Also, on a practical level, she realized that her converting was necessary to build Jewish momentum in their home. "To just affiliate, with Bruce not being at all involved in Judaism, would have made no sense for our family. We would have just been on the border. If he had been a strong Jewish influence it would have been one thing. One of us had to take the lead."

Cindy is typical of many converts to Judaism in the mixture of personal meanings, intellectual excitement, and family considerations that drew her to the religion. Rather than coming to accept a belief, she found a world view, a way of life, that she felt could affirm and strengthen the path she had already chosen, the person she had already become.

Understand Your Own Motivations If you are drawn toward the idea of conversion, it's important to recognize your motivations. There are both positive and negative reasons for wanting to convert. Some motivations provide a strong base for your new religious identity; some provide a much weaker foundation. Look into yourself for any of the following negative motivations: unresolved anger at your own family or heritage; too much eagerness to please; a desire to submerge into the new family; or a desperate acquiescence in order to put an end to the pressure from your fiancé or his family.

The desire to please is a matter of degree. Of course you want to please your spouse or fiancé and to be accepted by his family. But this alone is not a valid motivation. Conversion demands so much change of you that unless it has intrinsic satisfactions, it can throw off your inner balance. It can make you feel your life-style is out of synch with the real inner you.

Unresolved anger is also a matter of degree. Every convert, by definition, has found her religion of birth unsatisfying. But if the dissatisfaction has become disgust or rage, a conversion is primarily a "statement" made in reaction to the past rather than a considered step made as part of adult development.

We recall one convert to Judaism who had been furious at the Catholic church of her childhood. But when her marriage fell apart, she found herself equally furious at Jews and Judaism and the pressure her ex-spouse's Jewish family had placed on her to convert. She explored other Christian churches and finally realized that, with all its problems, the Catholic church had shaped her and she belonged there. After struggling through her angers at the Church, she was able to find a place where she could comfortably participate as her own kind of Catholic.

Use the exercises in Chapter 9 (Your Spiritual Needs) to probe your feelings about religion. By defusing anger at the family, religion, and community of your childhood, you will be better able to decide if you belong in the new religion, the old one, or neither.

The "motivation to merge" is seductive and difficult to acknowledge. For people who have gone through a period of religious experimentation or personal tumult, immersion in a Christian faith community or a Jewish way of life can offer a welcome structure and stability. Jewish families often have a closeness that may be very attractive to a gentile who grew up in a more restrained family. On the other side, a Christian faith community may have a sense of coherence and a spiritual intensity that a Jew may find lacking in the Jewish world.

But you are crossing into risky territory if you feel that conversion will help you immerse in the marriage, the new family, or the new religious community.[6] There may come a point when you "wake up" and suddenly need to recapture that submerged self. Conversion should feel like a chance to become more fully your real self, not like a chance to transform or to leave your old self behind.

Finally, there is conversion as a way to get out from under family pressures. If you are thinking of converting because of persistent messages that that is the only way you'll ever really be part of your spouse's family, you are probably resentful. You know it's not fair to you. It's also not fair to the new religion or to your children. You are approaching the religion under a cloud and may not be able to consider it on its merits. You also are likely to give a child a mixed message and leave him ambivalent about his own identity.[7]

Stay in Touch with Your Partner Your decision on conversion has a major impact on your family's future life. It's vital that you know how your partner feels about the religion and that he know how you feel about it. He may, for example, press for a *pro forma* conversion but be dismayed to discover that you really *mean* it—you want to live the new religion you have chosen. Talk specifically about the kind of home life and community involvement you would want if you convert.

Get Counseling Talk through not only the spiritual issues, but the family issues. Be sure you understand your own motives and ambivalences. Then go with your partner. Let the counselor help you to open up issues that have not been explored. In particular, it's important to probe whether your partner either has pressured you to convert or is opposed to your conversion.

Because the spiritual and emotional issues are so intertwined in conversion, it can be helpful to talk to a pastoral counselor. Seek one who is not a member of either the religion you are leaving or the one you're joining (e.g. find a Protestant if you're a Jew converting to Catholicism). One woman, brought up Catholic, had been raising her children as Jews for several years, was active in the Reform synagogue, and taught in the Sunday school. When the rabbi asked if she was ready to convert, she was thrown into confusion. Feeling that a priest and a rabbi would have their own agendas, she consulted a Protestant minister. The minister asked her if she still believed in Jesus (she didn't) and if she enjoyed and was comfortable with her Jewish life-style and the ideas behind it (she was). "You already are Jewish," said the minister. "Why not reap the benefits? You're doing all the work. Why not get the credit?" The woman felt a rush of relief, as if she had been given permission, by this Christian minister, to leave Christianity—a move that psychologically and spiritually she had made years before.

Some counselors have a bias that conversion is psychologically impossible. Be sure you know where they stand before you enter into a counseling relationship.

Approach the Religion Realistically When people are considering a religious conversion, they often, like Cindy, go through an initial stage of "falling in love" or infatuation. That's healthy. A religious conversion, like a marriage, is a major life commitment and ought to be accompanied by a certain joy and passion. Just as falling in love helps you feel complete in certain new ways, the new religion should help you feel complete in certain ways.

But it's important to go into a marriage with a clear understanding of your partner's flaws as well as his virtues. In the same way, it's important to get a rounded picture of the new religion and religious community before you convert. Talk with members of the religion about what they see as its "downsides' as well as the "upsides." Consider the negative reactions you're likely to encounter, and decide if you're willing and able to accept them as part of the total package.

Also, talk with converts about their experiences. Try to find a convert who has your religious background.

Find a neutral but sympathetic observer and voice your doubts out loud. Talk them through to help decide if this is where you really belong.

IF YOU DECIDE NOT TO CONVERT

Should you decide against converting, you need an alternative position. That will make it easier for you to deal with pressures from your partner, his family, and his community. Keep these points in mind:

In ancient Israel, a non-Jew could have two different levels of relationship to the Jewish community. He could convert outright, and was then considered fully Jewish in every respect—a *ger tzedek*, a righteous convert. Or he could simply live as part of the community, participating in its celebrations and respecting its laws, but not converting. In that case, he was called a *ger toshav*, the stranger or outsider who lives among you. Both types of people were to be treated with respect and to receive the protection of the community's laws.[8]

If you do not have the personal conviction to convert to Judaism but are sympathetic to your partner's desire to raise the children as Jews, you can choose to be a supportive and respectful *ger toshav*. Similarly, if you are Jewish but have agreed to raise your children as Christians, you can take a supportive and respectful role without converting.

Your children can be converted at birth so their religious status won't depend on your conversion.[9]

If you are drawn toward conversion but don't feel ready yet, you could think of yourself as going through a novitiate, a period of trying out the new religion. Do not put a time limit or deadline on your novitiate. Take as long as you need.

Finally, you may not wish to participate in your partner's religion at all. You may want to have no religion or to practice some other religion.

Once you have decided on what relationship you want toward your partner's religion, talk it out with him. If you have decided to have a trial period or to be a *ger toshav*, make it clear that this hardly means you are rejecting his religion or ignoring his wishes and his religious convictions.

Here are some things that you can say to help him accept your decision, things that the two of you, together, can then say to your prospective in-laws. (Since the pressure is most likely to come from Jewish families, we've put the statements in Jewish terms, but similar points can be made to a Christian family.)

1. You are not saying you will never convert. You are saying you do not feel ready to convert at this time.

2. Even if you don't convert, the children can be raised as Jews. They can be given a conversion at birth and sent to Jewish religious school. Jewish holidays can be observed in the home.

3. You understand your in-laws dreamed of having a Jewish wedding. But that would be an empty gesture if you don't feel Jewish. You can have a civil wedding now and a Jewish wedding later, if you come to a point where you do feel ready to convert.

4. If your partner and his family think about their own relationship to Judaism, they'll find it complicated and multi-leveled. They should appreciate that you, raised a Christian, need time to develop the many strands of Jewish identity.

5. If the family consults their own rabbi, he'll tell them that the Jewish religion counsels against seeking conversions for the sake of marriage, even for the sake of family unity. Conversion must come from personal religious conviction. You are actually showing more respect for Judaism by refusing to have a paper conversion as a matter of convenience.

In the case of a Catholic family, have the family talk to the priest to get an update on the church's position on Jews and intermarriage. The priest can tell the family that neither the non-Catholic partner nor the children will be damned if there is no conversion, and the marriage can still be blessed by God. Similarly, with a traditional Protestant family, have a minister whom you trust talk to the family about the church's belief in God's special relationship with the Jews.

If your in-laws are unyielding in their pressure, tell them you consider their behavior disrespectful and that you and the grandchildren will not visit until they drop the subject.

If people in the Jewish community keep up the pressure, try mentioning the five points listed above. Tell them that you understand their concern for the unity and continuity of the Jewish community. Explain that it is out of respect for Judaism that you will not convert until the move feels genuine.

If people are unkind or persistent, gently but firmly shut them up. Say, "Conversion is a very personal and private matter. It's something I will have to decide for myself." Then walk away.

Finally, if you continue to be uncomfortable in the congregation you attend, go elsewhere. As you'll see in Chapter 17 (Affiliation), there are lots of options.

Your decision not to convert may leave you and your partner with some hurt and angry feelings. Consider getting counseling from an impartial outsider to help defuse the negative feelings. When you feel you are at a point where you can make decisions based on your needs and not your anger, negotiate a religious pattern for your home that satisfies both you and your partner.

IF YOU DECIDE TO CONVERT

You may conclude that conversion feels truly right and good. In that case, continue with your preparatory steps—growing into the lifestyle and learning from an informal mentor. But now there are some new practical considerations.

Select a Movement Carefully The Jewish world is currently deeply divided over the issues of intermarriage and conversion. If you are converting to Judaism, this controversy presents you with some difficult choices. If you choose some branches of Judaism, your conversion may not be seen as valid by others.

Orthodox and Conservative Judaism will only recognize conversions which contain the three elements prescribed by Jewish law: circumcision for the man, a rabbinical court and immersion in the *mikvah* for both men and women. Orthodox Jews will require a pledge that the candidate will follow all the commandments, especially observing the Sabbath and keeping a kosher home. Reform Judaism has substituted a public or private pledge to enter the covenant, establish a Jewish home, and be active in the synagogue. But no specific details of religious practice are required. Circumcision and immersion are optional. The Reconstructionist movement encourages converts to go through the traditional ritual, but also to have a public welcoming ceremony.

The split has gone so deep that many Orthodox rabbis will not accept a conversion done under Reform, Reconstructionist, or Conservative auspices even if all the traditional rituals were followed. They will require that you study again with an Orthodox rabbi and have a second, Orthodox conversion.

If your conversion is not accepted as valid, it could have consequences for both you and your children. Some *mohelim* (ritual circumcisers) will not perform a *bris* (Jewish circumcision) if they know the mother converted under nontraditional auspices. Also, if you go to Israel, the Orthodox rabbinate, which has legal control of all wedding ceremonies, might prevent you from getting married.

Traditional Jewish law says that only children of a Jewish mother are Jewish, which means that if your conversion is not considered valid the tradition will not recognize your children as Jews. Traditional Jews will not regard your children as Jewish even if you celebrate all holidays and provide a Jewish education and a bar or bat mitzvah. Further, if your child should fall in love with a Conservative or Orthodox Jew, that person's rabbi would probably refuse to conduct the wedding ceremony until your child underwent a conversion course and immersion in a *mikvah* (and in the case of a young man, had a symbolic recircumcision).

For a young person who has always considered himself a Jew, this challenge to his whole identity can be extremely upsetting. We talked with one young man, raised as a Reform Jew, whose mother's Reform conversion (and his own Reform circumcision) were not accepted by his fiancée's Conservative synagogue. Although he had completed a Reform religious school, he was required to take a conversion course, go through the *mikvah,* and have a ritual recircumcision before the synagogue's rabbi would officiate at the wedding. (Her parents were very anxious to have the ceremony at their synagogue, with their rabbi.) The young man was so angered by what he saw as absurd obstacles to his marriage that, after going through what he saw as a pro forma conversion, he and his bride boycotted: They stopped attending synagogue and observing Judaism in the home.

Some converts choose to avoid these problems by having an Orthodox conversion. But there are also strong arguments for undergoing conversion in one of the more liberal branches of Judaism. In Orthodoxy, you usually will study individually with a rabbi, while in the more liberal branches of Judaism you are almost certain to have a group conversion class, with a chance to meet other people who are going through the process. You will be introduced to a synagogue where you are likely to meet more mixed and conversionary couples. Particularly in the Reform and Reconstructionist movements, there is an emphasis on welcoming you, on accepting you where you are, and encouraging and teaching you. Reform Judaism has established a nationwide program to "advocate" for Judaism and to attract converts. Where Orthodox Judaism integrates the convert quietly and matter-of-factly, liberal Judaism is more likely to celebrate your entry and welcome your special insights. Some Reform synagogues offer support groups and other services to assist converts in making the transition. If your Hebrew skills and background are limited, you may find a Reform or Reconstructionist service more understandable, and you may find the approach to Jewish ideas and lifestyle more compatible with your way of thinking.

Before you decide where to enroll for conversion, talk with people who have done it under Reform auspices, under Orthodox auspices, and (if possible), under both.

It can be distressing, when you are interested in conversion to Judaism, to find yourself in the middle of this rather acrimonious controversy. Keep in mind that the same divisions occur in the Christian world, between Catholic and Protestant; and even among various Protestant denominations. If there's less furor than in the Jewish world, it's because the divisions in Christianity are more complete. Judaism is still struggling with how to remain one people despite denominational divisions.

Make Demands on Your Instructors Most conversion courses are academic and don't teach many "how-to" skills. Ask your teacher to show the class, or you individually, the skills needed in the sanctuary (e.g.

following the prayerbook, handling the Torah), in the home (saying grace, making a seder, preparing holiday meals) and in the social world (understanding the functions of communal and synagogue or church organizations).

Make the Most of the Moment A conversion, like a wedding, is a rite of passage: a bridge from an old way of life to a new one. Ritual is a way to help you cross the bridge. Use all the available rituals to make the moment as spiritually meaningful as possible. If you are converting to Judaism, go to the *mikvah*. If you are being baptized, see if full immersion is available. A sprinkling also can be powerful if you concentrate on the symbolism of the water. (Several people told us that baptismal immersions are more satisfying if done in private. Many people become too self-conscious and distracted if a crowd is watching.)

Your denomination will give you full details on the ritual. But among questions you may have been too embarrassed to ask: In Judaism, the immersion is done naked, in private, but with a person of the same sex acting as a witness. In full-immersion baptisms, you usually wear a white gown. Both nakedness and the white gown are powerful ways to symbolize the new beginning.

Have a Public Welcoming Even though the actual immersion in the *mikvah* or the baptism may be done in private, ask your rabbi or pastor if there can be some kind of public ceremony following it. A public ceremony is valuable for you and the congregation. It will offset any sense you might have of being a fringe person. The community will see you in an honored position. If some congregants are skeptical, you have the clergyperson at your side to remind them of your inspiring spirituality and your full status. Another option is to sponsor the regular reception after the service, whether it is the kiddush in the synagogue or cake and coffee in the church basement.

AFTER THE CONVERSION

Because conversion is a sharp fork in your life path, any convert must face some problems. The problems are somewhat different depending whether you are a gentile converting to Judaism or a Jew converting to Christianity. Although many of the strategies and solutions are similar, we have dealt with the problems in separate discussions.

Dealing with Your Family Many people have told us that the most difficult aspect of converting was telling their parents. Because of the many centuries when Jews were forcibly converted to Christianity, a Jew's voluntary conversion to Christianity is looked on by most other Jews with horror and incomprehension. Few Jews convert, and those who do often do not tell their parents.

The reaction of Christian parents to their children's conversion to Judaism varies widely. Some are supportive, since they think it is a good idea to have one religion in the home. Others are hostile, either because their religious training leads them to think Jews are damned, or because they grew up amid anti-Semitic stereotypes and had little contact with Jews. More often their reaction has nothing to do with religion, but with hurt that their way of life has been rejected. Cindy, the Southern Protestant who converted to Judaism, recalls: "It's been real difficult for my mother that I was so different from her and didn't share her values. So I said I still cared about her and kept communicating and explained that I wanted to keep things open. The other dynamic is the power game, the 'if you convert I won't love you.' I didn't play that. The thing is to keep the issues clear and not argue on that level."

Try to talk out the issues with your parents even before you convert. Be reassuring with them. Apply an extra dose of the balm we describe in Chapter 3 (Dealing with Parents). Affirm your love for them and your respect for their heritage, and show that they still have a vital role in your life. Here are a few more tips for heading off problems and handling them if they do occur:

1. Introduce your partner to your parents *before* you talk with them about converting.

2. Do not have your partner present when you tell your parents you intend to convert.

3. Inform them in person of your decision. A follow-up letter also is wise. Do not tell them on one of their religious holidays.

4. Tell them you wish to provide your children with a single, coherent religious tradition and with the advantages of a faith which is shared with spouse and children.[10]

Is it OK never to tell your parents? Sometimes, parents are so deeply troubled or difficult to deal with that keeping your conversion from them is appropriate. But usually you owe it to them to reveal such a deep change in your life. Be gentle. If your parents fall apart, remain reassuring. If weeks go by and they continue to fume, you may need to take a firmer approach. Tell them: "The conversion was right for me. I hope you can respect it." Don't permit a cutoff, even if they attempt one. Continue to call and visit. It will be a difficult time, but stay involved because your presence demonstrates your love.

Your parents may not be the only ones upset by your conversion. If you already have children, they may find it hard to accept a switch in their life-style. Cindy's son was only five when she converted, but he had grown accustomed to a full-blown Christmas in their home. She had to soothe his confusion and distress. When he became a Scrooge against Santa during a postconversion Christmas season, Cindy determined that this was his backhanded way of telling them he was missing the holiday. She resolved to expand and enliven their Hanukkah celebration.

In some families, the spouse is a central player, making clear his desire for a conversion and helping his mate in the transition. But Cindy's husband, Bruce, never expected her to convert and has been ambivalent about his new Jewish home. (He told us he is "just along for the ride.") As a result, Cindy is operating without a copilot much of the time, a situation that she finds wearing. "He'll feel there's too much ritual. Like around the Passover meal, he would rather just eat, not do an hour of stuff. There are times when I wish he'd be a little more solemn, not quite so light about certain things." She tries to be philosophical: "His healthy cynicism is good, an important Jewish strain to maintain." She also dismisses much of his sarcasm as "a pose" and says the customs have begun to grow on him.

To some extent, you simply have to ride out these reactions and accept people as they are. Not everyone has as difficult a time as Cindy. Gail, another convert to Judaism, has parents who are leaders in their Episcopal church. She expected that they would have trouble accepting her conversion and her keeping a kosher home. She decided not to expect total acceptance or enthusiastic support. But she made it a point to reassure them of her love and to answer their questions about Judaism and conversion matter-of-factly, without taking things personally. Now, her parents send out Hanukkah presents and Rosh Hashanah cards and she keeps them abreast of her Jewish activities.

Dealing with Community Reactions Although there may be pockets of anti-Semitism, the Jew who converts to Christianity is generally received with open arms by the Christian community. Reactions from the Jewish community, however, may be so hostile that Jews who convert to Christianity may cut off all contact with the Jewish community. If you convert to Christianity, you may find a few Jewish individuals who are open-minded enough to accept you on your own terms. Maintaining ties with them can help you not to feel totally cut off from your past. But be equally open-minded with them and refrain from proselytizing.

The gentile who converts to Judaism is likely to get little reaction from the Christian community, which will hardly notice her absence, but may get a mixed reception from her new Jewish community. Here are some tips for handling that:

Understand the Discomfort with Converts Just as you need to be patient with yourself, you need to be a bit patient with the frowners in your new community. Until the present generation, the Jewish community has been forced to be a rather tight and ingrown world. You may not look or act like other Jews they know. Your spiritual approach might intimidate them. They may flaunt their ethnicity to hide their religious illiteracy. Don't let the skepticism undercut you, but see it as a simple consequence of their experience.

In addition, some born-Jews scoff because they can't understand why anyone would voluntarily become Jewish and risk the perils of anti-Semitism.

Many converts have taken to calling themselves Jews-by-choice to emphasize their joyful embracing of the Jewish way of life. If a number of people in your synagogue don't seem to understand why anyone would take this step, ask your rabbi to arrange to have you, or an outside speaker, explain. This can be an affirmative experience for the whole congregation.

Confront the Discomfort Try to let someone's first insensitive comment or glance roll off your back. You are an emissary for all converts and need to keep your image in mind. At first, if confronted, be abtrusely polite or disarmingly direct: "Yes, I was born Jewish, but to Episcopalian parents." "Yes, I'm a convert. Have you known others of us?" "I converted and I'm trying to settle into it. Have any pointers?"

If the person is well-meaning, it should be easy to fall into pleasant conversation. But if she is scornful, you can turn on a bit more tartness. Tell her there are Irish Jews, Chinese Jews, blond Jews, black Jews—and there always have been. Tell her that Judaism honors you as a righteous convert.

As this is happening, remind yourself of the many people who *have* welcomed you into the religion. Try to redraw your friendship circle for awhile so that it brings you into contact with the welcomers and not the rejecters. Gail has felt suspicious glances from some parts of the community, but she has tried not to let them penetrate. "To some people I will never be Jewish," she says. "That's the way they feel. But that doesn't mean that I can't consider myself Jewish, just because one Jew in the whole world doesn't feel that I am Jewish."

Gail and her husband joined a synagogue where they were eagerly welcomed. It was a "very liberal" Conservative synagogue with many young families, including a number of mixed or conversionary couples. "We have been called to be on so many committees," she said. "They are hungry for people to be involved. . . . I have been very honest with people about being ignorant about some things. I really have never felt anyone is evaluating me or thinking that I don't have a place there."

Get Support Make it clear to your partner that you will need extra emotional support and encouragement during the transition and for awhile afterward. If your partner doesn't know how to be supportive, teach him. Tell him you want him with you at key times. Have little home ceremonies (such as a wine toast, or in Judaism saying *Shehehiyanu*, the "special events" blessing) to celebrate steps in your process, such as telling your parents, completing your conversion course, going through the ceremony, joining your first community group, even telling off the first person who insults you.

In addition to whatever support you get from your partner, you need outside sources of support. Continue your relationship with your mentor and your "adoptive family."

Find a Support Group Here, converts can commiserate about adjustment, swap ideas for dealing with parents, in-laws, spouse, and community, learn religious skills together. Unfortunately, no one we contacted in the Christian community knew of convert networks or of support groups for new converts in individual churches. In Judaism, the Reform movement has initiated a number of regional and synagogue-based "post-conversion *havurot*" (fellowships for study and worship). Some Conservative and Reconstructionist synagogues also have convert support groups, formed periodically at local initiative. It is well worth your trouble to find one or to start one if need be, at least in the first months after your conversion.

One permanent support group is the Jewish Converts Network, which has several hundred members in eight chapters. Four of the chapters are in the Philadelphia area. The others are in Ohio, Rhode Island, Utah, and suburban Washington, D.C. For information, contact its director, Lena Romanoff (see Chapter 19, Programs and Resources).

Understand Your Own Post-Conversion Reactions Many converts feel deflated after the ceremony. They feel a little bit Jewish, or a little bit Christian, but not as much as they wanted to be. Others feel panicked. They feel as if they need to take on the whole passel of observances at once, and they can't handle it. Some feel they have to prove themselves—as if no matter how hard they try, they won't be Jewish enough or Christian enough.

Our advice to people who have any of these feelings: Take your time, and be easy on yourself. Consider yourself a newborn. Give yourself time to crawl, then walk. Don't expect to know all the prayers at once, or to put on a complete celebration for every holiday, or to identify with your new group at every turn. Don't go into a tailspin at your first gaffe. This new identity will grow over the years.

There's a common cycle experienced by converts: infatuation, disillusion, equilibrium. Many converts at first are thrilled by the new religion, feeling they've finally found their spiritual home. Then comes a period when they learn about the "downside," and they may withdraw bitterly. If you are patient, and if you get enough support, you'll be able to ride out this disillusion and come to a balance where you have a realistic picture of the religion and the role you want it to play in your life.

Take an Active Role in the Religion Don't hide behind your partner. Don't use him as a cultural shield. The religion must be your own. You need to be proud of your decision to take it on and be able to practice it alone. This is doubly important if you are a woman, because your children will probably look primarily to you for religious guidance and nurturing.

Learn the Different Points of Entry If you've become a Christian but feel you've hit a wall in your thinking about Jesus, let go of that struggle for awhile. Many *born* Christians spend their whole lives defining and redefining Jesus and their relationship to Him. Concentrate on the church's social-action programs instead, or volunteer for its building committee. They are valued activities and will help you bond with the community.

If you are a Jew-by-choice and feel overwhelmed by the many ways to be Jewish, don't try to be them all at once. Take one that appeals to you—it might be Jewish history, or blessings, or keeping kosher—and work on it. Then move on to another.

* * *

Above all, you have to find the level of religious involvement that fits with you and your lifestyle. Many converts are spiritual seekers who want to belong and to be involved. Every religious community is hungry for doers and seekers. If you keep at it, you will find a place for yourself in your new world.

UNDERSTANDING YOUR CHILDREN

12. CHILDREN'S ADJUSTMENT:

Born of Harmony

As a mixed couple, you may have heard dire warnings about how certain religious child-rearing styles are guaranteed to leave your child troubled. Actually, no such sweeping claims can be made. What seems to be true, instead, is this: *Whether you raise your child in one religion, two religions or no religion has little or no impact on her mental health.*

But a crucial factor must be present: *Both parents must agree with and stand behind the religious pattern you have chosen for your home.*

In other words, the vital factor in whether your children are happy or unhappy, troubled or secure, is whether the two of you are in harmony. Your job as intermarried parents is to work out your differences and deal with each other in such a way that you both feel comfortable with the religious style of your home. You must then consciously convey your agreement to your children. Whether you raise them in one religion or two, you must let them know that the two of you, together, have decided that this is how they will be raised. This is your "family policy."[1]

Very little research has been done on the relationship between religious upbringing and mental health in children of intermarriage. But two studies, one in California by psychologist Karen Kaufman and one nationwide study by sociologist Egon Mayer, seem to point to this conclusion.[2]

This is not to say that some religious approaches, no matter how sincerely agreed upon, might not cause your child some *identity* confusion. Religious identity will be an issue in any dual-heritage home, as Chapter 14 will make clear. But you shouldn't, for the sake of giving your child a single religious identity, set up a home situation that causes tension or deep unhappiness for one of you. The identity confusion your child may feel is less a hazard to her mental health than having two warring parents.

DESTRUCTIVE PARENTAL PATTERNS

What if the two of you aren't in harmony? What are the consequences if you don't have a unified family policy? Not good. Here are some intermarriage patterns that can wreak havoc with a child's mental health. Children from families with these patterns are more likely to be insecure, depressed, or have behavior problems. In nearly all the cases, dissonance over religion is a symptom, not a cause, of problems in the parents' relationship.

Ask yourselves if your family fits any of these patterns:

1. The tug-of-war family, where parents compete for religious leadership of the family.

2. The triangle family, where parents talk through the children instead of talking to each other.

3. The "Daddy's wrong" family, where parents criticize or contradict each other's values.[3]

4. The takeover family, in which one parent dominates and the other is a submissive outsider.

5. The sneaky family, in which one parent gives conflicting religious messages behind the other's back.

6. The marionette family, in which relatives on one side or the other pull the strings and control the parents.

7. The you-get-yours-and-I'll-get-mine family, in which, for example, it's decided in advance that the boys will be Catholic and the girls Jewish.[4]

8. The hands-off family, in which there is no clear direction from the parents and the children are given responsibility for leading.[5]

9. The secretive family, where one parent has completely hidden his or her roots.

Children of intermarriage who grow up in these unhealthy atmospheres have a good chance of becoming neurotic. In some cases, the neurosis centers on religion. For example, Alan did not find out until he was eighteen, and did some genealogical research, that his father was Jewish. As an adult, Alan has been as secretive as his father—in reverse. He has lived his entire adult life as a Jew, hiding from his acquaintances the fact that he had been reared in a Protestant church and his mother was a devout Christian. Alan has even invented reminiscences of Jewish family holidays. He lives in terror of having his secret past discovered and losing his Jewish status. (He isn't willing to convert because he would first have to admit he isn't Jewish.) He also has suffered from bouts of acute depression. Fortunately, this pattern of the runaway Jewish parent is rare.

Wendy came from a "Daddy's wrong" family. Her Southern-Baptist mother was constantly either hurling ethnic insults at Wendy's Jewish father or nagging him to convert. He passively resisted. Wendy grew up feeling like a victim because, even though the insults were not directed at her, she identified with her father. She became an adult with little trust in the world and herself. "I always cry when I watch Mister Rogers" (the children's television show), she says. "What's he trying to tell these poor kids: I like you just the way you are. I always want to say, Mister Rogers, you're the only one!"

We suspect that the two most common destructive patterns in intermarried families are the tug-of-war family, where the parents compete, and the takeover family, where one parent calls the shots and the other sulks. If either is happening to you, it may be subtle and hard to discern. Ask yourself: Do I genuinely support the religious pattern we have chosen for our family? Does my partner as well, or does she have discomforts she's afraid to express? If one partner's needs are being suppressed, recognize that this is an unhealthy situation which may have painful consequences not only for that partner but for the children. You and your partner need to work out a more mutually acceptable family pattern. If you are trying to raise children in two religions, ask yourself: Do I genuinely appreciate my partner's religion? Do I know enough to teach it to the children? Or am I secretly trying to raise them in my religion, not hers?

Family therapy, with a spiritually sensitive but religiously neutral counselor, can help alter many of those destructive patterns. If your family fits one of the patterns, you have to ask yourself a hard question: Do I care enough about my children to resolve my problems with my partner? Or am I so invested in my present stance that I am willing to use religion as my tool for maintaining an unhealthy family system?

ADVICE: FOR THE CHILDREN'S SAKE

Running through the following suggestions are universal themes of family cohesiveness: mutual love, openness, tolerance, flexibility.

Emphasize Parental Harmony Base your teaching of your children on ideas you and your spouse share concerning the world and people's purpose in it. Study each other's religions or world views and find areas of common ground. Spell them out to the children.

Be Equally Involved Do not relegate a parent to the corner if his religious background is not the one chosen for the children. That parent has an obligation to be involved, while the other has a responsibility not to exclude. Think of yourselves as allies in their religious upbringing. Even if you are what we call the "out-parent" (the parent who doesn't share their religion), take a role in their celebrations. Go to their place of worship, at least occasionally. And occasionally, have everyone come as a family to your place of worship.

See That Your Children Know Other Mixed Children If you are moving, add this to your list of questions for prospective neighbors. If you are affiliating or looking for a religious education program for your children, find out how many mixed families there are. Socialize with other mixed families, so that regardless of how you choose to affiliate, your children will know other children whose situation is similar to theirs.

Make Sure Your Children Know Both Sets of Grandparents The love of a grandparent can be precious to a child, and can give her a vital sense of having roots on both sides of her family. As long as the grandparents are not undercutting your religious approach, keep the road to their house open.

Introduce a Loving God, Not a Harsh One The concept of a loving God enhances a child's self-esteem and the concept of a harsh God undermines it. If a child lives in fear of God's punishment, he will be insecure and the world will seem a forbidding place.

Show Respect for Differences Acknowledge the differences between your two religions while showing how they meet similar needs. Be able to explain to your children how they can learn different, but complementary things, from each of you and your religions and can grow up to be healthier, stronger, more complete people.

13. CHILDREN AND SPIRITUALITY:

Seeds of Wonder

S herry, a fast-talking, chain-smoking television producer, is a passionate atheist. Her grandparents—one a Unitarian and one a fundamentalist Christian—fought bitterly over religion. Her parents, in her eyes, were conventional and hypocritical in their church attendance. Sherry, now intermarried, thinks organized religion is responsible for a lot of the evil in the world. Her nine-year-old daughter, Roberta, agrees with her about organized religions: They're boring and they make people fight, she says. But God is another matter. Bertie has been talking with God since she was two years old, and she reports regularly on God's side of the conversation. It drives her mother to distraction. "I just hope she'll outgrow it," she groans.

It seems a fine piece of irony that a woman who finds the very mention of God offensive and who has deliberately avoided teaching her daughter about religion should have a daughter to whom God is so vividly alive.

Our interviews, and those of other researchers, have shown that children often develop a lively spiritual life regardless of what they are taught by their parents. Whether or not you're interested in thinking about God, death, and the meaning of life, your children will ask you, starting at about age three.

As intermarried parents, you may have special problems in dealing with these questions: You may not feel able to fall back on conventional religious teaching. You and your spouse may have very different answers to these questions. You may be uncertain how to talk honestly about your own, perhaps agnostic, view of the world without squelching your child's innocent faith. Further, you may be one of the many intermarried couples who want to devise their own religious education rather than leave the teaching to religious institutions. To figure out how to respond to your childrens' questions, you need to learn something about their spiritual development. That's the subject of this chapter.

AN INDEPENDENT SPIRITUAL LIFE

Children are theorizers—they need to make sense of their world, and particularly of such ultimate puzzles as death.[1] When they receive no spiritual training, they often "make up" a religion from whatever raw materials are available. Rev. James Fowler, a prominent religion re-searcher, has interviewed children who concocted religions based on things they saw on television: a theology based on a wedding on a cow-boy show, or built around a cartoon of David and Goliath.

Some researchers believe that because children haven't developed a full set of psychological defenses, spiritual and mystical experiences come more naturally to them.[2] Even when parents think they know their children well, the children may have a whole spiritual world of which their parents know nothing.

That was apparent when we interviewed Karen Diamond and her seven-year-old daughter, Eva. Eva is very close to her mother and perched on her lap during our interview. A thin child with wide eyes in a serious face, she had gone to a Jewish preschool and Reform Jewish Sunday school. She talked with assurance about Jewish holidays and beliefs. (Being Jewish, she said, means, "We should follow the rules we think are good, and we don't have to follow the other ones." It means "celebrating hol-idays, believing in God, and that there's only One.")

Then we asked her if she ever prayed. "Well," she said slowly, tuning in to a thoughtful inner place, "every night, when I remember, I say a prayer to my dog."

Karen (dumfounded): "TOBY?!" (She explained that Toby had died three years earlier.)

Eva: "Sometimes I tell him what happened that day. Sometimes how much I miss him."

We asked her where Toby is.

Eva: "Sometimes I think maybe there's a place dogs go to. He isn't around anymore. He left the earth."

Then we asked her what God is like.

Eva: "Like a swirl of wind. When people are having trouble deciding things, or trouble with situations, He helps them in His own way."

Your child, like Eva, sees the world through a child's eyes, with child logic. Her thoughts on spiritual life have not yet been shaped by adult categories about what is reasonable and appropriate. Influenced by you, but not constrained by what you teach, she will develop her own way of explaining the sadnesses, mysteries, and beauties of life.

UNFOLDING IN STAGES

Researchers have found that children's religious ideas evolve in stages just like their mental and emotional development. Rev James Fowler, one of America's foremost researchers on religion, believes that children go through three, or in some cases four, stages of religious development.[3]

Before a baby has any religious ideas at all, it is developing the emotional foundation, the soil in which religious ideas may grow. If the infant receives dependable feeding and loving, it develops what Fowler calls an "Undifferentiated Faith"—a basic trust in its parents, and through that experience, a trust in life and in the world.

The child's first notions of God, religion, and morality develop between ages two and seven. At this stage, children are little transcendentalists. They are trying to figure out how the world works. They may ask ultimate questions about death and the nature of the world which stun and challenge you. Part of the challenge is figuring out what the child wants to know. The child who asked, "Why is she a baby?" may have wanted to know, "Why are there babies? Why do people have to be babies first? Why can't babies do as much as bigger kids? How did it happen that she is a baby, while I am a boy?"

The child's thinking at this stage is concrete, practical and magical—all at the same time. When your preschool child asks a question about God, remember that she may take your answer very literally. One four-year-old whose mother was pregnant asked, "Mommy, since the baby is in your tummy and God is in your heart, can they talk to each other?"

Because the child thinks concretely, she imagines God behaving, thinking, and reacting like the most powerful people she knows: her parents. Because she's practical and egocentric and understands only present time, she conceives of right and wrong not as abstractions but on the basis of whether she's likely to be punished or rewarded.

The child's thinking is also magical: The world is full of new things, mysteries, and arbitrary surprises. She doesn't understand cause and effect. Like Eva, who thought of God as a swirl of wind, the young child is naturally in tune with concepts of an invisible, shapeless, all-powerful, all-present God. It's not hard for her to imagine God being all over the world at the same time. At this stage she "imagines" God the way she imagines monsters—as a projection of her own powerful urges and fears. There is a danger at this stage of terrifying the child with images of a punitive God.

The child is likely to identify with the characters in religious stories—with the vulnerable new-born Baby Jesus, or Noah and his family shut into the ark with a lot of animals while it rained and rained and everything else was washed away.

At the preschool age, the child has a hard time distinguishing fantasy from reality. This puzzle underlies four-year-old Sammy's question, "Is God real, or is he real like He-Man?" By age six, Sam couldn't believe he had ever asked such a question. That's because, by age six, he was beginning to pin down the line between fantasy and reality.

From about age seven to age twelve, children go through a second, very different stage of spiritual development. Religiously, they're fundamentalists. Spiritually, they're storytellers. Children in this phase still want to know why and are still very literal. But instead of seeing everything concretely, they see the world in terms of structures, of rules. They believe deeply in values such as justice and fairness. They tend to apply rules of right and wrong rigidly. They believe in an anthropomorphic God and take religious stories as literally true. It's important for them to find cause and effect and reasons for things. They love to hear and to tell stories, which give structure and sense to experience.

At age six, Sammy no longer worried about whether God was real. God was real because he learned it in Sunday school, and because people were real and somebody must have created them. At age four, Sam was a transcendentalist; by age six, he was an orthodox creationist who conducted a mini-Scopes trial, scoffing at a playmate who thought people were descended from monkeys and not created directly by God. Sam's parents were religious skeptics, but for Sam, who was at the second, or fundamentalist stage of religious development, Bible stories must be real.

From about age thirteen to twenty, young people generally move into a third stage of faith development—conventional religiosity. Unlike the "story" religiosity of Stage 2, this is a fully developed religion with values and beliefs linked to an ideology and a theology, an explanation of the world. The ideology (usually that of one's parents, peers, and religion of birth) is accepted without much questioning. The ideology provides comfort because it explains the world and one's place in it. These beliefs are seen as true and inherent in the nature of the world.

People who don't hold the ideology are seen as alien.

Young people in this third stage of faith development may hold any variety of religious belief: fundamentalism, religious liberalism, skepticism, agnosticism, or atheism. The relevant criterion is not the content of the belief but the way it is arrived at. A person is at Stage 3 faith if he simply duplicates the views of his parents or takes on without question the tenets of the religion in which he was brought up. This is the religious development level at which many adults stop.

In America and other Western cultures, many teenagers or young adults go on to reject the conventional religion of their parents and enter a rationalist phase, a state of demythologizing. This often occurs when the individual is in his twenties. He leaves home not only physically but psychologically and spiritually as well. He begins to question the beliefs with which he was brought up and turns the microscope on his own assumptions, too. The existential questions asked in childhood come up again, but with new urgency: What is the meaning of life—my life? For some, this stage leads to agnosticism or atheism. For others (particularly girls and young women), it leads to an intense involvement with religion—a fascination with the spiritual or the occult.[4]

Different Strokes for Different Stages The stages of faith are sequential. You can't skip a stage. Even if you are a rationalist, your child cannot start out that way no matter what you try to teach him.

Faith development is also cumulative. "The previous stage isn't totally dismantled," says Fowler. "The child's first images of God remain intact in the psyche. Each stage adds a new repertoire." (This applies to you as well as your child: You haven't lost your earlier beliefs and images of God; they remain as nuggets, buried in your later concepts.)

Your child will go through these stages whether or not you give her any religious training or expose her to any religious institutions. But if you choose to try to influence your child's ideas or to nurture her spiritual capacities, you need to do it with sensitivity to her stage of development.

Very young children, in the first level of faith development, need things, not ideas. Their awe and imagination are excited by the Christmas tree or the Sabbath candles.

To a child in the second stage, religion is stories. If you want him to feel a connection to a religious tradition, you will tell him the stories of that tradition. You will use stories to explain religious ideas and morality.

Although there are limits to children's understanding at these first two stages, we must make it clear that even very young children can have profound spiritual intuitions. They can have deep insights, which they feel vividly but are unable to express in the abstract language of adults. When your children express notions of God and the universe, however quaint they may seem to you, try not to laugh, but listen with respect.

To a youngster in the third stage of development, religion is ideology. He is now ready to understand when you talk to him about how ethics, right and wrong, are connected to belief, to your understanding of how the world operates. Making this connection gives the youngster a sense of wholeness about the world. The moral world is not just an arbitrary collection of "you ought to do this and you shouldn't do that," but there's a central understanding of the world that connects all these disparate pieces. Certainly one can teach a child values without connecting them to a religious faith. But when ethics are imbedded in a religious tradition, comments Fowler, "morality is not just arbitrary; it has a cosmic resonance."

A child who hears his parents grappling with issues of religion and morality learns to do moral reasoning, just as a child who hears his parents talk about how they feel learns to express feelings. A child who doesn't hear people talking about their feelings often has trouble not only expressing feelings, but even being aware of them and how they color his behavior. Similarly, a child who lives in a home where morality is not discussed may be insensitive to when moral issues are at stake.

Even if you don't believe in or want to teach your child a particular theology, it's important to share your feeling for the spiritual rather than material dimension of existence, to give the child a sense of meaning in life.

Religion offers a sustaining spiritual system. This is particularly important in periods of questioning and personal crisis. Religion, says Fowler, "can help one feel at home in the world . . . In the face of death, the existential questions, it can give a sense of assurance. It gives a language for staying in the presence of mystery—not only to tolerate it but to relish it."

SPIRITUALITY AND FAMILY

As you learned when you explored your own religious beliefs in Chapter 9, children's spiritual outlook and choices are intertwined with family dynamics. In your children's early years, you are more than just authority figures—you are their God-image. If you are a believer, you certainly should talk about a loving God. But more important, you must *be* a loving God.

Several intermarried people told us how a cynical parent had turned a blowtorch to their budding spiritual feelings, leaving them feeling scorched and resentful for years. One woman, raised in the South, recalls how her yearnings were stifled by her fallen-away Protestant parents and particularly her father, a sarcastic atheist who insisted that one totally accept a faith system or stay away from it altogether. "I felt that I had to believe something or that there had to be something. I thought it was the love of mankind, that is what I thought at nine years old. I remember saying, 'I know what God is.' Then they laughed. When they laughed, I said 'never mind' and I wouldn't say. Now that I am forty, actually I think that that [God as love of mankind] makes a lot of sense to me."

Looking Elsewhere Children are resourceful. If they do not find access to spirituality from you—or if they just want an extra dose of it—they may seek and find it from another adult. It might be a teacher, a neighbor, a friend's parent, an aunt, or uncle. Often, we found, it is a grandparent.

Particularly in homes with little or no religion, or homes with mixed messages about religion, grandparents can be an important spiritual influence. What children seem to pick up from the grandparent is not so much a specific religious identity as a feeling that faith and the spiritual dimension are sources of strength, comfort, and meaning.

One woman, child of a feuding Baptist mother and Jewish father, escaped the cold war in her parents' city apartment every summer by visiting her grandmother in the Deep South. Her memories of those summers are a happy mélange of picnics, running in the woods, her grandmother's strict but warm parenting, and a chorus of amens from a country church. As an adult, this woman became a Unitarian. Although she rejected her grandmother's theology, she did take on her deep spirituality. She became a teacher in her church, believes in God, prays regularly, and is devoted to protecting the environment and "witnessing for peace."

Children vary widely in their spiritual needs. If you are a nonbeliever and not affiliated with any religious institution, some children will adapt happily to your ways. But others will develop a hunger for religion. Some youngsters who were given little or no exposure to religion develop a need for a "remedial experience of God," according to Fowler, and turn to cults or fundamentalist sects as teenagers or young adults.

ADVICE: HOW TO NURTURE SPIRITUALITY

Must you have a belief in God in order to foster your child's spiritual development? We don't think so. But it is important to have an openness to, and appreciation of, the spiritual dimension of life. Here are some ways to convey that:

Show How Your Beliefs or Principles Inspire You If you are a believer, let your children see that your faith gives you pleasure and meaning and connectedness. Show how it guides your everyday acts. Let them hear you praying or otherwise affirming your faith. Let them know how religion gives you strength when you need it or impels you to specific good deeds.

If you are a nonbeliever, talk with your children about how your principles inspire your actions and help you keep going when things get tough.

Expose Children to the Awe of Nature Your child probably already has a sense of wonder at the world. You need only affirm and articulate it. Point out the rhythms of the days and the seasons, the interdependence of life, the regeneration of the injured body. Intermarried couples who do not believe in a traditional God can still give a sense of reverence, a feeling for humanity's link to nature, a sense of cosmic connectedness.

Help Them Find Inspiration in Human Strivings Surround your children with lovely music, art, and poetry. Talk about the impulse to create beauty which inspires such works. The everyday, too, has its inspired: bridges and hospitals and poverty programs, which can be seen as strivings for the common good.

Share the Events That Move You If you find inspiration in religious services, take your children for an appropriate portion of the service. Children are very serious small beings, and they love to participate in things adults take seriously. The formality, dignity, pageantry—the awesomeness—of a religious service are very special gifts to share with a child. They give her a glimpse of mysteries, and a sense that people can act in many different ways, not just in the everyday.

If you are a nonbeliever, find ways through drama, music, dance, and mime of exposing your child to grandeur, ineffability—the many dimensions of human experience.

Don't Push Your Agenda Present your point of view, but don't insist that your children adopt it as their own. If you are an atheist, you don't have to persuade them of the nonexistence of God. If you are a believer, you don't have to mold the children into your set of beliefs. Recognize that the way you see things is not necessarily the truth but was shaped by your family history and circumstance.

Be Prepared to Learn from Your Children Respect your children's spirituality as different from your own. Let them provoke you to fresh thinking. If you are an atheist and your child talks of God, find it in yourself to ask sincerely, "Do you feel like you speak to God? What is it like? Where do you see God?" The answers may sound silly—or they may strike you as profound. Psychiatrist Annette Hollander writes, "Our children can help *us* enter into 'beginner's mind'—that state before defenses, concepts, and conditioning insulate us from experiencing directly."[5]

Find Out What Your Child is REALLY Asking When young children ask about God, death, and religion, they're not necessarily looking for a succinct statement of your philosophy and theology. Often, they have fears and worries, and what they need is reassurance. Before you leap into an answer, ask a few questions of your own, and get a better idea about what's on their minds. You might say, "What do *you* think?" or, "Why do you ask?" or, "Are you feeling scared or worried about something?"

Gear Religious or Moral Training to a Child's Temperament If your child is a bustling, generous doer, let her learn about religion through service projects. If she's a dreamer, tell her stories from your tradition. If she's a thinker, speculate with her about the paradoxes and mysteries of science and the cosmos. Each child needs a taste of each of these activities. But what you do should accord with her special personality.[6]

Encourage Appreciation Teach your child to be aware of and to enjoy the many ways in which his life is blessed. At bedtime, have the child look back at the day, pick out the thing he liked best, and think about how he felt when it happened. If he dwells on what you find crass, such as new toys, build on that by pointing out how good the world has been to him. Take a few moments to reflect on your own day and talk about your own best moment with your child.

Consider the Bible as a Resource for Teaching Whether you are a believer or nonbeliever, you can use the Bible as a framework for talking with your children about morality and about the ultimate questions of life and death. They can realize that the same questions they are asking were being asked by people thousands of years ago. They can become familiar with the stories and traditions that shaped their family and society. They can get a sense of the music, reverence, and sweep of the psalms. If you are a skeptic, use the stories as a framework for discussion: Would you have done it this way? Do you think this is fair? You can help your children be religiously literate and to cherish a tradition without making them believe every word of it.

Create a Home That is Contemplative Set aside regular quiet times to be together as a family, and for each parent to be alone with each child. Through music or family rituals, give the child a chance to be lifted out of the hecticness and grumblings of everyday life.

14. CHILDREN'S IDENTITY:

Knowing Who They Are

From an early age, children try earnestly to figure out who they are and where they belong. As their horizons expand and they become aware of a world beyond their family, they feel a need to define their place in it.

For many children, and for many adults, religion is an important part of that self-definition. Religion gives people a common history, values, traditions, rituals, stories, jokes. This shared system gives them an anchor in the world—an identity.

What's the difference between religious identity and religious faith? Identity is not what you believe; it's where you belong. For many people, this is a more important function of religion than its belief system. They stay with the religion of their childhood not because they still believe all of its particular dogma but because it is their community, their home.

People who are raised without a clear sense of religious belonging may feel a void in their lives. Leslie Goodman-Malamuth is one of those people. Her Jewish father and gentile mother were scornful skeptics "who made it real clear that religion didn't have any place in their life, and as long as I was living under their roof it didn't have anything to do with mine." Leslie remembers, when she was only five years old, envying a playmate from a strongly observant Jewish family. Even though she was so young, she felt that her friend's life had "a kind of continuity and feeling of something larger than yourself. My family was very individualistic and we seemed to lack that. We didn't tap into anything larger than ourselves."

Leslie vowed to join Judaism when she grew up. And she did. After struggling to attain a sense of Jewish literacy, she officially converted a few years ago. She also went on to co-found Pareveh, a network of support groups to help adult children of intermarriage deal with identity issues.[1]

We talked with many children of intermarriage who, like Leslie, have a longing to belong to a religion. While some children of nonreligious homes seem content remaining undefined secularists, the many yearners have such a longing that they will find a religious community despite what their parents do or don't do.

Based on those interviews and our talks with professionals, we have come to feel it is not satisfactory to raise a child with no group identification, no experience of belonging. By allying with a religious or secular community, you will be giving your child a way of understanding and explaining who she is. Because you can add to her sense of security by giving her a place to belong, and because a well-chosen community can enrich her in many other ways, we recommend that you give her a clear grounding in a specific tradition.

We have also come to the conclusion that children feel more secure if they are brought up in one religion, not two—if they have one clear religious identity. That doesn't mean the child can't be exposed to the religious background and celebrations of the other parent. But the child raised in one religion knows who he is. He has a definite, unambiguous label, and that label has some content. It is tied to some practices, some values, and a community of people with whom he is familiar.

Children who don't get a clear message about their religious identity can end up struggling for much of their lives to sort it out. Take Trudy, for example. Millie and Stan, a mixed couple who raised Trudy and her brother in Unitarianism, like to tell about a conversation they overheard when Trudy was five. They had just gotten the children a puppy from the Humane Society. A playmate happened to ask Trudy what religion she was. Her reply: "I'm half Jewish and half terrier."

Although Millie and Stan chuckle now about the incident, their daughter was struggling with what, to her, was a very important issue: defining her religious and cultural identity. Trudy's experience shows that even when parents are in harmony and are able to work out a compromise for their family, if they don't transmit a clear religious message, the children may end up floundering. Trudy's parents celebrated both Jewish and Christian holidays in the home. The parental harmony helped her to become the basically happy, emotionally healthy person she is today. But because her parents transmitted a mixed message through the holidays, Trudy, now twenty-one, still feels like a religious mongrel. She is uneasy—more so during periods of stress—with the feeling that she can't decide what to call herself: doesn't know, in a religious sense, who she is.

We found a number of adult children of two-religion or two-holiday homes who longed to commit themselves to a single religious identity, but remained suspended, tied up in knots of religious indecision.

The identity issue is painful when it seems to pit a child's needs against her parents'—her needs for a single identity against her parents' principled desire to practice both religions or no religion. Even though we think it is ideal to have a single identity for the child and for the household, you should not rush into this approach if it means suppressing the needs of one parent and creating tension or unhappiness in the family. That can produce the child-adjustment problems we described in Chapter 12. Later in this chapter you will hear about alternatives which can help your children develop a clear religious identity while permitting you to be true to yourselves.

We want to mention here one important way to ease tension on the identity issue: We suggest that while giving your child a clear single *religious* identity, you transmit an appreciation of her dual *cultural* heritage. Affirm to the child, "You are Jewish, and your ethnic roots are Polish and Italian," or, "You are Catholic, and your ethnic roots are Irish and Jewish."

It's easier to have a dual cultural identity than a dual religious identity. The religions, although they share many of the same moral values, contradict each other on matters of belief and doctrine. In that sense, they are mutually exclusive. But cultural traditions can complement each other and blend with either religion. In pluralist America, your children will not be alone in having multiple cultural roots. In addition, being aware of their ethnic mix can broaden your children and make them especially sensitive to others.

IDENTITY AND CHILD DEVELOPMENT

In order to foster a clear religious identity for your children, you need to be sensitive to their feelings and needs at different ages. As with spiritual development, children pass through several major stages in identity formation. Religious group identity plays a different role at each stage.[2]

Stage One: Feeling Like Part of One's Parents In the beginning, the child's thinking is very concrete. Trudy, the "half terrier," told us that as a little girl she imagined a line down the middle of her body. One half of her was Jewish and the other half was "something else."

Because young children are concrete in their thinking, they define Jewish or Christian identity in terms of the visible rituals and celebrations in the home. Christians are people who have Christmas trees. Jews are people who light Sabbath candles. If the home is happy, warm feelings will be associated with the rituals, and these can generalize to an overall positive feeling about the identity that is associated with the rituals.

On the other hand, if you tell a child he's Jewish but give him a Christmas tree, he won't hear what you say; he'll see what you do. Further, if you tell a child he belongs to a particular religion but don't give him concrete rituals, objects, and celebrations, what you say will have little meaning to him.

If the home contains symbols of two religions, the young child's most fundamental feelings are likely to be of having two religious identities. We think of one boy whose parents sent him to Jewish religious school and actively celebrated all the Jewish holidays but had a Christmas tree. He described himself as "mostly Jewish but a little percent Christian."

In thinking about identity development, parents need to reckon not only with the young child's concrete thinking style but also with her emotional needs. The preschool child feels that she can depend on her parents to take care of her if she is like them, is part of them. For this reason, if a child is being raised in one religion but her parents practice two different religions, she may describe herself during the early years as being half and half. Don't flatly contradict a child who says this. Be gentle: Affirm to her that she is culturally "both" even though the two of you have agreed to raise her in one religion.

Stage Two: Acquiring Competence During the elementary school years, the child's major concern is acquiring mastery or competence. Children of this age—especially boys—become very concerned about rules. They form rather rigid definitions of "who's like us" and "who's different." In school, children ask each other whether they are Jewish or Christian. A child who says he is both or neither might be given a difficult time.

Since mastery is an important concern at both elementary school and junior high school ages, children from marginally religious homes sometimes will find themselves in situations where they feel embarrassed and inadequate. They might go to a church or synagogue and not know what to do or how to follow the service. They might hear the other children talking about a holiday and not know what it's about. At this stage, some children try to bluff their way through by asserting a claim to one religion or the other.

If the child in late elementary school and junior high school is given a clear message by parents that he "belongs" in one religious camp or other, he is likely to accept that message and identify himself as a member of that camp.

A six-year-old who is raised to identify with one religion but says she is "both" Christian and Jewish is probably expressing comfort at being linked equally to both parents. A child of ten who says she is "both" may be feeling anxious about having to choose between two parents.[3] Reassure her that she can be identified with one religion without being cut off from the parent of the other religion.

Stage Three: Conformity and the Need to Belong During junior high school, peer relationships become more important. Some children of minimally religious homes begin to "tag along" with friends to a church or synagogue, trying to find an environment in which they are accepted as one of the group. Many will begin to identify with whatever religious group predominates in their school and neighborhood.

Children of nonreligious or mixed homes who are rebuffed by their peers at this stage can begin to think of themselves as outsiders to religion. A number of the children we talked to were initially attracted to Judaism but felt wounded when told by peers or Sunday school teachers that they "weren't really Jewish" because one parent (usually the mother) wasn't Jewish. Some children were sent to Jewish Sunday schools but, because the atmosphere of their home was not ethnically Jewish, felt they did not fit in with their Jewish classmates.

Stage Four: Rebellion and the Need to Separate During later adolescence (high school and college), the identity issue comes fully to the surface and can take on great urgency. Youngsters want to know "Who am I?" Part of defining themselves is separating from their parents. They may immerse themselves in a temporary identity (a club, a gang, a rock group) that is different from anything their parents would do. They'll try on identities like suits of clothes to see how each fits.

Among children of mixed marriage, loyalty issues can complicate this already-stormy stage. They're not able to rebel from their parents as a religious unit. Rebellion against either parent may feel like choosing one parent over the other.

During this stage, many children of intermarriage go through an intensive religious search. They read everything they can find about one or both of their heritages. (Indeed, some start intensively reading about religion in grade school.) They seek a spiritual guide or mentor. Finding Truth and finding themselves become closely linked tasks. If their parents are nonreligious or antireligious, simply going through this religious search may constitute a form of rebellion. For some, church or synagogue youth groups become an important home-away-from-home. Some youngsters end up following the religion of their home, while for others the resolution is no religion and no group identification. They may become loners. Still others choose a sect such as Buddhism which is different from the religion of either parent.

There are children of intermarriage who pass through all these phases of identity development relatively unscathed. If they are raised in a single-religion home and their parents give them a consistent and loving message about it, the children might feel comfortably settled on that identity. Or, if the parents are in harmony and the home is pleasantly but marginally religious, children may go through childhood happily identifying as both Christian and Jewish. If they live in an area where religious and ethnic issues are not strongly felt, they may not be grilled or rejected by their peers in elementary school or high school. They may feel no great drive in adolescence to find a religious niche.

But some of these peaceful people—particularly those raised in religiously minimalist homes—experience a delayed identity crisis when they become parents themselves. Among their other jobs, parents are religious leaders of their households. When children of religiously minimalist mixed homes become parents, they may find that they don't know enough about either Judaism or Christianity to pass on a religious value system to their children. Particularly if their family never affiliated, they may realize they have no grasp of either religion.

Jill is one of those people. She is the product of a basically harmonious mixed home—educated as a Protestant but with two sets of holidays in the home. Now, she is a well-adjusted woman, a teacher, and a partner in a stable marriage. But when Jill was pregnant with her second child, she went through a crisis of doubt. She'd had prenatal diagnosis and knew the baby was going to be a boy. For months, she vacillated about whether to give him a *bris,* the Jewish ritual circumcision that makes a male child an official member of the Jewish community. "This is the first time in my life I've been up in the air about being both [Jewish and Christian]," she said.

With a bright three-year-old daughter asking lots of questions and another child on the way, Jill was feeling that she needed to give her children some religious training. But when she tried to make a decision about what kind of training to give, she was immobilized. For at least six years, she hadn't set foot in a church. She and her Protestant husband went with her father to Jewish High Holiday services every fall, but that was their only connection to organized religion. Jill feels her beliefs are more Jewish than Christian, and both she and her husband feel more comfortable in a Reform Jewish service than in a church. "But I don't belong either place," she laments.

She also feels that she doesn't know much about either religion. "I don't know that I could talk very knowledgeably about either side when you get right down to it. . . . I have never been able to quote a Bible verse. And I have never been able to totally explain on the Jewish side what some of the holidays were all about. But I have always known I could go somewhere and find out. So it never bothered me. If I had a question about Judaism I would go to Dad. And if I had a question about anything else, I would go to Mom.

"I'm not sure it's all that bad to do it that way for the kids—to be both. But I feel like they need some specific teaching that I don't know if I can give them. . . . I think that they can get the things that I value from me. But I am not sure that that is enough to send a kid out on his life with . . . I guess I want to provide them with enough structure that they can make decisions for themselves. Based on some knowledge rather than just my example."

Though she'd like to learn more about Judaism, her efforts are fitful. "I have a drawerful of books about the history of Jews and what the Jews believe. I haven't read them yet." The problem is that to "claim" one religion, she feels she would have to "disclaim" the other.

She also doesn't want her children to miss the Christian festivities she had. "I can't imagine a kid growing up without Christmas and Easter. Not because Jesus was involved as much as the Easter Bunny or the Christmas tree . . . When I go to my Jewish friends' houses and they don't have the tree up and they [only] have signs that say Happy Hanukkah, I feel it is not complete."

A week before her son's birth, Jill felt that she was close to a decision. She called a Jewish clergyman to make some preliminary arrangements. She was pretty sure that she would have a *bris,* with a Jewish clergyman officiating. Patting her pregnant belly, she said, "This little guy is going to have a circumcision. And my reason is because someday, if this kid wants to be Jewish, he's ready."

But when the birth came, she hedged again. There was a hospital circumcision with no clergy present. She and her husband drank a cup of wine but there were no religious rituals. Jill remains immobilized on the issue of religion. Although she very much wants to bring up her children with the warmth and rootedness of tradition, she is so internally conflicted that she can't do anything at all.

The Perils of "Letting Them Decide" Many of the adult children of intermarriage we talked with had, like Jill, been given a taste of both Judaism and Christianity but remained outsiders to both. The parents had "exposed the children to both religions" and "left the choice up to them." It was a choice that they, now that they were grown, found daunting regardless of their longing for a permanent identity commitment. Like Jill, they vacillate or freeze.

We found three major problems in raising children religiously "both" or leaving them to choose: The children may have loyalty conflicts; they may feel like outsiders to the world of religion; and their decisions may be easily influenced by random outside factors.

For children of two-religion or no-religion homes, religious identity becomes intertwined with family dynamics. On a conscious or subconscious level, they may feel that to embrace one religion means rejecting the parent of the other religion. Even very young children feel the pressure of the loyalty dilemma. We asked one little girl whether she liked Christmas or Hanukkah better. "Christmas," she said, but then her eyes widened in alarm. "You promise you won't tell my Daddy that?"

Many of these children, particularly girls and young women, try to resolve the loyalty problem by saying they will take on the religion of the person they marry. The loyalty issue thus gets bound up with, and complicates, the choosing of a mate.

For one woman, the issue came to a head during college, when she found herself simultaneously dating two men: a Southern Protestant and a Midwestern Jew. "It's almost like my life was coming to this, having a Southern boyfriend and a Jewish boyfriend, my mother's part of the country and my father's part of the country. . . . I had to actually say to myself, 'What am I gonna choose? Am I gonna get mixed up with this Southerner and go live in the South and become a Southerner, or go with this Jew and become a Jew?' " She married the Jewish man and converted.

Partly because of ambivalence about identity, many children of mixed homes remain outside organized religion. Sociologist Egon Mayer found that the rate of affiliation with either church or synagogue is much lower among children of intermarriage than among their parents.[4]

When the religious messages you give are weak or contradictory, the scales of your children's religious identity can be tipped by seemingly minor influences: what we call "X-factors." We have heard accounts of how books, stray comments, random events, chance encounters, judgments of peers all have had an impact far beyond the expected.

"You have to let them know who they are," says Minister Stephan Papa of the First Universalist Church in Denver. "If you don't teach your children, someone else will. There are fundamentalists recruiting on playgrounds."

The Jewish Angle There is another identity factor to be aware of: your children's knowledge that they have a Jewish side. Jews are a minority—ridiculed or resented by some, lauded by others—but seen by most other Americans as "different." And indeed, whether reluctantly or proudly, most Jews see themselves as different from the mainstream in some ways.

The child of a mixed marriage must decide how to respond to that differentness. When anti-Semitic remarks are made, for example, the child must make a decision. One response is to hide the Jewish side and try to blend in, using the gentile side as camouflage. Harry and Helen Diamond chuckle about the time their daughter, Karen, then six, told her classmates she was a "Sanitarian." (She meant Unitarian. She'd heard her parents use that word when asked what religion they were. But she didn't understand it very well, which isn't surprising since she'd never been inside a Unitarian church.) Neither Karen nor the teacher who related the incident apparently told her parents about the circumstances that provoked the remark. Another child in the class had said, "You're Jewish—you killed Jesus." Karen replied in a panic, "I'm not Jewish, I'm a Sanitarian!"

A second response is to absorb the attitudes of the anti-Semites. Children who internalize these prejudices fall into a thicket of ambivalence or self-hate.

Even when the children are brought up as Christians and identify with the gentile parent, they still have to cope with the "differentness" posed by their Jewish half. If a mixed child has a Jewish last name and doesn't identify as a Jew, some Jews may see him as a traitor. Others may treat him like part of the club even though he feels uncomfortable at the uninvited and unreciprocated chumminess.

But Jewish differentness also has its attractions. Many children report feeling almost mystically pulled toward their Jewish part—compelled to learn about it and connect with it even if they were taught nothing about it by their parents. Some had Jewish last names or physical features or a cultural "flavor" that made others assume that they were Jewish. But others felt Jewish in their bones despite their "neutral" names, blond hair, blue eyes, or pug noses, and a cultural air that one adult child of intermarriage described ruefully as "really white bread."

Some of these now-grown children told us that encountering anti-

Semitism or learning about the Holocaust made them want to stand up and be counted as Jews. Karen Diamond, the "Sanitarian," said that by the time she reached high school, her response to anti-Semitic remarks had changed. Even though she had had no religious upbringing and no contact with Judaism, "I would take it personally. They were assuming I was Christian. I would say, 'Did you realize I'm Jewish?' "

Judaism seems to hold a special appeal for some youngsters from conflict-ridden, emotionally cold, or broken homes. They idealize the Jewish home, seeing in it a warmth, closeness, and rootedness their own homes lacked. If their difficult childhoods made them feel small and persecuted, they might also identify with Judaism for its smallness and history of persecution.

Some children of intermarriage, when they reach adulthood, go to great lengths to reclaim the "Jewish selves" which they feel connected to but know so little about. They study diligently. They work hard to overcome their discomfort at feeling like outsiders in the Jewish community. They listen carefully for the cultural clues like aliens learning the ways of a new planet. And they embrace Jewish religious practice with a passion that surpasses most Jews born of two Jewish parents.

But being accepted as a Jew can be complicated. According to traditional Jewish law, the child of a Jewish father and an unconverted gentile mother is not Jewish unless he is properly converted. Reform Judaism accepts the child of one Jewish parent as Jewish (even if the mother is an unconverted gentile), so long as the child is brought up as a Jew and given a Jewish education.

In our interviews it was clear that the children of intermarriage who chose Judaism didn't care whether they had a Jewish father or a Jewish mother. They chose Judaism because, regardless of what the traditional law said about their Jewish status, and often, regardless of what religious education they had received, they *felt* Jewish.

Leslie Goodman-Malamuth ultimately converted so no one could challenge her status as a Jew. But she says she and many other children of intermarriage believe "you should get some advance placement for having one Jewish parent. We're not like converts . . . . We're drawn to [Judaism] because we have Jewish relatives, we have Jewish heritage. We have one foot in *klal yisrael* [the community of Israel] and if we want to bring the other foot in with us, that shouldn't be such a big step."

HOME STYLES: LOOKING AT A VARIETY
OF OPTIONS

How will the home life you provide influence your child's sense of identity? We've talked about the hunger to belong that can plague a child from a totally nonreligious home. And we've talked about the feelings of loyalty conflict, ignorance and inadequacy, and outsiderness or marginality that can arise in a child from a two-religion home.

But "Doing Nothing" and "Doing Both" are not the only options available to intermarried parents. We saw couples trying a variety of other patterns. Here are accounts of several of them, and observations about their effects on child identity:

1. Parents Practicing Both Religions but Raising the Children in Only One This is a variation for parents who need their separate religions and who don't want their children to feel strung across the middle.

We think of one family in particular who has appeared to pull it off successfully. Vivian and Martin Bryant are the parents of three teenage boys. Martin is a devout Catholic and Vivian a committed Jew. At the outset, Vivian made it clear that she wanted the children to be raised as Jews. Martin, a resolute Irishman, assented. "I was aware from the beginning of the danger of religious rivalry and have tried to avoid it," he says. A Jewish upbringing made more sense, he recalls, because "our original supposition was that the mother was the nurturer. If the mother tried to nurture the kids in a religion that was foreign to her, it would be foreign to the kids."

Martin attends Mass every week, but (with one exception, as we'll see below) there are no Christian symbols or customs in the home. The boys went to religious school at a Reform temple, were bar mitzvahed, and continue to attend services there with their mother (and occasionally their father). Vivian and the boys have a Jewish home style. Martin is supportive, sitting at the *Shabbos* and seder tables and giving the children Hanukkah presents. He had a role on the *bimah* (stage) at their bar mitzvahs.

The boys are encouraged to ask their parents any questions about either religion and are free to accompany Martin to Mass. Vivian and the boys have gone to Christmas Mass "as a gift" to him. On Christmas Eve, they bring in a small evergreen in a pot as "Daddy's tree." They give him presents on Christmas, he gives them presents only at Hanukkah. To accommodate Martin's religious needs, the family eats fish rather than meat during Lent.

The sons, who were interviewed separately and privately, say they have emerged identifying religiously, but not ethnically, as Jews. The Judaism they identify with is not a race but a state of mind, an ethical system.

Because small children identify with concrete symbols, the Christmas tree in a Jewish home can undercut the solidity of the child's Jewish identity. But that doesn't seem to have happened to the Bryant boys. We think the family has been able to give the children a secure, single identity because of a combination of factors: They attend services regularly at a synagogue and gave the children Jewish schooling and bar mitzvahs; they practice only Judaism in the home, with Martin participating to the extent he feels comfortable; the Christmas tree is not an overpowering presence, and they make clear it is only Martin's; Vivian and Martin have supported each other and Martin has affirmed that his sons are Jewish. In addition, they didn't start having a tree in their own home until after Martin's parents had died. Before that time, they celebrated Christmas only at the grandparents' home.

At the same time, the Bryants have avoided doing things which would force the children to deny or be ashamed of their non-Jewish heritage. Their synagogue is accepting of mixed families. They live in a neighborhood that is largely Jewish but has other intermarrieds. Martin has his own strong relationship with the boys, which centers around nonreligious activities (he has a "specialty"—woodworking and other hobbies—with each of them). The Bryants have encouraged free inquiry about religion; by allowing the boys to accompany their father to Mass, they have prevented Catholicism from being "forbidden fruit." They have gone as a family to Mass from time to time so Martin does not feel totally isolated, and the boys can feel they are showing love and support for him.

Martin's stoic, chipper nature also helps greatly. "We share much more than we don't," he says. "In this kind of deal it's every man for himself. You figure out what's best for your family and take it from there."

Another important component in their success may be that the father is the one who does not practice the children's religion. The Bryants were correct in noticing that in our society, the mother tends to be the religious nurturer. Such an arrangement might easily feel dissonant to both mother and children if the mother were not the one taking the lead in religious upbringing.

The Bryants' arrangement shows that in some cases, by addressing the potential pitfalls, parents can each follow their religious bent without causing their children identity confusion.

2. Raising the Child in One Religion, with the Other Parent Not Practicing His Own Religion A mixed family is blessed—at least in an identity-building sense—if the "out-parent" is not committed to his religion of birth and will help raise the children in his spouse's religion. We call this unconverted but supportive parent the "associate Jew" in a Jewish home or "associate Christian" in a Christian home.

Fifteen-year-old Bridget and seventeen-year-old Susan have been raised as Catholics. Their mother is a quietly devout Catholic, their father a minimally practicing Jew (occasional High Holidays and Passover seder) who enjoys Christmas more than the Jewish holidays. Their father doesn't believe in Jesus but accompanies the family to Mass and supports their Christian upbringing. The girls were baptized, had first communion and were confirmed. They each go to weekly religious instruction as well as weekly Mass. Although now in public school, each spent a few years in Catholic parochial schools. They spend part of every Christmas with their mother's parents, and every Easter vacation they visit their Jewish grandparents for a seder.

Both girls say they are comfortable with Jews but clearly identify as Catholics. Susan, intending no pun, calls herself a "loose Catholic." She participates in the services but, like her mother, reserves the right to make up her own mind on matters of doctrine. She has dated a number of Jewish boys. A high school senior at the time of our interview, she had applied to both Catholic colleges and predominantly Jewish colleges, and eventually chose a school that had been founded by Protestants. Bridget, the younger sister, says she feels entirely Catholic in religion but half-Jewish ethnically. She says the ethnic feeling comes from attending so many seders and bar mitzvahs of Jewish cousins. "It's interesting to learn about the Jewish religion, and it has made me more interested in other religions," she says. "But I know that I'm Catholic, and that's where I belong."

If the parent whose religion is being practiced in the home is committed and observant, if his partner is genuinely supportive, if the home is uniformly one-faith, the family can greatly increase the chances that the child will identify with the religion his parents teach.

A special issue comes up in these homes: what to do about observing the "associate" parent's holidays. Susan and Bridget's parents take a common approach, observing them at the grandparents' house. Many counselors and clergy recommend that approach as best for guarding the clarity of a child's identity. We saw no evidence that having holidays with grandparents interferes with religious identity as long as there is one clear, strong religious identification in the children's home and the grandparents respect the parents' religious choices.

3. *Nontraditional Identities* Sometimes, when both parents are agnostic or are looking for a religious compromise, they turn to a group that is not in the mainstream of either religion. The two such affiliations we will consider here are Unitarian-Universalism and Ethical Culture. Both groups have a generosity of spirit: They look for universal values in all religions and teach children to respect different world views.

The problem is that they seem to have limitations as identities for children. There are few Unitarians and Ethical Culturists overall, so a child can easily feel isolated. Their intellectual thrust can be difficult for small children to grasp. It can be hard for a child to explain to peers what a Unitarian or Ethical Culturist is or believes. Neither group has the deep roots in history, or the distinctive, coherent belief system which make either Judaism or Catholicism such a powerful identity base. The two groups also have only begun to develop distinct rituals, traditions, and symbols, which are important building blocks of a child's identity.

Does "Unitarian" or "Ethical Culture" suffice as an answer to "What are you?" Sometimes yes, sometimes no.

Trudy, the girl who defined herself as half-terrier, says: "I guess I identified when I was growing up as Unitarian. I went to Sunday school and everything like that . . . But I was always interested more in the history of the Jewish religion, and it's weird because I think I consider myself half Jewish and half something else. Not necessarily Christian."

The number of equivocal responses like Trudy's left us uncertain about the vigor of a Unitarian identity for a child. The same holds for Ethical Culture. That movement has only two dozen chapters and a few thousand members nationwide. The Ethical Culture professionals we spoke with acknowledged that, although children raised in the group seem to become responsible, ethical adults, the majority fall away from Ethical Culture membership.

A nontraditional identity easily resembles being a Democrat or a Republican. It may be what a child thinks or stands for, but is not necessarily who she *is*. If it's important to you to give your child a sturdy identity as well as a values base, you will have to work doubly hard at explaining this affiliation to your child and showing its importance to her and to you.

4. *Actively Doing Both* Some couples, for reasons intrinsic to their marriage, will choose to bring up children within both religions. For those parents, we have two major pieces of advice.

First, examine your hearts to be sure that, even if you don't believe important pieces of your partner's theology, you can fully support each other's religion. If you are competing—if each of you secretly or openly hopes the children will adopt your path—it will set up a serious loyalty dilemma for them.

Second, practice both religions actively. Join congregations and go regularly. (Choose liberal congregations that will accept your children's mixed background.) See that your children get some religious training. Celebrate holidays in your home. Every religion has a language for talking about the world. As with any language, it takes immersion, a bathing in the words of the language, to become fluent in it. Don't leave a child in the painful position of speaking only fragments of both religious languages so that no matter where she goes, she feels self-conscious and embarrassed.

And let them know they are free to explore both religions. Reassure them that regardless of what religious life-style they follow, they will always be part of your family and you will always love them. Point out that just as you and your partner live lovingly and respectfully with your differences, you will do the same if your children's path diverges from yours.

5. One Parent Converting to the Other's Religion In about a third of all intermarriages, one partner converts. It's obviously easier to have a one-religion home if one parent adopts the other's religion. As we state in Chapter 11 (Conversion), you should convert *only* if it meets your personal religious needs. However, if you feel attracted toward your partner's religion, it may help in your decision-making to consider the impact converting is likely to have on the strength of your children's religious identity.

In general, children of converts have a more solid religious identity than children of mixed marriages. Sociologist Egon Mayer, for example, found that the conversion of one parent to Judaism greatly increases the chance that the children will identify as Jews (84 percent, compared with 24 percent of mixed children).[5]

If you do convert, there are two additional things you should do to help give your children a healthy identity. First, be open about having been born in a different religion and having chosen the religion you converted to. We spoke with several people whose parents had deceived them about the facts of their birth. They found out and proceeded to dive into the newfound religion as if it were buried treasure.

Second, actively practice your new religion in your home and in the community of your choice. Your children will see you and themselves as Jewish, or Christian, only if you act that way.

As you go through the process of deciding on a religious identity for your children, make sure that you and your partner have fully expressed your religious needs. Too often it is the more forceful partner or the one who holds power in the marriage, and not necessarily the more religiously committed one, who prevails. Be clear whether your positions are based on stubborn pride and a desire to "win" or on real commitment, on fear of hurting your parents or on your own, adult beliefs. Resentments are likely to emerge if a decision isn't worked out fairly.

The partner whose religion is chosen needs to appreciate—and openly acknowledge—the loss felt by the out-parent. (Don't be surprised if both partners in a "Doing Both" home feel like out-parents because no religion has been clearly chosen.)

One of the great dangers is that a resentful out-parent will poison the religious identity chosen for the children. If your partner is undermining your attempts to transmit an identity, confront her. But in doing so, commit yourself to try to create a home style which your partner feels she can accept and support, even if she can't fully participate in it.

ADVICE: MAXIMIZING YOUR CHANCES

Identity-building is difficult in the best of circumstances. It seems a matter of calculated chance, not certainty. In our complex era, even children of single-religion homes, with two parents born in the same faith, may not follow in their parents' footsteps.[6] No matter what home style you choose, having parents from two different backgrounds makes identity-building innately more complicated for your children.

However, there are steps you can take to nurture the process. Here are some:

Affiliate with a Community That Shares Your Values Whether you are believers or secularists, try to find a like-minded group or community that gathers regularly and has youth activities. Be sure the place includes other intermarried families and is comfortable with them. Go there as a family. The community shows your children that others value your lifestyle. It gives them and you legitimacy. In addition, it gives them a certain security. They know there is a community of caring adults who will provide for them and their family if necessary. Have them participate in activities by which the members care for each other.

Make a Positive Statement of What Your Group Stands For If you are bringing up the children as Jews, stress the values and achievements of Jews rather than the persecutions they have endured. If you are a secularist, talk about your humanism—your belief in the importance of the individual, and in people's ability to think logically and improve conditions—rather than focusing on your nonbelief in God. If you are a Christian, talk not only about redemption from sin but about the Christian principle of selfless, forgiving love. A positive statement makes your choice of religious identity more attractive. It also gives your children a better way to explain their identity to peers.

Have Symbols, Stories, and Celebrations in Your Home Rituals and symbols are tangible focal points for the child. They can be as simple as a grace over an evening meal or as elaborate as a full-fledged holiday celebration. The rituals and objects become part of the child, safe and familiar. They help give an identity that has staying power. Secularist parents and groups can create customs to weave a sense of community and dramatize values. See Chapter 15 (Holiday and Home Style) for ideas. If you're not telling the children Bible stories, tell them about your heroes as a humanist, and the heroes of your movement.

Let the Neighborhood Reinforce Your Identity Choice Although it's important to live in a neighborhood with other mixed children, try to pick one where a sizable number of families share your religious orientation. For much of their lives, your children's playmates and peers at school will be a powerful influence on the way they identify.

Consider Converting the Child at Birth Conversion gives the child undeniable standing in one community from the outset. If you are planning to bring the child up in one of the two traditional religions, we recommend you look seriously at this step. (Conversion at birth may not resolve the identity issue for all of the child's life, says writer Susan Jacoby, a child of intermarriage who was baptized but considers herself a half-and-half. Still, she says, conversion brings a secure foundation from which to explore.)[7]

Help the Children be Religiously Literate Give them enough exposure to the religion or religions in which they are brought up that they become fluent in the worship and celebration. Make religious discussion and expression a regular part of your home life. Participate actively in religious institutions so your children are familiar with the rituals. Enroll them in a stimulating religious school and give them opportunities through youth activities to develop confidence among their religious peers.

Support Your Child's Explorations If she seems attracted toward a religion or lifestyle different from what you're teaching, draw her out about her reasons. Make sure she is aware of movements that have the qualities she's attracted to within the religion you've chosen (for instance, encourage her to find out about the mystical wing of your religion, even if you're not attracted to it). But if she makes clear that she does want to try a different religion, give her the educational tools—and the permission—to follow it. Make clear that she can choose a different religious direction and still be close to you.

Gird Your Children Help them build patience and a thick skin. Regardless of what identity you choose to impart, your children will always be a minority within a minority. This is particularly so if you choose one of the secularist groups whose ways are less familiar to the public at large. Help your children to understand why other children, and some adults, may be curious, ignorant, even spiteful. From the time they enter elementary school and religious school, ask about whether they've run into any problems (they probably won't say unless you ask). Help them to practice dignified, strong, appropriate responses. Try role-playing, with you playing the bad kids and hamming it up. Let them say to you all the things they wish they had said to their peer. It will give them confidence in their own ability to deal with potential hurts.

Affirm Their Cultural Duality Teach them about your ancestors on both sides. Let them know, and share celebrations with, the grandparents on both sides. Incorporate nonreligious traditions from the out-parent's culture. Teach them the foods, the crafts, the stories, and the cultural values each of you grew up with. Let them know that America is full of ethnically mixed people and that they are hardly alone in that.

Though this message of a dual ethnic or cultural heritage might appear to undercut religious identity, it can actually enhance it. Affirming the bicultural heritage will make both parents feel represented even when only one parent's religion is practiced; that will improve marital harmony and head off any subversion by the religious out-parent. And affirming the dual heritage will defuse the loyalty issue. The child need not worry that having one religious identity cuts him off from the other parent; he can be satisfied knowing that both his parents want him to feel culturally "both" while religiously "one."

Like the Bryants, make sure that each child has some special non-religious activity to share with the out-parent. These strategies can reassure your children that, even though they are being raised in one religion, they "belong" to both of you and that both of your heritages belong to them.

Communicate Your Agreement Whether your choice is religious or secular, your children are likely to be in good shape if they know that the two of you are working together on it. Even if they move away from your home style, you will know that you have provided them with a basis, a structure, a foundation.

CHOOSING A
FAMILY STYLE

15. HOLIDAYS AND HOME STYLE:

Beyond the December Dilemma

Holidays are religion and family at the gut level. Because they are filled with concrete symbols and rituals, holidays, more than any other aspects of family life, shape your children's religious identity.

Holidays can be the jewels of family life—an opportunity to rise out of your workaday routine and celebrate together, pass on values to your children, reaffirm connections with extended family, get a sense of tradition and continuity. They can bind the family together and provide precious memories. But instead, holidays are often the crucible, the most difficult test, for all your good resolutions about how you will live as an intermarried family. Because holidays are potentially so enriching to families, it's worth working through the heavy emotional issues to arrive at a holiday pattern that your family can really enjoy. The purpose of this chapter is to help you do so.

The Christmas tree triggers the first crisis in many intermarriages. The problem is that the tree is as laden with emotional meanings as it is with decorations. And it means very different things to the Christian and to the Jew.

For most Christians, the tree symbolizes the best of family times: special sweets, warm family gatherings, carols, whispered secrets, the excitement of giving and receiving gifts, the beauty of lights and special decorations, and the special appeal of the Christmas story itself: the baby

Jesus, glittering kings coming to a humble manger, angel choruses. In Chapter 7 (The Lifetime Trajectory), we spoke of the tenacity of Jewish identity for most Jews, intermarried or not. Christmas is one area where the gentile often matches this intensity. Even when the gentile has no faith and no feeling for the Christian religion, the Christmas tree has its own special hold, its own enduring magic.

For the Jew, the tree often carries an opposite set of feelings: anxiety, ambivalence, anger. Christmas, in the childhood of many Jews, was a time of feeling left out, envious, self-conscious, defensive, resentful. The Christmas tree, more than any other object, symbolizes the difficulties of maintaining one's Jewish identity in the face of the overwhelming pressure of the majority Christian culture. Having a tree, to many Jews, means abandoning the struggle to stay Jewish.

"I think it was probably instilled in me, this is not something you do as a Jew," said one man who has reluctantly assented to having a tree in his home. "I have done a lot of things that aren't Jewish in my life. One of which is marrying a gentile. And going to the Universalist church. And lots of things like that." But having a tree, he says, is a particularly potent taboo, a mark of disloyalty. "The Christmas tree must be one level down from the cross. It is so symbolic of everything Christian. [It feels as if] we have a cross in my house."

As his children have grown, this man's discomfort with the tree has increased, rather than decreased. He refuses to buy, carry, or decorate it.

If an intermarried couple doesn't celebrate Christmas, the gentile may have feelings of loss, of being cut off from family, and of losing the right to engage in one of the most precious parts of parenting. If the couple does celebrate Christmas, the Jew may feel not only guilty, but eclipsed—that he has become alienated from his extended family and that his children are losing any shred of attachment to their Jewish roots.

Because the husband and wife often have such potent feelings pulling them in opposite directions, December is truly the worst month for many mixed couples. As a result it gets most of the attention. Professionals working with intermarried couples even have a name for it: the December Dilemma. But we want to point out two other seasons of holiday stress: Passover-Easter and the Jewish High Holidays.

At Passover, the Christian partner may feel overwhelmed by the all-embracing Jewish family. At the same time, if the gentile partner is an active Christian, she may be hurt by her Jewish partner's insensitivity and ignorance of the spiritual importance of Easter. Jews in America can't help but be aware of Christmas. They give much less consideration to Easter. (Although Easter is far more important theologically to Christianity, Christmas has folk culture and commercial dimensions that give it much more impact on secular, non-Christian society.) If an intermarried couple has decided to bring their children up as Christians, Easter is likely to be a very uncomfortable season for the Jewish partner since it faces him with the central theological tenet on which Judaism and Christianity differ—the Resurrection. In addition, the Easter liturgy in some churches contains passages which may sound anti-Semitic to the Jew—passages in which the Jews are portrayed as urging the killing of Jesus.

The Jewish High Holidays present a different set of dilemmas. Many Christian partners can enjoy sharing in holidays such as Passover and Hanukkah where there is a vivid symbolism, a concrete historical event being celebrated, and not too much theology. But the High Holidays—Rosh Hashanah (the New Year) and Yom Kippur (the Day of Atonement)—are somber, austere, and prayer-centered. Instead of taking place in the home, they involve all-day sojourns in the synagogue. The service may contain a lot of Hebrew, which is a barrier to many non-Jewish partners. The holidays' repeated confessions of sin are the last thing that will appeal to a lapsed Christian. And the sense of in-turning can leave the gentile feeling like he's facing a circle of covered wagons, all facing inward, while he stands alone on the outside.

GETTING IN TOUCH

Before you can resolve any problems you have with the holidays, each of you must be able to explain to your partner what the holidays have meant to you. So, before going forward, let's go back, with the help of a few exercises. (The exercises are taken from or modeled on the workshops conducted by Esther Perel, and have been adapted and recast for purposes of this book. Perel is a psychothcrapist working with intermarried couples and families and a consultant on Ethnicity and Mental Health to the American Jewish Committee in New York.)

EXERCISE 1: APPROACHING THE TREE

Place a chair in the middle of the floor. Imagine that it is a Christmas tree. Walk slowly toward it, focusing on your mental image of the tree. As you walk, talk about your memories of Christmas trees. If you were brought up with a tree in your home, what decorations did you put on it? How did you feel when you looked at it or decorated it? If you had no tree in your home, where did you see Christmas trees? How did seeing them make you feel? Did this change as you grew older?

Stop about three feet away from the "tree." Then walk forward, with your hand extended, and imagine yourself putting a decoration on the "tree." How does this make you feel? How does it make you feel about the idea of having a tree in your own home? If you are Christian, do you feel a stab of nostalgia? If you are Jewish, is there a limit to how close you can come to the tree? Does it feel as if you're breaking a taboo if you put a decoration on it?

EXERCISE 2: THE HOLIDAY DINNER TABLE

Write a description of the following scene, or describe it aloud to your partner or couples group.

Picture yourself at a typical holiday dinner during your childhood. What holiday is it? Who is at the table? Where do your parents sit? Where do you sit? What foods are eaten? What typical remarks are made? What rituals are performed, or prayers said? What typical family actions go on (squabbles, tickling, etc.)? Do you have any special role to play? How about your siblings? How do you feel? If you could use one word to describe the meaning of that scene, what would the word be?

Remember back to the several days before the holiday feast. What preparations were made? What did each of your parents do? What did your siblings do? What was your role? Were there special rituals or typical treats? Was there one year which stands out in your mind? What happened that holiday? How did you feel?

EXERCISE 3: TRANSLATING FEELINGS INTO NEEDS

What religious holidays were celebrated in your home when you were a child? List them.

Write down the positive feelings you associate with your childhood holidays (such as warmth, security, connectedness to family, anticipation, pride, fun). In addition, write down any positive feelings that were lacking in your family that you wish you could experience during the holidays. Then list any negative feelings you associate with the holidays (such as exclusion, vulnerability, boredom, disappointment). In addition, write down any negative feelings that you are worried about generating by choosing an approach that is different from your family's.

These feelings are the basis for your needs list. When you plan your holiday celebrations, think about the feelings you want to generate in your spouse, extended family, and yourself. Visualize also the situations or feelings you hope to avoid.

Now write out a paragraph about the outcomes you hope to create for your children: What feelings do you hope the holiday celebrations will trigger in your children? What feelings do you want to avoid triggering?

Compare your lists with your spouses'. What needs, fears, and hopes do you have in common? Which are different?

As a minimum, your lists for yourself and your child ought to include: feeling safe, feeling happy, and feeling proud. If these items are not on your list, add them.

After reading the descriptions of traditional and nontraditional holiday celebrations that follow, use your needs list and the negotiating techniques of Chapter 8 to help you and your partner come up with an agreement on holidays in your home.

EXERCISE 4: REVIEWING YOUR COMPROMISES

If you and your partner have already celebrated holidays together, list any compromises you feel you have made concerning them. Beside each compromise, list the feelings you have about it. List the compromises your spouse has made, and what feelings you think he or she has about each one.

Share your lists with your partner. Was each of you aware of what the other considered to be compromises? Was each of you accurately perceiving the other's feelings? How do you feel about the balance? Has there been some kind of compensation for or appreciation of the compromises made? Is the balance one that you both feel happy with?

FOUR APPROACHES TO THE HOLIDAYS

In deciding how you and your partner want to handle the holidays, it helps to consider four basic approaches. They parallel the overall lifestyle approaches outlined in Chapter 14, Children's Identity. We call them "traditional," "minimal," "actively doing both," and "nontraditional."

1. The Traditional Approach is to choose the holidays of one religion and celebrate them in a full-bodied way. Couples who follow this approach enjoy the folk customs of their chosen religion, and also attend a church or synagogue and talk with their children about the ethical teachings, and religious concepts associated with the holiday. Most would try to make the religion meaningful in their home not just at holidays, but year round.

If you choose this approach, don't ignore the holidays with which the other parent grew up. This is especially important if the other parent is what we call an "out-parent" (one who has not converted and is either practicing no religion or a religion different from the rest of the family). Let the children be familiar with the out-parent's holidays, but do it in a way that makes clear they're visiting on his turf: It's not their holiday.

For example, you can take Jewish children to their Christian grandparents' for Christmas, or accept a tree-decorating invitation from Christian friends. You will need to explain to the children that although this is not their holiday, they can enjoy sharing it with others. Similarly, you can occasionally invite one of the children's non-Jewish friends or cousins to share part of your holiday.

Even if you only practice one set of holidays in the home, both parents should be knowledgeable enough to answer questions about both sets of holidays.

If you choose the traditional approach, it is important to be sensitive to the emotional needs of the out-parent. If a holiday conflict (such as Easter and Passover falling at the same time) prevents you from spending the out-parent's holiday with his family, try to spend the weekend before the holiday with that set of grandparents. If Hanukkah and Christmas fall at the same time, pack up your menorah, take it to the Christian grandparents' house (if they're comfortable with this) and enjoy their tree. Make sure that a good proportion of nonreligious family times, such as Thanksgiving and Fourth of July, are also spent with these grandparents. If death or distance makes it impossible to spend holidays with grandparents, find another relative or friend to visit with.

During the holiday season, be sure that the out-parent has special times with the children. For example, he could take them shopping to buy gifts for relatives. He could take holiday foods or crafts from his own tradition and show the children how to adapt them to the holiday they do celebrate. For example, one mother who as a child had enjoyed making "stained-glass" Christmas cards out of colored tissue paper showed her children how to use the same techniques to make beautiful translucent paper menorahs to decorate the windows at Hanukkah. Then she offered her skills to the Jewish Sunday school and taught the craft to her child's class.

If you are the out-parent, make a conscious effort to enjoy the mood of your partner's holiday even if you don't believe in the theology. Permit yourself to get into the swing of the cultural aspects of the holiday, the gift-giving, baking, and crafts. You don't betray any theological precepts by doing so; you merely set an example of good cheer and open-mindedness for your child. Think about the more general and universal themes associated with the holiday and see if you can apply them to your own life. In the Appendix, we give examples of themes for each holiday. If you are flexible enough to reach toward your partner's holiday in these ways, you are likely to find you can make the holiday more personally meaningful and less alienating without violating your own principles.

We think that people who say they are raising their children Jewish, but have a tree and all celebrate Christmas, are in effect not raising them in one religion. In America, the tree is such a potent symbol that it alone introduces the second religion into the home. If you have a tree, you have as much Christianity in your home as many Christian families.

It may be possible to have a tree in a Jewish home if, like the Bryants (described in Chapter 14 on Children's Identity), you make clear that the tree is for one parent and doesn't belong to the children or the other parent. If you are raising your children Jewish but want to keep a tree for the gentile parent's sake, have a small tree and keep it up for as brief a time as possible given the gentile partner's needs. Celebrate Hanukkah enthusiastically. And have your Jewish life throughout the year be vibrant enough to outshine Christmas's once-a-year dazzle.

As said in the Children's Identity chapter, we think the traditional single-religion approach is best for giving children a clear group identity. But in choosing a holiday policy, you have to consider the emotional and spiritual needs of all members of the family. You may decide that because of both partners' emotional attachments to their holiday celebrations, or for other reasons, the single-religion approach is not the best for your family. If so, read on.

2. The Minimalist Approach is to celebrate only the major holidays, and only in a cultural fashion. A minimalist family might have a Christmas tree with presents, a Hanukkah menorah with presents, and an Easter basket, and might have a large Passover meal with family, but wouldn't talk about the religious meanings of the holidays. Many families will choose this path because it seems to minimize conflict or because it fits with their own temperaments and attitudes toward religion. The risk, though, is that children may feel a lack of group belonging, an emptiness of spiritual meaning, or conflicting identity tugs.

If you feel most comfortable with a minimalist approach, try to make the holidays as rich as possible for your children. Think of ways to talk about the ethical and emotional teachings of the holidays without getting into the theological realm. Explore folk customs and adapt them to your family's needs. Try to build your own nontraditional holiday celebrations. In this way you can abide by your own principles without sacrificing the color, drama, and meaning that the religious holidays offer.

3. Actively Doing Both means fully celebrating both sets of holidays: teaching the religious meanings, and engaging in the folk customs. This approach may cause identity confusion and conflicting loyalties, but it does give the child a richer upbringing than the minimalist approach.

If you choose either the minimalist or the "actively doing both" approach, we recommend that in addition to celebrating at home and with grandparents, you organize a group of like-minded families and celebrate holidays together. This gives your children a sense of being part of a bicultural community.

4. Nontraditional Approaches include secularist holiday celebrations, innovative forms, and celebrations drawn from other spiritual traditions, such as the Native American. Again, try to find a community, or organize a small group of families, to share these celebrations with you. Later in the chapter, we give more details on how to develop nontraditional celebrations.

MAKING MODIFICATIONS FROM A TRADITIONAL BASE

Whatever approach you choose, you will benefit by understanding the traditional Jewish and Christian holidays and home style. Be sure to use the descriptions of traditional holiday, community, and daily home observance in the Appendix as a basis for selecting and modifying your own approach. In the Notes and Recommended Reading, you will find books that give full accounts of holiday observances and crafts.

As you proceed, think of each holiday as having four intertwined components: the *tradition* (historical, theological or storytelling aspects—how the holiday connects with the central story or teachings of the religion); the *fun,* or *festival* aspects (the customs, foods, crafts, and relationships with extended family); the *universal themes,* having to do with ethics and nature; and the *emotional or spiritual themes.*

Even if you and your partner are religious skeptics, you will probably not find it hard to enjoy the festive aspects of the holidays. With a little thought, you can also use the other three elements in your own way to deepen the experience for yourself and your children. You can substitute your own interpretations for the traditional religious explanations of the holiday. You can use the holiday as a time to think and talk about certain universal ethical and natural themes. Even if you don't believe in God, you can meditate on the emotional themes associated with the holiday and how to apply them in your own life. For example, at Christmas, you could give free rein to and enjoy the loving and giving parts of yourself. You and your family could do community service— volunteering in a soup kitchen or hospital on Christmas Day, which would not only help the recipients of your work but would free some more religious people to be with their families or go to church. At Passover, you could cast off some enslaving habit or self-defeating way of thinking. You could get involved in a political action project aiding people struggling for freedom in the Third World. Doing such things together can help bond the family and bridge the gap between a religious and a nonreligious partner.

In addition to the actual holiday observances, the major holidays of each religion (Christmas, Easter, Passover, and the Jewish High Holidays) have prescribed preparation periods. These preparations build anticipation and can greatly increase the meaningfulness of the holiday. Check the Appendix for ideas.

If you have not done much in the way of holiday or home observance, you needn't jump in all at once. Experiment. Play with the ideas. Try adding one or two new elements to your holiday celebrations each year. Take a similarly gradual approach to any new daily or weekly home observances.

As you make your decisions, keep in mind that holidays play very different roles in the Jewish and Christian religions. Most Christian families—particularly "low-church" Protestant ones—celebrate, at most, two religious holidays: Christmas and Easter, while Judaism is built on a year-round cycle of holidays.

For the observant Christian, the day-to-day life-style is at least as important as the holidays. What is demanded of him is faith, as expressed through individual prayer and action and through participation in the church community. For the religious Jew, the holidays are at the core of the religion. Judaism is a way of life, a way that depends for its rhythms on the holidays. The committed Orthodox Jew, in fact, believes he is commanded by God to celebrate the holidays. As Rabbi Samson Raphael Hirsch, a German-Jewish scholar, said, "The catechism of the Jew is his calendar."[1]

The most important holiday in the Jewish calendar occurs every week: the Sabbath. The most important commandment of the Sabbath is to relax. You usher it in with blessings over lighted candles, bread and wine, and you make it a special, sweet, out-of-the-ordinary day.

The Jewish year also defines itself by seasons and by history. The year begins in the early spring with Passover, celebrating through story, song, and a sumptuous dinner the most important event in the history of the Jewish people: the liberation of the people from slavery in Egypt. Next comes a holiday of early summer, Shavuos, celebrating the second key event: the giving of the law at Mount Sinai. In the deadening heat of midsummer comes a holiday of mourning, Tisha B'Av, remembering the destruction of the Temple in Jerusalem, the exile of the Jews from Israel and the sufferings that have befallen them in many years since. As the summer heat dissipates into fall, Jews gather into their synagogues for the High Holidays: Rosh Hashanah (the New Year) and Yom Kippur (the Day of Atonement). The somber mood is dissipated by the joyous fall harvest festival, Sukkos, with its leafy rustic shelters decorated with fall produce. Sukkos ends, as autumn begins in earnest, with the joyfully abandoned dancing of Simchas Torah (Rejoicing in the Law), when the annual cycle of the Torah readings begins again with the creation story of Genesis. In cold, dark December, Judaism, like Christianity, has a festival of light, Hanukkah, which coincides with the winter solstice. Historically, the festival celebrates the victory of the Maccabees, in the second century before the Common or Christian Era, when the Jews reasserted their right to political and religious independence, throwing off a tyrannical ruler and establishing their own commonwealth. Finally, as winter nears its end, Jews have a zany carnival holiday, Purim.[2]

Christian holidays also have their roots in the seasons. But on a historical level, the most important holidays mark events in the life of Jesus, rather than of Christianity as a movement. The low-church denominations, such as the Baptists, generally celebrate only Christmas and Easter. The liturgical or high-church denominations, including the Catholic, Eastern Orthodox, Episcopalian, Lutheran, and some Presbyterian churches, observe a year-round cycle. However, the focus, except for Christmas, is far more on church activities than on home celebrations. The Christian year is divided into six months of festival time and six months of "ordinary time." The year begins at the end of November with Advent, four weeks of joyous preparation for Christmas. Christmas, on December 25, which celebrates the birth of Jesus, is for most Christians the pinnacle of the year, a holiday of gift-giving, warmth, and light at the darkest time of the year. Christians who are part of the renewal movement or attached to the Eastern church or one of the more traditional ethnic groups would celebrate Christmas as a twelve-day holiday, ending January 6 with the feast of the Epiphany, the celebration of the Wise Men's coming to visit the baby Jesus in the manger. The Sunday after

Epiphany celebrates Jesus' baptism as a young man by John the Baptist. Ash Wednesday, in February, begins a more solemn preparation period: Lent, the forty days leading up to Easter in the early spring. Easter itself is a week-long celebration. Holy Week begins with Palm Sunday, includes the somber Good Friday (commemorating Jesus' crucifixion and death) and climaxes with Easter, the celebration of Jesus' Resurrection. Fifty days after Easter comes Pentecost, which marks the time when Jesus' apostles, newly inspired, began to establish the church and to seek converts. The sense of a year-long cycle is more vivid in the liturgical churches, where the seasons are marked by changes in the colors of the priests' vestments, altar hangings, and banners: blue (the color of hope) for Advent, white for the festivals marking events in the life of Jesus, purple (the color of mourning) for Lent, red (for the blood of the martyrs) for festivals marking events in the life of the church, and green for the ordinary half of the church year, the summer and fall. During this "green time," the church reviews the life of Jesus and His teachings.

The Catholic calendar is also studded with saints' days. Some people who had a strongly Catholic upbringing will identify seasons and events by the saint's day occurring at that time. The feast day of their patron saint may be as important as their birthday. For example, we talked to one couple, a left-wing Jewish man and a lapsed Catholic woman, who chose their wedding date for an odd conjunction of reasons. The date was meaningful to her because it was her saint's day. It was congenial to him because it was the anniversary of the Cuban revolution.

You can't celebrate the holidays fully without a sense of the wealth of ideas, ideals, and customs which give them their richness (see the Appendix for these). A special tip: Look to the ethnic cultures for ideas, especially to the East European and Mediterranean cultures of both Jews and Christians. One important reason for holidays is to open ourselves to joy, fear, anticipation, and awe—all the human emotions. The ethnic cultures, being closer to the pagan nature festivals in which these holidays are rooted, can teach you a lot about how to really celebrate.

NONTRADITIONAL OPTIONS

1. Secular Approaches The Ethical Culture Society is strictly neutral on the question of God's existence. Therefore, its members do not display religious symbols in their meeting places. They do have seasonal celebrations, however, to enrich their community and to acknowledge that celebration is a natural human impulse. Diane Gross, director of religious education for the Ethical Culture Society of Bergen County, New

Jersey, says the group has a winter solstice festival that teaches that humans "in the coldest and darkest times of the year had a tradition of getting together with one another for warmth and comfort."

The Ethical Culture Society tries to stress the ethical dimension that might be associated with each of its holidays. During the winter solstice festival, they have a winter clothing drive. During the Thanksgiving season, they participate in the Oxfam Fast for World Harvest, giving up junk food and desserts, and sending the money saved to Oxfam. They break the fast with a simple, light dinner. Gross's family lights a candle and has broth and rice, which she reminds her children is "a luxurious meal by Third World standards."

The Jewish Folkshul movement seeks to give children a Jewish identity but not a God-oriented theology. Its members celebrate Jewish holidays, stressing the historical and ethical dimensions. Their "secular *Haggadahs*" for Passover emphasize the theme of freedom, tracing it from the days of the Hebrews in ancient Egypt to the struggle of a variety of peoples all over the world today.

2. Creative Alternatives Other intermarried couples, rather than joining a nontraditional movement, have simply developed creative holiday celebrations for their own family. One advantage of customs that you invent together: They allow both parents to have equal ownership of the religious atmosphere of the home. Even in a home following one religion, innovative customs give the out-parent more chance to shape and participate in the celebration. A disadvantage: Invented celebrations won't help your children to develop a religious identity, to feel connected to a larger culture. Still, custom-made rituals and celebrations perform the important functions of giving your life an aesthetic dimension and of expressing your family's value system.

Sam Mackintosh, founder of *Festivals* magazine, says families ought to find something to celebrate every day of the year. "Acknowledge just about anything that's available from any tradition," he says. "They're all variations on the same theme."

The Mackintosh family keeps a Supper Book in which they record every type of anniversary: the day the eldest boy got a bike, the day they moved into their house, the day the British marched down a street of their town, saints' days, anniversaries of deaths of relatives (similar to the Jewish custom of remembering a person on the anniversary of his death, rather than on his birthday). Before dinner every evening, they read from the book what is special about the coming day. Practices like this deepen your awareness, your sense of connection with the larger universe, says Mackintosh. "You have a history, a past, and therefore a future. You know where you've come from, and therefore you have a sense of where you are going. It locates you in the whole cosmic perspective."

The calendar, in short, gives you both a religious and a personal identity. Your holidays, celebrated year by year, become part of your personal and family history.

There are three key rules to remember about a holiday, whether you create it yourself or draw from some religious tradition. First, it should be fun. Second, it should involve food—some special kind of food. (The traditional Jewish and Christian holidays all have associated ethnic foods. If you're celebrating a personal holiday, such as the day your child reads her first book, let her choose her favorite meal or dessert for the day.) Third, the holiday needs a special environment. In some way make your home reflect the holiday. Decorate the house to reflect the seasonal meanings of the major Jewish or Christian holidays. For a winter holiday, try making arrangements of bare branches, dried herbs and citrus rinds.[3]

Rather than give you a list of premixed innovative customs, we'll give you strategies and examples. Think of them as the ingredients on your shelves: spices and fillings with which to whip up your own concoctions.

Modify the Traditional Celebration Use story, drama, song, or original readings to make the celebration your own. Susan Lieberman gives a number of examples in her book, *Let's Celebrate: Creating New Family Traditions.*[4] For example, one family, instead of using the *Haggadah* to tell the Passover story, put on their own play. Another supplemented its Christmas celebration with a birthday cake for Jesus, recalling the religious meaning of the holiday in a "non-churchy" way.

Lieberman's own family, which had become sick of the gift-getting emphasis of December, developed a "Hanukkah plan" for what they would do for the eight days of the holiday. Concocted in consultation with their children, the plan went like this:

> First night: "Big Gift Night" (parents give to children)
> Second night: "Mommy Night" (children give to mother)
> Third night: "Daddy Night" (children give to father)
> Fourth night: "Poem Night" (everyone recites an original poem)
> Fifth night: "Small Gift Night" (parents give to children)
> Sixth night: "Gift of Self Night" (non-monetary gift from each person to another or to the entire family)

Seventh Night: "Giving Night" (everyone gives a gift to a charity of his choosing, with the children's gifts matched by the parents)
Eighth night: "Word Night" (a game in which each person tries to stump the others with difficult words)[5]

Find Commonalities in the Jewish and Christian Celebrations Make a year-round family volunteer service schedule based on both the Jewish and Christian calendars. Talk about the values symbolized by each holiday and try to plan volunteer work to fulfill those values.

Emphasize the common historical roots. After your Passover seder, you might read about Jesus' Last Supper and how Jesus and Christianity reinterpreted the meaning of the seder. Or if you celebrate Easter, on Holy Thursday, you could use a Jewish *Haggadah* to retell the story of the Exodus from Egypt as Jews throughout ancient Israel were doing on the night Jesus and His disciples held the Last Supper.

Seek the Universal Impulses Which Underlie the Holidays Emphasize the seasonal more than the theological or historical aspects of the traditions. At Christmas, decorate a living tree outdoors with pine cones and bits of suet and bread for the birds. In December, talk about bringing light into darkness and even develop a light-into-darkness ritual which involves neither a menorah nor a Christmas tree, but some different source of light. Try building your own ritual around the spiritual meanings suggested by the seasonal pagan customs. At Purim, you could make masks expressing the "disguises" you wear in everyday life, then tear up the masks you want to discard.[6]

Look for Inspiration in Other Cultures Try reading about and adapting rituals from Native American, Celtic, or other nature-based traditions. The Catholic-oriented magazine *Festivals* has a series of stories and articles about Native American legends and practices that go with the seasons.[7]

Create Traditions Based on Your Family History One Holocaust survivor, for instance, held a family party on the anniversary of his liberation from Auschwitz. He sat his children on his lap and told them stories of the camp so that they would learn about it and never forget, and so they would learn about the heroism and strength of people he remembered, not only about the destruction. Then they had a special meal with prayers to thank God they now lived in a land of freedom and tolerance.

One family, described in Susan Lieberman's *Let's Celebrate,* had a "family cup." They asked a potter friend to make a special goblet, inscribed "The Kunkels Celebrate Life." It was passed from hand to hand to toast Kunkel family events such as birthdays, the first job, or the visit of a special friend.

One couple's holiday compromise illustrates several of the ideas we've been talking about. Burt is a union organizer who, like his immigrant Jewish parents, is a socialist and militant atheist. His wife, Vicki, an activist in reform politics, is the daughter of a minister. Although she became an agnostic as an adult, she needed a sense of ceremony and ritual in her life, and she wanted the children to have some framework of tradition. But Burt was adamantly opposed to religious ritual. Eventually, Vicki developed a way of celebrating holidays that was compatible with Burt's values and his anti-institutional reflexes.

They developed a ritual of holiday dinner discussions on ethical values. One Thanksgiving, for example, Vicki prepared a reading about the Indians. She talked about how this holiday was not really for the Indians because the Indians, unlike the Puritans and present-day Americans, were not really separate from nature in their daily life. Another year they talked about heroes. Everyone picked a hero and the family told stories or sang songs about them.

At Christmas, they talked about themes such as the struggle between good and evil, light and dark. Vicki's parents prepared a reading from World War II about hope in the face of Hitlerism. Vicki gave a reading about "putting Herod back into Christmas," saying that if you only talk about little babies and sweetness and light, you rob the holiday of a lot of its meaning. Burt gave a reading from Yevtushenko about positive and negative trends in the Soviet Union.

The most surprisingly effective ceremony has been a simple ritual: They light candles every night at dinner, then have each person recall a highlight of his or her day.

Vicki hastens to explain, "It's not religious."

But the candle-lighting creates a different atmosphere. Says Burt: "It's a way to avoid dinner conversations being mostly grumbling. It's a departure for conversation."

Ten years ago, he says, this simple ritual might have threatened him. Now he thinks it adds a great deal to their family life.

DECISION-MAKING

After discussing the options in this chapter and the holiday descriptions in the Appendix, sit down with your partner (and your children if they're old enough) and write out a tentative description of your holiday and home style: a blueprint for the year. Describe both everyday rituals and holiday celebrations, one by one. Specify what holidays you will spend in your own home and when you will go visiting.

Don't neglect the daily customs. Grace at meals, Sabbath blessings, and bedtime reflections are wonderful teaching times as well as sacred family moments. If you want to keep the traditional holidays, consider innovating with daily customs. Should you find yourselves disagreeing over the holidays, see if balance can be restored by letting one parent develop some daily customs that don't conflict with the main religious message of the household.

If you are celebrating the holidays of only one religion, consider reading your children books about the holidays, history, and ideas of the second parent's religion, so they will be literate about that religion even though it isn't their home base. Libraries and bookstores can introduce you to a variety of well-written children's books that tell the stories of each religion without being insensitive to the other. Reading with children is also a good way to plug gaps in your own knowledge about the religions. (Both parents should read about both sets of holidays, to be sure you don't fall into a subtle competition where the out-parent lobbies for his holidays through books.)

What details have to be attended to for your agreement to be successful? Make a list. Set dates for doing what needs to be done to put your plan into action. Decide who will be responsible for what and write it down.

Find a family whose pattern resembles the one you're considering. Spend some time talking and celebrating with them.

As you implement your plan, keep these principles in mind:

Make Your Family Policy Clear Be sure the children understand it. Let them know what is expected of them. Accept their feedback. Explain the policy to parents and in-laws. Let them know the limits or boundaries and expectations. Be specific. If you want them to give your children presents on Hanukkah rather than Christmas, and to wrap them in Hanukkah paper, say so explicitly. If you want your children to think of Christmas as being about the birth of Jesus, not about Santa Claus (this is something many believing Christians feel strongly about), tell your in-laws you'd rather they not emphasize Santa.

Educate and Involve Your Families Give them a calendar. Before and during each holiday, tell them about your plans and activities. If you celebrate Hanukkah and your parents celebrate Christmas, invite them to bring their favorite Christmas cookie to your Hanukkah celebration, but give them Hanukkah cookie cutters to shape the dough. If you celebrate Christmas, take your Jewish in-laws a box of your most delicious Christmas cookies (choose neutral shapes), invite them for a nonreligious dinner on Christmas Day, and be sure that, without pressuring, you've offered them a chance to participate in such holiday activities as tree-trimming, gift-giving, or watching their grandchildren perform in a play or pageant. (At the same time, show respect for their values by sending holiday cards, not only at Hanukkah, which occurs near Christmas, in your celebratory season, but at Rosh Hashanah, the fall New Year, which is a more important holiday for them. *Don't* send Jewish in-laws a Christmas card.)

Be Flexible Don't get frozen into roles. If you are the tentative parent, take on more responsibility as you grow more knowledgeable and more comfortable with the home style. And don't let yourself get stuck on a style that isn't working for you. Set a date for evaluation, about a month after each set of holidays. Be prepared to revise your arrangement, particularly if it triggers strong feelings of loss or betrayal in either of you.

Affirm What You Do Include special thanks for your strengths as a family. Thank your partner directly, both alone and in the presence of your children and extended family. If family members have made contributions from their different heritages, appreciate that.

It's not easy to struggle through the loaded emotions to a home style that's right for your family. But it's worth it. Holidays and family customs help you weave poetry into your lives.

16. RITES OF PASSAGE:

Birth and Beyond

Many mixed couples, when they decide to marry, put off or slide past the decision about what religion to choose for their children. They avoid the topic because of the potential for conflict. Even when they learn the woman is pregnant, many couples put off the discussion until the child is born.

Regrettably, this means that those couples—faced with the time crunch of an infant baptism or a *bris* (ritual circumcision)—will be making a major decision at the moment when they are least able to do so: the first week of the baby's life. That's when emotions are running wild, friends and relatives may be pouring in, the families are making their feelings known, the couple is facing a major life change, and both partners are exhausted. The potential for conflict and hurt is far greater than if the decision had been made earlier.

Some couples manage to fudge the decision at the time of the baby's birth and are pushed to make a decision at another inopportune time years later. They find themselves talking about whether to have a bar mitzvah or a confirmation at a moment when the entire family again is facing a major life change. A new person—a teenager—is entering the household to replace the child they thought they knew.

*   *   *

To see how these ceremonies can take on a dire urgency, consider the experience of Marv and Stacy. During Stacy's pregnancy they hadn't talked much about religion. It didn't seem necessary. Both were agnostics. Except for funerals and weddings, Stacy hadn't been back to Catholic church in years. But as the birth approached Marv began to go to synagogue again. It was his second marriage and, now in middle age, he found himself, for reasons he didn't fully understand, turning back toward Judaism.

The baby was a boy. Marv began making inquiries about having a *bris*. The rabbi of his Conservative synagogue tried to dissuade him. A *bris* wouldn't be legitimate, he said, because the boy's mother wasn't Jewish. The rabbi was citing Jewish tradition, which holds that a person is Jewish only if his mother is Jewish or if he is properly converted. Marv continued making inquiries and found a *mohel* (ritual circumcizer) who was willing to perform the circumcision but would note on the certificate that the *bris* would be valid only if the boy was later converted through immersion in a *mikvah* (ritual bath).

Meanwhile, pressure was coming from Marv's family about what to name the baby. Marv's mother insisted that he have the same name as his deceased grandfather, and that it must be the first name. Stacy's hackles rose: "It felt like the Jewish family was taking over." She and Marv eventually agreed on a name (Eugene, after the socialist hero Eugene Debs, with the grandfather's name used as the baby's Hebrew name rather than his English name).

The decision about the *bris* had to be made quickly so the ceremony could be held on the eighth day as required by Jewish law. Stacy agreed to have it. But she made up her mind that the boy would have a christening as well. Not because she believed in it, but for her parents' sake. If she were going to bend over backward to meet Marv's mother's needs, she could also do something for her own parents.

What with all the family pressures they were feeling, Stacy and Marv weren't communicating particularly well. Stacy thought it was perfectly logical to have both ceremonies. Since they hadn't decided how they would bring up the boy, she said, they should expose him to both religions. "But I *had* made a decision," Marv says. It was clear to him that he wanted to bring the boy up as a Jew and only as a Jew. He had very negative feelings about the christening and refused to go. But "I allowed it to happen."

The *bris* was held in their home. Stacy's father, a devout Catholic, didn't come. "I didn't even think about inviting him," she says. But her mother and sister did. The christening was later held at Stacy's father's church. None of Marv's family came. Stacy's mother was insulted since she had come to the *bris*.

It was nice to have her family at the christening, acting as god-parents to her son. But midway through the church ceremony, Stacy began to regret that she'd gone through with it. As she listened to the words, she thought, "I don't believe any of this. I cannot raise him as a Catholic." Even though she felt her parents knew she would not raise the boy as a Catholic, she thought the ceremony "raised false ex-pectations."

Marv and Stacy's turmoil and slapdash decision-making are not un-usual. Many mixed couples get stuck in either-or thinking, feeling des-perately caught between the two traditions and families, and they fight for one rite or the other even though they don't feel wholehearted about either. The tensions spoil what should be a true celebration.

A rite of passage is a very special kind of celebration. By giving you a moment elevated above the ordinary, it is supposed to help you make the transition to a new stage of life. In this chapter we offer ways to free up your thinking so you can have meaningful ceremonies for these change points in your family's life. First we will consider the birth ceremonies, then adolescent rites of passage. After describing the tradi-tional ceremonies and some innovative forms, we'll suggest ways to tai-lor an event to your circumstances.

I. BIRTH CEREMONIES

Every rite of passage has three elements: a separation from what went before, a transition, and an incorporation into the new status.[1]

In a birth ritual, the child is being separated from his previous unborn state. This element of the ceremony is primarily for the par-ents—to help them make the transition to seeing the child no longer as an extension of the mother's body, a hidden, satellite being, but as a new individual.

The child is also symbolically, and usually publicly, incorporated into the community. This welcome is preceded by a separation. The child is separated, set apart (often by a special sign) from all other com-munities, tribes, or religions.

There is a third factor in the birth ceremony: At least at the birth of the first child, it marks a change in the state of the new parents. Even more than the wedding, it marks the change in their status from adoles-cence to adulthood.

These elements are present in both the Christian baptism and the Jewish *bris* (for boys) or baby-naming (for girls).

Baptism Roman Catholics, Eastern Orthodox, Episcopalians, Lutherans, Methodists, and many other Christian denominations have ceremonies of infant baptism. Other denominations, such as Baptists and Disciples of Christ, baptize only when a child is considered to have come to an age of reasoned thinking, able to make a statement of faith, and a personal commitment.

Although baptism literally means dipping, infants are usually baptized either by sprinkling or by having water poured on their heads. Catholic infants may be immersed in the baptismal font. Often the child is dressed in a white "christening gown." The dipping itself performs the function of separating the child from what came before: in Christian belief, from original sin. Just as important is incorporation—bringing the child into the community. In all branches practicing infant baptism, this is accomplished by the parents' pledge to bring the child up in the faith and by the congregation's promise to nurture the child. Although the ceremony can take place in the home, it is generally held in the church to highlight this idea of incorporation.

Many Christians believe baptism is necessary for salvation. However, all branches of Christianity agree that baptism by itself is no guarantee of salvation; the child also must be brought up in the faith and adhere to it.

If you are Catholic, you might have been raised believing that babies who die without baptism are forever cut off from heaven. This does not mean they are condemned to hell; they are in limbo, "an eternal state of purely natural happiness" which is perfectly satisfactory to them since they don't know any better, but which falls short of the fullness of being in God's presence in heaven.[2] Although that is the prevailing belief, there is no Church doctrine on the matter. Especially since Vatican II, there is a widespread view among priests and other believing Catholics that God wants all humans to be saved and that He has His own ways of bringing unbaptized children to Him.

Bris The rite of consecration for a Jewish baby boy is called a *bris* or *b'rit milah*. The term means "covenant of circumcision." The main symbolic act of the ceremony is the circumcision, or the cutting away of the foreskin of the penis. This rite is among the oldest elements of Judaism still in practice. Circumcision marks the male indelibly as a member of the Jewish people.

According to the Bible, any Jew who does not circumcise his son will be "cut off from his people." Thus, the *bris* has a twofold significance: The son formally becomes part of the Jewish people, and the parent demonstrates his commitment to the Jewish covenant with God. Circumcision on the eighth day is considered so important that nothing must interfere except illness of the baby. Even if the eighth day occurs on the Sabbath (when other kinds of cutting are forbidden) or on Yom Kippur (the Day of Atonement, the holiest Jewish day), the ceremony must proceed.

The ritual circumcision is performed by a *mohel,* who has been trained in the medical and religious aspects of circumcision.[3] The *bris* is a public commitment and is intended to be performed before family and friends. It is also a family ceremony that generally takes place in the home and is followed by a feast (a buffet, in our day).

Traditionally, at the start of the ceremony the *mohel* places the child briefly in a chair which has been designated as the chair of Elijah. (The prophet Elijah, who will announce the coming of the Messiah, is said to attend all *bris* ceremonies.) The *mohel* hands the child to the father, who hands him to the *sandek* (a Jewish godfather). The circumcision follows. In our day, the penis is numbed with a topical anesthetic.[4] After the *mohel* cuts off the foreskin, the father (or the *sandek* if the father is gentile) recites a traditional blessing. All the people present bless the child in a loud voice, wishing him the three elements of a happy and complete Jewish life: "Just as he has entered into the covenant, so may he enter into [the study of] Torah, marriage, and [the performance of] good deeds." The baby is given a wad of wine-soaked cotton to suck. The foreskin is placed in a box containing sand or earth.

The *mohel* then takes a cup of wine, blesses it, and announces the baby's name in Hebrew and English. It is customary for the father to whisper the baby's name to the *mohel,* since no one is supposed to know the name until the *mohel* announces it. Everyone shouts "Mazel Tov" (congratulations, or literally good luck). The *mohel* signs a Hebrew certificate which is proof that the *bris* was in accordance with Jewish law.[5]

Jewish Baby-Naming The naming ceremony for a girl is much less elaborate. Her father is called to stand beside the Torah in the synagogue on the Sabbath following her birth, and she is blessed with a wish that she grow up to live the three elements of a full Jewish life: Torah, marriage, and good deeds. In a liberal synagogue, both parents are called to the Torah.

In our day, non-Orthodox Jews have tried to develop *b'rit* ceremonies for girls that have the power and significance of the ceremony for boys. A variety of ceremonies have been developed, but so far, none match the impact of the *b'rit milah*.

The Mark of the Law Circumcision is seen so strongly as a basic mark of being Jewish that nearly every Jewish parent will want to have a son circumcised even if he does not wish to have the *bris* ceremony. But note that even if a boy is not circumcised, he is still considered Jewish if born to a Jewish mother. That is automatic under Jewish law. For a boy born to a Jewish father and a non-Jewish mother, circumcision is necessary for his Jewish status, but it is only one of two steps that traditional Jews require. The other is immersion in a *mikvah*. A girl born to a gentile mother would only have to be immersed in the ritual bath to be considered Jewish. (Some Jewish authorities would say this step should not be taken until the child is old enough to understand; others would say it should be done in infancy so the child doesn't grow up with a confused identity.) We think if you both have agreed to raise the child as a Jew, immersion should be done in infancy.[6]

Reform Judaism considers a child Jewish if either parent is Jewish and the child receives a Jewish education and home life. Typically, a child of either sex is given only a simple naming ceremony in the synagogue. (A boy will generally be given a hospital circumcision.) No immersion in a *mikvah* is required for children of a gentile mother. However, it is unlikely that a Reform rabbi would be willing to let a boy have a bar mitzvah if he knew the youngster was uncircumcised.

If you decide on a conventional birth ceremony in either religion, be sure that both of you read over the ceremony well in advance and can agree to the commitments you are making.

EXPLORING: BEYOND THE USUAL

Perhaps both of you are comfortable having a conventional religious birth rite. But we also know that many mixed couples are interested in mixed or nontraditional ceremonies. Let's examine five possible approaches and the implications of each.

1. "Doing Both" We met one couple, Lou and Regina, who managed to find clergy who performed both a baptism and a Jewish naming for their daughter, Holly. Regina, a fervent Catholic, had insisted on the baptism. Lou, a nonpracticing but identified Jew, had an idea. Why not have both a baptism and a Jewish baby-naming? The girl would be welcomed into both communities. To Lou, faith had nothing to do with it. He wanted the naming as a way of "acknowledging [Holly] as a Jewish person."

They hoped they might get a rabbi and a priest to perform a ceremony together. If that didn't work, a few blocks from them a Catholic church and a synagogue stood only a few doors apart. Maybe they could schedule the ceremonies on the same day and just walk from one down the street to the other. The priest they spoke to was quite open to permitting a rabbi to say a few words. They were surprised to find that the rabbi was not only unwilling—he was outraged. Lou recalls, "It's kind of like, 'If you don't do it exactly the way we do it, then you can't play in our game and I won't come to yours, either.' I don't know why, I thought [they] would be more accepting."

Eventually, they were able to find a rabbi who performed a Hebrew naming ceremony in his office for Holly, even knowing that she was going to be baptized in a separate ceremony. (We suspect that most couples will not find a rabbi who will knowingly perform a naming ceremony under such circumstances.)

But Lou had not really thought through his own reaction to his daughter's baptism and what it might mean. Holly is now two years old. "I don't think of her as Catholic," he says. "I think of her as our child and I just think of her as Jewish. . . . My children would be bar mitzvahed or bat mitzvahed. Of course they would be. I didn't even think about it."

Regina and Lou are able to joke about their differences. "I've told Regina she can raise Holly Catholic on one condition—that Holly marries a Jewish guy," says Lou.

In seeking to minimize their differences and to respect and share each other's traditions, Lou and Regina were on the right track. But we don't think that having both a baptism and a *bris* or naming is a reasonable or honest way to move toward this goal. An essential part of the birth ceremony in each religion is incorporation into that specific community. Your child can't be truly consecrated to two different communities any more than you can be married, consecrated, to two partners at once. If you make two sets of wedding vows, both are violated. If you enter your child simultaneously into two religions, both traditions are being abused. Certainly, any child who is baptized and raised with a belief in the divinity of Jesus would not be considered Jewish by the great majority of Jews.

This is not to say children can't be taught about both traditions or the commonalities between the two. But the goal of having the child know both religions and identify with both parents can be met without having two birth ceremonies. There are other ways to have both of you represented.

2. A Single-Faith Rite, with Additions You can have a birth rite from one tradition but include the other parent and grandparents in the ceremony. That's what Felix did. Although Felix was raised as a Catholic by his mother, his father had scornfully boycotted religion. Largely as a result, Felix felt like an outsider unable to commit himself to any religion. He didn't want to do the same thing to his own son.

When his Jewish wife, Frances, had a son, they decided to have a traditional *bris*. But they added a few speeches, blessings, and stories which were read by them, their friends, and their families. Felix made a speech in which he pledged to support his son's Jewish upbringing. He and Frances gave their son an English name that reflected Felix's family history and a Hebrew name from Frances's family. Each of them talked about the relatives for whom the baby was named and spoke a bit about what in their backgrounds they wanted to pass on to the boy.

Another option is to give the Christian grandparents a brief role at a *bris*. Though Jewish law does not allow a gentile to hold the child in the capacity of *sandek* (godfather), you could have the gentile grandparents hold and pass the child at the very beginning of the ceremony, before the *mohel* has begun the blessings. You could also let them offer special good wishes after the ceremony. By doing so, you let them more fully share in the joy of welcoming your child to the world. You publicly signify that they are in an honored position, and that your decision to raise the child in Judaism is not intended to abridge their very important role as grandparents.

You could have a creative, alternative ceremony. We must say at the outset that this approach has a drawback. Because its language and symbolism do not resound across the generations, it will probably not have the elemental power of a traditional ceremony. Nevertheless, what you develop may feel like the only honest approach and may be less alien to your in-laws. It also can be beautiful. We want to describe several approaches.

3. A Single-Faith but Recreated Ceremony Some people choose one religious tradition but adapt the ceremony to fit their own needs. Among liberal Protestants and Jews, you will find a number of people who have developed modern birth ceremonies. For instance, parents who intend to raise their child in one of the liberal wings of Judaism could have a son medically circumcized in a hospital and later hold a naming ceremony in which they gave him some "equipment" for a Jewish life: a Bible and prayer book, a wine cup and candlesticks for Sabbath or a mezuzah for his bedroom doorpost. A non-Jewish parent who intends to assist in the child's Jewish upbringing can participate fully in the ceremony by giving the gifts, and a prayer or reading.

Parents who intend to raise their child in Christianity could also develop a welcoming ceremony rather than a traditional baptism. They could postpone baptism until the child was of an age to make a personal commitment to the faith, and instead hold a ceremony in which they gave the child "equipment" such as a children's Bible, prayer book or hymnal.

4. *A Ceremony That Isn't God-Oriented* Both the Unitarian-Universalists and the Ethical Culture Society have developed simple, humanistic ceremonies for welcoming a child. You will find them described in Chapter 17 (Affiliation). These ceremonies enter your child into a community of values without committing you or the child to any theology.

5. *A Self-Created Rite* You could develop a ceremony from scratch. That frees you to fuse elements from both backgrounds or to choose symbols or language that don't come from either.

But keep two things in mind. Let any symbols speak for themselves. If there are more words than action, you will lose what you came for: the power of ritual to bypass the brain and speak directly to the heart.[7] Also, make it short. Five to fifteen minutes is about right for the actual ceremony.

One couple who planned to raise their daughter as a Jew had a tree-planting because they knew a standard synagogue naming would be painful for the wife's Catholic family. (It is a custom among some Jews to plant a tree at a child's birth. When the child marries, the tree is cut down and used for the poles of the wedding canopy.) This couple chose a fruit tree and explained that they hoped their daughter would be not only healthy and lovely but also productive and giving to others. The grandparents were a bit mystified, but in general the ceremony went well.

Reconstructionist Rabbi Nancy Fuchs-Kreimer, who conducted that tree-planting ceremony, has also helped to write a naming and covenant ceremony based on the ancient custom of washing the feet. Instead of being brought specifically into the Jewish covenant (the covenant of Abraham), the child is brought into the covenant of Noah, which according to the Bible was a more ancient covenant between God and all human beings. The ceremony is described in Susan Weidman Schneider's book *Jewish and Female.*[8]

Robert Rice, a dance therapist at the Institute for Creation-Centered Spirituality at Holy Names College in Oakland, California, told us of a modern technique that you might adapt. Ask your friends to "birth" you into your role as parents. At the ceremony, have them make two double lines, one for men, one for women. Each of you passes through one of the lines, being gently helped and massaged. Do not emerge until you are ready. At the end, a friend or family member could hand you your child and say, "You have been reborn as a parent." Then the two of you together can welcome your child into your family and community.

Using such techniques from humanistic psychology requires a certain openness and willingness to experiment. But they can be quite powerful because they touch on universal themes of human existence and because they let you express change points through your body and not just through your mouth and head.

SIMPLE CEREMONIES, COMPLEX EMOTIONS

You and your spouse may find it surprisingly difficult to agree on a birth ceremony. You may not believe in the Trinity and your partner may not give a hoot about the covenant. Yet each of you feels strongly about having a rite that reflects your own, intact religious tradition. It's a gut feeling—beyond logic. What's going on here? In a word, *family.* That is the other factor in the equation.

Your own feelings are probably a reflection of the even stronger feelings of your parents and grandparents. For them, the birth ceremony may represent a visible symbol of their line continuing—of the bit of immortality that comes from parenting children and seeing them follow in one's footsteps. If you are putting into practice the traditions they taught, they can rest easy. But if you choose some other path, they may feel rejected, defensive and helpless.

EXERCISE: THE FORCE FIELD

To assess the forces you may be feeling from all around, try the following exercise:

Divide a sheet of paper into five columns. Label them in order:

"Me," "My spouse," "My parents," "My grandparents," and "History, Tradition, Belief."

In the column for your parents, write what they expect and want you to do to connect their grandchild to them (such as: carry on the family name, show your respect for the tradition, give them grandchildren to brag about). Write what feelings they would have if you gave the child a birth ceremony in their tradition, and their feelings if you had a ceremony in your partner's tradition.

Do the same under the label for your grandparents if they are living or if they strongly influenced you before they died.

In the "History, Tradition, Belief" column, write the messages you got about the birth rite in your tradition and what you were taught about your partner's tradition. Would having a ceremony in the other tradition be a betrayal? Would the child be seen as damned?

Now write under your spouse's label the wishes, feelings, and beliefs you think he or she has.

Finally, write under your own label. What are your feelings of obligation, loyalty, guilt? Your beliefs? Your fears? If you had no one else's feelings to consider, what would you do?

Now draw a large circle. Imagine that at the four points of the compass are magnets representing: your parents, grandparents, tradition, spouse. Add a point for your current beliefs if they differ from what you were brought up with. Put a dime in the middle of the circle to represent yourself. Move it toward each point and feel their relative strengths. Let the dime be pulled in the direction of the strongest forces, and leave it there. If you feel pulled in several directions, draw force lines with arrows to indicate that.

Check with your spouse as to his or her feelings and wishes. Did you accurately gauge the strength of those feelings?

Negotiating with Your Partner As we stated in Chapter 7 (The Lifetime Trajectory), the birth of a child may suddenly cause you to identify strongly with your parents and to want to please them. You may want to do things your parents' way, turning a blind eye to your partner's wishes. That is why it is important to talk about child-rearing and birth ceremonies before marriage, or at least well before the birth of children—before you get immersed in the welter of strong yet murky feelings.

Try to work your way to an early agreement, at least a tentative one, about a birth rite. Do this alone with your partner, as free as possible from the dictates of your families. Brainstorm about what you want the ceremony to convey. Then sketch out an event, keeping the following questions in mind: Do both of you have a clear and important role?

Is there something in the ceremony that represents each of your most precious values? (It may be a symbol, a blessing or poem, an action or a moment of silence.) Are both sets of grandparents given a role?

Remember that the event consists of two parts: the ceremony and the reception. If you decide on a single-faith ceremony, consider letting the parent and family members whose religion is not represented have a role at the reception, such as making a blessing or toast or reading a poem.

For many couples, choosing a birth ceremony is a tacit way of choosing a family religion. Don't let that larger decision slip by. It deserves its own full discussion. If you seem to be leaning toward a traditional, single-faith ceremony, be sure you both agree not only on the ceremony but on the family life-style that will follow. Don't let the more dominant person take charge of this important decision.

The best way to anticipate where the single-faith ceremony may lead you is to experience the religion together. Celebrate its holidays. Attend the church or synagogue you think you would use. Attend birth ceremonies. The tradition needs to feel comfortable to both of you.

There's a catch in negotiating ahead of time. You need to realize that as the birth approaches, your best-laid plan may have to be revised. One of you might have strong new feelings and opinions. It is important to see these not as betrayals or "going back on one's word" but as natural consequences of being thrust into your new life stage. Ambivalent and shifting feelings are part of the price of being intermarried. To ignore them could spell trouble later.

Be sure to review your plan together shortly before the ceremony. If you get a surge of doubt, tell your spouse. But be honest about what you want. If it is having your side be represented, remember there are ways to do that which might not require pitching your reasoned plan out the window.

Dealing with Family Once you both feel firm in the decision, inform your families. It's best to do this before the birth so they'll have time to adjust. If you have a role in mind for them at the ceremony, tell them what it is and be sure they are comfortable with it. You might be expecting them to participate in a way they would consider too far outside their tradition and values. They might be more comfortable contributing in another way: buying an outfit for the baby, giving a special gift, or speaking at the reception. (If they want to give a blessing, specify any ground rules about its religious content.)

If you are having a single-faith but innovative rite, you might be thinking of referring to the other religion during the ceremony. This can backfire by insulting the relatives of that religion rather than making them feel included. If you plan such a gesture, talk informally to them to see how they would react.

But certainly, during the ceremony or at the reception, mention ways in which you hope both sets of grandparents will help to teach and nurture the baby. And think of other inclusive gestures, such as having their favorite foods at the reception.

If your parents feel unable to come to the event, see if they can spend time with you in the few days after the baby's arrival getting to know the baby. Take pictures of them holding the baby and send the pictures to them. Whatever happens, keep the door open. Few people can resist the lure of grandparenting.

Dealing with Clergy If you want a Jewish ceremony, remember what we said earlier about the ways in which traditional and modern Judaism differ on the status of mixed children. You will save yourself a lot of pain by finding an appropriate officiant. Also, keep in mind that it is not necessary to have a rabbi at either a *bris* or a naming. Any Jew (in traditional Judaism, any adult male Jew) can serve as a witness.

The *mohel* is likely to come from the Orthodox Jewish world. He may be unwilling to perform a *bris* unless the gentile mother has received an Orthodox conversion to Judaism before the child's birth. One couple who had not had a thorough discussion with the *mohel* had a terrible experience. After the circumcision was complete, the *mohel* pointed at the wife and asked, "Has she been through the *mikvah?*" The answer was no. He tore up the certificate. Other *mohelim* would perform such a circumcision, with the clear understanding (perhaps noted on the certificate) that the baby must later be immersed in the *mikvah.*

Some *mohelim* are more flexible than others. Explain the roles that you wish to be played by a non-Jewish parent or relatives, as well as any modifications of the traditional ceremony you want to make. Make sure all parties understand what has been agreed to. The Reform movement in Judaism started its own *mohel* training program in 1983. There are now Reform *mohelim* in the Southern California, New York, and Boston areas, and they plan to expand the program throughout the United States. The *mohelim* are medical doctors (male or female) or nurse-midwives who are given a semester of training in the Jewish law and traditions concerning circumcision, pass an examination, and are certified by the B'rit Mila Board of Reform Judaism. Their circumcisions are recognized as valid by some, but not all, of the Orthodox community. Reform *mohelim* do not require a non-Jewish mother or her child to go through the *mikvah.* They are generally flexible about modifying the ceremony and including non-Jewish relatives. For more information, contact the nearest regional office of the Union of American Hebrew Congregations (see Appendix).

The same applies to working with Christian clergy. Most will be flexible since they view Judaism as part of their religious heritage. Ask to see the text of the ceremony and find out what you will be asked to say and do. There may be portions you want deleted. If the rite is unfamiliar to one set of grandparents, ask the clergyperson to meet with them to answer questions.

Finally, remember that regardless of what you do, the ceremony does not carve your household's future in stone. The birth rite is an important first step and it is a commitment. But it does not mean that you cannot later reconsider your path. And by itself it will not guarantee your child's sense of identity. It is what you do in the years that follow that counts.

II. ADOLESCENCE: THE COMING OF AGE

You recall Marv and Stacy from the beginning of the chapter. Stacy had a christening for Eugene but realized during the ceremony that she didn't want to raise him as a Christian. Let's pick up the story.

After the christening, Stacy accepted Marv's wish to raise Eugene as a Jew. However, she told Marv he would have to take responsibility: "I kind of put myself on the periphery."

Eugene is eleven now, an articulate and thoughtful young man who feels himself to be deeply Jewish and is looking forward to his bar mitzvah. As that big day approaches, though, Marv and Stacy have had to face a second round of decisions. At the Conservative synagogue where their son attends Hebrew school, the rabbi informed them that Eugene could not be bar mitzvahed unless he was immersed in the *mikvah* and formally converted to Judaism.

Marv was angry, feeling that Eugene was much more knowledgeable and involved and committed to Judaism than virtually any other child in the Hebrew school. He resolved that he was not going to have Eugene converted "just to please some black-hats" (his term for very Orthodox Jews, who wear black hats and coats).

Marv consulted a rabbi he trusted, and the rabbi invited him to attend a conversion ceremony to see what was involved. The convert took a dip in a pool out of Marv's sight, then spent some time talking with the *bet din* (rabbinical court). "It was a very nice thing," Marv recalls. "It was a simple and painless declaration that this is what I want to be—a confirmation, really." He began to worry that "possibly without it, at some point Eugene might say, maybe I should have done that." So he asked Eugene whether he wanted to go through a conversion.

Eugene was ambivalent but decided to do it. "I don't think I should have to confirm the fact that I'm Jewish," he says. "I'll do it just for the fact that I am, so there will be no disputing it anywhere."

The boy is far more nervous about his bar mitzvah. That is the big event coming up, and it means a lot to him.

What can an adolescent ceremony, at its best, signify to a youngster? We'll let Eugene say. Though he's describing a bar mitzvah, his words could apply to a Christian rite as well: "I don't think it will make me a man. I don't think it'll make me grow up. I can act grown-up now, but sometimes I still like to be little. [He gives a little baby "Waaa" as an illustration.] The bar mitzvah will help me to feel like I'm an adult Jewishly. That I can participate in services more. That I'm grown up enough to be part of the service. That I know what I'm doing."

PSYCHOLOGICAL AND COMMUNAL MEANINGS OF
THE CEREMONY

Planning a ceremony for an adolescent is very different from planning a birth ceremony. Your youngster, like Eugene, has independent thoughts and feelings about having a ceremony. He is not the oblivious baby who was presented at the birth rite. For the adolescent ceremony to be meaningful, you must be sure your youngster is genuinely involved in the planning and execution of the event and that his preferences are respected.

Sometimes, as with Eugene and his parents, everyone's needs and goals seem to mesh. All see the ceremony in basically the same way, as a celebration of their home's consistent, clear religious message. With other families, the religious message may have been fuzzy but the child is willing to comply with the parents' desires for a bar mitzvah or confirmation because he doesn't want to anger them or because he's happy to have a "coming-of-age" event like so many of his peers.

In still other families, however, everyone's goals don't overlap so smoothly. Sometimes it is the teenager who brings the issue to a head. He may pressure for a ceremony because he wants to have a clear identity—throwing the parents, who had been avoiding their religious differences, into turmoil and paralysis.

Other times it is an erstwhile-nonpracticing parent who is suddenly stirred to want a ceremony, while the child balks. Such a child, having plunged headlong into adolescence, might simply want to pull away from his parents, to be unconventional and independent; the last thing he wants is to be paraded around by and for his parents. In addition, if you haven't given him a clear identity message, he might fear that a ceremony will force him to choose between his two parents.

The Mid-Life Turnabout Let's look closer at the scenario in which a parent pushes for a ceremony. We saw that happening quite a bit. A number of couples told us they sidestepped the religion issue until their children neared the teenage years. They didn't feel strongly about having a birth ritual so they did nothing. They didn't feel strongly about religious education so they did nothing. Then, as the child reached age ten, eleven, or twelve, one parent began to feel strongly that he wanted a coming-of-age ceremony for his child. Even if the parent harbored memories of ostentatious receptions, rote memorization, dishonest promises, it didn't matter anymore. He wanted that ceremony for his kid.

This desire seems more likely to come from the Jewish partner than the Christian one because of the difference in what the two ceremonies represent. The Christian confirmation is a statement of faith. Many of the Christian partners we talked to had lost their own faith years earlier. They saw no particular reason to ask their children to make declarations of Christian faith. The Jewish ceremony, however, affirms identification with a people. The Jewish partner may have no faith yet still identify as a Jew. He wants his child to share in that identification.

The parent's mid-life turnabout, of course, is not unique to intermarried couples. Many minimally identified couples in which both partners are Jewish experience a new sense of urgency about religion as their child nears bar mitzvah age. But the turnabout for an intermarried couple poses four special questions:

First, how realistic is it for your child to develop a sense of religious identification when he is almost a teenager? If you have not been pointing him in any religious direction, he has probably identified with both of you in matters of religion. Though he may not have verbalized it, he probably sees himself as a secularist with roots in both Judaism and Christianity. This is particularly true if you had a Christmas tree and Easter baskets, Passover with the relatives, and no other observance.

Second, your spouse may neither understand nor feel much sympathy with the new urgency about the child's religious identity. The spouse may feel that you are upsetting the balance in what was previously an equal-time relationship.

Third, the non-Jewish grandparents may be upset by the sudden emergence of a Jewish identity in their child's household.

Fourth, you probably don't have a synagogue affiliation. Many of the rabbis you approach may be unwilling to arrange a bar mitzvah for a child who hasn't been a regular attender at religious school. In addition, as in Eugene's case, Conservative rabbis will be unwilling to accept the child of a gentile mother as a bar mitzvah candidate unless he converts.

You may well have repeated all these arguments to yourself. Yet you may still feel strongly that you want your child to have a bar or bat mitzvah. What should you do?

Working with Your Spouse Whether you have been looking forward for years to your child's bar/bat mitzvah or confirmation or whether you have just decided this is something you want to do, your first task is to sit down with your partner and talk about your needs and goals. (Keep in mind that an adolescent rite of passage commonly follows a period of preparation by the youngster. To minimize pressure, try to do your goal-sorting well in advance of the date by which you have to decide whether to have a ceremony.)

First, do the exercise from the birth-ceremony section of the chapter, adding another point of the compass to represent your child. Then, list the religious and values goals you want the ceremony to convey. These might be: demonstrating pride in your child, and affirming your own links to your faith or people.

After you are clear on your goals, read about the options that follow to see that there are many ways to structure both the preparation period and the event itself. Keep in mind that the event has three parts: preparation, ritual or ceremony, and reception. If you and your partner are feeling at odds about having both heritages represented, perhaps using the preparation or reception creatively will resolve the problem.

Working with Your Child Your youngster is old enough that the ceremony should represent a genuine milestone in his life, a meaningful achievement or decision. It ought to express his thoughtfully considered values. Thus, he must have a full voice in the final planning. If he doesn't, you'll undermine the very thing you ought to work toward: his movement to adulthood.

If he merely shrugs when you ask him what he wants, try to find out why. If he won't open up to you, suggest that he find an adult outside the family to talk over the decision. Have him do the circle exercise to help him clarify his feelings. If he would prefer to delay the ceremony until he's a bit older, tell him you'll respect his wishes.

If you and your partner have agreed you'd like a single-religion ceremony, assure the child that his taking part does not imply rejection of his other parent. It's best to have the parent of the other religion explain this.

If he fights the entire idea of a ceremony, make a deal. Insist that he try out the preparation or training program for a set period of time. Once he is under the tutelage of a stimulating teacher, he may change his mind. If he does, don't gloat. If he doesn't, don't insist. If he suddenly starts spouting his own ideas for the ceremony, don't be surprised. As long as the core of the event retains what you and your spouse want, let him have his expressions, too. It is all a way of helping him grow in competence, confidence, and maturity.

If he wants to delay the ceremony, find a clergyperson flexible enough to plan a special event when your child is older.

Considering Your Families As with the birth rite, when you've decided on your own general direction, take account of your parents' feelings in planning the details.

At the ceremony, your child could acknowledge the special contributions of the grandparents who do not share his religion.

Tell your parents what you're going to do. Explain your reasons, and tell how you want to include them. Keep them posted on how your child is preparing. Have the youngster personally invite them to the ceremony. If he has the time and inclination, ask him to write letters to them about his preparations.

When the day draws near, give them a printed program and walk them through the ceremony so they know what to expect. If you are having a bar mitzvah, invite the non-Jewish grandparents to attend services with you before the event so they will not be walking into a synagogue for the first time.

Use their strengths and aptitudes. If the grandmother has a gift for flower-arranging, ask her to provide the flowers. If the grandfather has a flair for carpentry, ask him to make a special gift (such as bookends) that he can present during the ceremony.

BAR MITZVAH, CONFIRMATION AND BEYOND

The atmosphere you want to create is one of warmth and sensitivity. Now, here are some specific paths you could take. First we will describe the traditional ones.

Bar/Bat Mitzvah Bar mitzvah typically takes place at or near the thirteenth birthday, after an extended period of study. In traditional Judaism, there is no elaborate ceremony. The regular Saturday morning service proceeds as it always does, but part of it is chanted by the boy rather than by the adults as is normally done. After he has performed this task, the youngster is considered an adult for religious purposes. This means he can be called upon to make a minyan (the quorum of ten men needed for public prayer) and can serve as a witness in religious functions such as a marriage. He is also obligated to observe all the commandments such as fasting on Yom Kippur.

The bar mitzvah ceremony does not deal with belief. It is an affirmation of full membership in the congregation, and of commitment to the Jewish people and way of life.

Traditionally, there was no rite of passage for girls because only male adults were obligated to participate in the congregation. However, most Conservative, Reform, and Reconstructionist synagogues now hold a bat mitzvah ceremony for a girl. In some Conservative synagogues, the service for a girl is held on Friday night, when the Torah is not chanted.

Partly in an attempt to stem the tide of youngsters who drop out of religious school after their bar mitzvah, Reform temples and some Conservative synagogues have added a group confirmation ceremony which occurs typically at age sixteen, when the teen graduates from religious school.

Confirmation Christian confirmation is similar to bar/bat mitzvah in some of its goals. But there is one crucial difference: Confirmation is an affirmation of belief in a particular doctrine. The person is confirming the faith to which his parents brought him at birth. The ceremony takes place during a Sunday service, with the individual making a personal statement or agreeing to a creedal vow stated by the clergyperson.

While the bar mitzvah is an individual performance, the confirmation is a group event. It takes place anytime from age seven to sixteen, and generally occurs at about twelve. The ceremony conveys full membership in the congregation.

You might find that you all feel best about a traditional, single-faith ceremony. Because it is "normal," it might spare your child from feeling peculiar. But interreligious families sometimes try variations on the standard course. Here are five:

1. *Crash Course in One Religion.* This occurs in the case of the midlife turnabout. In Judaism, your best bet for getting a crash course for your child is through a Reconstructionist, Reform, or liberal Conservative rabbi. Request two things: a gifted tutor who is willing to stress Jewish practice, history, and Bible more than Hebrew skills; and a family you can "buddy up" with that has a child the same age as your child. The family should be willing to celebrate holidays and occasional Sabbaths with you and to show you the ropes. Your child can play catch-up, but only if the entire family does, too.

You probably can't expect your child to "perform" by chanting the Torah and Prophets as would be done at a traditional bar or bat mitzvah. Instead, ask the tutor to develop a ceremony with your child that uses and demonstrates his new skills. Ask the rabbi to approve this adapted ceremony.

Such a plan will succeed only if the child is willing to put in a fair amount of effort. But don't expect him to come out of it with long-lasting identity or skills. It is not reasonable (except by spending the year in Israel!) to ask a child in a one- or two-year period to become proficient in both a foreign language and a culture that may be familiar to one of his parents but had been foreign to him.

2. Conventional Ceremony, with Modifications The approach here is to find a clergyperson who will let you add elements to the program that meet the needs of your child and your family. For example, some ministers are now suggesting that each confirmand in a Christian ceremony take a religious study project and give a talk about it. Your child might research part of the Old Testament and discuss the elements of Judaism that are a foundation for Christianity. (Discuss this idea with your child. The decision should be his.)

It is possible to modify a bar or bat mitzvah ceremony in ways which acknowledge and allow participation by the non-Jewish family. The youngster could choose a special project that would help him to become more familiar with his non-Jewish heritage and to integrate it into his Jewish identity. For example, he might research the changes in the Catholic Church's attitude toward Jews that have resulted from Vatican II. Or he could compare the Christian and Jewish views of a Biblical book such as Isaiah.

The youngster could also have a service project that he works on with the non-Jewish parent. (The Jewish parent could help the youngster with Hebrew skills, the non-Jewish partner with the service project.) It could be made clear that this project expresses values common to both traditions.

This must be done with care. Many Jews are hostile to introducing specifically Christian elements (or even references to Christianity) into a Jewish service.

What you can do in the ceremony itself depends on the synagogue you work with. Most Conservative synagogues and some Reform ones have rules limiting the role a non-Jew can play in the service. For example, the non-Jew might be permitted to read a speech from the pulpit but not to hold the Torah, stand beside the Torah, or open the Ark in which the Torah rests. Ask the rabbi what roles are permitted for the gentile parent and grandparents. See if some open acknowledgment can be made of their support.

3. A Nontheistic Ceremony Ethical Culture, Unitarian-Universalism, and secular Jewish groups have instituted adolescent rites that involve study and service projects and that culminate in a public address. A project might involve an aspect of ethics or an academic exploration of a topic that spans both heritages. These ceremonies are described in Chapter 18 (Religious Education).

Finally, you could create and host your own ceremony. The advantage of this approach: You can control every aspect, including what symbols you use and how old your child is when the ceremony occurs. You might, for example, have the ceremony when your child is fifteen or seventeen rather than thirteen. You could time it to an event in the youngster's life, such as the onset of menstruation, or getting a driver's license.

The disadvantages are the same as mentioned in the birth-rite section: little sense of history, no ongoing community to support you. Should you choose this approach, envision it as an expression of values, not identity.

There are two directions to go with this option, a theological ceremony and a non-theological ceremony.

4. A Creative Theological Ceremony We spoke with one mixed couple, Norman and Yvonne, who took this approach and ran with it. During their first decade as parents, Norman and Yvonne had had an on-and-off approach to religious education for their son and daughter. Then, as son Steve approached bar mitzvah age, they embarked on a course both regard as a high point of their marriage: They held a Jewish-Christian coming-of-age ceremony for both children. Steve refers to it as a "barfirmation."

Norman and Yvonne decided that what they wanted to teach their children was the Judeo-Christian history and worldview, with emphasis on the common ground. "Really, there is so much continuity" says Norman. "That is what we were searching for. We were not trying to pull out the differences."

To prepare for the ceremony, they instituted a weekly family discussion. They all read a particular Bible selection and focused on its ethical lessons. At Christmastime they read about Jesus' birth. At the Passover/Easter season they read about the seder and Jesus' Last Supper. They also for the first time as a family celebrated all the major holidays of both traditions.

At first the children resented the process. It seemed like just more schoolwork and it took up every Sunday morning. But eventually they were drawn in and a family spirit took root. Sometimes they would burst into song, singing the *Sh'ma* (The Jewish affirmation of God's oneness).

Then, after a year, came the ceremony. It was in a Quaker meetinghouse. Each of the two children picked one passage from the Hebrew Bible and one from the New Testament, read them aloud, and discussed their meanings and how they related to each other. They talked briefly about other experiences that had made them feel linked to both Jews and Christians. Their parents spoke about the qualities they appreciated in each of their offspring. Then, in Quaker style, family and friends added their blessings.

"The kids got a lot of strokes," says Norman. "They wrote everything without any coaching from us and they stood up on their own two feet."

5. A Creative Nontheological Ceremony This works best if you think of it as a coming-of-age project. Work with your child on developing a "growing plan." Choose one or more of these five areas: emotional maturity, skills, physical competence or strength, readiness for job, readiness for family. Have your child develop a one-year plan for how he will improve in the area he chooses. Let him select an adult as mentor and guide. At the end of a year, have a ceremony at which he demonstrates the skill or talks about what he learned.

Suppose he chooses "patience" under emotional maturity and "endurance" under physical competence. To develop his patience, he could volunteer once a week in a day-care center or old-age home, with a staff member supervising and charting his progress. To develop his endurance, he could get involved in long-distance running at school. At his ceremony, he could talk about what he learned. He could ask the adults he worked with to talk about changes they saw in him, and he could give them gifts. The Appendix contains suggestions for other projects, such as a Native-American-style "vision quest."

The creative ceremony is best if it is more than just words. Include a symbol or a ritual act to signify the transition. It could be putting on a new garment, using water, taking a new name, giving or receiving a gift. One way to find a symbol that has power for you is to build on things that you grew up with, but to change them slightly. For example, a girl's coming-of-age ceremony might include baking a *hallah* (braided bread) with a whole egg, still in the shell, inside it. At the ceremony, the *hallah* could be broken open and shared. It might include dipping pieces of *hallah* in honey and in various types of seeds, with blessings about the qualities represented by the different seeds.

Be careful about the symbolism you use and the project you choose. The object is to set out goals and experiences which will affirm your child's confidence in his growing maturity, not to set a task at which he is likely to fail. Even the symbols should tell him you understand that growth to adulthood is gradual—he doesn't have to do it all at once. If the symbol is a flame, choose a candle, not a torch. A torch can connote "the responsibility is all on your shoulders now."[9]

When All Else Fails Finally, if your son or daughter simply wants no part of a coming-of-age ceremony, consider having one for yourself. Besides being personally rewarding, this can help you to stop pressuring your child to do a ceremony for your sake.

You might reaffirm your wedding vows (with a new exchange of rings or other tokens, and readings about the growth you recognize in each other and in your marriage). Or you might be interested in the resources listed in the Appendix, such as the "fully coming of age ritual" developed by Kathryn North or the vision quest through Rites of Passage Inc. or Outward Bound.

Rites of passage are fruitful opportunities. Intermarriage adds a level to the planning, but with a bit of creativity you ought to be able to make the moment meaningful and inclusive.

MAKING
CONNECTIONS

17. AFFILIATION:

Finding a Community

There comes a time in life when many people who had steadfastly stayed outside the world of religion want to get back in. If this is your situation, or if you are just starting out in marriage and are looking for a community, you will find that a carefully chosen affiliation offers a number of benefits: a network of friendships; communal celebration of holidays and life-cycle events; an identity base for your children; a forum for you and the children to discuss the meaning of life; a comforting haven in times of crisis; a ready place for demonstrating values through social action.

If you and your spouse are nonbelievers, you may want to affiliate with a secular humanist community. A community which has ethics as its focus can add a dimension of meaning not found in other social centers such as a country club or sports program.

Don't expect to find a heaven on earth. Any community is inherently a blending of people with different views, so there are always trade-offs. Every institution needs some bureaucrats and organizers who may seem unspiritual but are good at getting things done. Every community also has hard-liners who want others to do as they do and think as they think. In any community, you are bound to find yourself uncomfortable with certain practices, dogmas, rituals, or people. But you don't have to accept every jot and tittle. Part of the beauty of community is the give-

and-take. You learn that your perspective is not unique, your truth is not the only one—and that you are not alone.

If you have decided to look for a religious community after years on the outside, you're doing so at a good time. There are many more options available to you, both as individuals and as partners in an intermarriage, than there were even a decade ago. This chapter describes some of the options, within and outside Judaism and Christianity. Addresses and phone numbers for a variety of groups appear in the Appendix at the back of the book.

New Options The decades since the 1960s have been a time of questioning, excitement, and spiritual search in America. There has been a great deal of experimentation with native religions, Eastern religions, and meditation. In addition, there has been a burst of energy in most mainstream religious denominations. The Second Vatican Council ignited imaginations and expanded the sense of possibility among Catholics. Within nearly every major Protestant denomination, there are groups experimenting with liturgy, social action, and new forms of organization. Broad waves of change have come from feminists and committed social activists such as church-based anti-nuclear groups. Ecumenicists are communicating across denominational barriers, between Catholics and Protestants, and between Christians and Jews.

Most of these new trends have been influenced by humanism. Humanistic religious communities are less heaven-directed and are deeply concerned with the needs and strivings of people in this world. They do not demand obedience and they respect freedom of conscience. Instead of emphasizing the risk of sin, they stress the possibility that people can achieve their full potential; instead of instilling guilt, they try to inspire creativity and hope. Christian humanists emphasize Jesus as man and teacher. Jewish humanists, such as those in Reform and Reconstructionism, encourage lay participation and see religion as a rich treasury of human experience rather than a set of divine commands.

The humanist religious option has been a boon to intermarried couples who are looking for a comfortable common ground, as well as to individuals who were alienated by the religion of their childhood but still feel a need for a spiritual connection.

Sarah, an intermarried woman who was in flight from a rigidly Orthodox immigrant family, found that she could fulfill her spiritual longings in one of the nondenominational New Age groups, and could make a positive reconnection with her Jewish heritage through a secularist *folkshul* (literally, people's school). It was a revelation to her when, "As an adult, I met Jews who loved being Jewish . . . and who really had a tremendous joy in it and were finding a lot of spiritual satisfaction in it. People whom I could take seriously as spiritual seekers, not just as people who were doing it because their parents did it."

If you are considering joining a mainstream religious congregation, it may help to realize that members who come from the post World War II generation, whether intermarried or not, are probably not that different from you in their spiritual outlook. Most have neither the simple faith nor the strong sense of obedience that were common two generations ago. They choose to become or remain part of a religious community for a complex mix of reasons. They may need a feeling of community; they may be looking for a place that will reinforce what they teach their children about ethics and values. They may hope for some connection with transcendence, some insights into the meaning of life. They may return to the religion of their childhood because they find a deep comfort, a feeling of being at home in its forms, even if they do not adhere to much of its theology. They reconcile the difference between the religion's worldview and their own by *reinterpreting* the religious language for themselves. They view the stories, blessings, and even dogmas as metaphors and use them as sources of meaning or inspiration.

Nancy Fuchs-Kreimer, a Reconstructionist rabbi and a scholar in Jewish-Christian theological dialogue, says she has seen much reinterpreting in both Judaism and Christianity. "In a liberal church," she says, "you might all stand and say the Apostles' Creed, but you and the minister and everybody else has an implicit understanding that you're saying these words but you're interpreting them the way you want to interpret them . . . Similarly there are Jews who sit there and say the prayers, but say them in quotes. Before they say each one, they sort of add in parentheses, 'As our ancestors used to say, quote.' "

Spiritual Intensity Some returnees approach the religion tentatively, like deer at a brook, and wade in only up to their ankles. Other returnees, however, want to plunge in to an observant life. They reject what they see as the "lukewarm," "conformist," or "hypocritical" religiosity of their parents' generation and seek an intense spiritual experience. If you have unfulfilled spiritual longings, you can find a variety of religious forms that may have greater intensity than the church or synagogue you grew up in.

A good example is the burgeoning Jewish *havurah* movement. *Havurot* are small, liberal fellowship groups that fuse lay leadership and egalitarianism with lively discussions and holiday celebrations. Another example is the Christian charismatic prayer-group movement, which emphasizes a direct, mystical experience of Jesus. Other spiritually intense forms are the new Jewish orthodoxy, Jewish "New Age" or mystical groups (such as P'nai Or), the Hindu or Buddhist mystical groups, and synthesis groups such as the Movement for Spiritual Inner Awareness and the Sufi Order of the West.

A university chaplain is likely to know about the intense Jewish and Christian groups. To find out about any of the New Age or "holistic" spiritual movements, look for a bookstore that specializes in the literature of this movement. At least twenty regional publications serve as clearinghouses for activities and groups in their part of the country.

What do you do if one of you is attracted to affiliating with a congregation or religious movement but the other is opposed? Try to be flexible enough to let each partner follow the path he or she is comfortable with. But stay in touch and keep talking about what you're doing. The partner who gets religiously involved should share thoughts and experiences, but not proselytize. The partner who chooses to remain outside can voice his skepticism and discomfort without being mocking, harshly critical, or hostile.

If you are the partner who is religiously involved, look for less formal settings such as retreats and holiday celebrations in which the nonreligious partner might feel comfortable. If you are the nonreligious one, go to some of those events. You would attend your child's piano recital even if you didn't enjoy the music. Make it clear that you intend to support your spouse's interest even if you do not share it. You may choose to be present but not participate in the rituals, songs, or prayers.

RECONNECTING: A LOOK AT SOME OPTIONS

Here is a sampling of the reception that awaits the wanderers who decide to join a religious or secular community. Most of the options that follow have proved popular with intermarrieds or are widely available.[1]

Converts have full standing in all of the movements, though the policies on mixed families vary. All of the groups offer religious schooling for children unless we state otherwise. (The content of the education is described in Chapter 18.) All the groups have some social-action programs. These may focus on the homeless, nuclear disarmament, ecology, housing discrimination, sanctuary for illegal aliens, interfaith and interracial programs, the sick and infirm. Jewish groups will add efforts for Israel and Soviet Jews and Christian groups will aid needy members of their communities.

Since the majority of intermarried couples who affiliate link up with a Jewish institution, we will present Jewish groups first, and then Christian and other options.

Reform and Reconstructionist Judaism

These two movements constitute the liberal end of "establishment" Judaism. In both, you will find a considerable number of intermarried members. (Reform congregations include anywhere from 10 to 50 percent intermarried families.)

Reform and Reconstructionism both have a more contemporary, less traditional feel. Women hold full equality, for instance, and Jewish law is seen as a guide, not a binding or unchangeable obligation.

The Reform service will probably not feel too foreign to a gentile. At many temples, the prayers are largely in English. A number are "universal" in tone and make no mention of Jews being a people specially chosen by God. Instrumental music is permitted. The Reform movement in the past threw off many Jewish traditions, such as dietary laws and special worship attire, as a matter of principle. But in recent years many Reform Jews are returning to those forms. As a result, you can expect to find a particularly wide spread nowadays in Reform Jews' levels of observance and intensity.

Reconstructionist Judaism took hold as an actual movement about twenty-five years ago, making it the youngest (and smallest) branch of establishment Judaism. Reconstructionism is an attempt to reinterpret, or reconstruct, Judaism for modern Jews who live in two cultures in America. It sees Judaism as an evolving religious civilization, with the past having "a vote but not a veto." It is *anthrocentric* rather than *theocentric,* meaning that God is seen not as a divine protector but rather as a source of inner strength, a force in people and the world that leads us toward the constructive and the good.

The movement encourages lay participation as a way to make Jewish practice meaningful to each individual. Many Reconstructionist congregations have produced their own prayer books. Services are informal and frequently experimental, with the rabbi rarely performing all the rituals. The ratio of Hebrew to English varies with the makeup of the congregation.

Reform and Reconstructionist synagogues are autonomous, meaning they are free to set their own bylaws on involvement of mixed couples. A few grant the gentile full membership rights and full involvement in the worship service. More commonly, though, a line is drawn. A congregation will permit the gentile to vote and serve on committees, for instance, but not to be an officer of the congregation. It might allow her to participate in certain rituals such as opening the ark (which holds the Torah scroll) but not to read from the Torah (a hallowed act traditionally reserved for Jews who have had a bar or bat mitzvah).

If you are a mixed couple where the woman is gentile, Reform and Reconstructionism have a feature that may be very attractive to you. Both movements depart from Jewish tradition by recognizing what is called patrilineal descent. That means that a child is considered Jewish by both movements if *either* of his parents is Jewish and he is actively raised and educated as a Jew. (Traditionally, a child has been seen as Jewish only if his mother is Jewish or if he is properly converted.) The new, and controversial, patrilineal policy is intended specifically to bring mixed families and their children into the community.

Both parents in a mixed couple can expect a role on the *bimah* (altar or platform) in their child's bar or bat mitzvah. In the Reform movement, the child of a non-Jewish mother does not have to be converted to qualify for a bar or bat mitzvah. The movement will consider the offspring of a mixed couple fully Jewish if they are entered on the "cradle-roll" of the religious school, complete the ten-year Sunday school course, and are then confirmed as Jews (a ceremony similar to graduation).[2]

Many Reconstructionist rabbis take that same approach to bar and bat mitzvah. But others do not. In spite of the movement's patrilineality policy, some Reconstructionist rabbis will call for the child of a non-Jewish mother to have a conversion (a ritual immersion and, for an already circumcised boy, a symbolic drawing of blood from the penis) prior to bar or bat mitzvah to satisfy more traditional Jews.

The Reform movement has been in the forefront of programming for intermarried families in recent years. In fact, the courses may be almost old-hat at the local temple. There was a burst of new programming in the early 1980s, so you may find that the mixed members who were interested have already gone through the process. Be assured that several models exist, at least on the books, for support groups, discussion groups, preconversion classes, and "adoptive family" programs. You may be able to activate them or locate where one is in progress. Some are run by local Reform temples, others by the regional offices.

Special groups or classes for intermarrieds are not widespread in Reconstructionism. Unlike the Reform movement, it has no national outreach program.

General adult-education classes abound in both camps. The Reform movement has found that many members have scant Jewish knowledge. As a result, "how-to" classes are popular: How to observe *Shabbos,* how to make Passover, how to cook Jewishly, how to follow the prayer service, how to celebrate life-cycle rites. Reconstructionism offers how-to education as part of its philosophy of "empowering the individual." As a skill is taught, its context is presented: What did the custom mean to ancient Judaism? What are the values behind it? How is it viable today?

Traditional Judaism

Orthodox and Conservative Judaism are the bulwarks of Jewish tradition. As a result, they firmly oppose the modern notion of patrilineal descent. Instead, they adhere to Jewish law, which holds that to be considered Jewish, a child must have a Jewish mother or be formally converted.

In Orthodox Judaism, a convert is fully and completely accepted as a member. But mixed-married families are not accepted. The gentile partner could not be a member and the couple would likely experience pressure for conversion of the gentile, or at least of the children. The children of a gentile mother would probably be denied enrollment in the religious school unless they and their mother underwent formal conversion.

The large Conservative movement occupies the broad middle ground between Orthodox and liberal Judaism, both in terms of liturgy and outreach. Though it extends a hand to mixed couples, the movement's central body, United Synagogues of America, imposes several rules that limit the right of a mixed family to participate in the congregation. The unbending rules are these: An unconverted gentile cannot be a member (the Jewish spouse can, though many congregations have not allowed the intermarried Jew to serve as an officer or board member); the unconverted gentile cannot read from the Torah or open the ark; the child of a non-Jewish mother cannot have a bar or bat mitzvah without first being converted according to Jewish law. Also, though congregations are expected to welcome individual mixed couples, don't be surprised to find the desire expressed, by the rabbi or congregants, that the gentile will eventually convert to Judaism.

The gentile may be able to assist in program activities on an unofficial basis. In most Conservative congregations, the gentile partner would be given some role in a bar or bat mitzvah. For instance, he might be allowed on the *bimah* and permitted to give a celebratory, but non-liturgical, reading.

Don't expect to see much official outreach to mixed families in the Conservative movement. Some congregations have organized support groups at their own initiative. But there has not been a central push for them.[3]

Adult-education classes may start at a fairly advanced level. The assumption is that members have had a Jewish education, so you will not find as many "how-to" primer classes.

Conservative Judaism has what is referred to as a "right-wing" and a "center wing" (there is no left wing). Right or center usually refers to the liturgical styles. On the right, one can expect to find the complete prayer service performed, mostly in Hebrew. In terms of the prayers recited and the length of service, it would be indistinguishable from an Orthodox ceremony. True to tradition, the services have less English and less participation by women (though men and women are not seated separately as in an Orthodox service).

Moving to the center, one sees shorter services, more English, more involvement of women. (Also, increasing use of cantors, choirs, and organs.) At either end, one might find a *havurah* subgroup, which prefers an informal service and considerable membership participation. These subgroups often experiment with liturgy and tend to be spiritually intense.

Secular Judaism

For mixed families who want a Jewish identity but not God-oriented liturgy and prayer, this is an alternative to consider. Secular Judaism is nontheistic, meaning it is neutral on the matter of God and a divine hand in Jewish history. Its focus instead is Jewish peoplehood, culture, and values. We found two small movements within secular Judaism: the Society for Humanistic Judaism and the *folkshul* groups.

The *folkshul* approach is the older of the two. It is the product of a nationalist movement born three or four generations ago as Yiddish-speaking Jews from the ghettos of Eastern Europe began to move into the modern world. Secular Judaism moved beyond the world of the synagogue while still embracing Yiddish culture and Jewish ethics. In this country, its socialist-leaning adherents formed a network of schools, many of them called *folkshuln,* to propagate Yiddish culture. Organizations sprang up with names like the Workmen's Circle, the Sholom Aleichem Club, the I. L. Peretz School.

Now, decades later, their memberships are a sometimes-uneasy mix of aging Old Left Yiddishists and secularized young parents who have joined simply to have their children learn some Jewish culture, divorced from ritual and theism. The curriculum emphasizes Jewish history, holidays, literature, music, art, and language (some Hebrew and a touch of Yiddish).

The *folkshul* groups, allied loosely in the Congress of Secular Jewish Organizations, generally provide little for the parents. They exist solely to be parent-run schools for children, with no regular adult service or meetings and no clergy. Sometimes there will be adult-education sessions or life-style discussions, but they'll probably be on a one-shot basis.

A more ongoing structure for adults is offered by the Society for Humanistic Judaism. Its congregations, known as groups, are free to set the style and frequency of services. The smaller ones might meet one Friday a month in a rented space or a living room for adult education or a holiday gathering, and offer no schooling and other programming. The several larger ones function as synagogues with buildings, weekly services, religious leaders, choirs, and regular schooling. A service (or meeting, as it may be called) often centers on a theme, such as brotherhood, humanism, or a seasonal event. The theme is opened up through poems, readings, even a dramatic presentation.

Although they may not believe in God, many of the Society's congregations do promote a sense of the transcendent and are probably more comfortable than *folkshul* groups with using spiritual language. The traditional Friday night candle-lighting blessing ("Blessed art Thou, Lord our God . . .") has been modified to, "Blessed be the light of the world, blessed be the light of humanity and blessed be the light of *Shabbos.*"

A feature of both movements is the nontraditional or secular bar/bat mitzvah. (See Chapter 18, Religious Education, for more details on this.)

Intermarriage and patrilineality are nonissues in secular Judaism. Most places will have intermarried members (the Society estimates that 25 percent of its members are), and the issue of your religious mix probably won't even be raised. In fact, Humanistic Judaism holds that a person becomes a Jew merely through voluntary association with the religion. Its gentile congregants are considered full members, with no conversion or declaration required. Similarly, the children are presumed Jewish regardless of parentage or conversion.

The larger groups in the Society have offered interfaith workshops covering communications and family issues.

"New Age" Judaism

If you are drawn toward mysticism, you may be interested in one of the "New Age" Judaism groups. They are few in number but are high-energy and thriving where they do exist. You can expect to find some intermarrieds worshipping there—many of them observant new converts—even though there are unlikely to be special programs for mixed couples.

Services will begin from a Jewish base and end at a Jewish base, but along the way might bring in elements from many traditions and philosophies. P'nai Or, a loose alliance of twelve of the groups, says it is "a network of spiritual seekers and communities" that "combines traditional study of Torah, mystical Kabbalistic and Hassidic traditions, meditation, singing, prayer, and current techniques of humanistic and transpersonal psychology." Efforts are made during the services to explain the exercises and goals.

Community events often focus on the holidays. At Passover, members might bake matzoh together and have a large communal seder. On Sukkos, people may eat together nightly in the group's sukkah. Expect lively family events on Purim and Hanukkah and all-night study sessions on occasion.

Each fellowship is autonomous, with no rules imposed about non-Jewish participation or any other matter. Because the groups try to be open, a gentile could expect to be given membership. If she is a regular worshipper, known and trusted by the others, she would probably be allowed to lead part of a service. Some groups might even let her read from the Torah. The spirit of patrilineality probably would also prevail: If her children had been raised as Jews, they would be welcomed for bar or bat mitzvahs even if they or she had never converted.

This is the only one of the affiliation options we describe that does not have organized religious schooling for children.

P'nai Or (formerly called B'nai Or) is known for the weekend retreats and weeklong summer institutes that it organizes. The retreats, which focus on personal prayer, are open to anyone. The group also offers adult classes in such topics as understanding the prayer book and learning mystical concepts and techniques.

The Jewish options we have described thus far have been movements. But you might also look into the handful of independent, single congregations; these nonaffiliated congregations have maverick rabbis that serve a large proportion of marginal and/or intermarried couples. (None of them offers religious schooling, although they will provide individualized bar or bat mitzvah training.) Several contacts are listed in the Appendix at the back of the book.

Liberal Protestantism

The Protestant denominations generally mentioned as having vibrant liberal wings are Presbyterian, United Methodist, United Church of Christ,

Episcopalian, Disciples of Christ, American Baptist, and Lutheran.

While liberal Protestants can have a deep faith in Jesus, they also concentrate on the social gospel (good works) and have rejected evangelical Christianity's hope of converting the world. Judaism is accorded legitimacy.

A liberal minister might suggest that congregants can redefine Jesus in their own terms. But the traditional theology has only been loosened, not dropped. Jesus is still the heart of the liturgy. He will be called the Christ and the Son of God. Creeds ("I believe in . . .") will be recited in unison and hymns of salvation sung. At Eastertime, Gospel passages from the Book of John (Chapters 18 and 19) that accuse the Jewish Pharisees of complicity in Jesus' death are likely to be read.

The best way to find a church where you can be comfortable as a mixed couple is to attend services and listen for the nuances. Does the pastor speak respectfully of Judaism? Does he talk more of Jesus as inspiration than as Savior? Do the adult education classes take an inquisitive rather than doctrinaire approach to Bible and belief?

The interreligious mix in any church is more likely to be Protestant-Catholic than Protestant-Jewish. Don't be surprised if you are the only Christian-Jewish family. We did not hear of any Protestant programs for or about intermarried couples.

The unconverted Jew should not expect to be given full church membership. Some churches have categories (such as "constituent member" or "prospective member") that recognize the supportive spouse but withhold the right to vote or hold office. The Jew probably could serve on project committees, be in the choir, perhaps help teach a Sunday school session.

Liberal churches practice infant baptism. A Jewish parent would probably be welcome at the altar during the baptism, and a Hebrew blessing might be welcome as well. The child of a mixed family (in fact, any child in the church) is expected to be baptized prior to his adolescent confirmation ceremony.

Social action is a deeply held value of liberal Protestantism, and you can expect to find a wealth of it. One possible sore point involves the Middle East. In recent years the National Council of Churches, acting on behalf of mainline Protestantism, has taken positions on the Middle East that have antagonized Jewish organizations.

Finding a mainline Protestant church in your area should be no problem. Finding a liberal one might be harder. University communities are usually havens for liberal worship. Get names from the university chaplain and from other ministers or friends.

Roman Catholicism

If you are uncomfortable with ritual, a Catholic Mass may start all your alarm buttons flashing and beeping. Here, Christian iconography and pageantry are full-blown. An aura of the supernatural surrounds you, with incense, bells, and holy water. People supplicate themselves in worship and confession. The priesthood is the voice of authority. But if the Catholic Church is home to your partner, you may be able to find a liberal, activist parish that will also be congenial to you.

Do not expect the form of worship itself to be diluted regardless of where you go. The Church requires an official liturgy, with its set Gospel, Epistle, Hebrew scripture passages, and communion. Within that structure, however, there are points where a priest has flexibility. A traditional priest might focus his homily on basic Catholic truths. A more liberal one, aware of the mix in his congregation, might praise pluralism and emphasize the need for social action.

Some moments in the standard liturgy may be surprisingly familiar to a Jew. Some of the prayers are similar to Hebrew prayers. The Mass refers to "our father Abraham."

Judaism is accorded official respect. The Second Vatican Council in the 1960s renounced attempts to proselytize Jews and emphasized the validity of God's covenant with the Jews and of the Hebrew Bible, independent of the New Testament. Still, because the Church also sees Christianity as the fulfillment of Judaism, you may encounter vestiges of chauvinism. Arm yourself with knowledge of the Vatican II declarations.[4]

An unbaptized Jew can't be a member of a Catholic church. She can enjoy other aspects of parish life, however, joining study groups and assisting informally on projects. She cannot partake of the sacraments (such as taking communion and being anointed by a priest during sickness).

The child of mixed parents would have to be baptized before enrolling in the catechism classes that lead up to confirmation.

Programming for mixed couples exists in some localities, as you'll see in Chapter 19. The Church does encourage general marriage-communications classes and retreats. And there are interfaith dialogue groups in which the two of you could explore your backgrounds in a structured way.

A caution on social action: The Vatican has no diplomatic ties with Israel but does with the Arab nations.

The advice on locating a comfortable church is the same as for Protestantism. Find a liberal community, visit a service, and watch for the nuances in tone and emphasis. Talk to an active Catholic whose social views and politics you share; he might know about subtle differences among parishes that would be important to you. Liberal Catholics often congregate near universities. Get referrals from a priest at a campus Newman center.

Society of Friends (Quakers)

The Society of Friends developed in a Christian context, and many Friends consider themselves Christian and Jesus as divine. But because freedom of belief is at the core of Quakerism, and because it has no dogma, an equal number of Friends would not call themselves Christian. That lack of dogma, together with its pacifist and nonhierarchical principles, has made the movement a home for many mixed families and "religious refugees."

The Quaker form of worship is spare by design. The movement began in seventeenth-century England as a reaction against what it regarded as excessive ritual and formalism in the established church. The early Friends felt they could experience God directly, through the quiet "inner voice," without benefit of liturgy or clergy. The only outward expression of group belief is the "testimonies," which are generally liberal positions on a range of issues, among them: against war, capital punishment, slavery, discrimination and segregation, and in favor of penal reform, equality of women, and humane treatment of the mentally ill. The result is a movement today that is noted for its political activism and religious tolerance.

The Quakers have split off in different directions through the years. Though they are best-known for their "Silent Meetings," don't be surprised if the Meetings in your area are of another type that resembles standard Protestant services, with sermons, choirs, and responsive readings. Realize that some Friends are evangelicals and will attempt to proselytize the Jew. Even where the Meetings are politically liberal and the worship is silent and gentle, don't think that you have fallen in with agnostics. The silent form is deeply mystical and God-oriented and must be respected as such.

Of the four main groupings of Friends, the Friends General Conference, with its liberalism and silent, unprogrammed worship, has particularly appealed to intermarrieds. The silent "Meeting for Worship" is held Sundays (called First Day) and convenes in a traditional, unadorned meetinghouse or in a classroom or living room. There is no ordained minister, no sacrament, no fixed program. Congregants sit silently for at least twenty minutes, sometimes the entire hour, until someone is moved to share the inner message she has received. Others might then also speak, at a delicate pace that allows for silent reflection on each message. Then, at the appropriate time, the overseers of the service shake hands, signaling the conclusion.

The Friends consider holidays no more holy or special than any other days. There are no special rites at birth, only a smiling acknowledgment by the congregants at a weekly service.

Becoming a member is fairly straightforward. The outlook is: If you are drawn to the worship, it is for a reason that is honorable and sufficient. Once your application is approved, you are admitted without fanfare or conversion.

There are no official programs for intermarried couples. A caution on social action: The movement's action arm, the American Friends Service Committee, has a reputation in the Jewish community as "Arabist," or at least too neutral on Middle East questions.

Unitarian-Universalism

Unitarians have gone to great lengths to create an inclusive, nondogmatic system. You will find many mixed couples and religious refugees among its members anywhere.

Historically, Unitarianism stressed the idea of God as a unity rather than a trinity, while Universalists taught that God does not reserve salvation for a limited few but extends it universally to all people regardless of their belief or lack of it. The two traditions officially became one in 1961 when the Unitarian-Universalist Association was formed.

Though some people might find Unitarian tenets nebulous, others think they are ideal for a modern, broad mind. Unitarianism, as the movement is frequently called, tries to draw from all religions and does not limit its members to any one way. The goal is diversity, free inquiry, beliefs freely chosen and evolving. The approach is so free-form that other churches have ejected Unitarianism from the Christian fold. Because the movement does not affirm Jesus as savior, it has not been permitted to join the National Council of Churches (though it does work with the council).

Still, Unitarianism springs from Protestantism. Many Unitarian congregations continue to have a definite Christian feeling to them. They will be called churches. Their officiants are known as ministers. They will sing hymns, have responsive readings, refer frequently to Jesus, have an invocation and benediction, perhaps offer a form of communion. Other groups are leaderless, will call themselves a "society" or a "fellowship," and will be avowedly a-Christian.

Unitarians like to discuss and adapt traditions from a variety of religions, including Judaism. A service might have a Yom Kippur, Hanukkah, or Passover theme at the appropriate season, as well as acknowledging Christmas and Easter. Congregations often put on seders (but perhaps during Thanksgiving to point out Passover's commonality with that celebration).

The movement has only a few distinctive rituals. A flaming chalice, symbol of the Unitarian movement, often is lighted by the minister or a congregant and placed at the front of the altar, where it burns throughout the service, denoting the light of truth. Some congregations have a water ritual: Members bring vials of water from different sources (the ocean, a stream, a well, a faucet) and pour them into a central container during the service. Water is a symbol of life-giving energy, and the ritual is performed in autumn to help people draw strength for the winter ahead. A third ritual is the "flower communion," which is celebrated in springtime (and as part of Easter in the Christian-oriented congregations). Congregants bring flowers, which are gathered together and become the focus of readings and meditations on nature and renewal. As they leave the service, people take a different flower than the one they brought, symbolizing their unity with one another.

Life-cycle events are intended to "celebrate life," not (as with sacraments) to wash away sin or draw God closer. There is a naming ceremony, or "dedication," at which the parents, godparents, and other selected adults come forward with the baby. The parents receive a flower or other gift from the congregation. They may dip the flower in water and place it on the baby's forehead, saying something about the uniqueness of each human life. More traditional congregations might call the ceremony a christening and have a symbolic use of water. Adolescents, after a period of study, are welcomed into membership through a ceremony which is called a confirmation but is more a coming-of-age rite than an affirmation of any particular beliefs.

Families are free to shape the content of these rites. Unitarian officiants usually welcome the chance to custom-make celebrations for children. You would probably be allowed to say a Hebrew blessing at a naming ceremony, for instance, or even to have your child read from the Torah during his confirmation.

Becoming a member is a simple matter of signing a membership book. A short welcoming ceremony follows during a service.

Even though it has an abundance of mixed families (or perhaps because it does), the movement has no special support-group programming for intermarried couples. It does offer marriage-enrichment workshops and weekends.

One thing to keep in mind if you are considering a Unitarian affiliation: You should choose it if you find the ideas attractive, the community stimulating, and the services fulfilling. You should not choose it as a fall-back position, because you can't agree on anything else and are reluctant to explore your differences too deeply. If this is your stance, you probably won't be able to present the religion in a convincing way to your children. In addition, as we have stressed throughout, conflicting needs, when not adequately dealt with, have a habit of erupting into problems later.

Ethical Culture

While Unitarian-Universalists are non-dogmatic and tolerate a wide range of religious viewpoints including belief in God, Ethical Culturists are committed to a worldview that is not God-oriented. There are other secular humanist groups, the American Humanist Association chief among them. But Ethical Culture comes closest to a standard affiliation, having regular Sunday meetings and family events as well as religious schooling.

The Ethical Culture movement, founded in the 1870s, is intellectual and "dry" by choice. Many members might call themselves reverent agnostics (revering life and human worth), but they tend to reject anything that smacks of the supernatural such as ritual, prayer, and scripture.

The rationalist spirit is evident in their Sunday morning meetings, which usually are called "platforms." The centerpiece of the platform is an address by the Leader or by an invited speaker. The topic might be a point of scientific research or politics or international affairs; always with an emphasis on the ethical dimension. The sessions begin and end with music, which might be classical music, folk guitar, perhaps a choir. There is no congregational singing and no invocation.

Though ritual is shunned, most chapters have group customs: monthly meals, or an annual one-day fast for world hunger, with the food money saved being donated to a famine-relief organization. Seasonal festivals organized by the Sunday schools deal with universal themes. In winter, for instance, there will be a solstice festival to create warmth in a time of cold.

Rites of passage are celebrated secularly. Upon the birth of a child, the family and Leader can develop a naming ceremony. For instance, the child might be presented during a platform, the Leader will discuss the significance of a new person coming into the world, and the parents could comment about what the event means to them and their family. Another ceremony for children is the graduation. Upon completion of

Sunday schooling, usually at about age fourteen, each child gives a talk on a social issue such as peace or world hunger. A gift might then be presented.

As a parent, you may want to have a blessing said at one of these ceremonies. But references to God are problematic to the Society. One Leader might allow a blessing to be offered as a "reading," while the next Leader might refuse, knowing that so many members wheeze at the slightest whiff of God or church.

Joining the Ethical Society is straightforward and involves no vows or ritual. New members are introduced at a platform and presented with a small gift, such as a book or a flower.

A course for interfaith couples has been developed by Lois Kellerman, Leader of the Brooklyn and Queens, New York, chapters, and Arthur Dobrin of the Long Island chapter. The movement also offers a host of adult education classes which deal with ethical issues and interpersonal relations.

Making an Informed Decision In considering whether and where to affiliate, don't try to work out a decision prematurely, on paper, or over a cup of coffee together. Get out and *experience* the different styles. This chapter's descriptions can only give you an overview. Each denomination, within its ranks, has a diversity of approaches. To decide where you may be comfortable, you have to see the styles of worship first-hand.

As you explore, keep in mind a few practical tips: Be sure to talk to both the clergy and congregants. Hunt out the intermarried members. Examine the pamphlets and fliers on display in the vestibule. Go during a holiday, since that will show a congregation in full swing and will demonstrate how conventional or experimental it is. If a congregation seems almost right but not quite, try another congregation in that movement.

Above all, take your time. You might give yourself a set period, say three months of active looking, before approaching a choice. Don't get frozen into indecision even if no place feels perfect. Join the best one and give yourself a year to warm up to it. You always can switch affiliations later.

If your children are old enough, consider including them in the decision. After all, your goal in affiliating is to find a place where you can be a family among families.

18. RELIGIOUS EDUCATION:

Trying Harder

Religious school: It is the place where children develop a special peer group, find adult role models, build a framework of ethics, learn religious skills, solidify their identity.

Religious school: It is also a prospect that makes many an intermarried parent stiffen. Their memories are sour: stern teachers, boring lessons, rote memorizing, pat answers. Repeatedly we heard the associations. Now, the wheel has turned and the graduates have become the parents, facing the decision for their own children: to enroll or not to enroll.

This chapter will help you make an informed decision. We look at Sunday schools and (for Jewishly identifying families) Hebrew school. Though some of you might be willing to enroll your child in a full-day parochial school, we limit our discussion to the less intensive education that accompanies family affiliation with a congregation. We will describe the approaches being taken by the better Sunday schools and provide a satchel of information so you can evaluate programs on your own.

Often, we heard parents complaining that religious schools exist to indoctrinate, not to stimulate. It's certainly true that some schools or some individual teachers follow a doctrinaire, disciplinarian approach. They commit what theologian Paul Tillich called the fatal pedagogical error: tossing answers like stones at the heads of people who have yet to ask the questions.[1] But today's liberal administrators are quite aware of the problem and are trying to overcome it. Their message to the skeptical parent is: Give us a fresh look. Religious education has changed since your day.

WHAT MAKES THE GOOD SCHOOLS GOOD

What is a good religious school like today? There are at least six characteristics to notice in the better-run ones (and to push for in the others):

1. The Good Schools Encourage Self-Exploration They urge teachers to pose questions to the children more than to provide them with answers. A liberal Jewish teacher, for instance, might use Bible stories to draw out pupils' values, by emphasizing the actions of the human characters in the tales rather than the role attributed to God. Liberal Catholic teachers nowadays rely much more on classroom discussion than on memorization of theology. Many mainline Protestant denominations employ curricula that are "idea-centered." Explains Rev. Jean M. Jones, a Methodist minister and longtime religious educator in Georgia, "The appropriate Bible background is included, but there's a great emphasis on interpersonal relationships, on how we treat people, as being what religion is all about."

2. The Good Schools Are Experiential By shopping in the secular marketplace, they have developed ways to make learning and knowledge "come alive." Arts and crafts, even board games, will be used with the younger pupils. A school might have a semester-long theme (immigration, say, or charity) and develop it through drama, fairs, or carnivals. Older pupils might make clothing of the immigrant period, or initiate a class charity project. They will be encouraged to develop these ideas themselves and with their classmates, as the teacher oversees. They might be allowed to choose from several activities to give them a sense of "ownership" of the curriculum.

3. The Good Schools Have an "Age-Appropriate" Curriculum They will know how to teach differently to children at different ages. By applying the theories of Erikson and Piaget, they know that in the early grades, when children are still in the "magic years," affective (emotional) approaches are at least as important as cognitive (intellectual) ones. The educators are trying to build positive early associations with a given aspect of the religion rather than a deep understanding of it.

This might be considered mild indoctrination, but a good school will later reopen that same aspect to scrutiny with the older pupils. Although the holidays or Bible stories might at first be presented in fairy-tale form, they will later be analyzed for their values, messages, and historical context. The technique is called "spiral curriculum."

4. The Good Schools Involve the Family There will be "family days" when you can join in the learning and celebrating. The marginal parent will find these a good way to stay abreast of the information. The schools encourage these events for the message of family unity they give. The good schools also will be open to having a parent with special knowledge address a class, even if the parent is not of the religion.

5. The Good Schools Respect Other Belief Systems Educators from all the denominations told us their curricula had been changed in the last generation to delete negative references to other religions. Rev. Jones tells how the changes have penetrated liberal Protestant schools: "In the less conservative groups you will have some very positive things about Jewish people. You will have sessions on Jewish children celebrating Hanukkah, that this is a very important, positive aspect of their faith . . . We've moved to a more accepting and respectful attitude toward people who believe differently from what we believe in religious matters."

6. The Good Schools Are Sensitive to Mixed Families They will let mixed parents know they are accepted. They will attempt to head off awkwardness that a child of intermarriage might feel.

Reform Judaism is doing the most in this area. As part of its strong outreach effort to intermarrieds, the movement has written official guidelines for teachers and administrators, entitled "Developing Sensitivity to the Needs of Children Who Have Non-Jewish Relatives."[2] The 133-page publication, released in the autumn of 1986, presents lesson plans for teaching about the two religions and both sets of holidays. It describes a model workshop at which teachers explore their own attitudes about intermarriage. As part of the workshop, a number of scenarios are posed for healthy dealings with intermarried parents and with classroom dilemmas.

The tenets of the guidelines (and the Reform movement) are summed up in three of its statements: "Having a non-Jewish parent is not a shameful secret and should be treated matter-of-factly." "Children should not be made to be missionaries to their parents." "Avoid comparing our best with their worst."

Stepping Stones, a pilot program for intermarried families run by the Jewish community in Denver, is an example of many of these trends.

The program is built around hands-on experiences. Youngsters conduct a mock Jewish wedding, for instance, and make menorahs and holiday foods. Activities are aimed at particular age levels. Teachers are given sensitivity training in dealing respectfully with other religions. Stepping Stones is emphatic about parental involvement. Parents are required to attend at least six family sessions with their children.[3]

A Caution Most religious schools are likely to fall short somewhere with the six "enlightened" approaches. The schools are only as good as their classroom teachers. If the teachers are college students, seminarians, or volunteer parents, their skills may be meager and their style stiff. Even if the school has a budget to hire professionals, the teachers may drill rather than challenge. If the teachers are older or are not broadminded, they may parrot stale notions of the other religions that were inculcated in them when they were children.

Religious schools are not out of the woods yet. But the good ones are trying. Through informed looking, you can find a good school, or certainly an acceptable one, for your mixed child.

What Do You Want? What Don't You Want? Before setting out, you need to understand what you're looking for. Religious education has four elements that every school will promote in its own way: religious skills, religious identity, moral action, and a spiritual life. As a parent, you'll want to evaluate a school's relative emphases on the four. But you also need to reckon with where you yourselves stand on them.

Talk with each other about what areas you hope the school will emphasize, and any areas you'd prefer that it downplay. That process will help greatly in your dealings with the administrator or teacher. Your questions will be more pointed and you can explore the areas of most concern to you.

As parents, you need to understand why you are sending your children to religious school and what sort of message you want to transmit to them about it. If the signal is weak, you'll be leaving yourself open to the same charge of hypocrisy that you might have leveled at your own parents when you were the schoolchild. Despite your determination to "do it better" with your children, you will be setting up the same poisoned cycle of resistance and resentment. Once you have selected a religious school, muster as much enthusiasm and involvement as you can.

The Age Question Sometimes parents' ambivalence results in their holding back on religious education until the child is nearing adolescence. That has its own drawback. Just as a dissonance between what he is learning and what you are practicing can leave the child cool to the religion, so might his commitment be limited if he is first enrolled when he is already beyond the "magic" early years. The reason is not your attitude so much as his own psychological state.

Rabbi Jeffrey Schein, director of education at Reconstructionist Rabbinical College, emphasizes the value of exposure to religious symbols and holidays in the early years. "If we get a nine-year-old coming in and he doesn't have that base of wonder, then he begins to master things that don't make sense to him. . . . If it hasn't hooked someone already, then [his] rationality is going to be a cold rationality."

Though the child enrolled at nine or older will benefit from the knowledge, the chances of the religion taking a visceral hold on him are lessened. Don't expect more.

Nicole and her brother Michael, students in Denver's Stepping Stones, are a good example of this age-related difference. Nicole entered the program at age eight and came away with a greatly strengthened sense of Jewish identity. When asked about her religious identity, she enthusiastically said she was Jewish and glad to be so. Michael, who was enrolled at age fourteen, said the program was "interesting," but he basically felt like an observer toward both religions.[4]

EVALUATING A SCHOOL: LOOK AND LISTEN

Once you are ready to explore, how do you begin? How do you find a program you can trust and support? Here are some pointers.

Ask About the Approach to Mixed Families Does the school attempt to learn about its pupils' home experiences? What is the congregation's policy on membership of mixed families? Would your child have to be converted prior to enrollment? Prior to the movement's adolescent ritual (confirmation or bar/bat mitzvah)? Are there other mixed children in the school? Could the parent of the other religion be involved in classroom teaching? Could she be on the school's policy-making board? Are efforts made to sensitize the staff to mixed children?

Study the Curricular Goals Get a copy of them prior to your interview with the administrator to help you formulate questions. See if the lessons are age-appropriate. Are the teachers encouraged to innovate? If there are no curricular goals in writing, ask the administrator to explain them.

Ask About the Relative Emphasis on the Four Essentials We're referring to skills, identity, morals, and spirituality. Which are most important? How does the school promote them? What does it mean by them?

Learn About the Faculty Who are the teachers? How well are they trained in classroom techniques? How versed are they in the religion? Are they paid? How is their performance evaluated? Is there much staff turnover?

See a Classroom in Action Preferably, make it the one where your child would be placed. Is the room cheerful and lively? Is there a good pupil-teacher ratio? Are there hands-on projects? Does the teacher give the children praise? Does she converse, or does she lecture? Does she incorporate experiences from the children's daily lives?

Pose Concrete Situations Don't be afraid to ask questions of the administrator or the teacher. Here are a few: What would your child's class be taught about God? About the other religion? If it is a Jewish school, what does it teach about Jewish law? If it is a Christian school, what does it teach about Jesus? If it is a secular school, what does it teach about organized religion? Are there community-action projects for children? Do they involve the wider community as well as that religious community?

Ask About Other Programs Do they have summer camps? What has the camp experience been like for mixed children? (Camps offer intensive dunkings in the religion, which might seem intimidating to a mixed couple. But realize that the effect on children varies. Camp produces a deep and lasting commitment in some children. For others, the fervor does not transfer from the woods, but washes away with the first autumn rain.)

Do they have a youth group? Are mixed children in it? What do the members do? Sometimes a youth group provides a forum for freewheeling discussions of social and personal issues that is not built in to a more structured classroom.

Talk to a Parent See if the administrator will give you an enrollment list. Contact a family who lives nearby. Better yet, contact another intermarried couple.

* * *

Here's a taste of the answers you'll get from denominational educators. What follows are summaries of the atmosphere in the religious groupings described in Chapter 17 (Affiliation).

The denominations all begin children in formal schooling at about age six and offer classes for them until about age sixteen. Church schools start young children with an hour-long class Sunday mornings and later might add an hour during the week. Jewish schools begin with two hours Sunday mornings and add as much as five hours on several weekday afternoons.

Reform Judaism will enroll your child whether you are a conversionary family or not, and won't require that the child be converted prior to bar or bat mitzvah. The movement is keen on having bar and bat mitzvah graduates continue classes until confirmation, at age sixteen. The age-related "spiral curriculum" is central to the Reform approach. The schools teach Hebrew, Bible, history, and holidays but also make a point of applying Jewish ethics from the pupils' personal lives.

Reconstructionist Judaism emphasizes the concept of community above even the Jewish curricular triad. Its schools resist focusing on one aspect of Judaism, whether it be prayer or Torah or the *mitzvot* (commandments), as the Jewish essential. While teaching those classic areas, it also adds large doses of folk customs and other peoplehood ideas. Community is fostered by having children celebrate with the rest of the congregation regularly and perform helpful tasks in the synagogue. Children of an unconverted gentile mother will be enrolled, but might be required to convert prior to bar or bat mitzvah.

Conservative Judaism is more, well, conservative, both pedagogically and socially. Many congregations will not enroll the child of an unconverted gentile mother. Others will, provided the child is converted within a certain period (perhaps a year, and certainly in time for bar or bat mitzvah). Conservative schools are in session several more hours a week than most Reform and Reconstructionist schools. The schools tend to have professional teachers and to be strong on the fundamental skills. A child will emerge from a Conservative school with a solid foundation in Hebrew, Bible, texts, and Jewish ethics.

Orthodox Judaism generally won't accept a child unless his mother was converted before his birth and the family follows an Orthodox lifestyle. Its schools provide a rigorous education in worship skills, texts, and *mitzvot.*

Secular Judaism emphasizes Jewish holidays, customs, values, and peoplehood. Its schools look at the Torah, other texts, and the blessings with a scientific objectivity. They probably won't teach worship skills.

Hebrew might be taught, but not extensively. The schools will probably involve the students in social-action projects. Children of intermarriage will be enrolled with no questions asked or conditions applied, and can be bar or bat mitzvahed without conversion. In the "secular bar mitzvah" (or bat mitzvah), the child chooses a project, works on it for a year or so, and then gives a presentation to the school and invited adults. The topic might be Eastern European Jewish music, or literature of the Holocaust, or Jewish ethics, or even Jews in sports. Members will probably be uncomfortable if the topic is Scripture-based.

Liberal Protestantism does promote a belief in Jesus, but a skilled teacher will make clear that the content of that belief can vary from person to person. You might be presenting the congregation with its first mixed child, so it may devise a policy as it goes along. Most churches are accustomed to children being baptized at birth. If your child was not, the church would probably want him to be baptized by the time of his confirmation.

Catholicism would require that a child of intermarriage be baptized prior to enrollment in catechesis classes. Catechism prepares children for First Communion and for later confirmation by teaching liturgy, faith, and morals. The Gospels will be taught as the word of God revealed through man. Liberal teachers, though, will explore the historic context of the Bible and will encourage open classroom discussion.

Society of Friends has three thrusts in its "First Day" schools: Bible stories, Quaker history, and mysticism. The special emphasis is on spirituality, felt through prayer and the personal "inner light" and expressed in life through simplicity and peace work. Some schools are explicitly Christian in their teaching; others are universalist. "Silent meeting" congregations try to incorporate children into the congregation by having pupils end their session and join the parents in the meetinghouse for worship just as the parents are ending their own period of silent meditation. Your child would be guaranteed enrollment; the movement is nonritualistic, so there is no baptism, conversion, or confirmation.

Unitarianism, in general, presents Jesus as a great teacher and downplays the theology in Bible stories. Though the movement has its roots in Christianity, its schools try to give children an appreciation of and experience with the customs of many religions, with Judaism being one of the favorites. Some congregations shy away from ritual and theism, emphasizing ethics and social action in the schools instead. Others dabble in ritual and might offer a brief worship service for the children. You can expect to find mixed children in any Unitarian school. They are given automatic entry and face no conversion requirement.

Ethical Culture automatically would enroll a mixed child. As a non-ritualistic movement, it has no equivalent to conversion. Its schools present the Bible as allegory laden with value lessons and Judaism and Christianity as worldviews, two among many. The schools teach self-respect, ethics, and conflict-resolution and organize social-action programs for the pupils.

WHEN NOWHERE IS SATISFACTORY

For some parents, nothing will feel right. You might have been put off by the answers to your questions about the curriculum or about you as a mixed family. If you live in a small town or rural area, your options may be paltry or you might not want to travel the distance to the school. You may find that your child would be sorely isolated as the only mixed child enrolled. You might feel OK about the school but not want to pay the tuition or the congregation's affiliation fee.

Do you go it alone? You can. By your daily example, you already are teaching your children about faith and values. But you will have to take on a more explicit role. Begin to articulate your beliefs, and to draw out your children's. You can teach them the ways of the religion. Brush up on the customs and teachings. Check with the denomination that comes closest to what you want: Can it provide any lay literature on its tenets and practices? (Addresses and phone numbers appear in the Appendix under the Affiliation heading.) Look over the home religious education packets listed in our Appendix. Browse the religion sections of libraries and bookstores for primer books. Learning together as a family can be enriching for parent as well as child.

One important element is missing from this approach, however: a community. Transmitting the skills and positive associations depends solely on your effectiveness. Even if you teach well, the enterprise will be sorely tested if, in adolescence, your child rebels against you and the religion that is so closely bound with you. Even if he does not rebel, the religion will lack scope. Bringing in others affirms to him that the religion has an importance to others. (And, on a practical level, including others makes the celebrations much more fun.)

Sometimes parents of young children form discussion groups. If you can locate one, see if its members are your type. Broach the idea to them of forming a self-styled religious school.

You might have to organize the discussion group yourselves. Invite parents whose orientation seems to resemble yours. Think of the group as a fellowship. Assess the members' religious needs and thresholds. Try to get a consensus on the goals and content. See if anyone is observant or knowledgeable enough to teach.

The teaching itself is a challenge. Though the group of children may be manageably small, their ages might vary considerably. The best approach is to have classes at least twice a month, but that requires commitment and stamina. The potential for burnout is always there. A better approach might be to hire a clergy student or college religion major as your teacher. Should you do that, use parents as aides and keep the fellowship functioning for adult discussion and holiday festivities.

We have seen several parent-run schools which were fresh and creative and got children much more excited about the religious tradition than most standard Sunday schools. Their drawback was that they were scattershot. In both skills and history they gave children only a spotty background.

In the Appendix, we list several practical guides for developing an informal curriculum.

Regardless of the route you take, remember that you are your children's primary religious educator. You may be ambivalent about religious school because you imagine it will take over as your child's principal religious role model. But *you* are the role model that counts, for better or worse.

19. PROGRAMS AND RESOURCES:

Where to Turn

A s you talk with your partner about your religious loyalties and needs, consider bringing an outside voice into the process. The fresh insights of a trained counselor, the support and feedback of intermarried peers, sometimes are necessary to jog you out of your fixed positions or give you the courage to follow your instincts together in the face of outside opposition. This chapter (and the Appendix) will tell you where those outside voices can be found.

If your differences seems significant, look into the options for individualized counseling that we list. But if your relationship is on solid ground and you just want more clarity on some mutually perplexing interreligious issues, check the programs specifically designed for intermarried couples. (As you will see, Christian institutions offer very few programs specifically for the intermarried. Nearly all of the programming comes from the Jewish community.)

The first and most immediate resource in your search for an outside voice can be a local, trusted clergyperson. If he or she is liberal, sensitive, and not too busy to provide sustained support, you need go no farther. But if that doesn't work, check out the variety of options—some religious, some not—listed below.

Pastoral Counseling A network of about five hundred pastoral counseling centers exists nationwide to help you discuss marital communications and religious issues. Pastoral counselors are clergy or religiously committed lay people, all of whom are accredited therapists. The centers are interfaith services that usually have both Jewish and Christian counselors.

The centers offer individual, family, and sometimes group counseling. Though there probably will not be a group specifically devoted to interreligious issues, you can expect the issues of religion and belief to be raised by any pastoral counselor in any setting. Because the counselors tend to be religious liberals, you can expect their guidance to be gentle and nonjudgmental.

To contact a nearby center, check the phone book under "Pastoral Counseling Center" or the *Yellow Pages* listing under "Counselors." Or get a referral from the American Association of Pastoral Counseling, 9508A Lee Highway, Fairfax, Va. 22031 (telephone: 703-385-6967).

Marriage Encounter This movement exists to help basically healthy couples strengthen their relationship. It also has a religious message: that in fully experiencing your unity as a couple, you experience a oneness with God.

Marriage Encounter began as a Catholic concept and now is offered in Jewish and Protestant forms as well. Its centerpiece is the intensive encounter weekend. The event is very structured, with no time for freewheeling group discussion. Here's a description of a Catholic session:[1]

The encounter takes place in a hotel or similar facility where each couple has a private room. A priest is on hand to lead prayers and Mass and to offer pastoral care if needed. The clergy and previously "encountered" couples give a number of talks which, progressively through the weekend, explain the purpose of Marriage Encounter: to help you realize that each of you has masks that prevent you from revealing your true selves to your partner; that you love your partner in ways you never express; that God has a place in your marriage and you have a place in God's plan. These talks are a buildup for the real work of the weekend, which is intensive communication between couples. Each person is given notebooks and questions to answer in writing ("What are my good points?" "What are my bad points?" "What are my feelings about what I find most attractive in you?" "What feeling do I find most difficult to face in myself and share with you?" "What are my reasons for wanting to go on living?").

You will spend most of the weekend writing out your answers to those and many other questions, swapping notebooks with your spouse, and sharing your feelings. This is done in strict privacy. For a couple who is open to the exercises, an intense intimacy builds. Marriage Encounter offers followup sessions to help couples keep that intimacy alive. These include monthly "regional renewals" as well as meetings in couples' homes.

The Protestant and Jewish forms of Marriage Encounter are similar in technique to a Catholic session. A Jewish weekend, however, might have a smaller religious component.

There is no national office to contact to get in touch with a Marriage Encounter group near you. Look in your phone book under "Marriage Encounter/Catholic," "Marriage Encounter/Jewish," etc. Check with a clergyperson or local council of churches, Catholic chancery, or board of rabbis. Keep an eye out for posters or newspaper listings of talks by Marriage Encounter speakers.

The Unitarian-Universalists offer a Couples Enrichment Program that is similar in style but eschews the religious tone.

Marriage Enrichment This is a widely available program that sometimes is offered by churches or synagogues and sometimes independently. The model differs from Marriage Encounter in two ways: First, Marriage Enrichment is not designed as a religious experience. If it has a religious element, it will be secondary to the marital-communications component. In keeping with that, the sessions are often led by trained couples, with no clergyperson on hand. Second, Marriage Enrichment centers on small-group talks rather than private encounters among couples.

There are more structured forms in which couples cover a set agenda and less structured ones in which the couples determine what issues will be covered. Topics typically include conflict-resolution, intimacy, communication styles, and goal-setting.

The sessions are normally weekend retreats. Occasionally the couples will be instructed to go off privately to share an exercise either in writing or orally. The emphasis, though, is on group discussion.

Retreats are organized across the country through the Association for Couples in Marriage Enrichment. The group trains leaders to conduct religion-sponsored sessions and publishes exercise books, pamphlets, and bibliographies on communications, intimacy, and conflict resolution. It also exists as a membership organization that couples join to attend followup sessions.

The group has fifty-two chapters. To get the name of a local contact or a list of publications, contact the Association for Couples in Marriage Enrichment, Box 10596, Winston-Salem, N.C. 27108 (telephone: 919-724-1526).

The Society of Friends (Quakers) has its own Couple Enrichment programs that follow this model, but with the Friends' emphasis on "the light within."

Reform Judaism This is the religious movement that, as part of its outreach to the intermarried, has the single most comprehensive program for mixed couples. Though the program is offered in a Jewish framework, the facilitators encourage open discussion and are likely to be sensitive to the Christian partner's loyalties. Often, in fact, the facilitators are intermarried people themselves who have chosen to have Jewish homes. It is as if you are gathering at the Jewish doorway; the leader will show you what's inside but won't pull you in.

We describe the three courses most available nationwide:

1. *"Times and Seasons"* This is a popular eight-week course designed for young interreligious couples. Usually, the couples have yet to marry or are newly married and without children. The course is designed to help them focus on the life-style issues that lie ahead. Topics for group discussion can cover the gamut, as listed in this course description: How can I become more tolerant of my partner's beliefs? How can we figure out which religion to raise our children? Will I regret raising them in the other religion? How do I maintain my integrity if my parents or in-laws are aggressively pressuring me? In what ways do Jewish and Christian beliefs differ? How is it possible to be Jewish if I do not believe in God? How should Christmas be handled if the children and one parent are Jewish? Is there a way to raise my children to be comfortable identifying with both religions without confusion? How do I teach my children to pray?

2. *"Bridge to Understanding"* This is an eight-session discussion group for couples who have different religious attitudes and values. People who sign up tend to have been together longer than "Times and Seasons" couples and to have experienced some interreligious difficulties. The group provides a supportive atmosphere for discussion of such issues as tensions within the extended family, holiday celebrations, religious education, and child-rearing.

3. *"Making Marriage Work"* This is a ten-week course, for engaged or newly married couples, that discusses both interreligious concerns and general marriage issues. General issues include marital communications, handling two careers, money and time management, sexuality, and decisions about child-rearing. Religious issues include problems of parents and in-laws and religious identification of children.

The three courses have some overlap. Check with a Reform staff person to see which one seems most appropriate for you. The decision might depend on which course is being offered. Although program models exist for all three courses, you might find that Bridge to Understanding and Making Marriage Work will only be offered when the demand is there. Times and Seasons seems to be more readily available in Reform regions around the country.

Some regions also arrange Times and Seasons "networks," which are informal gatherings for course graduates. The meetings, usually held monthly in people's homes, allow further discussion.

The Reform outreach coordinators often are available as well for private consultation with individuals or couples. This can be over the phone or in person. There will be no charge, but the counseling is not designed to be long-term.

To find out when courses are being presented, call a nearby Reform synagogue or contact your regional office of the Union of American Hebrew Congregations (Reform's official name). Check the Appendix, under the Affiliation heading, for the addresses of the regional offices.

Jewish Agencies The Jewish communities in most population centers have social-service agencies that provide programs for couples. Some of them are specifically for intermarried couples. For instance, you might find a six-session discussion group for the intermarried that covers child-rearing, negotiation, religious life-style, and personal-identity issues. The group will be led by a psychologist or counselor, with perhaps a rabbi on hand to address religious issues. The leader and rabbi are likely to be nonjudgmental, with the leader sometimes intermarried himself. Because of the agencies' mental-health orientation, you can expect the emphasis to be more on the health of your relationship than on a desired religious outcome.

These one hundred and forty agencies, through their family-life education programs, also provide general sessions to help married people. You might find your local agency facilitating support groups for couples that cover communication and conflict resolution. You might find workshops on effective parenting in both early childhood and adolescence. The agencies also all provide private counseling for individuals, couples, and families.

To locate the agency nearest you, look in the phone book under "Jewish Family Service," "Jewish Community Service" or "Jewish Social Service." If that doesn't work, get the name from the closest Federation of Jewish Agencies.

Jewish Converts Network This permanent support group was formed to help new and prospective converts in their transition. The organization also has a number of mixed-married couples, who often are graduates of Times and Seasons or some other formal course and want to continue with a group forum.

JCN has several hundred members in eight chapters. For information, contact Lena Romanoff, director, at 1112 Hagysford Road, Penn Valley, Pa. 19072 (telephone: 215-664-8112).

Protestant Denominations Some churches will run their own Marriage Enrichment workshops, but the quality and frequency depends on the initiative of the pastor and the lay leaders.

Catholic Dioceses Priests and dioceses automatically will refer couples interested in marriage enhancement to the local Marriage Encounter people. Dioceses, through their Family Life Bureaus, sometimes will augment Marriage Encounter as well. One-day workshops for newly married couples are given on a regular basis in many dioceses. These teach techniques of communications and family management. You might also find one-day workshops on effective parenting.

If you are engaged and having a church wedding, you might find a special workshop on interreligious issues offered. In Chapter 4 (The Wedding), we tell of the marriage-preparation classes that the Catholic Church requires for couples who wish to be married by a priest. In some dioceses, the church provides engaged Catholic-Protestant and Catholic-Jewish couples with extra preparation on interfaith issues: worshipping together, dealing with parents, deciding on child-rearing.

For information, contact a priest or Family Life Bureau.

In addition to these programs for couples are two resources we know of that are geared to the other members of your family who are affected—your children and your parents:

Pareveh This grassroots group, which officially calls itself Pareveh: The Alliance for Adult Children of Jewish-Gentile Intermarriage, sets up support groups, puts out a quarterly newsletter, and sells informational tapes and pamphlets. For information, contact: 3628 Windom Place, N.W., Washington, D.C. 20008 (telephone: 202-363-7266).

Parent Groups The Reform Jewish outreach offices, as well as a number of Jewish family-service or other social-service agencies and YM-YWHAs, present periodic workshops and support groups for the Jewish parents of intermarriers. These are usually run by professional counselors and are designed not as gripe sessions but as occasions for people to talk out their mixed feelings, broaden their viewpoint, and try to come to terms with the intermarriage.

Scattered around the country are permanent, single programs for intermarrieds. We list a few with which we are familiar:

Paulist Center Community This Catholic center in Boston has a standing support group for interfaith couples, most of whom are Catholic-Jewish. For a number of the members, the group exists as an ongoing community. The group's goal is to help people co-exist religiously. The discussions tend to center on child-rearing and life-style issues. The Paulist center is at 5 Park Street, Boston, Mass. 02108 (telephone: 617-742-4460).

Queens (N.Y.) Ethical Culture Society For several years, this group has conducted a four-session workshop for interfaith couples. Lois Kellerman, Leader of the Queens society, guides the groups through an exploration of individual credos and spiritual search, Jewish-Christian theological differences, religious child-rearing, and life-style decision-making. For information, contact Lois Kellerman, Ethical Culture Society of Queens, 152 Burns Street, Forest Hills, N.Y. 11375 (telephone 718-263-7260).

Ansche Chesed Synagogue This creative congregation in Manhattan has offered six-session workshops for intermarried couples several times a year since the mid-1980s. Religious, child, and family issues are covered. The synagogue is at 251 West 100th Street, New York, N.Y. 10025 (telephone: 212-865-0600).

The Rabbinic Center for Research and Counseling Irwin H. Fishbein, a psychotherapist and Reform rabbi, directs this center in northern New Jersey. He and his staff provide individual and couples counseling and offer sessions periodically on marriage enrichment, effective parenting, and parenting in an interfaith home. The center also has an ongoing, open-agenda support group in the form of a monthly "Sabbath couples' group." The rabbinic center is at 128 East Dudley Avenue, Westfield, N.J. 07090 (telephone: 201-233-0419).

Stepping Stones This innovative school for intermarried families sponsored by the Jewish community in Denver, has set up an ongoing parents' group, at the parents' request, that explores questions of Jewish identity. The school is at 51 Grape Street, Denver, Colo. 80220 (telephone: 303-388-4013).

* * *

In addition to those ongoing programs, you will find programs cropping up on a temporary, local basis. Many synagogues, for instance, sponsor their own support groups for intermarried couples or might know of ones that have been started independently by their members or people in the neighborhood. Check with synagogues near you, or with the local Board of Rabbis. Sometimes, Jewish YM-YWHAs will have support groups and workshops; New York's 92nd Street YM-YWHA has been a model of Jewish programming. A campus Hillel or Jewish Campus Activities Board often can refer you to programs. Local chapters of the American Jewish Committee have been involved in intermarriage programming around the country. Contact the Protestant council of churches or diocesan Jewish-Catholic liaison for their suggestions about local programs and groups.

You have another outlet in this search: creating your own support group. Perhaps none of the resources you locate feels comfortable. Perhaps the programs are simply not offered at a convenient time and place. Perhaps you want to shape the agenda well away from any institutional framework. Broach the idea to intermarried friends and acquaintances. Brainstorm an agenda. This book and its exercises will get you off to a good start. You might want the group to be limited in duration. Or you might want it to serve as your community, a place to share holidays, and teach yourselves and your children together.

Whether you choose individual counseling or a group setting, whether the group is temporary or permanent, using an outside voice will help you understand yourself and your partner better.

HANDLING SPECIAL DIFFICULTIES

20. DIVORCE AND REMARRIAGE:

Children in the Middle

Intermarriage and divorce do not go hand in hand, despite what some people would have you believe. But they definitely are acquaintances. Researchers have found that Jewish-Christian intermarriages are somewhat more likely than same-religion marriages to end in divorce. They also have found that remarriage and intermarriage are frequent partners: After someone divorces a person of her own religion, she is far more likely to marry outside the religion the second time around.[1]

Divorce and remarriage are always difficult, especially when children are involved—and the religious factor can easily complicate the situation. In researching this problem-laden issue, we found four key principles to keep in mind:[2]

First, when religion becomes the focus of continuing, bitter disputes during a divorce, it is actually a smokescreen masking other issues. Regardless of the religious convictions of the parties, conflicts over religion can be resolved unless the parties are invested in continuing the dispute.

Second, when you fight over religious training, the child is bound to be caught in the middle. One expert we consulted, clinical psychologist Emily Visher, recalls what one child said of her divorcing parents, "They're shooting arrows at each other and they're going right through me."

Third, exposing a child to more than one religion in the various households to which she is attached does not by itself cause her emotional stress or identity confusion. If her parents have come to an agreement about the religious patterns in their households, she will adapt.

Fourth, conflict can be reduced when each person feels he has some power in the situation. Feelings of powerlessness produce resistance and intransigence. Sharing power means compromising—even when you are sure you are right and where values dear to you are involved. You have to decide where religion fits into the total scheme of your values, including the value you place on your children's emotional health.

DIVORCE: COMPETITION OR COLLABORATION?

The main cause of problems in this arena is the failure to achieve an emotional divorce to accompany the legal one. The goal of the person who has not emotionally divorced is still "winning" or "punishing" his ex-spouse, and in that climate he can't see ways to reduce conflict for the child's sake.

When he has attained an emotional divorce, even if his ex-spouse has not changed, he will find himself acting in new ways that will lead both of them toward a resolution of the issues.

Herb learned that lesson the hard way, as the result of a painful divorce and custody fight. When he and Dottie had married a dozen years earlier, Dottie had converted to Judaism with what seemed genuine enthusiasm and had agreed that the children would be raised as Jews. But as their two sons grew, she felt more and more strongly that she still was a Catholic in her heart and that she wanted to raise the boys as Catholics. Dottie began going to church regularly and criticizing Herb for insisting that the boys attend Hebrew school.

The marriage was tense from nearly the beginning, with religion one of many difficulties. They hung on for a number of years, but eventually it was clear they weren't going to patch things up. When the boys were ten and seven, Herb and Dottie separated. In the separation agreement, Dottie was given temporary custody, and she agreed in turn that she would continue to take the boys to Hebrew school and give them bar mitzvahs.

But the fight only got worse. Dottie resisted their Hebrew training and began taking them to church. Herb and his lawyer were in court frequently to enforce the separation agreement. The boys began to identify as Catholics. After protracted divorce proceedings, Herb sued for custody of the boys. He won. But after six weeks he returned them to Dottie, saying they were spiteful and made it clear they did not want to live with him and did not want to be Jews. In the end, the boys were raised as Catholics.

Herb felt Dottie had "poisoned" the boys against him and against Judaism. But he was determined not to lose his relationship with them. For the next five years, they visited him one day a week, every week, whether they wanted to or not. He talked to them on the phone between visits. He tried to convince them by action and example that he loved them and was a good person. It took years, but a new father-son relationship developed. When the boys became teenagers, Herb let them decide whether to continue visiting every week—and they voluntarily kept coming. The relationship is now an affectionate one.

Looking back on the court battle, Herb has two strong and opposite feelings. On the one hand, he feels he'd do it again. Had he not attempted to see that his sons were raised Jewish, he says, he would have been "selling them down the river." Although they may not understand now why he did it, he thinks someday they'll appreciate his Jewish commitment.

On the other hand, he says, the impact of the dispute on the children was "devastating. My older son is still scarred." The younger one, by the time he was ten, "had spent twenty-five percent of his life listening to his mother and father tear each other up in court." His advice now, both to the person who is thinking of a religious reversion or of a religious challenge in court, is, "Consider the children."

That's what people were saying to him at the time, and he just couldn't listen. "Everyone says, 'Get the divorce over, get away from each other, but try to do it with some dignity. And quickly.' But when you're in the throes of the thing, you don't think as rationally . . . Neither of you wants to give in. You've invested all this money and time and emotion."

Now, his priorities are different. He still doesn't like his ex-wife very much, but they have a civil relationship. His anger at her is not the center of his life. He doesn't have to spend all his time and emotional energy getting back at her.

"The bottom line is, my kids are not Jewish, but they are my kids, and they care about me and we have a good relationship. The bottom line is to preserve the relationship" with them.

If you have not achieved an emotional divorce, you may be tempted, out of vindictiveness, to use religion as a weapon against your ex-spouse. If you do, you are likely to harm your child in the process. Here are four possible situations.

1. Using Religion to Undermine Your Ex-Spouse's Relationship with the Children In this scenario, both parents are now openly practicing separate religions, and they lock horns over the question of "double exposure" to the two faiths. Double exposure is likely to harm the emotional health of a child of divorce in only two situations, according to legal commentators and psychological assessments presented to the courts: first, when the religions are presented as mutually exclusive polar opposites; and second, when religion is used as a vehicle to criticize and undermine the authority of either parent.

Both behaviors illustrate the smokescreen pattern, because the parents are using religion as a handy way to retaliate against each other. What they might not realize is that since the child identifies with both parents, criticism of the religion—and by implication the values and personality—of either parent also undermines the child's own confidence and self-esteem.

Should your ex-spouse indulge in these destructive behaviors, you need to call her hand. But don't do it in the presence of your children. When speaking with the children, muster as much equanimity as you can. Do it not to score points as the "better" parent but to show them that there is a middle ground that everyone can be aiming for. Tell them that even though you and their mother have had disagreements, you are going to look for the merit in her ideas and you hope she will look for the merit in yours. Add that different religions all have something to teach and that you hope that, even if the children embrace one religion, they will grow up open-minded enough to learn from the best of the other.

If your ex-spouse presents the religions as irreconcilable and opposed, you can point out the similarities and common ground. (Chapter 10 and the Notes and Recommended Reading sections can help you acquire the background needed to give a thoughtful and balanced response.)

2. The Hoarding of Custody In this scenario, the custodial parent takes away holiday or weekend visiting time from the noncustodial parent in the name of the children's religious training (going to church, synagogue, or Sunday school, and celebrating the holidays of her religion).

Sometimes the custodial parent will do this out of sincere belief that the child will be confused if she is exposed to two religions. If you feel that way, understand that keeping the child from one side of her family at holiday times denies her precious contact with one side of herself.

At least as often, the custodial parent hoards custody not for the child's sake but to get emotional revenge at his ex-spouse. The behavior is another smokescreen.

You may be tempted to fight out the issue in court. Be aware that the general response of the courts, in all states, is not to interfere with the custodial parent's decisions concerning details of upbringing unless the child is threatened with serious harm. In addition, for constitutional reasons courts are reluctant to intervene in religious disputes. They are usually unwilling to change or even review custody or visitation orders where the alleged harm has to do with religious teaching. This means that while the custodial parent is free to teach what he wants when the child is with him, the noncustodial parent is entitled to do the same.

If you are the custodial parent and you truly feel your child needs religious training on weekends, come to an agreement about a comparably valuable time for your ex-spouse to be with the child, a time that is satisfying to both of them.

3. *Conversion-Reversion* If you had converted, you may feel very lonely trying to bring up your child in that religion after the break-up of your marriage. This is a time when it is crucial to find support in raising your child in the new religion. Seek out the programs for single parents in your church or synagogue—there is an increasing number of them—as well as networking organizations for converts. Try to establish a close relationship with one or two families who can serve as your connection—your substitute relatives. If you don't know such a family, ask your clergyperson to introduce you to one. Or try to "adopt" an older person in the congregation who can assist you and who will appreciate your company. If possible, also preserve a cordial relationship with your former spouse's relatives and see that they spend time with their grandchild.

If you had been pressured into converting for the sake of marriage, you may be thinking about reverting. Your former religion and community may seem to offer the emotional support you need. The experts we consulted suggest that, if your child is relatively young, a religious change will not by itself cause her to undergo identity confusion or emotional stress. If your child is older (e.g. mid-grammar school) and has had several years of religious school, your reversion is likely to be troubling to her. She will have begun to form her own religious identity.

Either way, reversion is not a decision to make impulsively. Examine your own commitments and be sure you are not reverting to retaliate. Be aware that reversion can inflame your former spouse, as happened with Herb and Dottie. Keep the issues clear. Tell your ex-spouse that you are doing what you need to for your own sake but that you intend to speak respectfully about his religion to the child. To your child, explain that each person needs spiritual nourishment, and that in this difficult time you found that the best comfort was the religion you grew up in. Explain that the new religion wasn't as familiar so you didn't find it as helpful, but that people who grew up with it find it very helpful and comforting.

Resist the temptation to turn your personal need into a competitive situation. That's hard to do in the midst of a divorce, so consider delaying any shift in religious affiliation until you have worked through the emotional divorce and have settled into a stable new relationship toward your ex-spouse.

4. *The Escalation of the Loyalty Issue* The three preceding patterns, at their ugliest, will heighten a child's identity-loyalty predicament. Religious differences that she could integrate when the family was together now appear polarized between the two parents. She may have felt "both" before (or "one," in the case of a conversion), but the open rift of divorce now makes her feel pressured to choose one or the other religion.

If you fight vehemently to have your child follow your religious heritage, you could achieve the opposite effect: He may associate religion with conflict and thus reject all religion. We recall one nine-year-old whose parents were competing over religion and associated visiting times. The boy announced one day, "When I grow up, I'm not going to believe in God."

If you and your former spouse are pursuing two different religious paths, what is a healthy way to approach your child's religious identity? Psychologist Emily Visher and psychiatrist Sheldon Frank emphasize that the approach must depend on the age of the child. Preschool children take their identity from the parent who cares for them most of the time. They want to be like that parent and are confused if someone tells them they are different. This is also true, but to a lesser extent, of elementary-school children.

A child generally feels more secure if raised in the custodial parent's religion. But it is important to support the identity the child feels. The older a child, the more developed will be her own preferences on holidays and religious training, and the more you need to take those preferences into account. A teenager should not be asked to make a religious switch, even to the religion of the custodial parent, unless the youngster initiates the idea.

One caution: You can't always determine the child's sense of identity by asking her outright. If she believes religious labels will be seen as expressions of loyalty to one parent or the other, she may feel pressured to take on the religion of the parent she is most afraid to lose, or to hurt. If you were sensitive to her when the family was together and have tried to continue being so, you will sense how she identifies. You can explore identity issues without presenting it as "choosing."

What if the child is not being raised in the custodial parent's religion? That parent can still take the child to religious school, help with homework to the extent possible, and express pride in his achievements. At the same time, the parent can certainly practice her own religion and let the child share as much of it as he wishes. The key is to be noncompetitive.

Regardless of what religion each parent follows after the divorce, it is important for the child to spend holiday time with both parents and to have both parents present at life-cycle events. Your child has lost an intact family. Try to ensure that she loses as little as possible of the pleasures of the seasons and the life cycle that are normally part of family life.

In all cases, let this be the identity message: No matter what disagreements you may have with your ex-spouse, your child will always be your child. You will love and respect her no matter what she believes and practices, and you hope she will do the same for you. If she doubts you, she need only notice that you have many friendships with people with whom you have disagreements. You are able to learn from them and they from you.

Parents often fear that religious identity will be a wedge between themselves and their child. You may worry that if your child follows your ex-spouse's religion, you and she will become so different that you can no longer communicate. But children learn to speak many languages. Religion is only one of them. If you are speaking to your child in the language of love—the language of nurturing, of attention to her feelings and needs, of dependability—your child will understand.

REMARRIAGE: BLENDING AT LOW SPEED

Remarriage presents a different set of issues. While the task of divorce is to separate without polarization, the task of remarriage is to integrate the new family members without denying their preexisting ties and loyalties. There are many ambiguous relationships, such as those between the children who live in the home and those who visit on weekends, or between the step-parent and the child's grandparents from the previous marriage.

As a result of a remarriage, the child may feel pulled in opposite directions. There may be competing demands for time and for group loyalty from the parent, step-parent, and noncustodial parent. The child may wish to belong to the new family but feel that to do so means losing what was precious in the old family. Not only have her parents split up, but she might have lost the holiday traditions that used to make them feel like a family.

There are also age-related issues. A younger child is working on taking her parents into herself—becoming like them and sorting out the differences in the ways she is attached to her mother and her father. In the midst of this modeling, along comes a new parent, and she must decide which parts of this new person to incorporate as well. For a teenager, the issues are different. She is trying to pull away from parents, to become her own person. Suddenly in the midst of this pulling away, she is part of a new recombined family with a strong message to pull together. Emily Visher tells how one frustrated teen summarized the dilemma: "Two parents are two too many. Who wants any more?"

In this situation, Visher offers several guidelines:

Change Slowly In religious terms, this means not discarding the traditions of either family right away. Regardless of your own convictions, it may be necessary to combine traditions for a time so all the children feel they have a place in the new family but have not lost things that were important in the old family.

Plan Together Each member of the family needs to feel the security of knowing what's going to happen next, and needs to feel he has some input into the situation. In a remarriage, the family expectations have been uprooted and no one knows what to expect next. An interfaith remarriage adds one more piece of disruption: even those dependable treats, the holidays, are called into question. The family can restore security about what lies ahead by planning together. Let each family member talk about how things used to be at the holiday season in their "old" family. This gives each person a chance to voice her vision of the way things should be. Then the family can jointly plan how they will celebrate the upcoming season. Children should not be allowed to call the shots in this, although their views need to be listened to and incorporated in the final plan.

The same goes for coordinating with the ex-spouses where the children will be for the various holidays. Children's views should be heard and holiday celebrations multiplied as many times as necessary to meet their needs. But in the end, the children need to see that you and your ex-spouses have set the terms.

Develop Family Customs Create some customs that weren't part of either previous household. Customs make a family feel like a family. Develop secular rituals for birthdays, Fourth of July, or just for supper-times, bedtimes, or weekends. The members will value these rituals as expressions of the new family they are all helping to create.[3]

We met one blended family that was especially good at modifying the holidays to make them meaningful to that family. We'll call the family the Curtises. They had been next-door neighbors, one family Jewish and the other Christian. When the father of one family married the mother of the other, the new family had twelve children—half of them having grown up with Christmas and the other half with Hanukkah. Before the remarriage, the parents had agreed that while each child would be free to follow whichever religion she wished, the family as a whole would celebrate the Jewish holidays.

But they didn't want the children who had grown up with Christmas to feel deprived. They brainstormed about their December dilemma. They agreed that they disliked the commercialism of the Christmas season. And besides, with twelve children and a pinched family budget, they simply couldn't afford expensive presents or gift-giving at both Christmas and Hanukkah. They didn't want relatives to feel obliged to give gifts to all twelve children, but to have them give only to the ones they were related to before the remarriage would be divisive.

Their solution was "the December fund." Uncles, aunts, and grandparents from both sides of the family were asked not to give holiday presents, but instead to give money sometime before December to the December fund. Everyone in the family also contributed part of the money he had earned during the year. The December fund was used to buy not presents but events: special treats that the family otherwise could not afford. They found it exciting to talk as a family about how they would spend their December fund. One year they went to a restaurant together. One year they went to a play. Often they would reminisce about the special things they had done with the December fund. This holiday custom helped the new family pull together and become one.

Use a Light Touch with the Children Each child in the family should receive a measure of independence appropriate to her age and personality. At the same time, each child should be given a clear and strong invitation to belong or take part. We recall a youngster who was eleven when his gentile mother was remarried to a Jewish man. When they went out to a restaurant together with the man's relatives, the boy ordered ham and said, "I'm not Jewish. I don't keep kosher." His mother replied, "That's right. We do not bring nonkosher foods into our house, but when you're away from home you have the right to eat what you want." When they joined the man's extended family for Passover, the boy was always brought along. But he was free to leave the seder and go to an adjoining room to read the newspaper.

For younger children, a feeling of belonging to the new family and the new step-parent is uppermost. One of the women we talked to, a lapsed Catholic named Rosa, remarried when her daughter was six. The daughter said, "Now that you're married to Mike, am I part-Jewish?" Rosa sensed that her daughter needed some concrete symbol that she was now attached to her stepfather, that she belonged to him as well as to her mother. She bought a Hanukkah menorah and began lighting it. This, as well as the Christmas tree, became part of their family's traditions.

One way to help the family integrate is for each person to spend one-on-one time with every other person. Holidays can be particularly hectic in a remarried family, but try to carve out some private times just before or during a holiday. You might make a ritual of one-on-one time during holiday preparations.

If you and your new spouse want to establish a family religion in which all the children will be raised, you will find that that works best if the children are younger than about six. You will be getting them before the rules-oriented latency stage, when identity feelings have begun to solidify. According to Dr. Sheldon Frank, if you establish a family religion, it is a good idea to convert the children so the change will be concrete and they will have no doubt about belonging. But, as mentioned earlier, if your children are older (teenagers or in some cases preteens), don't even suggest conversion, and pursue it only if a child initiates the discussion. At the same time, even though teenagers are on their way out of the family, they need to get a strong invitation to belong. They need to be invited to each event, and to participate in each tradition.

Don't Isolate the Children As with a divorce, recognize that your children must integrate beliefs, ideas, and practices from the different worlds to which they have attachments. Don't make this more difficult by insisting on one way as right and another as wrong. Don't cut your child off from ex-spouses or grandparents; permit them to share in the holidays of those families even if they are different from yours. With your help, they can see the differences as enriching rather than divisive.

Don't be surprised or hurt if your child—like many children from intact families—follows a religious path different from any of her parents.

Finally, says Visher: "Don't get hung up as though religion was the only thing in life. Find out what the similarities are and focus on them."

21. SEXUAL PROBLEMS:

Getting Your Signals Crossed

Sex is like a boxing ring for marital conflict. If there are overall problems in the relationship, they often express themselves in the sexual arena.

Are interfaith couples more likely to have sexual problems? It's a question not easily answered. We have found no research on this question. Sex researchers William Masters and Virginia Johnson think that religious background is such an important influence on sexuality that they keep a theologian on their clinic staff. A few therapists we talked to think that interfaith or interethnic couples are more likely to have sexual problems; others said that when interfaith couples had sexual problems, it had nothing to do with religious backgrounds; still others think that more severe sexual problems may show up in some marriages between those of the *same religion,* (specifically, among a portion of those raised in orthodoxy or fundamentalism).

Our educated hunch is that interfaith couples are not more likely overall to have sexual difficulties, but that those who do will tend toward certain types of problems—problems which may be closely related to other intermarriage issues.

If you and your partner *are* having sexual problems, they can be anguishing and seem intractable. But it is definitely possible to heal a sexual relationship that has gone awry. In this chapter, we describe problems that may occur among interfaith couples and present remedies that sex therapists would suggest.

Sex problems can enter the marriage in one of three ways: First, they can grow out of a more general level of conflict in the marriage. If you're not getting along, it can ruin your sex life. Second, they can grow out of unresolved problems in either partner's relationship with parents. In some marriages, a parent problem may show in difficulties over handling money, in some it may show up in the physical illness of one partner, and in some it may show up as a sexual problem.[1]

Third, differences in ethnic background or religious teachings can affect the sexual relationship even when the emotional relationship is sound. Let's examine that issue first.

Jewish Views of Sexuality Judaism traditionally has considered sexual pleasure as a healthy and beautiful part of marriage. Sex is necessary not only for procreation, but to fulfill the marital relationship. Although the wife is supposed to be modest, she is also seen as naturally having sexual desires, even more intense desires than her husband. One of the husband's duties in marriage is to satisfy his wife sexually.

According to the traditional Jewish view, God showed love for human beings by giving them sex for their pleasure and emotional bonding as well as for the procreation of children. In fact, the erotic Biblical book *Song of Songs* is seen as an extended allegory for the passionate love between God and the people of Israel.

Within marriage, particular sexual practices are not seen as good or bad in themselves but in terms of how they contribute to the love between husband and wife. Contraception has been permitted for reasons such as preserving the marital relationship by many (though not all) Jewish authorities. In fact, contraception is required when it would be physically dangerous to the woman to have a baby. There are restrictions: In traditional Orthodox Judaism, masturbation is not acceptable. And menstruation is considered to render a woman unclean; sex is prohibited during the period and for seven days afterward, and a woman's husband is only permitted to have sex with her following this time if she has bathed in the *mikvah* (ritual bath). Intercourse outside of marriage is not acceptable, but the responses to it have varied widely depending on the circumstances. Adultery in the Bible was punishable by death—a sentence rarely enacted since there had to be witnesses to the act—but if the man and woman were both unmarried, the "punishment" for premarital sex, including rape, was that they be wed. Although the sex drive is sometimes called the *yetzer hara* (the evil impulse), the rabbis also taught that sexual energy can be channeled for either good or ill. Without this impulse, the rabbis said, a man would never build a house, marry a wife, father a child, or engage in business.[2]

This generally positive attitude has influenced many Jewish families to be fairly liberal sexually and fairly open in expressing affection. However, in some families, a sense of rules predominates—sex is OK in this circumstance but not that; masturbation is not OK; sexual fantasies about anyone other than one's wife are not OK—and guilt hampers people's ability to enjoy sex. In addition, the complex emotional dynamics described in Chapter 3 (Dealing with Parents) and Chapter 6 (Ethnic Ambivalence) can interfere with the Jewish partner's sex life.

Christian Views of Sexuality Christian attitudes toward sex developed in a very different direction. Although Jesus is not recorded as having married, He in no way condemned sexual pleasure. But Saint Paul had a grudging attitude toward sex ("It is better to marry than to burn"). The attitudes of the early Christian Church toward sex were shaped not primarily by the Hebrew Bible nor even by the New Testament, but by Greek Stoic philosophers. The Stoics thought of the rational mind as pure and supreme and infinitely superior to the body. Early Christian authorities were attracted by this asceticism and rejection of the demands of the body. Saint Augustine taught that intercourse was only fully moral when it was for procreation (although it was permissible to acquiesce in sex to relieve one spouse's sexual needs). Pope Gregory the Great said that even when having sex for procreation, couples were sinning if they felt any physical pleasure.[3]

Many Catholics, and many Protestants reared in fundamentalist or conservative churches, grew up with such teachings. The Catholic Church did not change its basic teaching that sex was primarily for procreation until the Second Vatican Council in the 1960s. Contraception (through any means other than abstaining during the fertile parts of the woman's cycle) remains forbidden by the Catholic Church. However, a number of the sex therapists we talked to said that today's Catholics don't seem for the most part to be sexually inhibited by the Church's teachings. They are able to compartmentalize—to disregard the Church's teachings about sex and contraception, while drawing strength from its other spiritual teachings. Whether your Church's teachings affect your sexual reactions may depend partly on what region you were brought up in and how much that region was dominated by a particular religious outlook.

Assessing Your "Sexual Theology" A critical factor in sexual relationships today is the individual's personal "sexual theology," notes sex therapist William R. Stayton, an ordained American Baptist minister. Some people, regardless of their religious background or their feelings about God, have a "relationship theology." They look at sex in the context of relationships. They don't see an act, such as masturbation or homosexuality, as good or bad in itself, but judge it by whether it nurtures a loving relationship. Other people have an "acts theology." They see certain sexual practices, such as anal intercourse, as inherently good or bad regardless of the quality of the relationship in which they take place.[4]

Where do the two of you stand? Are all sex practices possible or does one of you see certain types as bad? Where does sex fit in your relationship? Is it a vital aspect to both of you, or does one of you feel it should not get a high priority?

Look to your past for clues. What messages did you receive from your family and your religious group? How much physical affection was there in your family? How much did your parents tell you about sex, and what did they convey? Did they regard sexual pleasure as good, or as dirty, as something good people only do for procreation? Were there "bad girls" and "good girls"?

How did the messages affect you? Do you enjoy physical intimacy? Are you at ease talking about sex? How do you feel about your body? Are you comfortable being naked? Do you feel sexually attractive? Are you comfortable looking at and touching your own and your partner's sex organs?

Where did you learn about the facts of life, and how accurate was the first information you got? How would you want to teach about sex to your children?

In discussing sex with your partner, be as open as you can about your own feelings and your memories of family and religious institutions. But—except in the case of a traumatic experience like rape or sexual abuse, which must be discussed—don't talk about particular sexual experiences or relationships you have had. That can be a "turnoff" for either partner.

Sex therapists we talked to mentioned a variety of problems that may stem from religious or cultural backgrounds.[5]

The Madonna/Whore Syndrome Occasionally, someone from a religiously orthodox background, whether Protestant, Catholic, or Jewish, may be able to have sexual feelings, or lust, only for people who are "off-limits" as marriage partners. A couple may have a good sexual relationship before marriage. But the desire of one or both partners may drop off precipitously after the marriage or after the birth of the first or second child. (They may feel subconsciously that mothers are not supposed to be sexy or to be sex objects.) If both partners come from the same religious background, they may share the same attitudes and be content to coexist in a largely celibate marriage. But in an intermarriage, where partners come from different backgrounds, at least one is likely to be very distressed by this turn of events. In this situation, the intermarriage may be a healthful factor since it pushes the couple to get help with the sexual problem.

Ethnic Ambivalence In Chapter 6, we talk about ethnic self-hate and ethnic prejudices. These can affect the sexual relationship in a number of ways. First, the person who is ashamed of his or her ethnic group may feel unattractive and consequently may have trouble expressing sexual feelings. Jews may see themselves through the distorting lens of anti-Semitism in the larger culture. Christians may have absorbed a cultural message which sees individuals as sinful and tells the child, "Why should you think you're special?" Consequently, they may not allow themselves the right to have sexual feelings.

Second, the partner may have chosen a mate from outside his ethnic group because she symbolizes certain things to him. He may be unable to perceive and respond to her as a real person. He may see her as the unattainable Ice Maiden. Even though they're married and she's sexually interested in him, he may be unable to express sexual feelings toward her. Or, because he has married her and she's now attainable, she may no longer be attractive.

A sex therapist told us about how several of his clients projected their self-hate and prejudice onto their partners. One man from an anti-Semitic Protestant family rebelled by marrying a very attractive Jewish woman. Once they were married, he unleashed all his family's prejudices on her, calling her a frigid, dependent Jewish princess. The woman had been excited by her husband, but in response to his hateful remarks she froze emotionally, so his accusations became self-fulfilling. In therapy, the man's task was to understand how he had used his wife as a tool against his family and to learn to see her instead as a real person, with understandable feelings and needs.

This therapist was also seeing a gay Protestant man who had been unable to have sex with his Jewish lover. In individual sessions, it became clear that this man shared his family's stereotypes of Jews. He had chosen this Jewish partner because he hadn't come to terms with his own homosexuality. He acted out his self-loathing by choosing a partner who was on the bottom in his family's scale of values. Until he started liking himself, he couldn't choose a partner he could respect and be attracted to and he couldn't have a healthy relationship.

We have heard similar stories about Jewish men who married gentile women and then, because of their ambivalence about being Jewish, proceeded to ridicule them.

Sex as the Arena for Larger Family Conflicts One therapist told us about a Jewish man who was having problems of premature ejaculation, which left his gentile wife sexually unsatisfied. Out of bed, they were fighting because he remained closely attached to his mother. His wife was vocally angry about this tie. The man was not able to express his anger at his wife. The premature ejaculation was his indirect and largely unconscious way of getting back at her. When they dealt with the larger problem in their marriage, the sexual problem disappeared.

Ethnic Differences in Expressing Affection In Chapter 5, we mention that intermarriages often involve partners who are emotional opposites. This can lead to a vicious circle in the sexual relationship that is similar to the ones in verbal arguments. Helene and Gil found that out.

Gil was from an emotionally restrained WASP family. He estimates that he has seen his parents kiss three times in his life. Helene was from an expressive Jewish family. Sometimes her parents nagged or yelled at each other or at her, but they were also affectionate and open in talking about sex. Many times she had seen her parents kiss, hug, or pat each other's bottoms. They talked proudly about how sexy they found each other.

During their courtship, Helene and Gil had problems with sex, but both attributed it to the tension of a commuter relationship between two cities. After their marriage, Helene said, she was shocked. She had stocked up on sexy negligees and was looking forward to having a regular sexual relationship with Gil. But he saw her eagerness and seductiveness as frontal assaults, and he retreated. He felt that she was forcing him to have sex whether he was in the mood or not, and was restricting his independence. He began to sound like the stereotype of a frigid house-wife—always too tired or having a headache.

Helene was bitterly frustrated. She says she now realizes that she became shrill and accusing, which worsened the cycle. Gil became less and less attracted to Helene, and Helene squelched her own sexual feelings in self-defense. As she tells it, she so thoroughly snuffed her emotional fires that she didn't even get turned on during the romantic parts of movies.

They sought sex therapy but didn't find it helpful. Eventually, they began to work things out on their own. Once they had tacitly agreed not to deal with sex for a while, they realized how much they had in common in other areas. Helene saw that she trusted Gil deeply in talking about all the other aspects of her life. She willed herself simply to trust that if she didn't push him and he didn't feel threatened, Gil would learn to behave in a sexually loving way toward her.

In this quieter atmosphere, they concentrated first on talking. They talked a lot about their backgrounds and the expectations of sex life that they had coming into the marriage. Gil told Helene more about what things she did that made him feel like withdrawing sexually. She has agreed to let him take the initiative and do things at his own pace. They have agreed to enjoy gentle touching even if it doesn't lead to intercourse. The approach seems to work for them.

ADVICE: SOME HEALING TOUCHES

Even though they didn't make much progress during their sex therapy sessions, Gil and Helene's self-prescription follows the recommendations made by most of the sex therapists we talked to. Here are some of the most important strategies:

Work on Two Tracks: The Physical and the Emotional Gil and Helene learned to be sensitive to each other by talking about their backgrounds, their expectations, and their feelings. They were specific about what each found attractive or comfortable or pleasurable, and unattractive, uncomfortable, or unpleasant. (If, like Gil, you come from a culture that doesn't talk about such things, this will feel awkward at first.) At the same time, Gil and Helene got "unstuck" by changing what they were *doing* sexually. Some sex therapists show films of specific touching exercises to couples and give them "homework" so they have actual experience with new behaviors. One caution: Although sexual fantasy is an important part of developing a better sexual relationship, do not talk about your fantasies with your partner. It's precisely because your fantasy life is private that it's a safe place to express your sexual desires.

Have a Policy of Gradualism Gil and Helene followed the suggestions of sex therapists by beginning with non-threatening, non-sexual kinds of touching. They allowed the partner who was feeling the most threatened and uncomfortable to set the pace. Many therapists suggest touching places like the arms, back, shins, hair, learning all the textures of all the parts of your partner's body. Think of it as play, not sex. If you are from a family that didn't touch much, this gentle play will help you develop a "vocabulary" for communicating affection through touch.

Work at Expressing All Your Feelings, Not Just Sexual Ones Marriage partners need to be able to say to each other, "I'm depressed, and

I need you to hold me in your arms for awhile," or "I'm feeling anxious and I need to just lie here quietly with you for awhile," or "I'm angry about something that happened at work, and I need to be by myself for awhile." Practice expressing your happy feelings, too: "I'm feeling great and I want to hug you."

If you come from a culture that doesn't generally express feelings, you'll have to work at this, too. Resolve that you won't make your partner guess about what you're feeling and what you need. Also, work at asking about what your partner is feeling, about how her week has gone. Many people can't relax enough to have sex until they've dealt with the piled-up feelings of the week.

Appreciate Your Partner's Value System and Emotional Needs Gil and Helene were fortunate that, although they had absorbed very different attitudes about sex from their backgrounds, their beliefs about what was moral and permissible in a sexual relationship were not that different. At the same time, each of them was committed to the marriage and to developing a more satisfying relationship.

If you and your partner have different beliefs about sex, you can ease the tension by agreeing that neither of you will ask the other to do something which contradicts deeply held values. It's important to realize that no amount of arguing is likely to change these deep values. If your partner believes oral sex is wrong, you're not likely to change that by argument or demands. Concentrate instead on finding other mutually acceptable and pleasurable sexual practices.

Strongly held values and beliefs can affect behavior even when people want, intellectually, to ignore the feelings. One therapist treated an Orthodox Jewish man who was unable to have sex before marriage. His fiancée, who had had a fair amount of sexual experience, worried that the man might be impotent. He was certain that once they were married, sex would not be a problem. After much discussion and counseling, they decided to go ahead with the wedding. Once they were married, there were no sexual problems.

With all this said, it's important to realize that, in the sexual relationship, ethnic and religious controversies can be a smokescreen hiding more fundamental problems. One therapist treated a Catholic woman who found sex so threatening that she would hold her breath and go into a panic attack during intercourse. After weeks of therapy discussing the negative messages about sex she felt she had received in her religious upbringing, the woman finally revealed that she had been abused as a child. This, far more than what she was taught by her religion, was the cause of her fear and revulsion toward sex.

Even though we've talked about accepting and working within your partner's value system, that doesn't mean either of you has license to be inflexible or to make unilateral demands. Each partner, like Gil and Helene, has to be committed enough to the relationship to re-examine his or her own beliefs and behaviors and to look for areas of compromise and growth.

Regardless of what you learned about sex from the religious and parental authority figures of your childhood, don't cling to an accusatory rage at them. That prevents healing and growth. Realize that in reconstructing a damaged sex life, religion itself can be a force for good today. The liberal wings of both Judaism and Christianity affirm sexuality as part of the goodness and wholeness of human beings, created by God in God's image. In fact, one large study indicated that there's a positive correlation between religious convictions and a healthy sexual relationship.[6]

Seeing your sexual feelings as a positive part of your spiritual nature makes sexuality both more beautiful and more manageable. It doesn't become the be-all and end-all of your relationship. Neither is it a forbidden troll, always threatening to pop out and change love into leering lust. It's part of your emotional fuel as a human—in fact, the very emotional fuel that makes it possible for you to love your partner.

22. IN THE END:

Death and Burial

There is one event in the life cycle you can be certain you will have to deal with: death. And death, while traumatic in any family, creates unique dilemmas for the intermarried.

When death occurs in a family, the survivors often feel a strong need for tradition. They want to do what is right by the person who died. They feel numb, disoriented, unable to concentrate and make choices, and they want someone with moral or traditional authority to tell them what to do. But when death occurs in an intermarried family, people can find themselves in a no-man's land. They may even have to "invent the ceremony" at the very time they most need the comfort of familiar prescriptions.

In addition, death can force the two extended families to come together in ways that exacerbate their differences in values, beliefs, or expectations. People are already feeling hurt and angry because of the death itself, so the inherent risk of family conflict is heightened.

Nearly all burials, you will find, are done under the auspices of organized religion. People may have civil wedding ceremonies, decide not to have a religious naming for their children, and never affiliate—but nearly everyone turns to religions to bury their dead. Even avowed nonbelievers tend to arrange religious burials, because they feel it has more dignity or is simpler to arrange, or because the deceased person was religious. According to one survey of bereaved families, less than 1 percent had nondenominational burials.[1]

When you try to arrange a burial service, however, you may be confronted with some of the most rigid rules of religion, including some specific restrictions against intermarried families. Unless you are aware of these restrictions and know of alternatives, you can find yourself butting into a stone wall at a time when your emotions already are brittle. Taking care to find a liberal clergy person who feels entitled to temper application of the rules with empathy can save you much pain.

The Carters: Left Out in the Cold   Rachel Carter was shattered when the rabbi of the liberal Conservative congregation her Jewish mother had helped found refused to bury Rachel's gentile father. The family had known the rabbi for years and considered him a friend. Rachel and her brothers and sisters had all gone to Hebrew school and had bar or bat mitzvahs. Her father, raised as a Protestant, had become an atheist but still learned the Jewish blessings, participated in the home rituals, and enthusiastically supported his children's Jewish upbringing. Furthermore, he was estranged from his Christian family. His social and family world was Jewish. But when Rachel approached the rabbi about conducting a funeral service, he said, "I won't do it and you won't find a rabbi anywhere who will."

Rachel was in her early thirties when her father died suddenly of a heart attack in a distant city. She was the "organized person" in the family, so her dazed mother and siblings left the arrangements to her. She was the one who dealt with the funeral director (they had the body cremated) and helped her mother bring the remains home. She arranged to meet relatives at the airport and find places for them to stay. She lined up a caterer to bring food to the house after the burial.

But arranging for burial of the urn was the most difficult part, emotionally and practically. After being rejected by the rabbi, she was in a quandary. Her mother had always been actively Jewish and had always assumed she would be buried in a Jewish cemetery. But she wanted to be buried beside Rachel's father. Rachel made a number of phone calls, finally located a nondenominational cemetery and purchased a plot. She arranged to use a room in the local town hall for a memorial service. A friend who was active in the synagogue and whom she considered a spiritual person agreed to lead the memorial service, and some Jewish musicians she knew played traditional melodies. But at the graveside, she wanted a religious authority. She turned to the only religious person she felt would not turn her down: her sister's husband, a deacon in a Christian church. He said a few nondenominational prayers. In the traditional Jewish manner, each member of the family shoveled some dirt into the grave. The family and friends came back to the house. Her mother lit a *yahrzeit* (mourning) candle, then asked a neighbor who was active in a local Protestant church to say some prayers.

Rachel's family would have liked to "sit *shiva*"—the traditional Jewish mourning ritual—for her father. "As far as I was concerned, he was very Jewish," she said. But the family felt they didn't have the religion's permission.

Both Rachel and her mother are still bitter about the experience. Her mother, a daughter of immigrants who was raised in an Orthodox home, has not been back to a synagogue since the death. In fact, she has started going to a Unitarian church.

Rachel feels robbed in a different way. She says she was so busy making arrangements in the days after her father's death that she never got to go through the early period of mourning, and to work out her grief. While her brothers and sisters sorted through her father's belongings, reading old letters and reminiscing, she was on the phone trying to work out the logistics. There were terrible family fights. No one was satisfied with the arrangements she had made.

"We had to make it up ourselves," she said. "We would have loved to have someone say, 'Now you do this and then this.' You're just in a state of shock when someone dies. You can't make those decisions. That's what religion is for. It has traditions, ceremonies. It frees your mind to concentrate on the spiritual, not the detail."

BURIAL POLICIES AND OPTIONS

Rachel's family stumbled on a painful dilemma: Most intermarried people who choose a family religion choose Judaism—but the traditional branches of Judaism in general don't permit the burying of non-Jews in Jewish cemeteries.

If you are intermarried and eventually want to be buried next to your spouse, here are the religions' rules and some strategies for negotiating them:[2]

Judaism A Jew who intermarried, as long as he did not convert to some other religion, would be entitled to burial in a Jewish cemetery. But traditional (Orthodox and Conservative) authorities would not knowingly permit the burial of the non-Jewish spouse or of the child of a Jewish father and non-Jewish mother in the Jewish cemetery. Although there is no clear Jewish law on the subject, it is a longstanding tradition that has taken on the force of law.[3]

Reform Reconstructionist rabbis will generally agree to bury the non-Jewish spouses and their children as long as they were active members of the synagogue and did not practice Christianity or maintain a separate church affiliation. Reform, Conservative, and Orthodox Jews are generally all buried in the same cemeteries, but (as long as the cemetery is privately or corporately owned, rather than owned by a synagogue) cemetery officials generally won't inquire into the status of the dead person unless someone raises the issue. The rule of thumb is to use a Jewish funeral home, have a Jewish family member buy the plot and make the arrangements, and not mention that the deceased spouse is a gentile.[4] If you are unaffiliated, a big Jewish funeral home in a large city can usually provide the name of a Reform or liberal rabbi who will conduct the service. You may have problems in a small city, where the cemetery is likely to be owned directly by a synagogue that would enforce the rules.

Some Reform and Reconstructionist rabbis would conduct a nondenominational or Jewish service for a Jew being buried in a nondenominational or even a Christian cemetery. Conservative and Orthodox rabbis would not, feeling that a Jew should be buried among Jews. It would be almost impossible to find any rabbi who would co-officiate with a minister or priest, although some might be willing to speak a few words informally. A priest or minister would not be permitted into a Jewish cemetery to conduct a service for the non-Jewish spouse, nor could there be any Christian symbols or blessing of the grave. A priest or minister might be present at the funeral as a nonspeaking guest, sitting with and comforting the non-Jewish family. If Christian prayers are desired, they should be offered at a separate, home service for the non-Jewish family.

Catholicism Catholics have their own cemeteries, specially consecrated and blessed by clergy. Although formerly non-Catholics could be buried only in an unconsecrated portion of a Catholic cemetery, this restriction has been lifted.[5] A rabbi is even allowed to perform a Jewish funeral rite at the gravesite. A priest could also perform a funeral service (without Mass) for a Jew and a graveside ceremony based on Old Testament passages, with no references to Jesus. The funeral would generally be held in a religiously neutral site such as the funeral home rather than in the church. The grave could have a simple headstone with only the name and no cross. The same rules would apply to an unbaptized child who died after infancy.

Canon law since Vatican II has also become more open in regard to the intermarried Catholic partner. A person who was baptized as a Catholic can receive a Catholic funeral and burial in a Catholic cemetery even if he had been nonpracticing, had been married outside the church, or had been divorced. A funeral Mass would generally not be held. If a person who had converted from Catholicism to Judaism later decided she wished to return and be buried as a Catholic, she would only have to return or be reconciled with the Church. She would not have to be rebaptized.

There are also no Church barriers to having a priest officiate at a graveside ceremony for the Catholic in a nondenominational or Jewish cemetery. He can bless the grave individually. (However, as mentioned above, this would probably not be permitted by a Jewish cemetery.)

Protestantism Most ministers will bury persons of any religion, and will try to respect your desires as to place and manner of burial. There are no theological barriers to their doing so. Most ministers would not object to burying a Jew, and—with the possible exception of a few of the most conservative high-church Episcopalians or of the most fundamentalist low-church Protestants—they would have no problem in departing from their church's standard funeral service, eliminating references to Jesus and the Resurrection, and using whatever prayers or liturgy were suggested by the family.[6]

However, a minister might object to conducting a funeral for a practicing Jew if he thought it would be against the dead person's wishes. And some ministers may simply be too busy: Some do seven or eight funerals a week.

Secular You can choose a nonsectarian cemetery; some are listed in the Yellow Pages of phone books. You can ask a funeral director to help you arrange burial in a nonsectarian cemetery. Many of them can give you suggestions for readings, or even conduct a simple, nonsectarian good-bye at the graveside. You can also make the arrangements without a funeral director. If you want a memorial service, you can set it up as Rachel did in a religiously neutral spot (such as a town hall or college chapel) and ask friends to speak or play music.

If you run into problems finding a cemetery plot because you are not affiliated with a religion, check your state's laws. Some states prohibit discrimination by cemeteries that are corporately rather than privately owned. Some states have laws saying once you buy a plot, you can bury anyone you wish in it.

One option that may be suitable is cremation.[7] Cremation can take the ceremony out of the precincts of established religion. You don't have to bury the cremated remains in a cemetery and thus needn't deal with the questions of cemetery and funeral. You can have a memorial service on neutral ground at whatever time you choose, leaving several months to allow family and friends to make plans to attend. Or you can simply inscribe the name of the deceased in the crematory's memorial book, register the death with the state, and leave it at that. Cremation can be considerably cheaper than burial, and it leaves up to you whether you go through such rituals as receiving hours at a funeral parlor.

However, we have several cautions about cremation: First, as you'll see below, cremation is prohibited by traditional Judaism and fundamentalist Protestantism and was generally forbidden until recently by Catholicism. You may not be permitted to bury the urn in a Jewish cemetery. (This may have been an added factor in Rachel's difficulty in getting a rabbi to conduct a Jewish funeral and a Jewish cemetery to accept her father's remains.) Consider possible reactions of more religious family members.

Second, a cremation may short-circuit the mourning process. Traditional customs such as viewing the body or shoveling dirt on the grave force people to accept the finality of death. Cremation, being clean and impersonal, may make it harder for people to work through their grief.

Third, many people have a false idea of what cremation involves. Be sure you understand the procedure: Cremation is not instantaneous and does not reduce the body to a handful of ashes.[8]

CHRISTIAN AND JEWISH BELIEFS ABOUT DEATH

In addition to the practical difficulties of burial, Judaism and Christianity have differences of belief which can be stressful to deal with at the time of a funeral. These beliefs shape practices regarding the funeral and mourning.[9]

Concepts of the afterlife are central to Christian faith. The main tenet of traditional Christianity, both Protestant and Catholic, is that through Jesus' death and resurrection, eternal life was made available to all believers. For a believing Christian, there is no death: Death is a crossing over into eternal life, which is superior to life on earth.[10]

In Judaism, there is an idea of afterlife, "the world to come," but it is far less elaborated and emphasized. One can be a good Jew, even an Orthodox Jew, without a belief in the afterlife. The most pervasive Jewish belief about death is that a person's reputation—his good name—and his family are his immortality. If he lives a *menschlik* (decent and good) life, his deeds will live after him, and his family will treasure his memory. Traditional Judaism has an idea of the soul's return to God after death, but the nature of this return or of the afterlife are not specified.

While Christianity teaches that death is a violation of the natural order and came into the world only because of man's sin, Judaism teaches that death, however hard to understand and regrettable, is simply part of the human life cycle.

Difficulties can occur when members of an intermarried couple or their families have very different beliefs about death or the afterlife. When a death occurs, remind yourself of the cultural background of the people you will be dealing with, and prepare for what they are likely to say to you. Look for the humane intent under the formulas. And obviously, if you are in the position of comforter, don't try to dispute any beliefs which give comfort to the grieving person.

Another difficulty: At a time of death or serious illness, some people find themselves haunted by traditional ideas (e.g. heaven and hell) they thought they had rejected. Catholics can benefit from learning about some of the more liberal notions of afterlife that have emerged since Vatican II. Salvation, in Catholic theology, does not in any way depend on a person's having a Catholic funeral or burial. And even though it is preferable for a Catholic to receive the sacraments of Reconciliation (confession) and the Eucharist before death, modern post-Vatican II Catholicism teaches that each person is ultimately judged by God, who knows whether the person repented in his heart.[11]

As for the fate of the Jewish partner and any non-baptized children, the Church now teaches that God wants the salvation of all people and brings each person to Him in His own way.

BETWEEN DEATH AND BURIAL

Traditional Judaism has fairly detailed requirements on the handling of the body. While neither Catholic nor Protestant denominations have such requirements, there are a number of customs and traditions of which you may need to be aware.

Judaism The body must be buried within twenty-fours hours if possible. Embalming, cremation, organ donation, and autopsy are forbidden unless the latter would save a life. There are three reasons for these restrictions. First is the basic principle of respect for the body as having housed the soul of a human being created in God's image. After death, the body should be disturbed as little as possible. Second, all these processes interfere with the natural cycle of life and death. The body should be placed in the ground and permitted to return to the elements through the natural process of decay, neither hastened nor retarded. For this same reason, an unlined wooden coffin is preferred. Finally, traditional Judaism accepts the idea of resurrection of the body and teaches that the body should be kept intact for the day when the

Messiah comes. (See Maurice Lamm's *The Jewish Way in Death and Mourning* for more details.)

Reform Judaism has lifted virtually all these restrictions. Reconstructionist rabbis vary from quite traditional to very liberal.

In traditional Judaism, there is no wake. Some modern non-Orthodox Jews have adopted the American custom of having receiving hours at the funeral home. However, the idea of an open casket or viewing is alien to Jewish tradition. The casket is present, but traditionally not in the room where the receiving line is held. The casket would remain closed except if a member of the family who had not been present at the time of death wished to see the face of the deceased briefly in private. Gifts of flowers are not considered appropriate; donations to a charity in honor of the deceased are preferred.

Catholicism Burial is preferred over cremation, both because it imitates the burial of Jesus' body and is in line with the Church doctrine of resurrection of the body. Cremation was formerly generally forbidden but is now permitted.[12]

A vigil or wake, with its own prayer service, in the home, funeral chapel, or church, is customary for many Catholic ethnic groups. A large turnout is considered a sign of respect to the family and the deceased. Mass cards or condolence cards may be left in a large pile on the table. The content and atmosphere of a wake depends on ethnic traditions. Since a funeral brings together family and friends who may not have seen each other for years, there will be a certain amount of socializing and catching up on news. Some families are accustomed to defusing tension with jokes, so there may be a fair amount of levity. Usually there will be an open casket, and it may be an important sign of respect to have the deceased person attractively "laid out," for the viewing: well-dressed and with the face treated to look as healthy and youthful as possible. In a traditional ethnic family, elaborate flower arrangements often surround the casket in the funeral home. These would illustrate special interests of the deceased, such as a baseball cap made of flowers if he was a sports fan. There may also be clocks made of flowers, with hands set at the time of the person's death.

In traditional families, guests might be expected to file past the open casket, kneeling on a bench in front of the coffin to offer private prayers. Catholic guests might be asked to participate in a brief prayer service. Family and good friends might be expected to kiss the cheek of the deceased person, a tradition descended from the early Christian practice of showing affection for the departed and belief that he was still with his loved ones in spirit.

The open casket and the whole atmosphere of a wake may be

uncomfortable for a Jew. He may be particularly put off by the custom of kissing the dead person. Jews have been reluctant to touch corpses since ancient times, when it was considered ritually defiling.

Protestantism Although the wake was not a Protestant tradition, many Protestants today follow the custom of the family receiving friends at the funeral home before the burial for a visiting hour or viewing.

Funeral and burial rituals are designed to help people let go of someone they can no longer hold on to. The open casket in a Christian wake accomplishes this in one way by impressing on the viewers that the deceased is really dead. No matter how well embalmed, the corpse will never look alive. The shoveling of dirt onto the coffin in the traditional Jewish ritual drives home this reality in another way.

We suggest that before going to the funeral of a relative or planning the funeral of a family member, you read the description of that religion's funeral rite in the Appendix. Funerals are stressful, and it helps to know what to expect.

MOURNING CUSTOMS

Display of grief is culturally conditioned. In some cultures, outbursts of emotion are expected at a funeral: sobbing, or even throwing oneself upon the grave. Lack of emotionality might be interpreted as lack of caring. There are culturally conditioned turning points in the funeral which typically trigger displays of emotion. For example, at the close of a Christian graveside service, each member of the funeral party might be given a flower to throw on the grave, and this might be the occasion for family members to break down.

At a traditional Jewish funeral, this moment might come at the end of the brief graveside ceremony, when the coffin is lowered by hand into the grave and each member of the family shovels a spadeful of earth onto it. The moment also might come during *keriah* (the rending of the garments). Orthodox and some conservative mourners traditionally wear some item of clothing that can be torn (a sweater, a tie, a blouse) and make a ripping tear in it as a sign of grief. This torn garment is worn throughout the period of sitting *shiva,* the seven days of deepest mourning.[13]

Don't discount the emotion displayed at these key moments. The emotion is real, but you need to see it in context and not be overwhelmed. It is this culture's way of allowing mourners to express their anguish in a sanctioned, controlled way.

After a funeral in an ethnic family, you may encounter a number of other mourning customs. They include:[14] drawing all the blinds; or, conversely, opening the doors and windows; a wreath on the front door with white, purple, or black ribbons; stopping the clocks; covering the mirrors; washing the hands at a pitcher after leaving the graveside and before entering the home (this is a Jewish tradition); wearing black, gray, white, or a veil; covering plants or birdcages with black cloths; a mourner's meal after the funeral. The traditional Jewish mourners' meal includes round foods, such as hard-boiled eggs, bagels, and lentils, all symbolizing the roundness of the world and the cycle of life, in which death comes to all.

In contemporary America, Jews are the only sizable group which has preserved a set of mourning customs for some period after the funeral. During the seven days of sitting *shiva,* the family doesn't go out of the house and Orthodox Jews stop all the usual amenities, not bathing, shaving, or engaging in small talk. Traditional Jews would continue mourning practices at a less intense level for a full year.

SPECIAL DILEMMAS

Converts and people who have taken on their partner's religion, even though they have not formally converted, face some difficult situations at the time of a death.

The Religious Convert A convert has full status in Judaism and in all branches of Christianity. In the event of her death or the death of her child, the standard funeral rite and burial would be given without question.

But if the convert's parent dies, she may feel caught between two worlds. One convert to Judaism told us of dreading going to the wake of her Italian grandfather, the patriarch of the family. She didn't know what to do about the custom of kneeling and praying at the coffin, and of kissing the departed. If she knelt, she would feel she was dishonoring her new religion. If she didn't kneel or kiss the body, she thought it would be seen as disrespect for her grandfather, to whom she had been very close.

Other converts to Judaism spoke of feeling isolated and alone when they attended the funeral of a parent. They no longer derived comfort from the Christian funeral, but still did not feel it was appropriate to engage in Jewish mourning practices for a Christian parent.[15]

Conversely, if the convert dies, her family may be doubly upset that she's buried in what, to them, is an alien rite.

If you are a convert and in mourning, use any practices you find comforting or that feel like authentic expressions of your respect. When you are attending a funeral in a tradition that is no longer yours, appreciate how other family members are comforted by that ritual. In your own private time, use whatever prayers or rituals comfort you.[16]

The convert to Judaism, although not required to say kaddish for a non-Jewish parent or to light the *yahrzeit* candle, is permitted to do so if he wishes.[17] Or he may choose a modified mourning practice compatible with Judaism such as reciting psalms or studying a special passage of Torah on the anniversary of the death. Orthodox Jewish tradition would say that the convert should not hold a standard *shiva* ritual for the parent. But we think the convert could hold a modified *shiva,* inviting people to her house and giving readings and psalms in memory of the parent. In this way, she could draw on the support of the community and go through the psychological withdrawal and nurturing which are valuable parts of the *shiva.*

The same rules would apply to a Jewish man or woman, who, like Rachel, is mourning the death of a non-Jewish parent.

Similarly, the Jewish convert to Christianity can show respect for his Jewish parents in ways consonant with their values: contributing to charities in their memory, and sending in their names to be recited in their synagogue on their *yahrzeit* and to be inscribed in the memorial booklet at Yom Kippur. At the same time, he can offer his own prayers in his own church.

The Religious Straddler Another difficult situation is when the deceased had largely abandoned his own religion but had not converted to another. His spouse may wish to give him a burial rite in the church or synagogue they both attended, while his parents may feel that since he had not converted, he should still be buried by the religion in which he was raised. The best solution is to make clear each partner's wishes before a death occurs. A second approach would be to look for a service that reflects the deceased person's actual beliefs.

If this doesn't resolve the conflict, the person designated as next of kin, which would be the spouse in the case of a married couple, would have the right to make arrangements as she saw fit. In the case of an unmarried couple, whether gay or heterosexual, civil law gives the blood relations the right to decide on the manner of disposal of the body. But that should not prevent the mourner from asking a friend to help organize an independent memorial service where he can receive support from his own community.

Where mourners are coming from two different religious cultures, there are several ways to accommodate each family's needs. One is to hold a nondenominational memorial service, with readings acceptable to both religious groups, such as psalms. This can be supplemented with denominationally specific prayers on behalf of the deceased conducted by each family's clergy in their home. When clergy from the religious group of one side of the family conducts the funeral or graveside ritual, the other family's rabbi or pastor can accompany them to the graveside for moral support and stand silently beside them. (This should be agreed upon by everyone, including officiating clergy, prior to the burial.) Purely cultural customs such as the mourners' meal can be drawn from the traditions of both families.

A time of death is not, however, a good time for negotiation. One person should have full power to handle the arrangements, while remaining sensitive to the other family.

THE FINAL ANALYSIS: RECOMMENDATIONS

The handling of death is a major challenge of family life. We urge you as an intermarried couple to discuss what you plan to do about the funeral and burial well before there appears to be any risk of death in a family.

Talk It Out Discuss what you would want to happen in the event of the death of either partner, or the death of a child, and what kind of support you would want from your partner in the event of a parent's death.

Go over your beliefs about death and afterlife. Talk about what your parents and religion teachers taught you on the subject, what personal experiences with death and burial you had, and how those teachings and experiences have affected you.

Discuss what each of you wishes regarding burial: Do you want to be buried together? Do you want to be buried with your religious group or your family? What will you do if these two desires are in conflict? Do you want to be cremated? Do you want to donate organs? What traditions would you like to have followed in the funeral or in mourning?

If you find it hard to hold this conversation, make an appointment with a sensitive religious professional and have him or her guide your discussion.

Lay Some Groundwork When you are seeking an affiliation, ask the clergyperson directly: Would you bury us side by side? Would you bury our unconverted children? If you choose to affiliate with an institution that will not, you need to make alternative burial plans.

Think about prearranging your funeral with a funeral director. Write out what each of you wants: You may want to specify prayers, readings, or music. Prepayment for your cemetery lot, marker, coffin, etc., is also a good idea where feasible: It not only locks in your plans but can prevent the family from being pressured into extravagance, or being financially strained at the time of a death. (Detailed prearrangement may not be possible for a very mobile family.)

Talk with Your Children Discuss with your spouse what you would like to teach your children about death. How will you present and explain any differences in belief between the two of you? In the event of a death, it is important not to remain silent, leaving a child alone with his fears and with the feeling that death is taboo for discussion.[18]

Anticipate Family Reactions If some family members' beliefs or practices are very different from yours, consider their objections and how you will handle them. You might talk about your prearrangement plans with your parents once they are made. If your spouse dies, contact a sympathetic clergyperson of her parents' faith who can explain your plans to them.

Attend funerals of relatives, both for the sake of family solidarity (these are important times for building family ties) and so you experience their ways of mourning.

Realize that family fights during mourning are almost inevitable, including fights between you and your spouse. Even if they seem to be about religion, such fights are usually really about the anger and hurt of loss. Don't take them personally, but do take steps after the deepest period of mourning to reestablish relationships, so rifts don't harden into concrete.

If the person who dies is someone with whom you had been quarreling, or out of touch, you may feel a deep, painful guilt. It's better to use your guilt creatively to spur you to mend the quarrel or resume the relationship now, before a death occurs.

Allow Yourself to Grieve Look to the traditional burial, funeral, and mourning rites and draw from them whatever customs can help you go through your own period of mourning and letting go. If you come from a culture that has no mourning traditions after the funeral, consider borrowing some customs. Ask a friend to call other friends to bring you food after the funeral, and to gather on the third or seventh or thirtieth day to share with you in remembering the deceased person. Permit yourself at least a few days of withdrawal from your usual activities, and at the same time accept whatever help is offered.

APPENDIX

I. FINDING AN OFFICIANT: REFERRAL SERVICES

Rabbinic Center for Research and Counseling Rabbi Irwin Fishbein, the director of the center, makes available (for free, but donations appreciated) a list that he compiles of Reform Jewish rabbis who officiate at intermarriages without requiring a conversion. The list is updated approximately every six years, the latest being in June 1986. It includes rabbis in thirty-four states from Hawaii to North Carolina, the District of Columbia, and Quebec. It specifies which rabbis will co-officiate and what conditions each requires (such as a course of study in Judaism or commitment to raise the children Jewish). *Address:* 128 East Dudley Avenue, Westfield, N.J. 07090 (telephone: 201-233-0419).

Philadelphia Regional Office of the Union of American Hebrew Congregations Rabbi Richard Address, director of the office, says this is the only regional referral service under the auspices of one of the major Jewish denominations, the UAHC being the official organization of Reform Judaism. The office's outreach director will refer couples to rabbis who perform intermarriages (but only for couples who plan to raise children as Jews). *Address:* Architects Building, 17th and Sansom Streets, Philadelphia, Pa. 19102 (telephone: 215-563-8183 or 563-8726).

Practical Rabbinics Program, Reconstructionist Rabbinical College
The small Reconstructionist movement has an informal referral service directed by Rabbi Linda Holtzman. *Address:* Church Road and Greenwood Avenue, Wyncote, Pa. 19095 (telephone: 215-576-0800).

United Nations Chapel The chapel primarily makes referrals in the New York area but has handled calls from as far away as California and Ireland. Director Rev. Melvin Hawthorne will counsel couples, help plan the ceremony, and sometimes officiate. *Address:* 77 United Nations Plaza, New York, N.Y. 10017 (telephone: 212-661-1762).

Society for Humanistic Judaism Executive director Miriam Jerris makes referrals to rabbis with a secular humanist orientation. *Address:* 28611 West Twelve Mile Road, Farmington Hills, Mich. 48018 (telephone: 313-478-7610).

II. OFFICIAL POSITIONS OF THE RELIGIONS

Judaism

To understand the context in which rabbis operate, and to appreciate why a rabbi who considers doing an intermarriage often wrestles at length with his conscience, it's worth looking at the policies and prevailing climates in each of the Jewish movements.

Orthodox Judaism The Orthodox regard themselves as governed by Jewish law, which they believe is binding and immutable—and which prohibits intermarriage. Any Orthodox Jew would know not to approach an Orthodox rabbi about officiating at a mixed marriage. But should it happen, and should that rabbi perform it, he would probably be drummed out of the Rabbinical Council of America (the leading organization of Orthodox rabbis), and be fired by his congregation to boot.

If the gentile partner undergoes an acceptable conversion to Judaism, the rabbi can officiate without problem. Rabbi Marvin Goldman of Adath Zion Congregation in Philadelphia says the rabbi in that case is even free to invite the Christian family's minister or priest to stand under the *huppah,* so long as that clergyman doesn't wear clerical garb and it is clear he is only a guest.

Conservative Judaism The Conservative rabbinate also cites Jewish law and presents a united front against officiating if there has not been an acceptable conversion. In fact, the Rabbinical Assembly not only prohibits members from officiating, but also from attending, on the grounds that their mere presence confers legitimacy. Any member accused of violating the standard can be brought before a committee and warned, censured, or expelled from the Assembly. This has occurred in a handful of instances, with the accused being expelled for refusing to testify. The United Synagogue of America, to which most Conservative synagogues belong, forbids interfaith weddings on the property of its member synagogues, and will take steps that could culminate in expulsion of a congregation.

Reform Judaism Here is where there is open strife and change. Officially, the guidelines of the Central Conference of American Rabbis oppose having its members solemnize a mixed marriage. But the members are divided down the middle on the question, with impassioned argument erupting periodically and no settlement in sight. No sanctions can be brought against members who ignore the guidelines against officiation because the Reform movement grants its rabbis autonomy. And many *have* ignored the policy as the demand for the service of intermarrying rabbis has increased. A 1972 survey of its membership by the CCAR and a 1977 survey by Rabbi Irwin Fishbein both indicated that at least 40 percent have officiated at mixed marriages. The intermarrying rabbis generally offer a simple defense: Their presence at a mixed marriage, rather than weakening Judaism as traditionalists claim, is actually likely to strengthen it by giving the couple a positive experience and thereby improving the chance that they will eventually affiliate Jewishly.

However, their rabbinic officiation often comes with conditions. Many Reform rabbis require a pledge that you will take an Introduction to Judaism course, have a home that is exclusively Jewish, and raise any children as Jews.

In the lay community, the tide is turning toward accepting interfaith weddings. In many communities, rabbis are under strong pressure to officiate at mixed marriages. Congregational search committees, in selecting new rabbis, frequently cite the willingness to officiate as a requirement for the job.

Reconstructionism This movement, which is considered liberal, like Reform, but is considerably smaller, has pieced together a consensus guideline that allows a limited rabbinic role (in hopes of laying the groundwork for a couple's later affiliation), but that asks a rabbi to stop short of officiating. Premarital counseling of couples is encouraged, with the rabbi expected to be "as sympathetic and accepting as possible." If the rabbi has a special relationship with a couple or knows they will have a Jewish home, he or she is urged to suggest that they have a civil ceremony at which the rabbi will "offer appropriate remarks welcoming the couple into the Jewish community."

Officiation is discouraged. The guidelines of the Reconstructionist Rabbinical Association state that "The traditional rites of the Jewish wedding ceremony should be reserved for the marriage of a Jew to a Jew." The guidelines carry no sanctions, however, and a sizable minority of Reconstructionist rabbis have chosen not to follow them.

Christianity

In contrast to the ferment of Judaism stands Christianity, in calm repose. Here the question of officiation or co-officiation at mixed marriages seems to arouse little emotion. Only Greek Orthodoxy is flatly opposed. Roman Catholicism allows it if the rules are followed. Protestantism has little to say on the topic.

Protestantism   Not only has this question provoked no controversy, it has not even been the subject of official dialogue in most of the mainstream Protestant denominations. The percentage of members in any one denomination, and certainly in any church, who marry Jews is small, so this remains a nonissue for most ministers. Mainstream church leaders who have discussed interfaith marriages have regarded them as a simple fact of life or have looked fondly on them as an expression of ecumenicism. The Lutheran Church in America, for example, says that theologically, such marriages should be seen as "a witness to the oneness of humanity, under the one God, and as such should be fully accepted in both church and society."

All this bodes well if you intend to use a Protestant minister. Take the Methodist stance: Their clergy are free to marry anyone—a Methodist to a non-Methodist, even a Buddhist to a Jew—and to conduct the ceremony anywhere. There is no set liturgy for the wedding, and Jewish elements are not disallowed. The couple does not have to promise anything. This lack of rules applies to the other mainstream denominations as well, according to Rev. Perry Biddle, a Presbyterian minister in Nashville and author of the *Abingdon Marriage Manual*. He says ministers have always been left to their own judgment in such matters, and it is his impression that most mainstream Protestant clergy will take part in mixed-marriage ceremonies.

Still, be advised that you may encounter a range of attitudes in your search. An increasingly vocal evangelical element, certainly in the fundamentalist churches but also at one extreme of the mainstream denominations, wants all Jews to be converted and thus would oppose participation in a mixed ceremony. Other times a minister will decline if the marriage is not in the Christian fold or is not between members of his congregation. But a substantial number will officiate.

Episcopalian With one important exception, the Episcopal Church shares the approach of the other mainstream Protestant denominations. Its priests are free to decide whether and where to do a ceremony, whether to join with a rabbi and whether to delete references to Jesus. One requirement is made of all couples, however: that they sign a declaration that they will live a Christian life.

Catholicism The Roman Catholic Church once forbade Jewish-Catholic marriages. But now, out of a simple recognition that interfaith marriages are increasingly frequent, it does sanction them—if certain rules are followed. Should you want your marriage blessed by the church, here's what's in store:

The Catholic must obtain permission, called a dispensation, to marry a non-Catholic. These are routinely granted for a nominal fee. The couple must then agree to wait a set time, such as six months, before being wed, and must take a premarital (Pre-Cana) course, which covers communication, finances, sexuality, and adjustment issues. The courses vary in length, with some as short as one day, and in price, with some being free. The Catholic is required to attend and the non-Catholic is strongly encouraged. Both of you will be asked to study each other's religion.

Prior to the wedding, the Catholic must declare, either orally or in writing, to a priest or deacon, that he believes in Jesus and will continue to be a practicing Catholic, and will do all in his power to have any children baptized and raised as Catholics. These promises no longer need to be signed by the Catholic, and no longer are required at all of the non-Catholic. In addition, the Church has become somewhat flexible in interpreting the promise: While the Catholic is expected to try strongly to have the children raised as Catholics, if she realizes later that insisting on this would jeopardize the marriage, she is excused.

Once these preliminary steps are taken, the priest can officiate at the wedding. The Church makes available alternate liturgy that omits references to Jesus, using instead references to God from the Hebrew Bible (Old Testament). A rabbi is free to take part as a guest and to offer blessings and words of advice.

Some dioceses require that if a priest is to officiate, the wedding must take place inside a Catholic church. Other dioceses allow their priests to officiate in a nonchurch site—a chapel, a home, a catering hall—if the priest feels he can create a "sacred setting."

But realize that even if a priest does officiate, the Church will not consider it a normal, "sacramental" wedding since one of the parties has not been baptized. Under Catholic law, the priest merely functions as an official witness as the couple exchanges the vows in the name of the Church. That is the essence of the Catholic wedding rite, and if one party has never been baptized, it does not matter what he says; the wedding cannot be a sacrament. The Church considers it valid, just not sacramental.

If the couple doesn't wish to have a priest officiate, a second dispensation should be obtained, also generally a routine matter. The couple is then free to arrange the ceremony with a non-Catholic officiant, be he a rabbi, judge, or whoever. The ceremony can be conducted anywhere, including in a synagogue. A priest is free to attend as a guest and to offer blessings or greetings. Priests are not allowed to share in the asking of the vows. This constitutes co-officiation, and the Church's rule is: One ceremony, one officiant.

The Church does not allow a second religious ceremony. Some couples have apparently tried to do back-to-back ceremonies, one in each faith, but the Church regards that as a clear abuse of the dispensation.

If you do not obtain dispensation and the Catholic has later regrets about not having the marriage blessed by the Church, you have recourse. Through a procedure called convalidation, you can restore official sanction by going through the steps we have outlined previously, then having a priest officiate as you repeat your vows in another, usually low-key, Church ceremony.

Greek Orthodox Officially, the Church takes a very hard line against marriage between one of its members and anyone who is not a baptized Christian. Should a member marry a Jew, he is regarded as having committed self-excommunication and is prohibited from taking Communion and sponsoring anyone at a wedding. Though he is allowed to attend services, the marriage is not recognized and the person is considered to have negated his baptism and confirmation. Should a Greek Orthodox priest officiate at an intermarriage, he would face suspension for violating canon law and for insubordination.

This stance comes partly from a minority culture's concern about assimilation. More than half of Greek Orthodox marriages are to non-Greeks. The Church does sanction marriages between a member and a baptized Catholic so long as dispensations have been granted and the ceremony is performed in a Greek Orthodox Church.

III. SAMPLE CEREMONY

To accommodate couples who intend to raise their children as Jews but where the gentile does not intend to convert to Judaism, some Reconstructionist rabbis have designed a "universalist" wedding ceremony which draws from Jewish tradition but bears little resemblance to the forms of the standard Jewish wedding. This ceremony is based on God's covenant with Noah, which in the Hebrew Bible predates God's covenant with Abraham, father of the Jewish people. According to Jewish tradition, the laws given at Sinai are binding only on the Jews, while the covenant of Noah given after the Flood is binding on all humans. Thus, only the Jews are obligated to keep kosher and the Sabbath, but everyone is obligated to set up courts of justice and is prohibited from murder, adultery, idolatry, theft, incest, and blasphemy. (The rabbis deduced these commands from Genesis 9:1–7.)

Since the Noahite covenant prohibited adultery, the rabbis concluded that God was commanding marriage as the basis of all families. The following ceremony is adapted from one given to us by Rabbi Moshe Halfon.

According to Rabbi Halfon, this is a universalist ceremony with Jewish content. It is a non-halakhic ceremony, meaning that it would not be considered valid under Jewish law. Rabbi Halfon agreed to perform the ceremony only once, for a couple who met specific conditions: the non-Jewish partner had a positive relationship with Judaism and was considering studying for later conversion. The non-Jewish partner was alienated from the religion of birth and was not affiliated with any church. Both partners were committed to observing Judaism in the home and to converting the children to Judaism.

1. Instrumental Music. *Huppah* holders bring in *huppah* (canopy).

2. Officiant: verses adapted from *Song of Songs* (may be chanted in Hebrew and translated):

> My love is mine, and I am his
> He who browses among the lilies.
> My beloved spoke thus to me:
> "Arise, my darling:
> My fair one, come away!
> For now the winter is past,
> The rains are over and gone.

The song of the turtle dove
Is heard in our land
The green figs form on the fig tree,
The vines in blossom give off fragrance.
Arise, my darling,
My fair one, come away! (2:16, 2:10–13)
Set me as a seal upon your heart,
Like a stamp upon your hand
For love is stronger than death,
Its passion is mightier than Eternity
Its sparks flame up into a blazing fire.
Vast floods cannot quench love,
Nor rivers drown it." (8:6)

3. Statement by bride and groom.

4. Covenant statement by officiant:

Since the dawn of recorded history, women and men have chosen to consecrate the act of choosing a mate and beginning a life together. Each religious tradition records this in its own unique way. Thus it was even when the world was young. The rabbis tell a story, or midrash, to show us what an honor and special deed it is to accompany the bride and groom and assist in their celebration. They say that God braided Eve's hair and bedecked her in fine garments in preparation for her betrothal to Adam. Thus the first primeval pairing of souls was celebrated and performed in a public manner, in the presence of a loving witness. You two are children of Adam and Eve, of Noah and Naamah, and you carry on that tradition. And so, in the presence of your family, your friends, and of God, I ask the two of you:

Do you, (groom), join in covenant with (bride) as your wife, promising to love, respect, and sustain her, and to build a home with her based upon the traditions of the Jewish people? If so, say "I do."

(Repeat vow with bride.)

Officiant: As a token of this love and devotion for each other, and of this covenant of marriage which you are entering into, I ask each of you to recite the words of the prophet Hosea, and to place a ring onto the finger of your betrothed as you do so:

With this ring, I betroth you to me eternally.
I betroth you in righteousness and justice,

In loyalty and compassion.
And I betroth you to me in faithfulness.

5. Officiant reads the written agreement of the couple.

6. Selected guests read four blessings, in English:

   A. We praise you, Source of All Blessings, Who has fashioned all human beings in the image of God. (Amen)
   B. We praise you, Source of All Blessings, Who has made it possible for humans to meet, to love and to care for one another, and to carry on your process of creating and caring for the world. (Amen)
   C. May this couple find peace, strength, and contentment in each other, and build a home blessed with harmony and joy. May they be blessed with patience, understanding, and a long life together. (Amen)
   D. May their home radiate with the celebrations, teachings, and beauty of Judaism. We praise you, Source of All Blessings, for the opportunity to share the joy of this moment together, and to rejoice in the joining of these two souls. (Amen)

7. Blessing over wine is said (first in English by a guest, then chanted in Hebrew by officiant). Two glasses are prepared, then the couple pours each into a third and drink together from the one.

8. Officiant makes remarks to the couple and blesses them:

   If you will truly hear God's voice, and keep these obligations enjoined upon you this day, then may all these blessings and more come upon you: You shall be blessed in the city and in the country; you shall be blessed in product and progeny; you shall be blessed in the fruit of your labor and the harvest of your dreams; you shall be blessed in your coming and in your going. (Based on Dt.28:1–6)

9. Statement by the congregants:

   We, the assembled family and community, hereby sanctify and affirm the marriage of this couple. Through the covenant of God with Noah's children and with all of us, we now declare you man and wife. Mazal tov!

IV. OTHER SOURCES

1. We know of several other Jewishly oriented universalistic ceremonies. One, by Arthur Waskow and Rabbis Linda Holtzman and Rebecca Alpert, appeared in the November 1983 *Reconstructionist* magazine. Another, developed by Rabbi Albert Axelrad, chaplain and B'nai B'rith Hillel director at Brandeis University, appeared in the July–August 1986 *Reconstructionist* magazine.

2. For a copy of a lovely ceremony that is reverent but totally nontheistic, write Judith Espenschied, Leader of the Philadelphia Ethical Culture Society, 1906 South Rittenhouse Square, Philadelphia, Pa. 19103.

3. Books
   Biddle, Perry, *The Abingdon Marriage Manual* (Protestant), Nashville, Tenn.: Abingdon Press, 1987.
   Brill, Mordechai L., Marlene Halpin, and William H. Genne, *Write Your Own Wedding,* Chicago: Association Press/Follett Publishing, 1979.
   Goodman, Philip and Hanna, *The Jewish Marriage Anthology,* Philadelphia: Jewish Publication Society, 1965.
   Newman, Carol, *Your Wedding, Your Way,* Garden City, N.Y.: Doubleday and Co., 1975.
   Seaburg, Carl, ed., *Great Occasions: Readings for Birth, Coming-of-Age, Marriage and Death,* Boston: Beacon Press, 1968.

CHAPTER 11: CONVERSION PROCEDURES

JUDAISM

The Jewish movements differ in their procedures, with traditionalists adhering closely to Jewish law and liberals less so. Three things are consistent: In the four major branches, you will be required to study under rabbinic supervision for at least several months; you will be expected to attend services and participate in Jewish ritual observances during the preparation; and you will be given a Hebrew name upon conversion.
   Here are the standard procedures in the four movements:

Orthodox Some Orthodox rabbis may still adhere to the longtime practice of turning away a prospective convert two times before accepting her on the third. This practice grew out of grim historical realities. While Christianity held political power in Europe, Jews were forbidden under penalty of death to seek converts. Any Christians who converted to Judaism were also liable to be burned at the stake. They had to be questioned to be sure they comprehended the risks of being Jewish.

Nowadays, if you express a desire to convert you will probably not be turned away but rather be invited into the rabbi's study for a talk about your reasons and beliefs. Usually, you will then be tutored personally by the rabbi, learning mostly about Jewish law and observance. You will learn some Hebrew, either from him or another teacher. The preparation period commonly lasts at least a year so you experience the Jewish calendar cycle.

For a male candidate comes the requirement of *milah* (circumcision). If you have never been circumcised, you must undergo the surgical procedure, usually in a hospital. If you were circumcised as a child, a drop of blood *dam ha-brit,* the "blood of the covenant") is taken from the place where your foreskin would be.

Once the rabbi feels you know enough to become a Jew, you will go before a *beth din,* a court of three knowledgeable Jews, to be tested for your motivation and knowledge. You will be asked whether you are prepared to throw in your lot with the Jewish people and to live a traditionally observant Jewish life. It is called *kabbalat mitzvot* (welcoming or acceptance of the yoke of the commandments). You will be expected to abide by the laws of Jewish living, with two of the *mitzvot* being essential: keeping the Sabbath and keeping a kosher home.

The third requirement, after *milah* and *kabbalat mitzvot,* is *tevilah.* This is immersion in the *mikvah,* a special ritual bath or any flowing body of water. The immersion culminates the event. It is the moment at which you officially become a Jew. The rabbi then presents you with a certificate of conversion.

None of this is done in front of your new congregation. The Orthodox custom is quietly to integrate the proselyte into the community. You are to be indistinguishable from all other Jews.

Conservative Read the Orthodox description and you get a rough picture of the Conservative process as well. Desiring to adhere to Jewish law as Orthodoxy does, it requires the same three things of a person: *kabbalat mitzvot, milah,* and *tevilah.* But there are several differences. First, you are almost certain to do your study in a formal, group conversion class (while also meeting individually with your sponsoring rabbi). Second, the content of the instruction is broader; you will learn about Jewish history and modern community characteristics as well as about observance. Third, the preparation period is usually not quite as long. Fourth, though you must promise to practice Jewish living, the expectation is not that you will take on strong observance from the outset but that you will make it a goal.

Once you have completed the formal course of study and your sponsoring rabbi has determined that your "thoughts, feelings, and actions are Jewish," he will take you before the *beth din,* according to Rabbi Stephen C. Lerner, director of the Center for Conversion to Judaism and rabbi of Temple Emanuel in Ridgefield Park, New Jersey. The *beth din* will cover the same ground that your rabbi did, such as: What led you to convert? What do you see as the primary differences between Judaism and Christianity? How difficult will it be for you to give up Christian beliefs? A few questions about your Jewish knowledge and Hebrew proficiency also are asked. Sometimes, at the conclusion of the questioning, a private ceremony is held at which you state a declaration of Judaism and recite the essential Jewish prayer called the *Sh'ma,* and the rabbi reads your document of conversion and might address a few remarks to you. The *mikvah* generally follows. In other localities, the procedure might be *beth din,* then *mikvah,* then ceremony, and might take place over several days instead of all in one day.

Followup and enrichment efforts vary by locality. Rabbi Lerner's conversion center holds weekend retreats for candidates and new Jews, giving them an opportunity for intensive Jewish living. Support groups for converts also are offered by some Conservative synagogues.

Reconstructionist This movement, the smallest of the four, suggests that preparation last for at least six months. You will either study in a group setting or individually with a rabbi, depending on local circumstance. The rabbi is expected both to teach you and discuss your emotional and religious needs.

Most Reconstructionist rabbis will require immersion and the circumcision or *dam ha-brit.* There is a *beth din,* though its function has been modified. The Reconstructionist Rabbinical Association guidelines state that the court operates not "to put the candidate through a 'dissertation defense' type of examination, but to elicit from him/her thoughts and feelings . . . [It] should be warm and memorable."

In keeping with the traditional Jewish custom at all special occasions, you will be encouraged to make a *tzedakah* offering (charitable contribution) to a Jewish cause.

The movement has been promoting the idea of public ceremonies or welcomings for the sake of both the congregation and the convert. If you are unable for some compelling reason to have an immersion, the congregational welcoming might serve as the official moment of your conversion. Otherwise, the ceremony would serve as a public welcoming after the fact of conversion. "The [public] ceremony should include a 'Declaration of acceptance of Judaism' on the part of the convert," the guidelines say. "The rabbi or a member of the congregation may wish to address the candidate, who, in turn, might want to make a personal statement."

Reform The first step is study, occasionally one-on-one but usually in a group setting as part of the movement's eighteen-week Introduction to Judaism course. You will learn the fundamentals—theology, rituals, holidays, life-cycle events, history, some Hebrew. At the end of the eighteen weeks, there usually are several group sessions with a social worker to discuss the interpersonal and community dynamics of conversion. Your sponsoring rabbi also will meet with you regularly to provide advice and counseling. Reform's Central Conference of American Rabbis recommends that the period last from four to twelve months. The norm approaches the shorter end.

Preparatory study is where the movement places its emphasis. Years ago, it dropped the requirements of ritual immersion and circumcision as anachronistic. Today, those rites are optional (and many Reform candidates are electing to undergo them).

One likelihood is that you will go before a sort of *beth din* composed of three adult witnesses. In their presence, you declare your acceptance of Judaism. You also have the opportunity to discuss the conversion process. The Reform rabbinate intends that your appearance before the group be positive, stating in its guidelines on proselytism: "This should not take on a critical or defensive tone, for the rabbi should already be aware of the (candidate's) knowledge and commitment."

Like Reconstructionism, the Reform movement has developed a conversion ceremony that every candidate undergoes, whether or not you go to the *mikvah* as well. The candidate has the option of whether to have the ceremony be private; before family and friends; or public at a *Shabbos* service. It consists of either your responding to six specific questions that the rabbi asks you, or of your stating a formal pledge.

The questions are along these lines: "Do you choose to enter the covenant between God and the people of Israel and to become a Jew of your own free will?" "Do you promise to establish a Jewish home and to participate actively in the life of the synagogue and of the Jewish community?" Should you choose to state the pledge, you speak alone: "I choose to become a Jew of my own free will. . ."

Afterward, the rabbi is expected to continue his tutelage and may encourage you to join a synagogue and enroll in adult education classes.

A number of Reform congregations also offer support groups for new Jews.

CHRISTIANITY

Catholicism The ceremony is standardized but the instruction is not. In a small parish, the priest might give you a small amount of reading, meet with you once a week for ten weeks, and declare you ready after a modicum of pastoral care. In a large parish or a more progressive one, there would be a formal class, counseling, and perhaps retreats and service projects.

The baptism ceremony will be public. Until the past twenty years, Catholic baptisms tended to be private and to be held sporadically through the year. But the church has since revived an old custom of having public, group baptisms on the night before Easter, at a Mass called the Holy Saturday Vigil Service. Each candidate must stand before the congregation and respond to a series of creedal questions to this effect: Do you believe in God? Do you believe in Jesus? Do you believe in the Holy Spirit? Do you believe in the importance of the church and the sacraments? Do you promise to pray? Do you promise to be of Christian service? After those questions have been answered, the congregation makes a creedal reaffirmation of faith. The priest sprinkles each candidate with water, culminating the conversion.

Protestantism Local autonomy prevails in nearly all matters in Protestantism, and conversion is no exception. Few denominations have guidelines that tell a minister what you should study and how your readiness should be measured. That is left to the pastor's discretion. There are so many divisions and subdivisions in Protestantism that we can't describe them all. Instead, we summarize the process in a less liturgical locale (Riverside Church) and a more liturgical one (Presbyterianism).

Riverside Church: This massive congregation in Manhattan has long been a pillar of liberal Protestantism. Its affiliation is jointly United Church of Christ and American Baptist. Rev. Eleanor Scott Meyers, a professor at Union Theological Seminary, described the straightforward process she experienced when she transferred her membership to Riverside. First came six group sessions. (The students in the membership class were "Hindus, American Indians, Buddhists, Confucians, American Baptists, United Church of Christ, Roman Catholics, Jews.") They were taught the structure and history of Riverside and its parent denominations, as well as the liturgy and its theological underpinnings. Someone converting from another religion would be given extra pastoral attention. When it is felt you are ready to convert, you would be expected to sign a statement to the effect, "I believe Jesus Christ is the lord of my life." Beyond that, there is no creedal affirmation. Then comes the baptism, usually public and usually a sprinkling.

Presbyterian: We spoke with officials in this denomination as well as in Lutheranism and Episcopalianism and felt the Presbyterian approach loosely represents all three. As a Presbyterian conversion candidate, you would join a ten- to twelve-week adult communicants' class or, if you were the only person, would be tutored one-on-one by the pastor. The standard topics covered are Judaism, Christian history and theology, Presbyterian history and theology, and the workings of the denomination and local church. Prior to that, or concurrent with it, you would receive some additional pastoral care as someone new to Christianity. Rev. T. Michael Dawson, a Presbyterian pastoral counselor, says most ministers would be alert to a Jew's "struggles of identity." Readiness for baptism depends "not so much on what the person knew but on how the person felt, whether the person felt they were ready." Once ready, you would be baptized during a regular Sunday service. First comes a series of questions, among them, "Do you believe in Jesus Christ as your Lord and Savior?" "Will you seek to support the fellow members of the community in faith and love?" Once answered, the congregation declares that it will nurture you as a "brother or sister in Christ." A baptism by sprinkling culminates the ceremony. You are then customarily enrolled in an adult church-school class to continue your development.

CHAPTER 15: HOLIDAYS AND HOME STYLE

The following descriptions give the traditional content and themes of the holidays of Judaism and Christianity.

JUDAISM

The Sabbath *Shabbos,* the weekly day of rest, is one of Judaism's most important contributions to world civilization. The late Rabbi Abraham Joshua Heschel, a giant of contemporary Judaism, said in his book, *The Sabbath:* "The Sabbaths are our great Cathedrals; and our Holy of Holies is a shrine that neither the Romans nor the Germans were able to burn."

Observed with a joyful and reverent spirit, *Shabbos* (or Shabbat) should be beautiful, nurturing and fun—a real holiday. We can't overstress the importance of this weekly holiday for creating a Jewish home and Jewish identities for the children. Ahad Ha-Am, A European Jewish writer of the last generation, said in *Al Parashat Derakhim:* "More than the Jews have kept the Sabbath, the Sabbath has preserved the Jews."

Traditional aspects: The Sabbath is a day of complete rest. It commemorates God's resting after the creation of the world, as described in the Biblical book of Genesis. Like all Jewish holidays, *Shabbos* starts at sundown of the previous evening. It begins with lighting of candles, partaking of wine and bread, and thanking God for these rituals, which give an aura of holiness to the day. At synagogue services on Friday evening and Saturday morning, there are prayers of praise. On the Sabbath, observant Jews have long leisurely meals, visit with friends, take short walks, nap, and relax. In an Orthodox home, no work is done. People refrain from such workaday activities as writing, cooking (all the food is prepared ahead of time), and riding in cars.

Festival aspects: *Shabbos* begins with a festive meal. The table is set with the best cloth (usually white), candlesticks, a braided egg bread (*hallah*) covered by a special cloth, and a special wine cup (the *kiddush* cup). People dress in their best clothes. The meal usually begins and ends with songs. *Shabbos* ends when darkness falls on Saturday night with the ceremony of *Havdalah (separation* between the holy and the routine). Lighting a torch-like braided candle, partaking of wine, and breathing the scent from a box of fragrant spices, Jews again thank God for the opportunity to set apart the Sabbath. There are more songs.

Universal values: The central value of the Sabbath is family. The holiday is centered in the home; it consecrates and uplifts the home. At the start of the Sabbath meal, parents ask God to bless their children. The husband often recites a special prayer honoring his wife. It is considered especially praiseworthy for a husband to make love to his wife on Friday night. The Sabbath is thought of as a lovely bride who on this day is a special guest, bringing grace to the Jewish home.

Emotional and spiritual themes: The goal of the Sabbath is harmony. It's a time for consciously letting go of worries, plans, ambitions. For twenty-four hours, you accept the world exactly as it is and don't try to change anything. You don't even mow your lawn. You live in balance with nature.

Passover The Jewish year begins in the spring with Passover (*Pesah*). This usually occurs in April (because Jews use a combination of lunar and solar time, the date of the holiday varies somewhat from the Julian or solar calendar). For nearly all Jews, *Pesah* is the most important and beloved holiday. It is as central to being Jewish as Christmas is to being Christian.

Traditional meanings: Passover celebrates God's miraculous freeing of the Israelites from the slavery of Egypt, as told in the Book of Exodus. During the eight days of the festival (seven days in Israel and in Reform Judaism) Jews eat only matzoh (unleavened bread). The matzoh is a reminder of their hasty flight from Egypt, when they didn't have time to let the bread for the journey rise before it was baked.

The story of the Exodus is retold during the Passover seder, an elaborate meal which is also a religious ritual or service. The story is read from a special book (the *Haggadah*) and is dramatized through the eating of matzoh and other special foods, such as *haroses* (an apple-nut mixture that symbolizes the mortar used by the slaves to make bricks), horseradish (a reminder of the bitterness of slavery), and salt water (a reminder of the tears of slavery).

Also on the seder plate is an egg and a roasted lamb shank, the *Pesah,* which is not eaten. They symbolize the Passover sacrifice and the festive meal. The Egyptian Pharaoh wasn't willing to let the Jewish slaves leave Egypt until, in the tenth plague, the angel of death came and took all the first-born sons of the Egyptians. Each Jewish family had been commanded by God to kill a lamb and sprinkle some of its blood on the doorway as a signal to the angel of death to "pass over" that house. The family was then to feast on the lamb, until by morning not a scrap was left. As long as the Temple stood in the land of Israel, each year at Passover every family commemorated the miracle by bringing to the Temple a lamb, which was sacrificed by the priests and returned to the family for its Passover feast. Once the Temple was destroyed, the sacrifice was no longer possible. This one bone is a reminder of the original miracle and of the Temple sacrifice.

According to Jewish tradition, Passover is the birthday of the Jewish people. When the Jews emerged from Egypt, they were born as a distinct people with a special relationship to God.

Keep in mind that the purpose of the holiday is to tell a story to children. (The Biblical commandment in Exodus 13 says, "You shall tell your son on that day, 'This is because of what God did for me when I came out from Egypt.' ") Be sure at least one of your seders is at your children's level in language and in length. There are coloring-book-style children's *Haggadahs* to help you do this. Or you can adapt the seder yourself, writing your own *Haggadah* with illustrations by your children.

Festival aspects: Seders are held on the first one or two days of the holiday. Customarily, the whole extended family gathers together, along with a few invited guests. People lean on pillows as if they were Roman nobles. The symbolic foods for the service include four cups of wine for each person. In the middle of the story, the family takes a break and eats a hearty meal. Each family has its favorite Passover foods, depending where the family emigrated from. Then the service continues. There are many special roles for children. The seder begins with the chanting, by the youngest child who is able, of four questions about the meaning of the celebration. The meal ends with a treasure hunt: Children look for the *afikomen* (a special piece of matzoh), and the finder gets a reward. At the end of the evening, the children open the door for Elijah, the prophet who, Jews traditionally say, will usher in the Messiah. Throughout the evening, there are songs, many of them game songs for children.

Preparation: According to the Biblical commandment, during the eight days there is to be no *hametz* (leavening or grains) in the house. In the traditional Jewish home, the house is cleaned from top to bottom. The stove is sterilized to burn away any trace of leavening. All the usual dishes, pots, and pans are sterilized or locked away in a basement cabinet. Special dishes are brought out that are used only at Passover and have never touched yeasted bread or other grains.

It adds to the anticipation of the holiday to get children involved in the cleanup. You can explain that this hard work lets you feel for a short while what it was like to be a slave, who had to work this hard every day. Children can also help prepare some of the special seder foods.

On the evening before the first seder comes the *hametz* search. With the aid of a lighted wax candle, the child peers into all the crannies of the house, looking for crumbs. Any that are found are swept with a feather or small brush into a paper bag. Often the parents will hide a half piece of bread for the searchers to find. The next morning these last specks of *hametz* are burned, and a special blessing is said telling God that the family has really tried to rid the house of leavening, and asking that they be excused for anything they have overlooked.

Universal themes: Passover stresses the ethical theme of freedom and justice, and of solidarity with the oppressed. It's a Passover tradition to talk into the night about these ideals and how they might be achieved. If you gear one seder to the children, let the other seder be a night for adult discussion, and let the kids play around the edges and eavesdrop as they wish. Some *Haggadahs* have excellent selections to read aloud and to stimulate debate. It's also a time-honored Passover tradition to bring in readings and commentaries from outside sources.

The second major theme of Passover is spring, with its accompanying renewal, blossoming, and hopefulness. Passover is one of three agricultural festivals in the Jewish calendar. They are called "pilgrim festivals" because in ancient Israel, the population would converge on Jerusalem from all over the country, bringing offerings from their flocks and fields.

A hard-boiled egg on the seder plate symbolizes these seasonal sacrifices. The plate also contains parsley, representing the greenery of spring.

During the seder and in the synagogue service, lush verses from the biblical book Song of Songs, celebrating young love and spring, are recited or sung. One of the recurring themes of Judaism is the marriage between the people of Israel and God. Passover is the time of betrothal, of passionate commitment.

Emotional and spiritual tasks: The two tasks of Passover are self-cleansing and personal liberation. During the days leading up to Passover, while you are cleaning your house, you can also muse about the "crumby" aspects of your character that you would like to change: meanness or vanity, enslavement to negative or self-defeating habits. Imagine scrubbing your own soul and starting over, shiny and new. The holiday is a time for hope, of renewing faith in the ability to make personal transformations.

Shavuos From the second day of Passover there is a fifty-day countdown to the holiday of Shavuos. The second of the three ancient agricultural festivals, it falls in May or June.

Traditional aspects: Shavuos commemorates the giving of the law at Mount Sinai. As Passover is the birthday of the Jewish people, Shavuos is the birthday of the Jewish religion. In the relationship between the Jewish people and God, as Passover represents the betrothal, Shavuos represents the signing of the marriage contract. At this time, according to the Bible, God revealed Himself to the assembled Jewish people, speaking aloud and making His presence known through lightning and thunder and the blast of a heavenly ram's horn. Traditional Jews believe that not only the Ten Commandments, but also all of the Torah and later wisdom handed down orally by the rabbis, was dictated by God to Moses during the forty days he stayed on Mount Sinai.

During synagogue services on Shavuos, the Book of Ruth is read. Ruth, a Moabite woman who married an Israelite, became the ancestress of King David and thus the forerunner of the Messiah. She is generally regarded as the most famous convert to Judaism. Traditional Jews believe all Jewish souls, including those not yet born and those who convert to Judaism, were present at Mount Sinai when God revealed Himself. According to Jewish tradition, just as the Jewish people voluntarily accepted the Torah at Mount Sinai, and as Ruth voluntarily joined herself with the Jewish people in ancient Israel, (saying "thy people shall be my people and thy God my God"), so each Jew must personally make a commitment to the Jewish way of life.

Festival aspects: As during all of the agricultural or pilgrim festivals, psalms of praise are sung. In Reform and Conservative synagogues, there is a confirmation service during this season at which the sixteen-year-old students graduate from religious school and declare their Jewish commitment.

If a member of your family has converted to Judaism, this might be a time to have a special family celebration of that event and to acknowledge the gifts the person has brought to the Jewish people.

On the night of Shavuos, some Conservative and Orthodox Jews hold an all-night study session called a *tikkun* (mending). According to a traditional story, the Jews fell asleep at Mount Sinai and were late for the giving of the Ten Commandments. To make certain they won't miss it again, they stay up all night. At dawn, they take out the Torah scroll and read—reaffirming their commitment to the law.

Universal meanings: This is a time for thinking about the laws of right behavior and what it might mean, in practical terms, to recommit oneself to an ethical way of life.

Spiritual and emotional themes: Shavuos is a time for reflecting on what it means to be open to revelation.

Tisha B'Av In the parching heat of July or August comes Tisha B'Av, the ninth of the month of Av, a fast day.

Traditional meaning: Tisha B'Av is a day of mourning for the destruction of the Temple in Jerusalem and for all the other persecutions suffered by the Jews. At this time, Jews try not only to remember, but to relive, the sufferings of the Jews who were expelled from Spain in 1492 (which occurred on Tisha B'Av) or killed in the pogroms of Russia and the Holocaust. In the evening, members of the congregation gather at the synagogue, sit on the floor, barefoot in the dark, and by the light of memorial candles read the Book of Lamentations, which is chanted to a mournful melody. The scripture tells of the siege of Jerusalem, with a famine so desperate that mothers ate their babies.

Universal meanings: Tisha B'Av is a fast day, but it is a working day rather than a holiday. Working all day on an empty stomach, without even a glass of water in the summer heat, one can feel a visceral connection with poor people all over the world and can renew the determination to ease their suffering.

Emotional and spiritual themes: Ponder the meaning of suffering; try to understand one's relationship to God in a world in which suffering continues daily. But the tradition also says the Messiah will be born on Tisha B'Av—that deliverance will come at the point of most intense suffering. (For this reason, the Sabbath after the holiday is a time of exhilaration.) So Tisha B'Av is also a time to seek hope in the midst of suffering.

The High Holidays The Jewish month of Tishri, which coincides with September and October, includes a month-long cycle of holidays. During the first half of the month come the two holiest days of the calendar, Rosh Hashanah and Yom Kippur.

Traditional meanings: As Passover was the birthday of the Jewish people and Shavuos the birthday of the Jewish religion, Rosh Hashanah, the New Year, is the birthday of the world, the anniversary of creation. Rather than being a time of giddy abandon, it is a time of rededication, of trying to begin fresh as if both you and the world were new and unspoiled. The New Year is also a time of judgment. The tradition says that during this time, God looks over your actions from the last year and determines your fate in the year to come. You can sway the decision by repenting any sins you have committed and making amends for any wrongs done. Rosh Hashanah begins the Ten Days of Awe, an intensive period of self-assessment. By the time of Yom Kippur, the Day of Atonement, each person is to have made amends to the extent possible for all sins against human beings, so that the only things to be dealt with will be the sins against God.

Yom Kippur is a fast day, but a fast of purification rather than of mourning. People customarily dress in white, wear no jewelry or leather (so as to avoid participating even indirectly in the killing of anything or in selfish luxury), and spend all day in confessional prayers, which close with one last wail of the ram's horn. If you have done your best to make amends, your true repentance and prayers on this day will be accepted and you will be purified and given a clean slate in the New Year. Jews who do not come to synagogue any other time of the year find their way there on Yom Kippur, and synagogues are so jammed that many can admit only those who are members or have special tickets. Folding chairs may be set up in classrooms or even in neighboring buildings to accommodate the overflow. At the end of the day, the solemnity gives way to jubilation. The ram's horn signals that one's prayers for forgiveness have been accepted.

Emotional or spiritual themes: It's hard to let go of guilt, regret, and self-condemnation and to really experience a sense of being forgiven. Yom Kippur is a day dedicated to dealing with the guilt and arriving at that sense.

Preparation: The High Holidays are preceded by Elul, a month of intense in-turning and self-evaluation. During Elul, the lonely blast of a ram's horn is heard in the synagogue each day except *Shabbos*. People are supposed to do everything they can to make amends with other people—pay outstanding debts, resolve family quarrels, make apologies, and the like. They donate to charity. Just before Rosh Hashanah comes the ceremony of *Selihos*—midnight confessional prayers at the synagogue.

The High Holiday period is a good time to talk with your partner about how your marriage is going and to devise new approaches to any problem areas.

Preparing children for the High Holidays is a delicate task. Without scaring them, you can help them understand the idea of reconciliation. Ask them to think of all the people they are mad at, and all the people who might be mad at them, and why. They might start by going up to other people they have hurt, apologizing and asking if they can have a hug and be forgiven. Then they can go to the people they are mad at, tell them why they are mad, ask "Did you mean to hurt me?" and say, "If you'll say you're sorry, I'll give you a hug and stop being mad at you." (Try having them deal with the adults they're mad at first, so that if they get rejections from their peers, they'll still have something good to remember.)

Festival aspects: The High Holidays are a time for homecoming in many Jewish families. On the night when Rosh Hashanah begins, a festive meal is held. Apples are dipped in honey and eaten to symbolize the hope for a sweet and fruitful New Year. People also gather at the end of Yom Kippur to break the fast together, traditionally with a light dairy meal.

Sukkos This fall harvest festival begins five days after Yom Kippur. It is the third of the three ancient pilgrim festivals and the one which most clearly recalls the people's agricultural roots.

Traditional meanings: The day after Yom Kippur, observant Jewish families begin building a rustic outdoor booth (*sukkah*) with a thatched roof of branches or cornstalks. During the seven days of Sukkos, they are to dwell in this booth—to take their meals there, and, weather permitting, even to sleep there—a modified camp-out. The holiday commemorates the historical period when the Jews were wandering in the desert, having received the Torah but not yet having come to the promised land of Israel. The booth also recalls the shelters used during the harvest seasons by the farmers of ancient Israel. It is a time to rejoice in the ancientness and continuity of Jewish roots. It's also a time to feel at one with the patriarchs and sages of Jewish history; a different one is invited each night to come into the shelter and to join the family at the table.

Festival aspects: Sukkos is one of the most vivid holidays, appealing to the senses. The rustic booth is decorated with all kinds of fall produce as well as with children's drawings. Eating there at night, the family is supposed to take time to look up and see the stars through the branches of the roof. In the synagogue, the congregation parades in seven circles, chanting and waving fronds of palm, myrtle, and willow trees and fragrant citrus fruits. In a dance-like prayer, the fronds and fruits are waved toward all points of the compass.

Universal meanings: It is a time for appreciating the bounty of nature. Another theme is hospitality. Just as the code of the desert decreed that no stranger could be turned away from your threshhold, so at Sukkos all the nations of the world are to be invited to dine in your tent. It's a good time for inviting the children's friends to join them in the *sukkah*. (It also can introduce non-Jews to the idea that there are other festive Jewish holidays besides Hanukkah and Passover.)

Emotional or spiritual themes: In the fragile openness of the *sukkah,* it's appropriate to consider how, though we feel secure when hedged about by our possessions, this is an illusion: We are ultimately vulnerable, or ultimately dependent on the grace of God. Sukkos is also a time for thinking about how to live during interims—when one has a notion of what one is supposed to do but hasn't reached the promised land, the Messianic age when humans will be inwardly and outwardly in harmony.

Simchas Torah After seven days of modified camping-out, Sukkos culminates in Shemini Atzeres (the Assembly of the Eighth Day) and Simchas Torah (the Rejoicing in the Law), when the cycle of Torah readings begins again in Genesis, with the story of God's Creation of the world.

Traditional meanings: In certain Hasidic communities, as Passover is the betrothal and Shavuos the signing of the wedding contract, Simchas Torah is the wedding celebration for the relationship between Jews and God or between Jews and the Torah.

Festival aspects: At the front of the synagogue, a *tallis* (prayer shawl) is held overhead and all the children gather under it, where, under the wings of the adults, they can be close to and touch the Torah. This is the one time during the year when children under bar mitzvah age can be called to the Torah. In some Hasidic communities, the ritual takes on a joyous resemblance to a wedding celebration. The *tallis* held overhead is similar to the bridal canopy. An honored member of the community, called the *hasan Torah* (the groom of the Torah), is called to stand beside the Torah while it is read, and then dances with it. Wedding-style dances are danced, whiskey toasts are drunk, and the men of the community, carrying the Torahs, make a parade of seven circular marches, a ritual reminiscent of the Jewish wedding custom of the bride circling the groom seven times. Children ride on their parents' shoulders, waving apples and Israeli flags. (You can have the children make little scrolls with pictures of the seven days of creation, which they can carry in the procession.)

Emotional or spiritual work: In Jewish mystical tradition, it is a time for ecstatic union with God. During the seven circular marches, people may meditate on different aspects of God.

Except for Tisha B'Av, the holidays from Passover through the end of Sukkos are decreed, and their dates spelled out, in the Torah. (After the Temple in Jerusalem was destroyed about two thousand years ago, the sacrifices of farm animals and grains prescribed in the Bible could no longer be offered, and the rabbis spelled out new forms of prayer and home observance, which are the framework for today's holiday observances.)

From Sukkos to Passover, during the winter months, there are no holidays prescribed in the Torah. But during these dark cold days there are two light-hearted holidays (Hanukkah and Purim), both rooted in pagan nature celebrations. Both holidays commemorate later periods of Jewish history when the Jewish people won victories over those who sought to exterminate them and their way of life.

Hanukkah Hanukkah, which generally falls in December, is the festival of lights.

Traditional meanings: Hanukkah celebrates both a political and a spiritual victory of the Jewish people. Through an armed rebellion led by the Maccabee brothers, the Jews maintained their way of life not only against a Hellenistic (Syrian-Greek) ruler who tried to outlaw their religion, but also against assimilationists among the Jews who were ready to abandon it. The Maccabees founded a dynasty which ruled Israel as an independent or semi-independent nation for about a century in the second and first centuries before the Christian era. Hanukkah, which means *dedication,* celebrates the rededication of the Temple by the Maccabees after they drove out those who had polluted it.

Festival aspects: Hanukkah is celebrated by the lighting of an eight-branched candlestick, the *hanukkiyah,* or *menorah*. The eight candles symbolize a miracle that occurred during the rededication of the Temple in Jerusalem, when a one-day supply of oil lasted for the eight days it took to get a new, untainted supply of oil.

During Hanukkah, children get coins (or chocolate coins—Hanukkah *gelt*) from their relatives: the equivalent of trick-or-treating. Home holiday traditions include making *latkes* (potato pancakes) and playing a gambling game with a four-sided top, the *dreidel*. The letters on the four sides of the *dreidel* spell out a reference to the story of Hanukkah: a Great Miracle Happened There.

Universal meanings: As the theme of Passover is liberation and redress of injustice, so the theme of Hanukkah is self-determination: the ability to stand up for what one believes, for the right to be oneself. Politically, it is a time to renew one's conviction that a dedicated few can triumph over tremendous odds, that an individual or group has the right to maintain its own way in the face of an oppressive majority.

Hanukkah is also a festival of lights. Like Christmas, it is a holiday of brightness at the darkest time of year, and allows one to look forward to the return of longer, warmer days.

Emotional or spiritual themes: One often-overlooked aspect of Hanukkah is that it affirms the ability of ideals and faith to triumph over material power. During the Sabbath of the holiday, a portion is read from the prophet Zechariah: "Not by might, and not by power, but by my spirit, says the Lord."

Tu B'Shvat In February, there is a minor holiday, Tu B'Shvat, the New Year or Birthday of the Trees. The Talmud (the commentary on the Bible in which most of the laws of Judaism were spelled out) designates this date as the basis for calculating the tithing of fruits. It is the moment when, in Israel, the sap begins to rise in the trees.

Festival aspects: Children may plant seeds in cups, to be transferred outdoors later in the spring.

The sixteenth century mystics of the hillside town of Sfat in Israel saw deep meanings in this holiday and devised their own way of celebrating it. Paralleling the Passover seder, they held a Tu B'Shvat seder, a ceremonial "tree meal" of fruits, nuts, and wines. Their goal was ecstatic union with God. They let each type of fruit, nut, and wine represent a transition to different levels of holiness and connection with different aspects of God.

Spiritual and emotional themes: Although the trees are still bare and there's no visible sign of the regeneration which has just begun, this February day is the moment, according to Jewish tradition, when spring really begins. It is a time for thinking about hope in the face of despair.

Purim In the next month, Adar, which coincides roughly with March, comes Purim. It is a joyous dip into silliness, analogous to the late-winter carnivals of many cultures. It may have been a Jewish adaptation of a Persian fertility festival.

Traditional meanings: The Book of Esther is read, retelling how a beautiful young Jewish woman, Esther, became the bride of the Persian king and foiled a plot by the villain Haman to destroy the Jews. Haman becomes the prototype of all the enemies, down to Hitler, who have tried to wipe out the Jews.

Festival aspects: Children and adults "blot out" Haman by shaking noisemakers to drown out the sound of his name whenever it appears during the reading. Children and adults dress up in costumes and, in a sort of reverse trick-or-treating, leave bags of sweets on neighbors' doorsteps. Adults traditionally toast the end of each chapter of the story with hard liquor. This and Simchas Torah are the only two holidays on which drunkenness is actually encouraged (men are supposed to get so drunk they can't tell the difference between the hero and the villain). There are comic skits and poking fun at community leaders. In some synagogues, parts of the scroll are chanted in a parody of the chants used at all other times of the year. The special three-cornered sweet cookies of Purim, *hamantaschen,* (representing Haman's hat, according to some) are traditionally the last things baked at home during the year except the regular Sabbath *hallah* (bread). After Purim, it's time to start cleaning the house for Passover, when the cycle begins again.

Universal meanings: The holiday has much in common with the carnival seasons of many cultures, which celebrate the death of winter, the triumph over forces of evil, the rebirth of fertility, youth, and beauty.

Emotional or spiritual themes: This is a time to learn not to take yourself too seriously.

Daily Practices Two kinds of observance especially mark a traditional Jewish household: blessings and keeping kosher. If you choose to say them, Judaism has blessings for nearly every action and event of the day. The concept: Life, including everyday life, is holy. All creatures, objects, and events are testimony to the presence of God in the world. Thus, there are blessings for washing hands and for putting on clothes. There are blessings for eating fruit, for seeing a rainbow, seeing lightning, and seeing trees in blossom.

Keeping kosher emphasizes the dual holiness of food. On the one hand, it is holy because it sustains life. On the other hand, we should never idly kill anything, so if we eat meat, we should treat it with reverence and appreciate that this animal gave its life so we might sustain ours. Certain meats and fish are prohibited. Because mixing of meat and milk is prohibited, the household has two sets of dishes and pots, one designated only for meat meals, the other only for dairy meals. Meat has to be slaughtered in a prescribed way which is supposed to be more humane for the animal, and all traces of blood must be removed before eating, because the blood represents the animal's life. (*The Jewish Catalog* and other references in the Recommended Reading and Notes sections give information on how to keep kosher.)

Communal Life The Jewish community has a great variety of organizations, and an active Jewish family will probably belong to several and give money to several Jewish charities. Help to others and active involvement in the community are seen as hallmarks of the good person, the *mensch*. (A few key Jewish communal organizations are described in Lydia Kukoff's *Choosing Judaism,* which also is listed in the Notes.)

CHRISTIANITY

The early Christian church had holidays growing out of all the major Jewish holidays, as well as Christian refashionings of the pagan holidays. But America's early culture was shaped by several groups that were opposed to ritual and the folk culture of religion: the Puritans and Congregationalists, who were low-church Protestants, and the Unitarians, who were deists. As a consequence, there is much less emphasis on holidays in America than in the European countries from which much of the population came. Many American Christians celebrate only two holidays—Christmas and Easter. Devout members of the liturgical churches (Roman Catholics, Eastern Orthodox, Episcopalians, and Lutherans) may celebrate some of the other holidays, so we have described the major ones briefly. Folk customs associated with the holidays vary depending on which countries people came from. We have described a number because interfaith families may find that emphasizing folk customs is a way to permit the joy of holiday celebrations without the divisiveness of theological differences.

Sunday Sunday is the Lord's day. For many Protestants, Sunday, like the Jewish Sabbath, is a day of rest. But more important, all Christians see it as the day on which Jesus' resurrection occurred, making it the appropriate time for reaffirming faith in the redemption. Many Christians feel an obligation to be in church every Sunday. It is a day for being part of the community of Christians, which is seen as Christ's earthly body continuing his work. In Roman Catholicism, Sunday is the day for taking the Eucharist, or communion. (Many Protestants take communion only on the first Sunday of the month.)

Christmas Although Easter is much older and has more theological significance, Christmas has become *the* major holiday of Christianity. Even
people who have fallen away from every other aspect of Christian practice are likely to observe Christmas folk customs.

Traditional meanings: Christmas (Christ's Mass) is the Feast of the
Nativity, the celebration of the birth of Jesus. At this time, God gave His
only Son to the world. God became incarnate—took on human form.
The Christmas liturgy contains passages from the Gospels telling of Jesus' birth to Mary, the young virgin wife of the carpenter Joseph. In the
Roman Catholic Church, Christmas begins with a Vigil Mass on Christmas
Eve. (On Sundays and sacred days, Catholicism and an increasing number of Protestant churches consider the day as beginning at sundown on
the previous evening.) Additional Masses follow at midnight, traditionally
regarded as the hour of Jesus' birth, at dawn, and on Christmas day. The
priests wear vestments of white. Protestant churches may begin the
Christmas Eve service with a procession of congregants, singing carols
and carrying candles as they enter the darkened church. There are also
services on Christmas day.

Festival aspects: Five Christmas traditions are widespread among
American Christians: the Christmas tree; the giving of gifts; the Christmas
feast; the manger or crèche; and the singing of carols. The Christmas
tree is a descendant of the evergreen Yule tree which pagans brought
into their house at this season to reassure themselves that not all of
nature had died. To this was added the tradition of the Paradise tree. On
Christmas Eve in medieval times, many parishes had plays in which Adam
and Eve were depicted as sinning by eating the apple from the forbidden Tree of Knowledge. As they were ejected from Paradise, an angel
would tell them that Christ would eventually come to redeem the world
from their sin. The Paradise tree was decorated with bright red apples
(or apple-shaped glass balls). Added were candles, symbolizing Christ as
Light for a dark, sinful world. Under the tree was usually the crèche or
crib, with a scene depicting the Baby Jesus and the animals in the manger. Christmas trees are actually a late addition to the celebration. They
didn't migrate from Germany to America and the other countries of Europe until the last half of the nineteenth century. Gift-giving at this season was started by the pagan Romans for their own holiday, but Christians
reinterpreted the gifts as emulation of God's giving of his Son and of
the three Wise Men's gifts to the Baby Jesus. In most parts of Europe,
children were told that gifts came to them from the Child Jesus, and
they wrote letters to the Child Jesus asking for what they wanted. Each
region of Europe had special cakes and cookies for the holiday. Al-

though symbolizing the sweetness of redemption, they grow out of an earlier pagan tradition of making sweets to persuade the grain goddess to bless the winter wheat.

Universal aspects: Underlying Christmas are two nature themes: the evergreen, which does not die even when all else in nature dies, and light: light and warmth coming into the world at a time of cold and darkness. It was not clear from scripture when Jesus' real birthdate was. According to a common theory, the early church decided to give its blessing to holding the holiday on the festival of the winter solstice, December 25, birthday of the Roman sun god. (The solstice had earlier been celebrated January 6, which is the Feast of the Epiphany and is the traditional gift-giving day for the Eastern church.) In England, the pagans also had a holiday of light: Yule, with its traditional bonfire.

Candles, symbolizing Jesus as the Light of the World, are a recurrent symbol of Christmas. In its light theme, Christmas has a kinship to Hanukkah, which is also a solstice festival of light. Santa Claus is part of this theme of light and warmth. Christianity adopted this folk figure by fusing one of its own legends with the pagan story of the rotund, jovial German god of the hearth, Thor. Thor, who comes down chimneys to warm the peasant family, wears red because fire is his element. He lives in the North where he battles the demons of ice and snow, but occasionally rides southward in a sled drawn by two white goats. The name Santa Claus comes from a Christian figure: Saint Nicholas, a fourth-century bishop noted for his generosity to the poor, especially providing dowries for poor girls.

Spiritual and emotional themes: A central spiritual direction for both Christians and nonbelievers at this season is to rise above the commercialism and keep focused on the "Christmas spirit" of sharing, giving, and togetherness. Christmas is also a time for humility. An important part of the Christmas story is that the angels told the shepherds first about Jesus' coming. The kings or wise men didn't get there till later. Christmas is a time to try to see everyone as possibly an angel, a special messenger with something to tell you, or as Jesus Himself. There is a tradition that Christ comes back at this season as a beggar. Believers can say to themselves that if God was willing to lower Himself to become human, we ought to be able to identify with and share the feelings of the most wretched among us. For believers, there is an additional spiritual task: to focus on the idea of incarnation, that God was willing to see life through human eyes.

Preparation: Advent means "coming." The four-week Advent season preceding Christmas brings excitement and meaning to the holiday. Since the Christian year celebrates the major events in Jesus' life, and then in the life of the church, Advent opens the Christian year. In addition to the gift-shopping, the Christmas pageants, the baking of cookies and gradual decorating of the house, there are a number of special Advent traditions that many families follow.

The Advent wreath: This horizontal wreath, used both in church and in homes, contains four upright candles, representing qualities such as joy and peace. The first week of Advent one candle is lit each night, the second week two, and so forth. There are often Bible readings concerning the special quality of the new candle for the week.

Advent calendar: This contains twenty-eight windows and one door. Each day of the month, a window is opened to reveal a little picture, from the Bible or of a little animal, etc., until on Christmas Eve the door is opened, showing the Nativity scene.

Jesse tree: This is a table-sized tree on which, each day, an ornament is hung (e.g. a little boat for Noah) representing Biblical events from creation to the time of Jesus' birth.

Many families add to this sense of the gradual unfolding toward Christmas with their own traditions: One family we talked to has a special box of Christmas stories that they bring up from the basement on the second week of Advent.

Caroling: A few days before Christmas, a parade of singers goes from house to house in the neighborhood, with a stop at one house or the church afterward for hot chocolate or cider.

Advent is a time when churches strongly feel themselves as communities. There are musical programs, plays, pageants. In Protestant churches, there may be special study sessions, with potluck dinners during the week in addition to Sunday services.

Advent is also a time for reaching out to the unfortunate. Churches gather toys for poor children. As part of Advent in one family we talked to, the children go through their toys, choosing ones that are still in good shape but that they don't really play with, to donate to the toy drive.

The individual spiritual work of Advent is about waiting. For children, it's hard to wait for Christmas. Parents can tell them that the harder it is to wait, the sweeter it's likely to be when it gets there. For adult believers, the spiritual work is about trying to understand why it takes so long for the Christian covenant to be fulfilled by the Second Coming of Christ, and having faith that just as Christmas comes, that day of greater joy will also come. It's a time for focusing on three phases of coming: the first coming of Jesus; the promised Second Coming, which is still in the future; and the present coming, which is God's grace shining in people's hearts today.

Easter Easter celebrates the Resurrection of Jesus and is thus the central festival in the Christian calendar. Along with Sunday, it is the oldest celebration in Christendom, dating back to the earliest days of the church.

Traditional meanings: In many countries, Easter is called *Pasch, Paques,* or other words derived from the Jewish *Pesah,* or Passover. Just as when the Jews were freed from the slavery of Egypt, a lamb was sacrificed by each family and its blood used as a signal to keep away the angel of death during the tenth plague, so Jesus is seen as the "Lamb of God" who willingly sacrificed His life on the cross to redeem human beings from punishment for their sins. His resurrection gave the promise of triumph over death, of eternal life, of victory over sin. The nine Bible readings in the Roman Catholic Easter service span the whole of history as understood by Christians. The seven Old Testament readings—from the creation story in Genesis, through God's promise to Abraham to create a great nation through which the world would be redeemed, to the prophets who talked of a Redeemer who would come—all are seen as stages leading toward the eventual coming of Jesus. The Epistle from Romans, which talks about how, through baptism, Christians participate in Jesus' death, and Matthew's Gospel account of the Resurrection are seen as the fulfillment of the earlier history and prophecy.

An Easter sunrise service is traditional in many churches; an Easter vigil the evening before is gaining in popularity. In earlier periods of Christianity, Easter was the time for baptism of new converts—the time at which they make a full commitment to Christian faith. This practice has now been revived in the Roman Catholic Church. An increasing number of Catholic churches have returned to the practice of full-immersion baptism. The converts have been studying together for nine months or a year and often have developed an intense sense of community. In the Catholic church, they go into the baptismal pool in brown robes. After they have dried off, they put on new white robes. From this developed the tradition of new clothes for Easter, as a sign that all Christians are renewing their baptism.

Preparation: There are two stages of preparation for Easter. The first is Lent, a forty-day period of semi-fasting, and the second is Holy Week, the week before Easter. In the early days of the church, Lent was a final and intensive period of testing for the new converts, capping an average of three years of preparation. Because it was risky to become a Christian in those days, they had to be tested to be sure they were ready to endure the possible penalties, including loss of livelihood, imprisonment, or death. Christians believed that in the final forty days before their baptism, Satan would do everything he could to tempt these souls away from their resolve. So as they fasted, prayed, and prepared themselves, the community supported their resolve by fasting with them and intensifying works of charity. In the Middle Ages, Lent was a time for exorcisms and public penitence. Sinners would come to the church barefoot (it was February or March) in sackcloth, and would be given manual labor to perform as penitence. Nowadays during Lent, many Christians engage in physical or spiritual self-discipline, giving up a self-indulgence or having a regular period of prayer. It is a time to develop self-restraint. If Jesus could give up His life for others, you could reform a bad habit.

Since the reform of the Catholic liturgy in the 1960s, the concept of Lent and Eastertime as spiritual preparation for baptism and consolidation of the conversion has been revived. In addition to baptism for new converts to Christianity, there is a process of "coming into full union with the Catholic Church" (not a rebaptism) for people who were baptized in some other branch of Christianity and were not raised in the Catholic Church.

In earlier times, the Lenten fast meant giving up meat, cheese, fatty fish, oils, bacon, and alcohol. On Mardi Gras, "Fat Tuesday," the day before the start of Lent, people splurged and used up all those items. In England, this meant frying up a big batch of pancakes with lard. In some more southerly climes, it means a no-holds-barred carnival. In Eastern churches, the kitchen and pots and pans are thoroughly scoured, as Jews do at Passover. But instead of removing leavening, they remove all traces of fat from the utensils. Since the 1960s, Catholics are required to observe only two fast days, on which no meat is eaten: Ash Wednesday, the first day of Lent, and Good Friday. On Ash Wednesday, a Catholic comes to Mass. The priest marks an ashen cross on each parishioner's forehead, intoning: "Turn away from sin and be faithful to the gospel," or "Remember, man, you are dust and to dust you will return."

In some Protestant churches, on every Wednesday beginning with Ash Wednesday there is a fasting supper of bread and soup, followed by a Bible study session and discussion. Sunday schools may focus on the Easter story and related themes such as the Eucharist. In one Presbyterian church, the children had a "catacomb Eucharist" in the church basement, with "Roman soldiers" breaking things up in the middle, so the children could feel what it was like to be an early Christian, worshipping in secret and at great risk.

Because of the history of meatless fast days during Lent, there are many meatless Lenten dishes, which are part of the anticipation of Easter. Hot cross buns, decorated with a white sugar-frosted cross, have also been traditional Lenten fare.

Holy Week, the week before Easter, is a reliving of the events in Jesus' life during the week before His death and resurrection. On Palm Sunday, the congregation parades with palm fronds through the church, reenacting Jesus' triumphant entry into Jerusalem. The way may be paved with special cloths and carpets and strewn with flowers. Holy Thursday commemorates Jesus' Last Supper, which was a Passover feast. Some churches have a congregational dinner, or a modified seder, with the symbols reinterpreted according to Christian beliefs. Some people eat matzoh at home. During the Holy Thursday service, the priest washes the feet of twelve parishioners in imitation of the wry and humble pacifism of Jesus. At the Last Supper, Jesus interrupted the petty quarreling of the disciples about who would be most important after His death by quietly washing their feet. In some congregations, there is a chain of footwashings: The priest washes the feet of a deacon, who in turn washes the feet of a parishioner, who in turn washes the feet of another parishioner, and so on. Holy Thursday is also called Maundy Thursday because of Jesus' *mandatum* (command) (in John 13:34) issued on that day to "love one another." In the Roman Catholic church it is a day of pageantry. The altar, tabernacle, and crucifix are draped in white; the priests are dressed in white. At the end of the Mass, the Eucharist is placed in a side chapel, where it remains until the communion service of Good Friday. Then the church is stripped bare of all its decorations. The door of the tabernacle (which usually contains the consecrated Eucharist) is left open to reveal it empty. The church bells don't ring. The lights are turned off. Parishioners file out silently, in contrast to the usual recessional with music. This barrenness helps many Christians identify with Jesus' arrest, suffering, and death.

Good Friday is the anniversary of Jesus' death. People come quietly into the bare church for personal prayer. The Eucharist is not celebrated at the usual time. In Catholic churches, Biblical passages describing Jesus' suffering and death are read. Then comes the ceremony of adoration of the cross, where people file up to kneel and kiss the foot of the cross. Afterward, the Eucharist is brought back from its place of repose and people receive Holy Communion. (In Lutheran churches, there is no Holy Communion on Good Friday.) Good Friday is a fast day. Some people eat only dry bread and water, or rice boiled in milk. Some people eat standing, in silence. It is a day, said one person we talked to, "to think about the death of God, the absence of God. I've had the experience of God being gone in my life. Until you've had that, you can't know what it feels like to have God be around."

Holy Saturday is a quiet time, with no church service. In ancient times, a thirty-hour fast was held until the night service of Easter.

Festival aspects: On Saturday night, the eve of Easter, in Catholic and some Protestant churches, a bonfire is lit. From it the Easter candle is lit. People move into the darkened church, one by one the candles are lit, and light spreads throughout the church. In Europe, entire villages were darkened, their lamps snuffed out, their hearths extinguished. Then a boy or girl from each household grabbed a flaming brand from the Easter bonfire, ran home and lit the stove and all the lamps in the house. All the church bells, which had been silent for three days and had not been tolling the hours, began ringing at once. Easter burst into the village through all the senses. The whole village was alight, warm, and full of music. People embraced and kissed.

Home customs include the decorating and hiding of Easter eggs, a basket of Easter candy which is said to be brought by the Easter bunny, decorating the house with flowers, and in some communities a big ham dinner with relatives or friends.

Universal aspects: As the eggs and bunny reveal, Easter, like Passover, has roots partly in pagan agricultural celebrations of fertility and the arrival of spring. The name Easter is believed to have come from the name of an Anglo-Saxon spring goddess or from an Old High German word meaning *dawns.*

Spiritual and emotional themes: Easter, like Passover, is about personal renewal and hope.

Although most American Christians don't celebrate the other holidays of the Christian year, traces of the original celebrations can be found in the liturgical churches.

Pentecost, which parallels the Jewish holiday of Shavuos, occurs fifty days after Easter. After Jesus' Resurrection, according to Christian tradition, His presence remained with the apostles in various ways. As they gradually came to understand and accept His Resurrection, He withdrew from them in a bodily sense. On Pentecost, the Holy Ghost came in a rush of wind and flames, and they began to speak in foreign tongues that they had not known. Thus, they came to understand the form Jesus' presence and inspiration would take as He helped them to spread His message. That moment is considered the birthdate of the Christian church. The vestments for Pentecost are red, to commemorate not only the blood of Christian martyrs but the flaming visitation of the Holy Ghost. In European churches, rains of flowers or coveys of pigeons were released from church ceilings during Pentecost to symbolize the event. (Some churches tried to use flames, but this was stopped after too many parishioners and their churches caught fire.) One Episcopal church in Connecticut holds a Sunday school picnic, with a birthday cake for the Christian church and the release of hot-air balloons.

In many parochial schools at the time the current adult generation was growing up, May was also celebrated as the month of Mary, Jesus' mother. A girl would be crowned with a wreath of flowers, and in a procession the students would bring her bouquets. May was also often the time of First Communion when youngsters in feathery white dresses or crisp new suits received the Eucharist for the first time. These May celebrations—springing more from popular religious culture than from official church teaching—have a universal connection to the traditional spring flower celebrations of many cultures.

Halloween (October 31), All Saints' Day (November 1), and All Souls' Day (November 2) have similar agricultural roots. Many cultures have a harvest festival or a last burst of zany merriment before winter sets in. Halloween stems from the pagan festivals of the dead and the festivals for the witches and demons who were said to claim winter as their season.

All Saints' Day and All Souls' Day are days for remembering and feeling connected to those who have died. In Christian belief they are not dead, but are alive in heaven where they watch over the living. People pray that they may have eternal rest. The custom is to decorate graves of relatives, often by spreading white gravel in front of them and placing candles protected by small glass lanterns.

Some Christians have chosen to embrace the harvest festival aspect of the holidays, decorating their homes with pumpkins and dried herbs and flowers and having potluck dinners of fall produce and fruits.

Daily and Weekly Routines For many Christians, particularly Protestants, the essence of religious life is not so much in the holidays but in their ongoing involvement in a church community. People we talked to are involved in committees of their churches and in teaching Sunday School. Presbyterians serve as elders, and Catholics as ministers or deacons, lay people who build a sense of community by reaching out to isolated members of the congregation, passing out communion, perhaps planning liturgical innovations in the service. (Catholic lay ministers help plan drama and dance services within the Mass. Presbyterian services have lay members involved in every service.)

Many also weave religion quietly into their daily home lives. They have grace before meals and bedtime prayers such as the Lord's Prayer. Some sing or have periodic Bible readings. They do these things in a spirit of celebration rather than solemnity, and their children seem to look forward to them.

Sources for the Appendix material on Jewish holidays were: Eliyahu Kitov, *The Book of Our Heritage: The Jewish Year and Its Days of Significance,* revised edition, translated from the Hebrew by Nathan Bulman, New York: Feldheim Publishers, 1978; and Arthur I. Waskow, *Seasons of Our Joy: A Handbook of Jewish Festivals,* New York: Bantam Books, 1982.

Sources for Christian holiday material were: Francis X. Weiser, *Handbook of Christian Feasts and Customs: The Year of the Lord in Liturgy and Folklore,* New York: Harcourt, Brace and Co., 1958; J. G. Davies, ed., *The New Westminster Dictionary of Liturgy and Worship,* Philadelphia: Westminster Press, 1986; *The New Catholic Encyclopedia,* Vol. III, New York: McGraw-Hill, 1967.

CHAPTER 16: RITES OF PASSAGE RESOURCES

1. *Festivals,* a Catholic-oriented magazine dedicated to creation of family ritual. It is published by Resource Publications Inc., 160 East Virginia Street #290, San Jose, Calif. 95112 (telephone: 408-286-8505).

2. *Let's Celebrate: Creating New Family Traditions* by Susan Lieberman, New York: Perigee Books, Putnam, 1984.

3. *Great Occasions,* edited by Carl Seaburg, Boston: Unitarian Universalist Association, 1968. The book has poetry and readings for life-cycle events.

4. Nontraditional Jewish ceremonies are available through the *Creative Symbolism* Series (Rabbi Alvin J. Reines, editor) of the Institute of Creative Judaism, Box 20044, Cincinnati, Ohio 45220 (telephone: 513-221-1875). This is the telephone of the Hebrew Union College-Jewish Institute of Religion. Ask for Rabbi Reines's office.

5. *Coming-of-Age and Celebration Programs,* a booklet which details a challenging program for children ages twelve to fourteen, as developed by one Unitarian congregation. Available from Unitarian Universalist Association Bookstore, 25 Beacon Street, Boston, Mass. 02108 (telephone: 617-742-2100).

6. The Institute for Creation-Centered Spirituality at Holy Names College, 3500 Mountain Blvd., Oakland, Calif. 94619 (telephone: 415-436-0111) is a resource for Christians, for Jews, and for people who no longer feel a connection to either tradition but who are seeking a spiritual life. Founder Matthew Fox believes that the creation tradition, which emphasizes the goodness in life, has been lost or overwhelmed in Christianity by the fall-redemption tradition, which emphasizes sin. The institute's magazine, *Creation,* includes examples of rituals and rites of passage growing from a creation-centered spirituality. The institute periodically gives seminars or workshops around the country and can put you in touch with networks of its graduates in the various regions.

7. Psychotherapist Dr. Kathryn North, A.C.S.W., developed a ceremony marking her fortieth birthday. The event is described in "Celebrating Entry into Full Adulthood" in *Family Festivals* magazine (April/May 1985, Vol. 4, No. 2). The magazine is now called *Festivals.* A copy is available from Resource Publications, 160 East Virginia Street #290, San Jose, Calif. 95112 (telephone: 408-286-8505).

8. The Reconstructionist Rabbinical College Liturgy project, charging only for duplicating and postage, will send you copies of a variety of creative bris, naming, adoption, and bar or bat mitzvah ceremonies developed by other families. Director Marcia Prager will also consult by telephone with families on how to build on Jewish tradition in putting together their own ceremonies, and will send "raw materials" such as readings. The liturgy project, which encourages readers to send in their own ceremonies to share with others, also has creative holiday liturgies, peace services, and sample ceremonies for a variety of other life-cycle events, ranging from weddings to miscarriage and menopause. Contact: The Liturgy Project, Reconstructionist Rabbinical College, Church Road and Greenwood Avenue, Wyncote, Pa. 19095 (telephone: 215-576-0800).

A course for teenagers on rites of passage has been developed by Rabbi Nancy Fuchs-Kreimer at Reconstructionist Rabbinical College. Students learn about the rites of passage practiced by a number of cultures as well as in secular America. In the final session, they design and perform their own creative Jewish rite. Course materials are available from her at Reconstructionist Rabbinical College.

9. A ceremony for *menarche* (the first appearance of menstruation in a young woman) was developed by Phyllis Berman and her daughter Morissa. The ceremony is described in *Menorah* (now *New Menorah*) magazine (November–December 1985, Vol. VI, Nos. 1–2). It can be used instead of or in addition to bat mitzvah or confirmation. It blends feminist, Native American, and Jewish elements, and could easily be adapted to a nonsectarian or Christian format. For copies or further information, contact: Phyllis Berman or Arthur Waskow, ed., *New Menorah,* Beyt P'nai Or, 6723 Emlen Street, Philadelphia, Pa. 19119 (telephone: 215-849-5385).

10. The Wilderness Fasting Quest with Rites of Passage Inc., Novato, Calif. 94947 (telephone: 415-892-5371). This nonprofit organization leads small groups of people (ages sixteen to sixty) on a three-day "fasting quest" that is partly based on the Native American vision quest. The program requires no special wilderness skills or physical strength. Participants go through four preparatory meetings over a month's time, where they are given psychological and conceptual tools for their three days of solitude. Says Michael Bodkin, a psychotherapist who leads the program, "I think the essence of rites of passage is to make oneself responsible—not only to oneself but to the larger community, to somebody you leave behind and come back to . . . Whether or not you believe in the idea of a creator, one becomes very clear on the importance of creation."

CHAPTER 17: AFFILIATION ADDRESSES

Reform Judaism Eight hundred congregations. *Headquarters*: Union of American Hebrew Congregations, 838 Fifth Avenue, New York, N.Y. 10021 (telephone: 212-249-0100). *Regional offices*: New York; Chicago; Los Angeles; Philadelphia; Washington; St. Louis; San Francisco; Miami; Dallas; Toronto; Brookline, Mass.; Beachwood, Ohio; Paramus, N.J. *Yellow Pages listing*: Synagogues—Reform.

Conservative Judaism Eight hundred fifty congregations. *Headquarters*: United Synagogue of America, 155 Fifth Avenue, New York, N.Y. 10010 (telephone: 212-533-7800). *Regional offices*: New York; Los Angeles; Chicago; Houston; Philadelphia; Toronto; Montreal; Oakland, Calif.; Rockville, Md.; Hillside, N.J.; Milton, Mass.; Plantation, Fla.; Farmington Hills, Mich.; Amsterdam, N.Y.; West Hartford, Conn.; Sioux City, Iowa. *Yellow Pages listing*: Synagogues—Conservative.

Reconstructionist Judaism Seventy congregations, located in most major Jewish population centers. *Headquarters*: Federation of Reconstructionist Congregations and Havurot, Church Road and Greenwood Avenue, Wyncote, Pa. 19095 (telephone: 215-887-1988).

Havurah Judaism National Havurah Committee. *Headquarters*: 270 West 89th Street, New York, N.Y. 10024 (telephone: 212-496-0055).

Society for Humanistic Judaism Sixteen groups and several standing synagogues. *Headquarters*: 28611 West Twelve Mile Road, Farmington Hills, Mich. 48018 (telephone: 313-478-7610). The Society's largest groups are the Birmingham Temple in Farmington Hills, Mich. (telephone: 313-477-1410); Congregation Beth Or in Deerfield, Ill. (telephone: 312-945-0477); and Beth Adam in Cincinnati (telephone: 513-396-7730). Other groups can be reached by calling the home of the area contact person. The groups and their telephone numbers are: Beth Chai, in Washington, D.C. area (telephone: 703-525-8032); Machar, Washington area Society for Humanistic Judaism, Bethesda, Md. (telephone: 301-469-0865); Congregation for Humanistic Judaism, Fairfield, Conn. (telephone: 203-333-8479); Gulf Coast Society for Humanistic Judaism, Clearwater, Fla. (telephone: 813-797-2892); Humanistic Jews of Minneapolis-St. Paul (telephone: 612-822-8000); Kahal Breira, Boston Congregation for Humanistic Judaism, Newton Center, Mass. (telephone: 617-964-8409); Los Angeles Society for Humanistic Judaism, Culver City, Calif. (telephone: 213-870-4961; Marin County Society for Humanistic Judaism, San Rafael, Calif. (telephone: 415-479-3115); San Diego Society for Humanistic Judaism, Leucadia, Calif. (telephone: 619-436-6850); Northern New Jersey Society for Humanistic Judaism, Elmwood Park, N.J. (telephone: 201-796-1968; Long Island Havurah for Humanistic Judaism, Long Beach, N.Y. (telephone: 516-889-8337); Rochester, New York Society for Humanistic Judaism, Pittsford, N.Y. (telephone: 716-381-0920); Syracuse Society for Humanistic Judaism, Fayetteville, N.Y. (telephone: 315-637-6983); Israel Association for Secular Humanistic Judaism, Jerusalem, (telephone: 02-238897).

Congress of Secular Jewish Organizations About fifteen member organizations nationwide. *Contact*: Geraldine Revzin, executive director, 1130 South Michigan Avenue, #2101, Chicago, Ill. 60605 (telephone: 312-922-0386). The organizations include: in Los Angeles, the Sholom Community Organization; in Buena Park, Calif., the Orange County Kindershul; in Vancouver, the Vancouver Peretz School; in Toronto, the Secular Jewish Association and School; in Detroit, the Jewish Parents' Institute; in Ann Arbor, Mich., the Jewish Community Group; in Cleveland, the Jewish Secular Community; in Chicago, the North Shore School of Jewish Studies; in Rockville, Md., the Bethesda–Chevy Chase Jewish Community Group; in Philadelphia, the Sholom Aleichem Club and the Jewish Children's Folkshul; in Upper Montclair, N.J., the Suburban Jewish School; on Long Island, the Jewish Secular Shule of Suffolk County; in Stoughton, Mass., The Sunday School. (In addition are the Workmen's Circle groups, which emphasize Yiddish in their schools and are not part of the secular federation.)

"New Age" Judaism The handful of groups can best be located through P'nai Or. *Headquarters*: P'nai Or House, 6723 Emlen Street, Philadelphia, Pa. 19119 (telephone: 215-849-5385). Its affiliate groups are in Philadelphia; Milwaukee; Minneapolis; Boston; Mansfield, Connecticut; New York; Baltimore; Chicago; Poughkeepsie, N.Y.; Berkeley, Calif.; Gainesville, Fla.; Fort Lauderdale, Fla.; Basel, Switzerland. Other "New Age" groups exist independently in Berkeley; Boulder, Colo.; and Ashland, Ore., among other places.

Jewish Independents The following are single, nonaffiliated congregations that welcome mixed families. *Contact*:

Congregation Daat Elohim (the Temple of Universal Judaism) in New York. Led by Rabbi Roy Rosenberg, it is a congregation "for Jewish interfaith families and others in search." 1010 Park Avenue, New York, N.Y. 10028 (telephone: 212-535-0187).

The Rabbinic Center in Westfield, N.J. Rabbi Irwin H. Fishbein began the synagogue as a way station for couples who have come to his Rabbinical Center for Research and Counseling. 128 East Dudley Avenue, Westfield, N.J. 07090 (telephone: 201-233-0419).

Temple Micah in Denver. Leader: Cantor Uri Neil. 2600 Leyden Street, Denver, Colo. 80207 (telephone: 303-388-4239).

Temple Kal Ha Amim (All Peoples Synagogue) in Miami Beach. Leader: Rabbi Emmett Frank. 7455 Collins Avenue, Miami Beach, Fla. 33141 (telephone: 305-861-5554).

Temple Micah in Wyncote, Pa. Leader: Rabbi Robert A. Alper. Suite 300, 116 Greenwood Avenue, Wyncote, Pa. 19095. (telephone: 215-887-4300).

Conference on Judaism in Rural New England Counterculture or country families might find a way to link up with a fellowship through this group. Many participants at its annual two-day gathering are intermarried (in 1985, the session concentrated on the topic of mixed marriage). *Contact*: R. D. Eno, Thistle Hill Road, Cabot, Vt. 05647 (telephone: 802-563-2486).

Society of Jewish Science This small organization, centered in New York and claiming a few hundred members, is designed to supplement a synagogue affiliation. It provides a method of prayer, serenity, and spiritual healing. Box 484, Plainview, N.Y. 11803 (telephone: 516-349-0022).

Christian Charismatic There are networks of spiritually intense, grassroots prayer groups nationwide. *Contact*: North American Renewal Service Committee, 237 North Michigan Avenue, South Bend, Ind. 46601 (telephone: 219-234-6021). The committee offers a directory of Catholic prayer groups and can put you in touch with contact people in specific Protestant denominations.

Unitarian About a thousand congregations, most in the Northeast and others in urban areas and university towns nationwide. *Headquarters*: Unitarian Universalist Association, 25 Beacon Street, Boston, Mass. 02108 (telephone: 617-742-2100). *Yellow Pages listing*: Both "Unitarian" and "Universalist."

Society of Friends About 125,000 Quakers nationwide in three separate groupings. *Headquarters*: Friends General Conference, 1520-B Race

Street, Philadelphia, Pa. 19102 (telephone: 215-241-7270); Friends United Meeting, 101 Quaker Hill Drive, Richmond, Ind. 47374 (telephone: 317-962-7573); Evangelical Friends Alliance, with two regional offices, one at 1201 30th Street N.W., Canton, Ohio 44709 (telephone: 216-493-1660), and one at Friends Church Headquarters, Mid-America Yearly Meeting, 2018 Maple Street, Wichita, Kansas 67213 (telephone: 316-267-0391). The Friends General Conference is more universalist in orientation; the other groups are more avowedly Christian. *Yellow Pages listing*: "Society of Friends" or "Religious Society of Friends."

Ethical Society About twenty chapters, most in the New York metropolitan area. *Headquarters*: American Ethical Union, 2 West 64th Street, New York, N.Y. 10023 (telephone: 212-873-6500). Member groups are in New York; Baltimore; Boston; Chicago; Cleveland; Los Angeles; Philadelphia; St. Louis; Washington. Other chapters are in Brooklyn, N.Y.; Long Island, N.Y.; Northern Westchester, N.Y.; Queens, N.Y.; Riverdale-Yonkers, N.Y.; Suffolk, N.Y.; Westchester County, N.Y.; Bergen County, N.J.; Essex County, N.J.; Lakeland, N.J.; Monmouth County, N.J.; Columbia, Md.

American Humanist Association Eighty chapters nationwide. *Headquarters*: P.O. Box 146, Amherst, N.Y. 14226 (telephone: 716-839-5080).

Feminist Spirituality Around the country are isolated women's caucuses and worship groups that experiment with nonsexist and Goddess-centered liturgy. *Contact*:

Feminists of Faith (interreligious) c/o Annette Daum, Union of American Hebrew Congregations, 838 Fifth Avenue, New York, N.Y. 10021 (telephone: 212-249-0100).

Jewish Feminist Ritual Group, c/o Sheila Weinberg, 6909 Greene Street, Philadelphia, Pa. 19119 (telephone: 215-849-5584).

WATER—Women's Alliance for Theology, Ethics and Ritual (predominantly Christian), 8035 13th Street, Silver Spring, Md. 20910 (telephone: 301-589-2509).

Grailville (Christian), 9320 Bannonville Road, Loveland, Ohio 45140 (telephone: 513-683-2340).

See also listings in "The Jewish Woman's Networking Directory" in Susan Weidman Schneider, *Jewish and Female: Choices and Changes in Our Lives Today,* New York: Simon and Schuster, 1984. Check *Lilith* magazine, 250 West 57th St., Suite 2432, New York, N.Y. 10019. Check *Ruach,* newsletter of the Episcopal Women's Caucus, Box 187 Edinboro, Pa. 16412. Check *Daughters of Sarah,* a Christian feminist magazine, 3801 North Keeler, Dept. 1414, Chicago, Ill. 60641.

Political/Social Activists The following membership organizations work on a progressive agenda of peace, disarmament, and social change. *Contact*:

New Jewish Agenda. Has chapters in forty-seven cities. *Headquarters*: 64 Fulton Street, Suite 1100, New York, N.Y. 10038 (telephone: 212-227-5885).

Clergy and Laity Concerned. Has fifty chapters nationwide, composed of both Jews and Christians. *Headquarters*: 198 Broadway, Room 302, New York, N.Y. 10038 (telephone: 212-964-6730).

Fellowship of Reconciliation. Composed predominantly of Christians, with ninety groups around the country. *Headquarters*: Box 271, Nyack, N.Y., 10960 (telephone: 914-358-4601).

Holistic or "New Age" Spirituality A number of centers offer spirituality courses and workshops. Among the larger ones, *Contact*:

Institute for Creation-Centered Spirituality. Holy Names College, 3500 Mountain Blvd., Oakland, Calif. 94619 (telephone: 415-436-0111).

New York Open Center. 83 Spring Street, New York, N.Y. 10012 (telephone: 212-219-2527).

Interface. 552 Main Street, Watertown, Mass. 02172 (telephone: 617-924-1100).

Esalen Institute. Big Sur, Calif. 93920 (telephone: 408-667-3000).

Chinook Learning Center. Box 57, Clinton, Wash. 98236 (telephone: 206-321-1884).

Wainwright House. 260 East Stuyvesant Avenue, Rye, N.Y. 10580 (telephone: 914-967-6080).

Omega Institute. In session summers only. Lake Drive, R.D. 2, Box 377, Rhinebeck, N.Y. 12572 (telephones: 914-266-4301 May–September; 914-338-6030 September–May).

A Special Guide We know of only one locality that has a congregational guide for intermarried couples. In Washington, D.C., the American Jewish Committee chapter polled area synagogues in 1983 about their policies regarding interfaith families. The information was presented in a booklet that can be gotten from the chapter's office: 2027 Massachusetts Avenue, N.W., Washington, D.C. 20036 (telephone: 202-265-2000).

CHAPTER 18: RELIGIOUS EDUCATION

Here are some resources for parents who want to develop an informal home-based curriculum:

Behrman House, a Jewish-oriented publisher, offers "Home Start," a year-long learning package specially designed for children ages four to six whose parents are unaffiliated or barely observant. Each child is mailed activity kits (picture books, games, cutouts, and the like) seven times during the year. Most mailings are geared to upcoming holidays. The package also includes a parent handbook, a book of blessings, and a cassette tape of holiday stories and songs. The year-long program is $24. 235 Watchung Avenue, West Orange, N.J. 07052 (telephones: 212-689-2020; 201-669-0447; and 800-221-2755).

The Jewish Education Service of North America has an annotated guide for resources for family learning. 730 Broadway, New York, N.Y. 10003 (telephone: 212-529-2000). For a copy of the $10 guide, write to the service's National Educational Resource Center at the same address.

The Coalition for the Advancement of Jewish Education has a wealth of teaching material for schools and parents alike. To get it, you must join CAJE (the membership is $40). The coalition has a number of *havurot* (fellowship for study and worship) and intermarried people as members, who "network" at the group's high-energy national conference once a year or on a regional level more frequently. 468 Park Avenue South, Room 904, New York, N.Y. 10016 (telephone: 212-696-0740).

Paulist Press, on the Catholic front, has produced a highly regarded set of family-based materials. The publisher's catalogue lists dozens of books and booklets, priced from $2 to $10, for children and parents. 997 MacArthur Blvd., Mahwah, N.J. 07430 (telephone: 201-825-7300).

The Joint Educational Development Consortium, a Protestant Coalition, has developed a set of curriculum material that includes some home-based learning information. A catalogue is available on the curriculum, called "Christian Education: Shared Approaches." *Contact*: Westminster Press, 925 Chestnut Street, Philadelphia, Pa. 19107 (telephone: 215-928-2700).

The National Havurah Committee can give general information about forming a parent-run school or home-based learning group, and can put you in touch with individual groups. 270 West 89th Street, New York, N.Y. 10024 (telephone: 212-496-0055).

CHAPTER 22: DEATH AND BURIAL

I. THE TRADITIONAL FUNERAL CEREMONIES

Catholic As a result of a directive issued by Vatican II, a new Rite of Funerals published in 1969 shifted the emphasis from "the fears and sorrows of death and judgment" to "the victory and joy of resurrection." (P. F. Mulhern, "Office of the Dead," and A. Cornides, "Masses for the Dead" in the *New Catholic Encyclopedia,* Vol. XVII Supplement: Change in the Church.) The Funeral or Requiem Mass is now properly called the Mass of Christian Burial, but many Catholics call it the Mass of Resurrection. The theme is union with Christ in death. The ritual includes the Eucharist (Communion), a reenactment of Jesus' sacrificial death. The priest greets the family at the church door. The deceased's body is sprinkled with holy water to recall baptism, with its sharing in Jesus' death, burial, and resurrection.

Although the theology is different, some of the practices during the funeral are descended from ancient Jewish funeral practices, which the early Christian church continued to observe for some time after it separated from Judaism. A white cover, recalling the Jewish shroud and the Christian baptismal robe, may be placed on the casket. A lighted candle, symbol of the resurrection, is carried down the aisle with the casket and placed at its head during the Mass. Priests may wear white vestments (or black, or purple, the colors of mourning, which were formerly traditional). The priest gives a sermon, or homily, probably focusing on the Resurrection.

Some practices will seem foreign to a Jew: Incense may be used. There may be joyful songs with the theme of resurrection.

There is room in the new Catholic funeral rite for the family to suggest readings, psalms, and prayers. (J. L. Cunningham, "Funeral," in *New Catholic Encyclopedia,* Vol. XVI, pp. 183ff.) The liturgy contains a variety of possible selections from the Old and New Testaments, and the priest is urged to choose readings with consideration for the circumstances of death, the sorrow of the family, and the presence of those of other faiths. Eulogies are discouraged, as they are thought to invite exaggeration and hypocritical praise of the deceased.

There may be a funeral procession from the church to the cemetery. This custom dates from the early Christian church, when the dead person's body was paraded through the streets on a bier, head uncovered, to show the Christian's triumphal faith that death was a victory, not a defeat. In some families, the procession would honor the deceased and his family by going past his home, if it were feasible.

At the cemetery, a priest or layman leads a final prayer service. If the burial is not in a Catholic cemetery, the grave will be individually blessed.

If the person being buried were non-Catholic, the funeral would not generally be held in the church and there would generally be no Mass or communion service. But at the request of the family or of the dying person, a private Mass might be said later for the person's soul.

The new Code of Canon Law (in Canon 1185) appears to prohibit funeral Masses for non-Catholics, but it is ambiguous. The commentators mention two loopholes created by 1976 rulings of the Sacred Congregation for the Doctrine of the Faith. Both exemptions are explicitly for

"Non-Catholic Christians," however, and might not apply to Jews or other non-Christians. The loopholes are: 1) There is no problem with requesting a private Mass for a non-Catholic. 2) A public Mass may be celebrated if "expressly requested by members of the family, [or] by friends . . . out of a genuinely religious motive . . . [and if, in] the judgment of the ordinary, scandal on the part of the faithful is absent." (James A. Coriden, Thomas J. Green, and Donald E. Heintschel, eds., *The Code of Canon Law: A Text and Commentary* New York: Paulist Press, 1985, p. 840 [commissioned by the Canon Law Society of America].) Thus, it is up to the judgment of local clergy and how they react to your intermarriage.

Protestant A low-church Protestant funeral, such as in a Congregationalist church, would probably be relatively spare and simple. The minister would probably talk about the promise of eternal life but might also warn the living about "the transitoriness and accountability of human life" and emphasize the comfort to the mourners of being part of a church community. Many churches would hold a small prayer service just for family in the home of the mourners prior to a larger funeral service in the church.

A high-church funeral such as the Lutheran or Episcopal might include a funeral procession and communion, and might stress the sense of inseparable community and continuity between the living Christians and the deceased. In some churches, there might be a quartet or other group to sing at graveside as the casket is being lowered and the minister or funeral director might drop some earth or flower petals on the grave. (David Sibrey, "Burial, Congregationalist"; A. Niebergall and Gordon Lathrop, "Burial, Lutheran"; and B. B. Beach, "Burial, Seventh Day Adventist," all in J. G. Davies, ed., *The New Westminster Dictionary of Liturgy and Worship,* Philadelphia: The Westminster Press, 1986.)

Jewish The purpose of a Jewish funeral is not to comfort the mourner but to honor the one who has died. Jewish tradition says it is impossible to comfort the mourners while their dead lie before them. People simply share in and accept their grief.

Unlike the regulations on care of the body, the content of the funeral is not fixed. But it generally contains a eulogy, psalms, and a memorial prayer ("*Ayl Malay Rahamim* God, full of compassion, grant perfect rest to the soul of . . ."). It is a service of farewell and is generally quite brief. It is usually held in the home or funeral chapel or at the cemetery, and would only be in the synagogue in the case of an exceptional community leader. However, the funeral procession would pass in front of the synagogue and the cantor would chant prayers.

In traditional Judaism, people generally accompany the casket on foot at least part of the way from the funeral service to the gravesite. There would be pauses or hesitations on the way from the hearse to the grave, to symbolize the regret and difficulty in saying goodbye. The pall-bearers would generally be Jewish.

At the graveside, there is a prayer that affirms God as the true and righteous Judge: "The Lord gave, the Lord has taken away—blessed be the name of the Lord." Some Jews follow the custom of having each person place a stone on the grave and silently asking forgiveness of the deceased for any offenses against him.

If there is a *minyan* (ten or more Jewish men), the graveside service will close with the children of the deceased saying *kaddish,* a rhythmic affirmation of faith which is one of the most familiar prayers in Judaism.

As the mourners leave the cemetery, the community turns to the task of comforting them. The friends and more distant relatives form two parallel lines. The mourners pass through, and the people recite, in Hebrew, "May the Lord comfort you among the other mourners of Zion and Jerusalem."

A funeral and burial preferably is held in the morning. All the family then gathers at noon for a mourners' meal, and the first day of the mourning period begins that afternoon.

II. MOURNING RITUALS

Jewish Jewish mourning customs are obligatory for adults of the immediate family: the brothers and sisters, and most particularly the parents and/or children of the deceased. In traditional Judaism, there are four distinct stages of mourning: before the funeral; the first seven days after the funeral (sitting *shiva*); the first month; the first year.

During *shiva,* the traditional Jewish family sits, shoeless or just wearing slippers, on low stools, and simply experiences their grief. Friends come to visit. At least ten men must be there, morning and evening, for a regular religious service, so that the mourners can say the mourners' *kaddish.* A memorial candle burns for seven days.

If the mourner has lost a parent, he continues to refrain for a full year from engaging in entertainment, such as going to parties, and from buying new clothes (except as necessary for hygiene and social acceptability). He goes to synagogue and says the *kaddish* every day for eleven months, and from then on every year on the anniversary of the parent's death, and on specified holidays when services of remembrance are held. He lights a twenty-four-hour memorial candle every year on the *yahrzeit* (anniversary of the death). He may visit the grave at the end of *shiva,* at the end of *sheloshim* (thirty days), and on the *yahrzeit,* during or near the fall High Holiday season, and at moments of key life decisions.

Other than these remembrances, the period of mourning is not to be extended beyond the year. According to Jewish tradition, just as there is an appropriate time for weeping, there is also an appropriate time for completing the dealing with grief and returning to normal life. One way of symbolizing this ending of mourning is to unveil the tombstone. The unveiling can be held any time after the end of shiva, but is often held one year after the person's death.

Reform Jews might observe only the first three days of shiva and would be unlikely to observe the thirty-day and one-year stages of mourning. They would observe the *yahrzeit* with a memorial prayer at the synagogue.

(Material on Judaism is summarized or paraphrased from Maurice Lamm, *The Jewish Way in Death and Mourning,* New York: Jonathan David Publishers, 1969, with a supplementary interview on Reform Jewish practices with Rabbi Joel Alpert.)

Catholic A memorial mass may be said on the thirtieth day after death. Although this custom is less common today, the Catholic partner can use it as an opportunity to seek comfort and acknowledge the inner grieving that is still going on.

NOTES

INTRODUCTION

1. The National Jewish Population Study (NJPS), as cited in Charles Silberman, *A Certain People,* New York: Summit Books, 1985, estimated the national intermarriage rate at 5.9 percent in 1956–60. The 40 percent intermarriage figure is Brooklyn College sociologist Egon Mayer's current estimate based on his studies and review of other research. The NJPS conducted its own research and estimated the level at 31.7 percent in 1966–71. Charles Silberman, in *A Certain People,* reevaluated the existing research and calculated the national rate at 24 percent.

2. Egon Mayer, considered the leading researcher on Jewish-Christian marriage, provided us with these figures, which include conversionary as well as mixed couples. He said the half-million figure is based on periodic surveys of the adult Jewish population, chiefly Steven Cohen's national sampling for the American Jewish Committee. The forty thousand figure comes from applying Mayer's 40 percent intermarriage estimate to the hundred thousand Jews who marry every year.

3. According to the NJPS, 31 percent of Christian spouses in intermarriage convert to Judaism; 3 percent of Jewish spouses convert to Christianity. Egon Mayer's research showed that the level of the Jewish spouse's involvement in Judaism most often increased or remained the same after intermarriage; the Christian partner's involvement in Christianity was more likely to decrease.

According to the NJPS (cited in Rabbi Mark Winer, "Sociological Research on Jewish Intermarriage," in *Journal of Reform Judaism,* Summer 1985, p. 47), when the husband is Jewish, 60 percent of the children identify as Jews. When the wife in an intermarriage is Jewish, 98 percent of the children identify as Jews. And 70 percent of the intermarried couples intended to give their children a Jewish education.

CHAPTER 1: JEWISH-CHRISTIAN HISTORY

1. The history of early Christian-Jewish relations is from Father Edward H. Flannery, *The Anguish of the Jews,* New York: Macmillan, 1965, ch. 1–3. Eugene Fisher retells some of this material and gives perspective in *Homework for Christians: Preparing for Christian-Jewish Dialogue,* New York: National Conference of Christians and Jews, New York, 2nd rev. ed., 1986; and *Faith Without Prejudice: Rebuilding Christian Attitudes Toward Judaism,* New York: Paulist Press, 1977.

2. *Nostra Aetate* (Vatican II's reassessment of the relationship of Catholics to non-Catholics and non-Christian religions) is discussed by Fisher, *Faith,* pp. 23–26.

3. Flannery, *op. cit.,* p. 48.

4. Our perspective on this period was shaped in part by an interview with Dr. Eugene J. Fisher, Director of the Secretariat for Catholic-Jewish Relations of the National Conference of Catholic Bishops, as well as by Flannery's book.

5. The summary of legal restrictions is from Raul Hilberg, *The Destruction of the European Jews,* Chicago: Quadrangle, 1961, pp. 5–6, as cited in A. Roy Eckardt, *Elder and Younger Brothers: The Encounter of Jews and Christians,* New York: Charles Scribner's Sons, 1967, pp. 12–14. Parts are also cited in Fisher, *Homework,* p. 27. We have supplemented this summary from Flannery, *op. cit.*

6. Flannery, *op. cit.,* p. 75.

7. Flannery, *op. cit.,* p. 85.

8. Except where noted otherwise, the history of the persecutions is largely condensed and paraphrased from Chaim Potok, *Wanderings: Chaim Potok's History of the Jews,* New York: Fawcett Crest, 1978, and from

Flannery, *op. cit.* Some material also comes from Fisher, *Homework.*

9. From Fisher, *Homework,* p. 16.

10. *Ibid.,* p. 21.

11. *Ibid.,* p. 15. Even when the Jews won such a debate, it was at their peril. When the Jewish scholar Moses Nachmanides was ordered to debate Christian scholars before the king of Spain in 1263, the king declared Nachmanides' arguments more convincing. Within two years, the clergy succeeded in having him accused of blasphemy and exiled.

12. Potok, *op. cit.,* p. 435.

13. Max Leopold Margolis and Alexander Marx, *A History of the Jewish People,* New York: Harper & Row, 1965, p. 552.

14. Potok, *op. cit.,* p. 445.

15. Potok, *op. cit.,* p. 499.

16. The history of Christian leaders who protected the Jews is largely from Flannery, *op. cit.,* and from the interview with Fisher.

17. *Letter to the Duchess of Brabant,* cited in Flannery, *op. cit.,* p. 95.

18. *Encyclopedia Judaica,* Jerusalem: Keter Publishing (New York: Macmillan, 1st printing), 1971, Vol. 3, p. 202–3. In 1962, in considering an immigration petition from a Jew who had converted to Christianity and become a monk, the Israeli Supreme Court ruled that "apostasy to Christianity removes that person from this nationality." For an account of the case, see *Encyclopedia Judaica, ibid.,* p. 210.

19. A discussion of Vatican II's statements on the Jews can be found in Fisher's *Homework* and *Faith.* The text of *Nostra Aetate* and subsequent Catholic statements on relations to the Jews, as well as similar statements from the World Council of Churches and individual Protestant denominations, can be found in Helga Croner, *Stepping Stones to Further Jewish-Christian Relations: An Unabridged Collection of Christian Documents,* New York: Stimulus Books, 1977, and in Arthur Gilbert, *Homework for Jews: Preparing for Jewish-Christian Dialogue,* New York: National Conference of Christians and Jews (undated). Gilbert has an extensive discussion of recent changes in Christian churches.

20. *Nostra Aetate,* in Croner, *op. cit.,* p. 2.

21. "The Christian Approach to the Jews," First Assembly of the World

Council of Churches, Amsterdam, Holland, 1948, cited in Croner, *op. cit.,* p. 70.

22. Report of the Committee on the Church and the Jewish People to the Faith and Order Commission of the World Council of Churches, Geneva, Switzerland, 1968, cited in Croner, *op. cit.,* p. 78.

23. "Reflections and Suggestions for the Application of the Directives of *Nostra Aetate* (n.4)." Working Document prepared for the Holy See's Office for Catholic-Jewish Relations, by a special Commission. December 1969. Cited in Croner, *op. cit.,* p. 7.

CHAPTER 3: DEALING WITH PARENTS

1. Parents' attitudes were reported in Egon Mayer, *Love and Tradition: Marriage Between Jews and Christians,* New York: Plenum, 1985, p. 196. Some of the data were first reported in Egon Mayer and Carl Sheingold, *Intermarriage and the Jewish Future: A National Study in Summary,* New York: American Jewish Committee, 1979, pp. 12–13.

2. The first section of our discussion of parents' feelings is largely drawn from Rabbi Sanford Seltzer's booklet, *Jews and Non-Jews: Falling in Love,* New York: Union of American Hebrew Congregations, 1977. The second section comes chiefly from an interview with Sherri Alper, outreach coordinator for the UAHC's Philadelphia region.

3. Dr. Edwin H. Friedman, "The Myth of the Shiksa," paper delivered at the Third International Family Therapy Conference, Tel Aviv, July 1979. Friedman was then research associate and visiting faculty member at the Family Center, Georgetown University Medical Center, Washington, D.C. The paper was reprinted in *The Family,* October 1980, published by the Center for Family Learning, New Rochelle, N.Y. These passages are from pp. 13, 15.

4. *Ibid.,* p. 14.

5. Friedman, *op. cit.*

6. Ideas in this section on ethnic influences come from Barbara Breitman, a psychotherapist with the Jewish Family and Children's Agency of Philadelphia. She specializes in ethnotherapy, which involves helping people untangle their ambivalence about being a member of an ethnic minority.

7. Friedman, *op. cit.,* p. 14.

8. Mayer, *op. cit.,* p. 90.

9. Two books that contain helpful techniques for improving your relationship with your parents are: Harold H. Bloomfield, M.D., *Making Peace with Your Parents,* New York: Ballantine Books, 1983, and Howard M. Halpern, Ph.D., *Cutting Loose: An Adult Guide to Coming to Terms with Your Parents,* New York: Bantam Books, 1983. The emphasis on forgiveness and other strategies in this section of the chapter are drawn in large part from the Bloomfield book. This section of the chapter and the next ("Moving Ahead") draw heavily on interviews with Lena Romanoff, director of the Jewish Converts Network, and Sherri Alper, Philadelphia region outreach coordinator of the Union of American Hebrew Congregations.

10. Bloomfield, *ibid.,* and Halpern, *ibid.*

11. Bloomfield, *op. cit.,* p. 59.

<h2 style="text-align:center">CHAPTER 4: THE WEDDING</h2>

1. From Elizabeth A. Carter and Monica McGoldrick, eds., *The Family Life Cycle: A Framework for Family Therapy,* New York: Gardner Press, 1980, p. 94.

2. In the Bible, the commandment against intermarriage is seen as necessary for the maintenance of the Jewish people and the Jewish religion. When the Israelites are about to enter Canaan, God has Moses warn them not to intermarry with the Canaanites and other peoples: "Thy daughter thou shalt not give unto his son, nor his daughter shalt thou take unto thy son. For he will turn away thy son from following Me. . . . For thou art a holy people unto the Lord thy God: The Lord thy God hath chosen thee to be His own treasure, out of all peoples that are upon the face of the earth" (Deuteronomy 7:3–6).

3. Traditionally, in the Jewish wedding contract the man states what he will agree to pay in case of divorce. In fact, the Jewish wedding contract was virtually the only document until modern times which guaranteed a woman a financial settlement in the event of a divorce.

4. This understanding of the limitations of the Catholic pledge was clarified by several Catholic officials.

5. Traditionally, Orthodox rabbis could be ordained either by a yeshiva (a seminary) or privately, by studying with an ordained rabbi. This second method was common in Europe, but private ordination is often impossible to verify and has fallen out of favor in America.

6. From an interview with Monica McGoldrick, a family therapist at Rutgers University known for her writing on issues of ethnicity and cross-cultural marriage. This Irish-American Protestant, married to a European-reared Greek from a very traditional family, has personal experience in the issues of intermarriage.

7. Dr. Edwin H. Friedman, "Systems and Ceremonies: A Family View of Rites of Passage," in Carter and McGoldrick, *op. cit.,* p. 430.

8. These ideas came from an interview with Rabbi Linda Holtzman, director of practical rabbinics at the Reconstructionist Rabbinical College and rabbi of Beth Ahavah congregation in Philadelphia.

CHAPTER 5: ETHNIC BACKGROUND

1. Joel Crohn, *Ethnic Identity and Marital Conflict: Jews, Italians and WASPs,* New York: American Jewish Committee, 1985, pp. 12–13.

2. This exercise was developed with the assistance of Esther Perel, a psychotherapist working with intermarried couples and families and a consultant on Ethnicity and Mental Health to the American Jewish Committee, in New York. It is based on work by Carol and Peter Schreck, professors of pastoral care and counseling at Eastern Baptist Theological Seminary. Similar exercises have been developed by Joseph Giordano of the American Jewish Committee, Monica McGoldrick of the University of Medicine and Dentistry of New Jersey and Rutgers Medical School, and others.

3. Many of the generalizations in the WASP group will apply to assimilated Protestants from any Northern European country, and many of the generalizations on Italians will apply to other Mediterranean peoples such as Greeks, and to Hispanics from either side of the Atlantic. Black and Asian partners can use the categories and exercises here to develop their own cultural profiles to discuss with their Jewish mates.

4. Except where noted otherwise, these descriptions are largely distilled from Monica McGoldrick, John K. Pearce, and Joseph Giordano, *Ethnicity and Family Therapy,* New York: Guilford Press, 1982.

5. Crohn, *op cit.,* p. 26.

6. David McGill and John K. Pearce, "British Families," chapter in *Ethnicity and Family Therapy, op cit.,* p. 459.

7. Fredda M. Herz and Elliott J. Rosen, "Jewish Families," from *Ethnicity and Family Therapy, op cit.,* pp. 387–8.

8. Many ideas in this section came from interviews with Peter Schreck, cited above, as well as with Joel Crohn and psychologist Lori Santo, a consultant to the American Jewish Committee.

9. McGill and Pearce, *op cit.,* p. 458.

10. Herz and Rosen, *op cit.,* p. 372.

11. McGill and Pearce, *op cit.,* p. 460.

12. This idea came from an interview with Sally Green of the Marriage Council of Philadelphia.

13. This concept is from Sidney B. Simon, Leland W. Howe, and Howard Kirschenbaum, *Values Clarification: A Handbook of Practical Strategies for Teachers and Students,* New York: Hart Publishing, 1972, p. 19.

14. Many of these strategies came from our interviews with Peter Schreck, cited above.

15. Mark Zborowski, *People in Pain,* San Francisco: Jossey-Bass, 1969.

16. Ideas in this section were developed chiefly from an interview with Sally Green, cited above.

17. Crohn, *op cit.,* p. 17.

18. Ideas in this section come partly from an interview with Lori Santo, cited above.

19. Joel Crohn, from an address at the Second National Conference on Programs for the Intermarried, March 1986, in Los Angeles.

20. From Crohn address, cited above.

CHAPTER 6: ETHNIC AMBIVALENCE

1. This exercise was given to us by Robin Miller, a specialist in intergroup relations working for the Fellowship Commission of Philadelphia.

2. Joel Crohn, *Ethnic Identity and Marital Conflict: Jews, Italians and WASPs,* New York: American Jewish Committee, 1985, pp. 15, 28.

3. The term "internalized oppression" was coined in the Re-evaluation Counseling movement. RC uses co-counseling—in which pairs of people take turns listening to and drawing each other out—to help people uncover and discharge the emotions associated with past hurts. Black psychiatrist Price Cobbs first enunciated the ideas behind the term.

Much of our section, "The Forces of Shame," is based on an interview with ethnotherapist Barbara Breitman of the Jewish Family and Children's Agency of Philadelphia.

4. The term ethnotherapy was coined, and many of the techniques developed, by Judith Weinstein Klein. See Klein's booklet *Jewish Identity and Self-Esteem: Healing Wounds Through Ethnotherapy* in our Recommended Readings. Klein, in turn, expanded on ideas developed by black psychiatrist Price Cobbs. We learned about the internal process of these groups from a videotape produced by Klein through the American Jewish Committee, as well as from Breitman, Robin Miller, and Aileen Riotto Sirey, a New York psychotherapist who conducted several sessions for Italian-Americans.

CHAPTER 7: THE LIFETIME TRAJECTORY

1. Gail Sheehy, in *Passages: Predictable Crises of Adult Life,* Bantam: New York, 1980, popularized the notion of adult identity crises, which had been introduced by Erik Erikson and developed by Daniel J. Levinson and Roger Gould. An interview with psychologist Lori Santo, a consultant to the American Jewish Committee, helped us crystallize ideas on how relationship to cultural roots can vary over the life cycle. Other concepts came from *The Family Life Cycle: A Framework for Family Therapy* (New York: Gardner Press, 1980), which was edited by Elizabeth A. Carter and Monica McGoldrick.

2. Fowler's theory of faith development over the life cycle is based on the ideas of Erik Erikson, Jean Piaget, and Lawrence Kohlberg and on three hundred fifty-nine interviews with children and adults that he and his associates conducted from 1972 to 1981. It is presented in: James W. Fowler, *Stages of Faith: The Psychology of Human Development and the Quest for Faith,* San Francisco: Harper & Row, 1981.

3. The strategies in this section came largely from an interview with Robert Garfield, a psychiatrist who is intermarried.

CHAPTER 8: LEARNING TO NEGOTIATE

1. The negotiation approach outlined in this chapter was spelled out in Roger Fisher and William Ury's classic book, *Getting to Yes,* Boston: Houghton Mifflin, 1981. Roger Fisher, of the Harvard Law School Center for Conflict Resolution, was an adviser to President Jimmy Carter during the Camp David negotiations.

Some of the suggestions also came from Peter Schreck, a professor in the program on marriage and family at Eastern Baptist Theological Seminary, and Robin Miller of the Fellowship Commission.

2. Ethnic differences in response to conflict come from various chapters of Monica McGoldrick, John K. Pearce, and Joseph Giordano, *Ethnicity and Family Therapy,* New York: Guilford Press, 1982, and an interview with psychologist Lori Santo, a consultant to the American Jewish Committee.

CHAPTER 9: YOUR SPIRITUAL NEEDS

1. James W. Fowler, *Stages of Faith: The Psychology of Human Development and the Quest for Faith,* San Francisco: Harper & Row, 1981, p. 4.

2. This exercise and the next were adapted by Lois Kellerman, leader of the Ethical Culture Society of Brooklyn and Queens, N.Y., from: Richard S. Gilbert, *Building Your Own Theology,* Boston: Unitarian Universalist Association, copyright 1983, used by permission. Kellerman, herself intermarried, conducts classes for interfaith couples. We in turn have made some adaptations of Kellerman's work.

3. Adapted from Bernard Reisman, *Jewish Experiential Book: The Quest for Jewish Identity,* Hoboken, N.J.: Ktav Publishing House, 1979. Used by permission.

4. Bernard Spilka and Peter Benson, "God-Image as a Function of Self-Esteem and Locus of Control," *Journal for the Scientific Study of Religion,* 1973, Vol. 12, No. 3, pp. 297–310. (Spilka, in an interview, noted that the God-image is not always simply a reflection of the parent. In your first decade your parents were primary, but later the image might have become generalized, based on many adults in your life.)

5. From an interview with psychiatrist Thomas Fogarty, associate director of the Center for Family Learning, Rye, N.Y.

6. Harold H. Bloomfield, M.D., *Making Peace with Your Parents,* New York: Ballantine Books, 1983, pp. 19–47.

7. From an interview with Rabbi Neil Comess-Daniels of Temple Shir Sholom, a heavily intermarried Reform congregation in Venice, Calif.

8. The following are prominent titles by those religious thinkers: Harold Kushner, *When Bad Things Happen to Good People,* New York: Schocken, 1981; Eugene B. Borowitz, *Choices in Modern Jewish Thought,* New York: Behrman House, 1983; Martin Buber, *I and Thou,* New York: Charles Scribner's Sons, 1970; Abraham Joshua Heschel, *The Sabbath: Its Meaning for Modern Man,* New York: Farrar, Straus & Giroux, 1983; Paul Tillich, *The Dynamics of Faith,* New York: Harper & Row, 1958; Henri Nouwen, *Reaching Out: The Three Movements of the Spiritual Life,* New York: Doubleday, 1986; Hans Kung, *Does God Exist?,* New York: Random House, 1981. Also, check Marilyn Ferguson, *The Aquarian Conspiracy,* Los Angeles: J. P. Tarcher, 1981; and Paul Kurtz, *In Defense of Secular Humanism,* Buffalo, N.Y.: Prometheus Books, 1983.

9. Gordon Allport, *Becoming,* New Haven: Yale University Press, 1955, p. 17.

CHAPTER 10: HOW THE RELIGIONS SHAPED YOU

1. The idea of religion as a "reality map" was suggested by the Rev. Timothy Lull, chairman of the theology department at Lutheran Theological Seminary in Philadelphia. The idea of Jewish and Christian "master stories" is developed in Michael Goldberg, *Jews and Christians— Getting Our Stories Straight: The Exodus and the Passion-Resurrection,* Nashville: Abingdon Press, 1985. The stories of Judaism and Christianity are spelled out succinctly in Rabbi Samuel Sandmel's book, *When a Jew and Christian Marry,* Philadelphia: Fortress Press, 1977, which is out of print but available in some libraries. Also useful are Huston Smith, *The Religions of Man,* New York: Mentor Books, 1959, and Samuel Sandmel, *We Jews and You Christians: An Inquiry Into Attitudes,* Philadelphia: J. B. Lippincott, 1967.

2. Dean M. Kelley and Bernhard E. Olson, *The Meaning and Conduct of Dialogue,* p. 4. The booklet is available from the National Conference of Christians and Jews, 43 West 57th Street, New York, N.Y. 10019.

3. As a result of the new ecumenicism and tolerance in the wake of Vatican II, nearly every Catholic diocese or archdiocese in America has sponsored periodic interfaith dialogue groups involving Catholics, Protestants, and Jews. Intermarried partners can join those groups or organize their own dialogue group. The Kelley and Olson booklet cited above, *The Meaning and Conduct of Dialogue,* tells how.

4. Father William McGowan, who counseled many engaged interfaith couples during his tenure as pastor of the Newman Center at the University of Pennsylvania, calls this task "building a theology of marriage and relationship." If you're a nonbeliever, you could call it defining your ideal of a loving relationship.

CHAPTER 11: CONVERSION

1. Christians traditionally believe that baptism was "commanded by God and instituted by Jesus Christ . . . and [is] normally necessary for salvation." But baptism does not by itself ensure salvation. Salvation is achieved by faith, and baptism "calls forth" faith in the recipient, child, or adult. "The entire Christian life, with its struggle against sin, is a constant return to one's baptism." Conservative Christians believe that salvation is available only to those who believe in Jesus. Liberal Christians hold that baptism opens the way to salvation through Jesus, but that God has already assured the salvation of all people regardless of belief. (Quotations are from spokesmen of a variety of denominations and are taken from the *Westminster Dictionary of Worship,* Philadelphia: Westminster Press, 1979.)

2. According to the National Jewish Population Study, 31 percent of Christian spouses in intermarriage convert to Judaism, compared with 3 percent of Jewish spouses who convert to Christianity. The preponderance of women converts, and the connection to the impending wedding, have been established by several researchers, chief among them Steven Huberman. See: Steven Huberman, "From Christianity to Judaism: Religion Changers in American Society," *Conservative Judaism,* Autumn 1982, p. 14.

3. Dr. Edwin H. Friedman, "Conversion, Love and Togetherness," *Reconstructionist,* May 1973, p. 18.

4. Some Jews may resolve the potential conflict between a Jewish ethnic identity and a Christian faith by joining Jews for Jesus or similar organizations.

5. Rabbi Michael Paley, dean of the chapel at Columbia University and director of the university's Earl Hall Center for Religious and Volunteer Services, pointed out to us this distinction between an epiphanic Christian conversion experience and the accumulation of Jewish identity.

6. Friedman warns in his article "Conversion, Love and Togetherness," *op cit.,* p. 16, that those who are most eager to convert are often those who wish to "lose themselves" in the family system of their partner.

7. Egon Mayer has found that children of conversionary families experienced a bit more personal stress in choosing ethnic identity than did children of mixed families. In *Children of Intermarriage* (New York: American Jewish Committee, 1983, p. 37), he states: "It is possible that since in conversionary families religion is of greater significance than in mixed marriages, children of the former are somewhat more prone to experience symptoms of marginality than children of the latter." We speculate it may be because at least some of the conversions occurred under pressure, with resulting ambivalences and mixed messages to the children.

8. David Max Eichhorn, *Conversion to Judaism: A History and Analysis,* Hoboken, N.J.: Ktav Publishing, 1965, p. 34. Jacob B. Agus "The Mitzvah of Keruv," in *Conservative Judaism,* Vol. XXXV, No. 4, Summer 1982, p. 35.

9. There is debate in traditional Judaism about the rules for converting children of Jewish fathers and gentile mothers. The established practice has been to convert a child only if the parents promise to lead a traditionally observant life-style. A prominent Orthodox rabbi in Los Angeles has shaken up the establishment, however, by publicly arguing that the children of mixed marriages should be converted without any precondition for religious observance. The rabbi, Jack Simcha Cohen, says he has found Talmudic grounding for his position—and besides, he says, many Orthodox rabbis in outlying parts of the country had been taking his approach anyway. Some Orthodox rabbis agree with Cohen's scholarship and many don't. The point may not be the official outcome so much as his assertion that Orthodox conversions already are not as difficult to obtain as generally believed. You might find you can have your child converted under universally recognized Orthodox auspices without making promises that would be unacceptably strict for you.

10. Many of these tips came from Lena Romanoff, director of the Jewish Converts Network.

CHAPTER 12: CHILDREN'S ADJUSTMENT

1. This concept came from child psychiatrist Robert H. Abramovitz, chief psychiatrist at the Jewish Board of Family and Children's Services of New York City.

2. As part of a doctoral dissertation completed in May 1986, psychologist Karen Kaufman of Berkeley, Calif., surveyed ninety-five intermarried couples who reported themselves in agreement about their religious child-rearing. Some of the couples were raising their children Christian, some Jewish, some both, and some nothing formal. Kaufman looked for evidence of depression or self-destructive or antisocial behavior in the children. Her finding: There were no significant differences in the behavior patterns of the children regardless of how they were being raised. Furthermore, whether the family chose one religion, two religions, or no religion, there seemed to be no significant difference in the families' feelings of togetherness.

Egon Mayer of Brooklyn College came to roughly the same conclusions in a 1983 study he did for the American Jewish Committee. He found that children of intermarriage felt well liked and enjoyed family gatherings. They were confident about the future and knew what they wanted out of life. Very few felt they lacked roots or would have wanted to be born as someone else. Mayer did not ask families specifically whether they raised their children with one religion, two, or none. But he did compare mixed marriages, where neither partner converted to the other's religion, to marriages where one partner had converted. Children of mixed marriages seemed no more confused about what their parents expected than did children of conversionary marriages.

3. Nos. 1–3 come from a study of interethnic families by Dr. John F. McDermott, Jr., Thomas W. Maretzki and Dr. Wen-Shing Tseng. Results reported in *Adjustment in Intercultural Marriage,* Honolulu: University of Hawaii Press, 1977.

4. Nos. 5–8 come from James H. Bossard and Eleanor S. Boll, *One Marriage, Two Faiths: Guidance on Interfaith Marriage,* New York: Ronald Press, 1957.

5. There is debate about this. Kaufman did not seem to find that children come out of such a home maladjusted if the parents are in agreement.

CHAPTER 13: CHILDREN AND SPIRITUALITY

1. This concept was emphasized to us by both child psychiatrist Robert H. Abramovitz, chief psychiatrist at the Jewish Board of Family and Children's Services of New York, and Rev. James Fowler, the pioneering religion researcher.

2. See the discussion in psychiatrist Annette Hollander's guide, *How to Help Your Child Have a Spiritual Life: A Parent's Guide to Inner Development,* New York: Bantam New Age, 1982, pp. 20–38.

3. Fowler, in describing the stages of spiritual development, applied the findings of famed psychology theorists Erik Erikson, Jean Piaget, and Lawrence Kohlberg. In translating Fowler's stages, we have in most cases substituted our terms for his.

4. Fowler focuses on the rationalists, who tend to be boys and men. The spiritualists are primarily girls and women.

5. Hollander, *op cit.,* p. 139.

6. Ibid., pp. 190–192.

CHAPTER 14: CHILDREN'S IDENTITY

1. Leslie Goodman-Malamuth and Robin Margolis are co-founders of Pareveh: The Alliance for Adult Children of Jewish-Gentile Intermarriage. For information, contact: 3628 Windom Place N.W., Washington, D.C. 20008 (telephone: 202-363-7266).

2. The account of identity stages is based on interviews with psychologist Lori Santo, a consultant to the American Jewish Committee, and child psychiatrist Robert H. Abramovitz, chief psychiatrist at the Jewish Board of Family and Children's Services of New York.

3. This observation is from psychiatrist Samuel C. Klagsbrun, professor of pastoral psychiatry at Jewish Theology Seminary and professor of psychiatry at Columbia University Medical School.

4. According to Egon Mayer's research, in mixed marriages where neither partner converted, 36 percent of the parents belonged to churches, compared with only 21 percent of their grown children. Of the mixed marrieds, 9 percent belonged to synagogues, but only 3 percent of their children did so. Even where one parent had converted to the other's religion, the children tended not to affiliate. While 86 percent of the Jewish conversionary families affiliated with a synagogue, only 38 percent of the children did so. Though critics such as Steven Cohen, author of *Jewish Identity and Modernity,* New York: Methuen, 1983, have said the synagogue dropoff is merely due to the relative youthfulness of the offspring in the study, Mayer's "educated hunch" is that many of the children of intermarriage will remain nonjoiners.

5. Egon Mayer, *Love and Tradition: Marriage Between Christians and Jews,* New York: Plenum, 1985, p. 253.

6. The uncertainties of the identity-shaping process became clear to an American Jewish Committee task force, led by psychiatrist Samuel Klagsbrun, which studied the formation of Jewish identity. The task force found that the most important factors in whether people remained active in Judaism as adults were not home style or religious education, but where they lived after they grew up. If they were in a town where the country club was the focus of social life, they might remain aloof from religion. If the synagogue was the center of social activity, they were more likely to be drawn into a Jewish life-style.

7. Susan Jacoby, "I am a Half-Jew, American-Born," *Present Tense,* Autumn 1983.

CHAPTER 15: HOLIDAYS AND HOME STYLE

1. Rabbi Samson Raphael Hirsch, *Betrachtungen zum judische Kalendarjahr.* Cited in *A Treasury of Jewish Quotations,* edited by Leo Rosten, New York: Crown, 1956, p. 39.

2. Traditional Jews celebrate most holidays for two days and week-long holidays for eight days, while Reform Jews and people in Israel observe one-day and seven-day holidays.

3. These holiday guidelines come from an interview with Sam Mackintosh.

4. Susan Lieberman, *Let's Celebrate: Creating New Family Traditions,* New York: Perigee Books, Putnam, 1984, pp. 57, 64.

5. Lieberman, *op cit.,* p. 59.

6. This idea came from the Jewish women's Rosh Hodesh (new month or new moon) group of Philadelphia.

7. For an index to *Festivals* magazine, and back issues, see the address listed under Rites of Passage (Chapter 6 in our Appendix).

CHAPTER 16: RITES OF PASSAGE

1. These three elements were articulated by Arnold van Gennep, a Belgian folklorist who defined the term "rites of passage" in 1908. He said these rites allow people to pass officially from one stage of life to another. See: Arnold van Gennep, *The Rites of Passage,* Chicago: University of Chicago Press, 1960, pp. 2, 3 and 11 (originally published in French in 1909).

2. From Rev. Donald W. Hendricks, "What Is a Catholic?", an essay in *Religions in America,* edited by Leo Rosten, New York: Simon and Schuster, 1975, p. 49.

3. Some authorities say that if necessary, the ritual circumcision can be performed by a doctor, even a non-Jewish doctor, as long as a Jewish man is present and says the proper blessing. Others say that a *mohel* must perform the rite for it to be valid.

4. Is circumcision physically or emotionally traumatic for the baby? There has been some debate on this issue in the medical and psychological worlds. The bulk of opinion says no. However, complications are possible, especially when the procedure is performed by someone who is not expert. These can range from infections or scarring to—in extremely rare cases—loss of the penis. Complications, ironically, are more likely to occur in a hospital, where the procedure may be considered a minor one and relegated to an inexperienced intern or resident, than when performed by a *mohel,* who may do hundreds of circumcisions every year. For the last four or five decades, circumcision has been standard practice in most American hospitals. It was believed to promote cleanliness and prevent infection for both the man and the woman who might someday be his sexual partner. Researchers even found a higher incidence of cancer of the cervix among women who had uncircumcised sexual partners. In the last decade, medical opinion reversed slightly. The American Academy of Pediatrics Task Force on Circumcision stated in 1971 and again in 1975, after reviewing the medical literature, that there was no medical need for circumcision. However, because of new studies showing a lower rate of urinary tract infections among circumcised boys, in 1988 the Task Force was reconvened to reevaluate the evidence. The medical arguments are not forceful either way and are likely to pale next to the parents' compelling feelings about the rite. Just as some Jews may feel they can't stand the idea of repudiating the tradition by not having a son circumcised, some non-Jews and even some Jews find the very idea of circumcision repugnant. For a strong statement of the arguments against circumcision, see the pregnancy-and-birth handbook *Right from the Start,* by Gail Sforza Brewer and Janice Presser Greene, Emmaus, Pa.: Rodale Press, 1981, pp. 120–128.

5. If the woman's first baby is a boy, there is also traditionally a ceremony called *pidyon ha-ben* (redemption of the first-born son) on the thirty-first day after the birth. Consult a prayer book or rabbi if you wish to follow this tradition.

6. Delaying baptism until confirmation is consistent with a Christian identity, which involves a conscious acceptance of faith by the young adult. It's not consistent with Jewish identity, which usually involves a cumulative sense of being part of the people from one's birth.

7. These suggestions come from an interview with Sam Mackintosh, founder of *Festivals* (formerly *Family Festivals),* a magazine for creative ritual.

8. Susan Weidman Schneider, *Jewish and Female: Choices and Changes in Our Lives Today,* New York: Simon and Schuster, 1984, p. 124–127.

9. This suggestion is from Robert Rice of the Institute for Creation-Centered Spirituality in Oakland, Calif.

CHAPTER 17: AFFILIATION

1. This information came from officials of the various denominations and from Leo Rosten, *Religions of America: Ferment and Faith in an Age of Crisis: A New Guide and Almanac,* New York: Simon and Schuster, 1975.

2. The Reform movement's Central Conference of American Rabbis has held that "the ceremony of Confirmation at the end of the school course shall be considered in lieu of a conversion ceremony." The CCAR endorsed that policy in adopting the March 15, 1983, Report of the Committee on Patrilineal Descent on the Status of Children of Mixed Marriages.

3. The Conservative movement is experimenting with outreach. In early 1987, the movement held its first conference on intermarriage and issued a call for all its regions to adopt the "Project Joseph" model. Project Joseph had been launched two years earlier as a pilot program by the movement's northern New Jersey region. Much of the project's effort has been to try to stem mixed marriage by organizing Jewish singles groups and advertising conversion classes. But it also has tried to develop educational and support-group programs for intermarrieds. Inquire about the status of this project in your Conservative region or synagogue.

4. Get a copy from your diocese of the Vatican II declaration *Nostra Aetate* and the subsequently issued guidelines for implementing it. For a good brief discussion of the change in the church's position, see Eugene Fisher, *Faith Without Prejudice: Rebuilding Christian Attitudes Toward Judaism*, New York: Paulist Press, 1977.

CHAPTER 18: RELIGIOUS EDUCATION

1. George Brown, *Human Teachings for Human Learning,* New York: Viking Press, 1971. Cited in *Creative Jewish Education: A Reconstructionist Perspective,* edited by Jeffrey L. Schein and Jacob J. Staub, Chappaqua, N.Y.: Reconstructionist Rabbinical College Press and Rossel Books, 1985, p. 21.

2. For information about the Reform guidelines, contact the Union of American Hebrew Congregations, Department of Education, 838 Fifth Avenue, New York, N.Y. 10021.

3. Stepping Stones is unique in several ways. First, it is fully funded by the Jewish Federation and thus is tuition-free to families. Second, it is only for the children of intermarried and unaffiliated couples. Third, its program lasts only two years. By that time, parents must decide whether to "mainstream" their children in a synagogue or not. Though Stepping Stones teaches skills and customs, its main purpose is to provide positive associations and "Jewish memories" for the children.

4. Stepping Stones is a two-year immersion course. At the end of the first year, although Nicole had a positive feeling about Judaism, she had a somewhat garbled sense of what Judaism is. She told us, for example, that Yom Kippur was a holiday on which you eat matzoh.

CHAPTER 19: PROGRAMS AND RESOURCES

1. Condensed from *44 Hours to Change Your Life* by Henry P. Durkin, New York: Paulist Press, 1977.

CHAPTER 20: DIVORCE AND REMARRIAGE

1. There have been only a few studies of divorce and remarriage in intermarriage. One, by Harold Christensen and Kenneth Barber in Indiana, showed a divorce rate for Jewish-Christian couples that was nearly six times that for Jewish-Jewish couples and nearly twice the overall U.S. rate. The study was cited by Egon Mayer in *Love and Tradition,* New York: Plenum, 1985, p. 135.

Another study, a survey of intermarried couples by sociologist Mayer, found that 22 percent of born-Jewish spouses and about 15 percent of born-Christian spouses had been previously married.

A third study surveyed Jews in Indiana and Iowa and found that second marriages were about 50 percent more likely to be intermarriages than were first marriages. The Indiana-Iowa study, conducted by Erich Rosenthal in 1970, also was cited in *Love and Tradition,* p. 90.

2. Many of the concepts and suggestions in this chapter come from three experts we consulted, all of whom have personal and professional experience with divorce-remarriage issues. Clinical psychologist Emily Visher of Palo Alto, Calif., has been working with and doing research and writing on stepfamilies for twenty-five years. She is also the veteran of a successful remarriage. Long Island psychiatrist Sheldon Frank has a caseload that consists largely of families in various stages of separation, divorce, and remarriage. Dr. Frank was married, widowed, and married a second time, each time to women who had previously been married and had children. Psychiatrist Andrew S. Watson is a professor of family law at the University of Michigan Law School. He was raised a Methodist and is now in an interfaith remarriage. His Jewish wife brought two grammar-school-age sons to the marriage.

3. It is probably for a similar reason that researchers have found that stepfamilies tend to work better when the two step-parents conceive a child of their own. The new child is someone whom everyone in the family feels an attachment to. At a subconscious level, the child symbolizes that this family has its own identity.

CHAPTER 21: SEXUAL PROBLEMS

1. Rabbi and family therapist Dr. Edwin H. Friedman stresses that this is the key underlying pattern in cases he has seen in his work with intermarried couples—regardless of whether the overt symptom is sexual difficulty.

2. Sources on Jewish attitudes and theology toward sex: Rabbi Balfour Brickner, "Judaism and Contemporary Sexuality," in the *SIECUS* (Sex Information and Education Council of the United States Report, Vol. XV, No. 5, May–June 1987); Robert Gordis, *Love and Sex: A Modern Jewish Perspective,* Farrar, Straus & Giroux, 1978; David M. Feldman, *Marital Relations, Birth Control and Abortion in Jewish Law,* New York: Schocken Books, 1978. The quote on the *yetzer hara* (Feldman, p. 88), is from Genesis Rabbah, 9:9.

3. Source on Christian attitudes and theology toward sex: Daniel C. Maguire, professor of moral theology, Marquette University, Milwaukee, "Catholic Sexual and Reproductive Ethics: A Historical Perspective," in the May–June 1987 *SIECUS* Report, *op cit.*

Saint Augustine's views on satisfying sexual need were cited in Feldman, *op cit.*

4. William R. Stayton, Th.D., (assistant professor of psychiatry and human behavior, Jefferson Medical College), "Alternative Lifestyles: Marital Options," in Daniel C. Goldberg, ed., *Contemporary Marriage,* Homewood, Ill.: The Dorsey Press, 1985. Stayton elaborated these ideas in our interview with him.

5. Sex therapists and researchers interviewed for this chapter include: Dr. William Masters and resident theologian Rev. William Young of the Masters and Johnson Institute, St. Louis; Dr. Harold Lief, professor of psychiatry at the University of Pennsylvania School of Medicine and editor of *Sexual Problems in Medical Practice,* American Medical Association, 1981; Dr. Nathan Turner, an American Baptist minister, formerly a staff member at the denominational headquarters and a professor in the University of Pennsylvania's program in human sexuality, and now a sex therapist and psychotherapist in private practice; Dr. Michael Metz, of the program in human sexuality at the University of Minnesota; Dr. Julian Slowinski of Pennsylvania Hospital (a former Benedictine monk); Dr. William Stayton, professor at Jefferson Medical School and in the human sexuality program at the University of Pennsylvania, lecturer at Eastern Baptist Seminary, and LaSalle Pastoral Counseling Program; and Terence Tafoia of Evergreen College in Olympia, Wash.

6. *The Redbook Report on Female Sexuality,* New York: Delacorte Press, 1975, p. 99.

CHAPTER 22: DEATH AND BURIAL

1. Geoffrey Gorer, *Death, Grief, and Mourning,* New York: Doubleday, 1965, p. 20. Gorer's survey of 359 bereaved people was conducted in Great Britain in 1963. He believes most of the findings are also applicable to the U.S. He found that less than a third of those surveyed went to a religious service once a month or more and only about 3 percent held traditional religious beliefs concerning afterlife. But over 90 percent still considered themselves members of a religious denomination, and when a member of their family died, that's where they turned. Even of the 6 percent who considered themselves not members of any religious group, only two people chose not to have a religious burial service for a family member who had died.

2. In the discussion of burial policies, the Jewish section is based on interviews with Rabbi Joel Alpert, associate rabbi and director of education for Reform Congregation Keneseth Israel in Elkins Park, Pa., and Rabbi Joel Roth, associate professor of Talmud and rabbinics and dean of the Rabbinical School, Jewish Theological Seminary. Alpert's father was the funeral director of Park West Chapel, a large Jewish funeral home in New York. Roth is a member of the Conservative movement's Rabbinical Assembly Committee on Jewish Law and Standards.

The Catholic section is based on an interview with Msgr. Joseph F. Rebman, director of cemeteries for the Diocese of Wilmington, Del. Additional sources: C. W. Kerin, "Burial, Canon Law of," and C. M. Power, "Cemeteries, Canon Law of," in *New Catholic Encyclopedia,* New York: McGraw-Hill, 1967; and James A. Coriden, Thomas J. Green, Donald E. Heintschel, eds., *The Code of Canon Law: A Text and Commentary,* commissioned by the Canon Law Society of America, New York: Paulist Press, 1985.

The Protestant section is based primarily on an interview with the Rev. Timothy Lull, chairman of the theology department, Lutheran Theological Seminary, Philadelphia.

3. Once in 1956, the (Conservative) Rabbinical Assembly's Committee on Law and Standards ruled that a non-Jewish spouse could be buried in a Jewish cemetery if the non-Jew "had considered him or herself as part of the Jewish community, educated the children as Jews, and had attended synagogue services." However, the committee ruled that the grave should be distinguished from other graves by shrubbery or a railing and should be separated on all sides from other graves by the space of one grave. Liberal Conservative rabbis could cite that precedent. But except for the most liberal, they probably won't do it. Rabbi Kassel Abelson "The Status of a Non-Jewish Spouse and Children of a Mixed-Marriage in the Synagogue," in *Conservative Judaism,* Vol. XXXV, No. 4, Summer 1982, p. 45.

4. We caution that if you are dealing with a Reform rabbi you don't know, don't rub his nose in the fact that the deceased is not a Jew. The rabbi then may feel obligated to decline conducting the funeral or burial service. But if you don't bring up the issue, most Reform rabbis will be governed by the principles of *shalom bait* (peace in the house) and of comforting the mourner, and will not ask painful questions. Ironically, some Reform rabbis who would not perform a wedding for an inter-married couple would be willing to perform the funeral. There are two reasons: First, though Jewish law clearly forbids an interfaith wedding, there is no equally clear law on funerals. The wedding is a legal event, the consummation of a contract. A funeral does not have the same legal status. Second, there is no longer a question of encouraging intermar-riage. The intermarriage has already taken place, and the rabbi may feel that he or she is simply enabling the family to remain within the Jewish fold as it handles the sad as well as the happy events of the life cycle.

5. The post-Vatican II revision of canon law contains no explicit state-ment regarding the unbaptized person. Canon 1183 ("Rites for . . . Non Catholics") allows clergy to exercise their own judgment in burying a baptized non-Catholic in a Catholic cemetery "unless it is evidently con-trary to their will and provided their own minister is unavailable." How-ever, in practice, according to Msgr. Rebman, the canon on baptized non-Catholics has been extended to include Jews. Canon 1184 "Those to Whom Ecclesiastical Funeral Rites Are Denied" calls for excluding from Catholic burial "apostates, heretics and schismatics" and "manifest sinners." Apostates and heretics refers specifically to baptized former Catholics who have either converted to some other religion or publicly denied some aspect of Catholic doctrine.

Canon 1180 of the new code gives every Catholic the right to choose his or her own place of burial. Coriden *et al, op. cit.* Note, however, that when you buy a plot in a Catholic cemetery, you do not own the plot; you only acquire an easement or license to bury someone there. When you purchase a lot in a cemetery operated by a religious organization, your title is subject to the rules of that organization even if the rules are changed after you buy the plot. U.S. courts have accepted the Church's jurisdiction in this area. For example, the courts ruled that an arch-bishop could have a woman disinterred who, it was found after burial, had been married outside the Church. "Cemeteries, U.S. Law of," in *New Catholic Encyclopedia, op. cit.*

6. The Protestant flexibility is rooted in history. When the Protestant Reformation rejected the idea of purgatory, the funeral service was greatly abbreviated; prayers for the departed were eliminated since the soul was not seen as requiring any special pleadings on its behalf. In fact, the Puritans went on to forbid all burial services: Bodies were to be buried "without ceremony, prayer, scripture or preaching." As the practice of funerals was revived, services remained brief, informal, and flexible. This Protestant flexibility has continued to the present day, with innovations such as the use of nonsexist language in referring to both God and humans during the funeral service. C. O. Buchanan, "Burial, Anglican" in J. G. Davies, ed., *The New Westminster Dictionary of Liturgy and Worship,* Philadelphia: Westminster Press, 1986, pp. 120–122.

7. Technical information on cremation is based primarily on an interview with Philadelphia funeral director William Cavanagh. Additional source: Walter F. Naedele, "Funeral Traditions Fading, Cremations on the Rise," *Philadelphia Inquirer,* Dec. 7, 1987, p. 1.

8. Cremation simply burns the flesh off the bones, leaving a full skeleton. The body is inserted into a furnace, and the process takes several hours. The skeleton is then pulverized by machine, leaving a quantity of powdered bone which fills a container of about six inches by eight inches by four inches. Catholicism would generally require that the urn be buried rather than the contents be scattered.

9. The chief sources for the discussion which follows are: John Hick, "Life After Death," in Alan Richardson and John Bowden, eds., *The Westminster Dictionary of Christian Theology,* Philadelphia: Westminster Press, 1983; F. W. McGuire, "Burial with Christ," in *New Catholic Encyclopedia, op. cit.*; and Maurice Lamm, *The Jewish Way in Death and Mourning,* New York: Jonathan David Publishers, 1969. Except as previously noted, Lamm is the source of all detailed information on Jewish beliefs and practices in this chapter.

10. M. A. Hofer, "Mourning Customs (In the Bible)," in *New Catholic Encyclopedia, op. cit.*

11. From an interview with Msgr. Joseph F. Rebman, cited above.

12. C. A. Kerin, "Burial, Canon Law of," A. C. Rush, "Burial, II (Early Christian)," and R. P. Funke, "Cremation," all in *New Catholic Encyclopedia, op. cit.*

13. Some funeral homes supply mourners with black ribbons to be pinned on the clothes and torn, but according to Lamm, *op cit.,* this alteration of the custom often does not allow the full venting of grief.

14. Some of these customs are described by Gorer, *op cit.* Most are described by E. S. Hartland, "Death and Disposal of the Dead," in James Hastings, ed., *Encyclopaedia of Religion and Ethics,* New York: Charles Scribner's Sons, 1955, Vol. 4, pp. 411ff.

After a traditional Jewish funeral, a pitcher, bowl, and towel are placed outside the front door, and mourners returning from the cemetery pour water over their hands before entering the house. In Judaism, this ritual is descended from the ancient practice of purification with water to remove the defilement from touching a dead body.

The explanation for the Jewish mourners' meal comes from Lamm, *op cit.* and Joan Nathan, *The Jewish Holiday Kitchen,* New York: Schocken Books, 1979, p. 250.

In virtually every culture, neighbors have a meal waiting for the mourners when they return from the burial.

15. As an example, look at Lydia Kukoff's description of her father's funeral in *Choosing Judaism*, New York: Union of American Hebrew Congregations, 1981, pp. 82–84.

16. Sherri Alper, a convert to Judaism from Catholicism, contributed her thoughts and experiences on this dilemma.

17. Lamm, *op cit.,* p. 82.

18. Gorer found that nearly half the bereaved parents in his survey didn't tell their children anything about death when one occurred in the family. Another third used a euphemism such as "gone to heaven" or "gone to Jesus" that they did not believe. Only one-fourth told their children the truth as they saw it. Gorer, *op cit.,* pp. 10–19.

RECOMMENDED READING

Asheri, Michael, *Living Jewish: The Lore and Law of the Practicing Jew,* New York: Everest House, 1978. A concise, comprehensive guide to Jewish life-style from a traditional point of view.

Bellah, Robert N., et.al., *Habits of the Heart: Individualism and Commitment in American Life,* Berkeley: University of California Press, 1985. This best-selling analysis of the modern American psyche explores, in part, how the culture of individualism limits community and commitment.

Borowitz, Eugene B., *Modern Varieties of Jewish Thought,* New York: Behrman House, 1981. A scholarly but accessible guide that describes both Orthodox and liberal changes.

Cowan, Paul and Rachel, *Mixed Blessings: Marriage Between Jews and Christians,* New York: Doubleday, 1987. An insightful discussion of common factors in intermarriage: the partners' social mobility, assimilation, and lack of communication on religious loyalties and needs. Has a Jewish orientation.

Eichhorn, David Max, *Conversion to Judaism: A History and Analysis,* Hoboken, N.J.: Ktav Publishing, 1965. Though growing out-of-date, this is an authoritative sourcebook. In addition to its scholarly narrative, the book includes profiles of a number of Jews-by-choice who recount their conversion experiences.

Gilbert, Richard S., *Building Your Own Theology,* Boston: Unitarian Universalist Association, 1983. An experiential and often inspiring teaching guide that helps people articulate their feelings about religion and God.

Gruzen, Lee, *Raising Your Jewish/Christian Child: Wise Choices for Inter-faith Parents,* New York: Dodd, Mead & Co., 1987. An intermarried writer offers a sensitive commentary about the difficulties and rewards of intermarriage. She urges people not to devalue their or their partner's heritages.

Hollander, Annette, M.D., *How to Help Your Child Have a Spiritual Life: A Parent's Guide to Inner Development,* New York: Bantam New Age, 1982. A "New Age" sourcebook that is rich in anecdotes, advice, and resources. The author, a psychiatrist, talks of new directions as much as traditional approaches.

Kaye, Evelyn, *Crosscurrents: Children, Families and Religion,* New York: Clarkson N. Potter, 1980. A mixed-married journalist analyzes religious child-rearing in intermarried homes. She discusses hostility to religion, parents' changes over the life cycle, and families' attempts to create their own solutions. Included are the text of ecumenical ceremonies and customs.

Klein, Judith Weinstein, *Jewish Identity and Self-Esteem: Healing Wounds Through Ethnotherapy,* New York: American Jewish Committee, 1980. This booklet by a prominent ethnotherapist is at once scholarly and grippingly direct.

Kukoff, Lydia, *Choosing Judaism,* New York: Union of American Hebrew Congregations, 1981. A prominent convert describes the psychological ground covered by converts and offers resources and strategies.

Kurtz, Paul, *In Defense of Secular Humanism,* Buffalo, N.Y.: Prometheus Books, 1983. A professor of philosophy's crisp description of the humanist platform.

Kushner, Harold, *When Children Ask About God,* New York: Schocken, 1976. A well-known liberal rabbi offers encouraging answers for parents. His view is of God as strength and inspiration, as all-good though not all-powerful.

Lewis, C. S., *Mere Christianity,* New York: Macmillan, 1964. A readable doctrinally orthodox argument for Christian belief.

Lieberman, Susan, *Let's Celebrate: Creating New Family Traditions,* New York: Perigee Books, Putnam, 1984. An idea book that is filled with inspiring anecdotes about ways busy modern families can custom-make ceremonies for themselves.

Mayer, Egon, *Love and Tradition: Marriage Between Jews and Christians,* New York: Plenum, 1985. Written *about* rather than *for* the intermarried. This book provides a wealth of information about the history, sociology, and psychology of intermarrying.

Miller, Donald E., *The Case for Liberal Christianity,* San Francisco: Harper & Row, 1981. A religion professor promotes the liberal church as a credible institution for the modern mind.

Nelson, Roberta and Christopher, *Parents as Resident Theologians,* Boston: Unitarian Universalist Association, 1984. Similar in tone and purpose to the previous *Building Your Own Theology.*

Potok, Chaim, *Wanderings: Chaim Potok's History of the Jews,* Fawcett Crest, 1978. A rich and readable history of the Jewish people from the earliest days to the present.

Rosten, Leo (ed.), *Religions of America: Ferment and Faith in an Age of Crisis: A New Guide and Almanac,* New York: Simon and Schuster, 1975. An encyclopedia of current religious thought and demography. A highlight is the profiling of the major denominations.

Sandmel, Samuel, *A Jewish Understanding of the New Testament,* Hoboken, N.J.: Ktav Publishing House, 1974. A leading Jewish scholar analyzes Christian writings.

Sandmel, Samuel, *When a Jew and Christian Marry,* Philadelphia: Fortress Press, 1977, which is out of print but available in some libraries. Fatherly in tone, but nonjudgmental and filled with important insights.

Schauss, Hayyim, *The Jewish Festivals: History and Observance,* New York: Schocken, 1978. The major and minor holidays are traced from ancient times to today, with a description of various customs used around the world.

Seltzer, Sanford, *Jews and Non-Jews: Falling in Love,* New York: Union of American Hebrew Congregations, 1977. This booklet provides a useful, if brief, discussion of the psychodynamics of intermarriage, as well as enunciating the Reform movement's positions on the issue.

Siegel, Richard, and Michael and Sharon Strassfeld, eds., *The Jewish Catalog: A Do-It-Yourself Kit,* Philadelphia: The Jewish Publication Society of America, 1973. A vibrant and informative guide to bringing Jewish customs alive in your home. It is overflowing with essays, references, and how-to advice, and has become the standard reference work of "New Age" Judaism.

Strassfeld, Sharon, and Green, Kathy, *The Jewish Family Book,* New York: Bantam, 1981. Though we object to some assertions in its chapter on intermarriage, this is a useful handbook that helps couples focus on the large parenting issues: rites of passage, home rituals, and education.

Weatherhead, Leslie D., *The Christian Agnostic,* Nashville: Abingdon Press, 1965. A senior Methodist minister in England makes the case against creedal faith. An accessible summary of modern, liberal Protestantism, the book was written to reassure the lay reader that Jesus would have wanted people to be inquisitive, not obedient.

Wiesel, Elie, *Night,* New York: Avon Books, Hearst, 1969. A moving personal account of the Holocaust by a man who spent part of his childhood in a concentration camp.

Weiser, Francis X., *Handbook of Christian Feasts and Customs: The Year of the Lord in Liturgy and Folklore,* New York: Harcourt, Brace, 1958.

A lively account of how Christian holidays have evolved from Jewish origins through early and medieval Christianity to modern liturgy, and from pagan rites to European folk customs and modern celebrations. A good source for families who want to enrich their celebrations.

Zborowski, Mark, and Herzog, Elizabeth, *Life Is with People: The Culture of the Shtetl,* Schocken, New York: 1962. Captures the flavor of life in the East European ghettoes.

Index

minority status of, 53, 89, 94, 201
stereotypes of, 98, 106, 108–110, 313
survival of, as a people, 43, 144, 148
John Chrysostom, Saint, 19
Johnson, Evan, 66–67, 71
Johnson, Virginia, 309
John the Baptist, 225
Jones, Jean M., 278, 279
Judaism:
appeal of, to gentile partner, 42–43, 44, 48,
106–107, 159–160
baptism and conversion as betrayal of, 29
beliefs central to, 138–139
burial policies of, 321–322, 324, 325–326
children of non-Jewish mothers and, 42,
153, 165, 202, 234, 321
Conservative, 65, 69, 143, 165, 171, 265–
266, 283, 321–322, 334–336, 343–344
conversion views within, 165–167
early Christian views on, 19
family central to, 65, 116, 139
holidays, 224–225, 359–371
intermarriage opposition in, 10, 41, 43, 64–
65
intermarriage policies of, 334–336
marriage tenets of, 64–65
"New Age," 157, 262, 267–268
Orthodox, 42, 45, 71, 165–166, 265–266,
283, 321–322, 334, 342–343
Reconstructionist, 65, 66–67, 138, 165–166,
171, 260, 263–265, 283, 335–336, 344–
345
Reform, 55, 65, 69, 70–71, 138, 165–166,
171, 202, 263–265, 279, 283, 290–291,
321–322, 335, 345–346
religious calendar of, 223–224
rituals of, 65, 72, 116, 171
secular, 266, 283–284
sexuality and, 310–311
symbols of, 63, 72, 74, 131, 149, 203
traditional wedding ceremonies of, 72–73,
74
world view of, 138–139
Judaism as a Civilization (Kaplan), 66
Judenschachter (Jew-slaughterers), 22
judges, 64, 66–67, 68, 74
Justin, Saint, 19

kabbalat mitzvot, 152
kaddish, 329, 377–378
Kaplan, Mordechai, 66, 67
Kaufman, Karen, 177
Kellerman, Lois, 293
Kelley, Dean M., 144–145
keriah, 327
kiddush, 149, 167
Kiddush Ha-Shem, 21
Kishinev pogrom, 27
klal yisrael, 202
Klein, Judith Weinstein, 85, 86
kosher, keeping, 65, 165, 172, 359–360

Kukoff, Lydia, 157
Kung, Hans, 135
Kurtz, Paul, 135
Kushner, Harold, 135

Lamm, Maurice, 326
Lateran Council, Fourth, 23
Lateran Council, Third, 21, 23
laws:
anti-Jewish, 20–29
Jewish, 138–139, 152, 165
moral, 140
Lent, 224–225, 363–365
*Let's Celebrate: Creating New Family Tradi-
tions* (Lieberman), 227, 228
Levine, Irving, 85
licenses, wedding, 74
Lieberman, Susan, 227, 228
Louis I (the Pious), emperor, 26
*Love and Tradition: Marriage Between Jews
and Christians* (Mayer), 51
loyalty:
of children of divorce, 302–303
dilemma of interfaith children, 200
ethnic group vs. spouse, 94–95
transference of, 39, 200
Lull, Timothy, 138
Luther, Martin, 24
Lutherans, 141, 224, 269

Maccabees, 224
McGill, David, 86, 88, 93
McGoldrick, Monica, 85
Mackintosh, Sam, 226–227
madonna/whore syndrome, 312–313
Making Peace with Your Parents (Bloomfield),
53, 132
marriage:
"good," definition of, 32
as ideal state, 65
of older man to younger woman, 113
reverence for, 149–150
marriage contracts, 35, 64–65, 72, 73, 117
Marriage Encounter, 288–289
Marriage Enrichment, 288–289
mass, Catholic, 134, 147, 203, 204, 205, 323
Masters, William, 309
masturbation, 310, 311, 312
matzohs, 22, 131
Mayer, Egon, 39–40, 51, 177, 200, 207
Mediterranean cultures, 44–45, 46, 121
menorahs, 131, 220, 221
menstruation, 310, 369
Messiah, 138, 140, 326
Methodists, 141–142
Middle Ages, 22–25, 27–28
Middle East, 139, 269
mikvah, 154, 165, 166, 167, 234, 238, 245, 246
milah, 154
ministers, 57, 64, 65–66, 72, 153
minority groups, 53, 90, 94–95, 107–110, 201